RADIANT

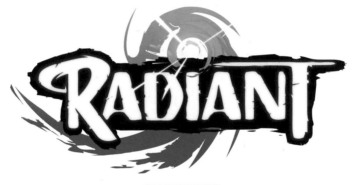

TONY VALENTE

CONTENTS

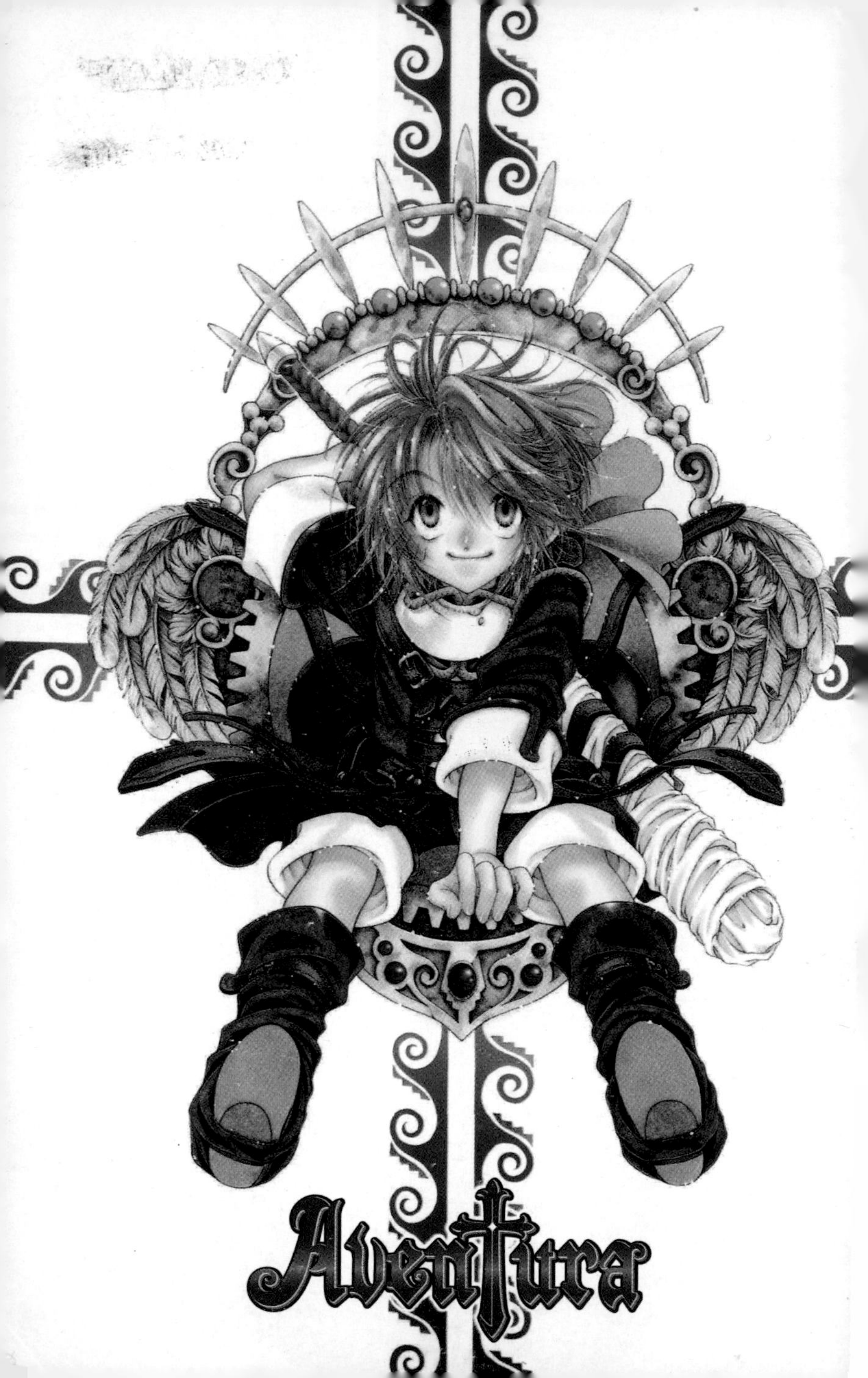
Aventura

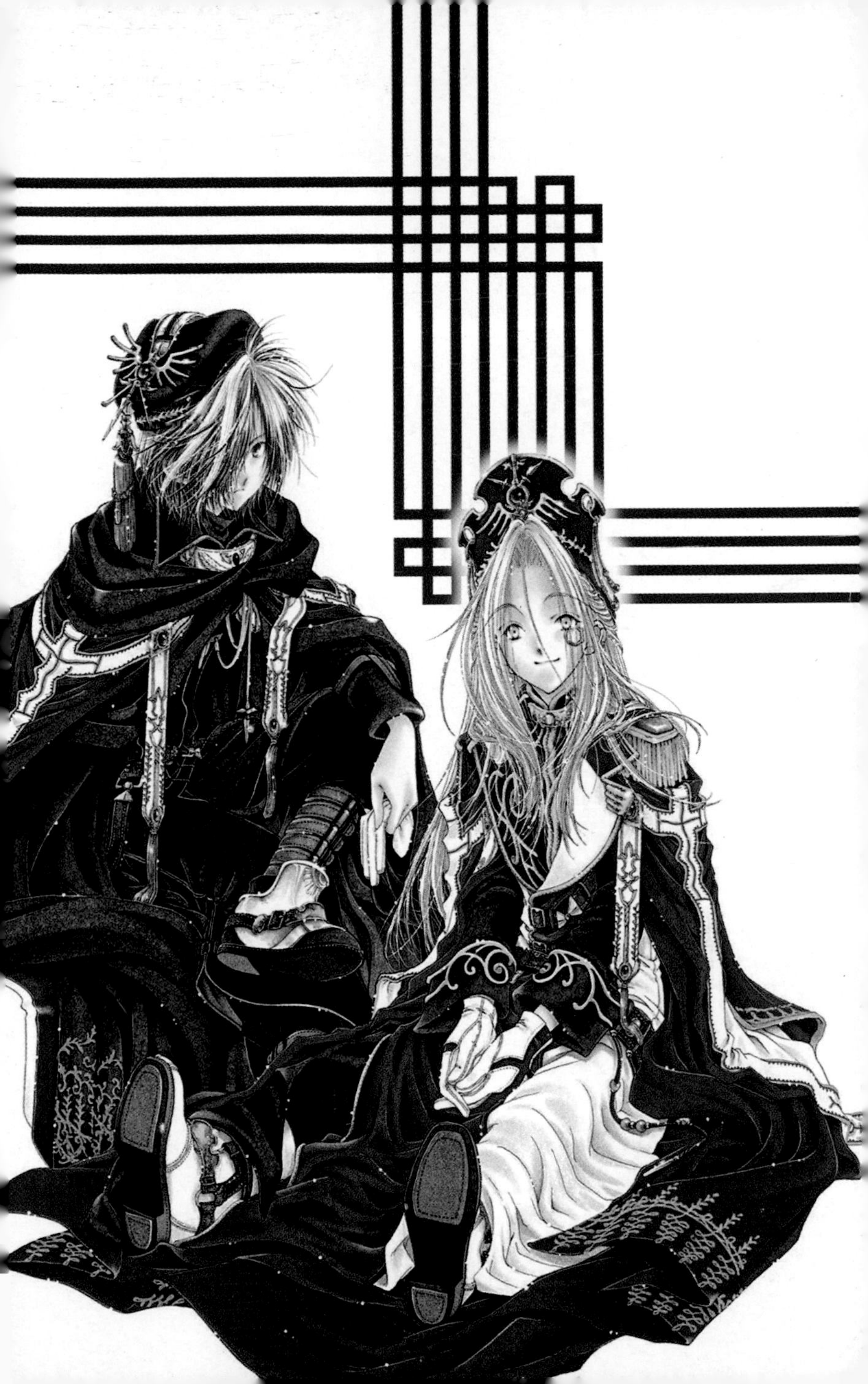

Aventura

1

SHIN MIDORIKAWA

TRANSLATED AND ADAPTED BY ELINA ISHIKAWA

LETTERED BY NORTH MARKET STREET GRAPHICS

BALLANTINE BOOKS · NEW YORK

Aventura volume 1 is a work of fiction. Names, characters, places, and incidents are the products of the author's imagination or are used fictitiously. Any resemblance to actual events, locales, or persons, living or dead, is entirely coincidental.

A Del Rey Trade Paperback Original

Published in the United States by Del Rey Books, an imprint of The Random House Publishing Group, a division of Random House, Inc., New York.

Publication rights arranged through Kodansha Ltd.

First published in Japan in 2006 by Kodansha Ltd., Tokyo

ISBN 978-0-345-49744-4

Printed in the United States of America

www.delreymanga.com

9 8 7 6 5 4 3 2 1

Translator/Adapter: Elina Ishikawa
Lettering: NMSG

Contents

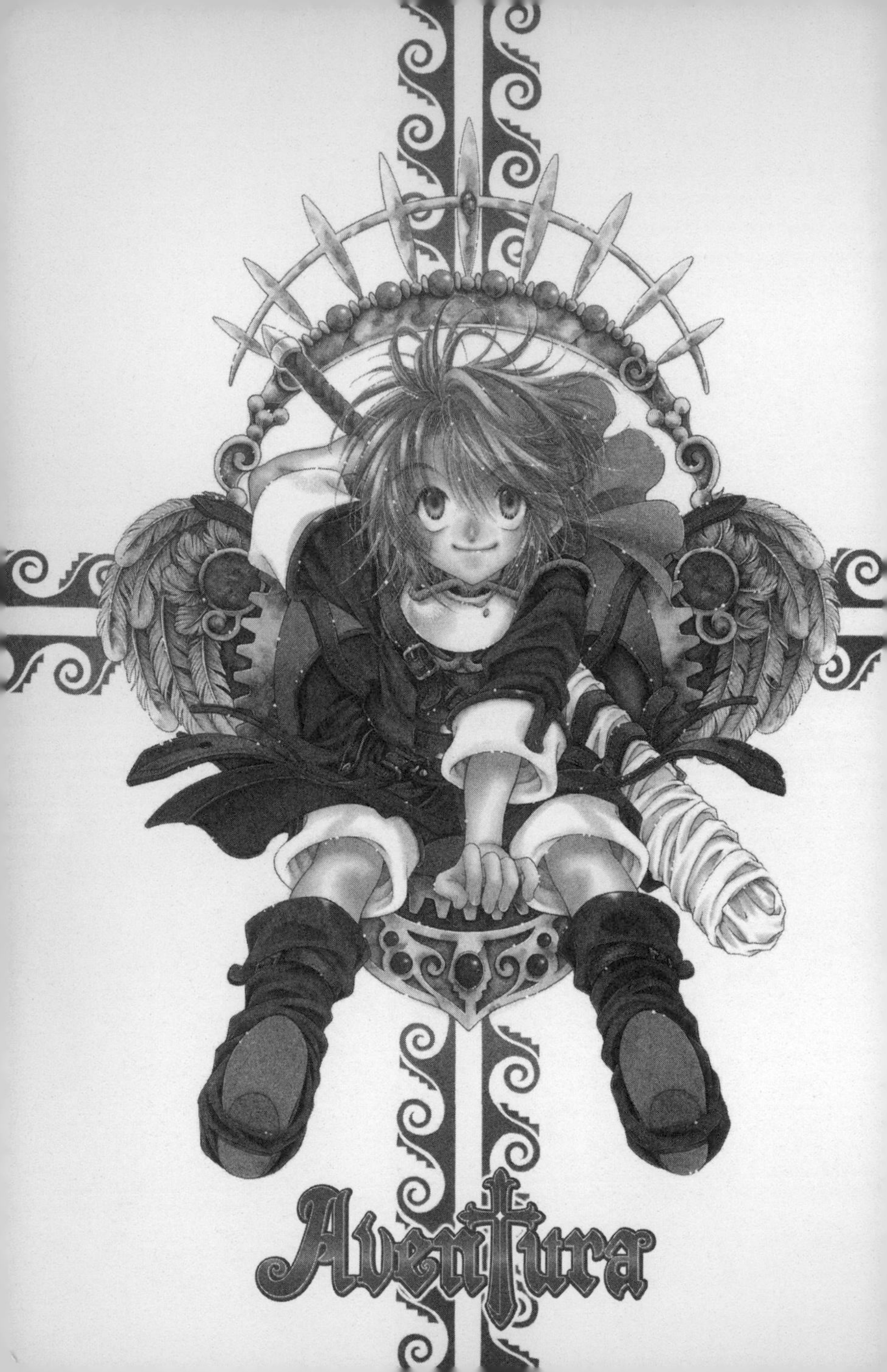
Aventura

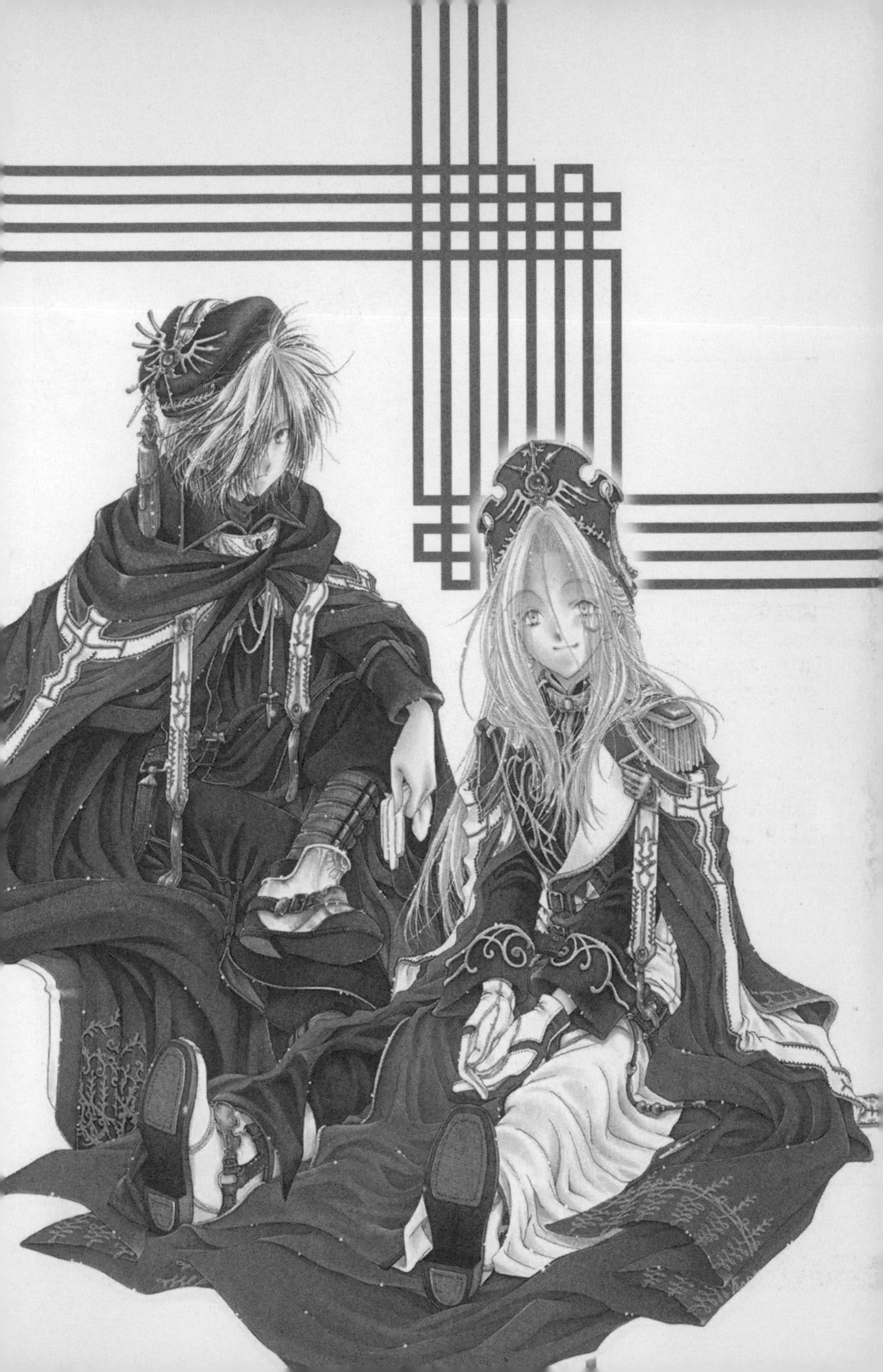

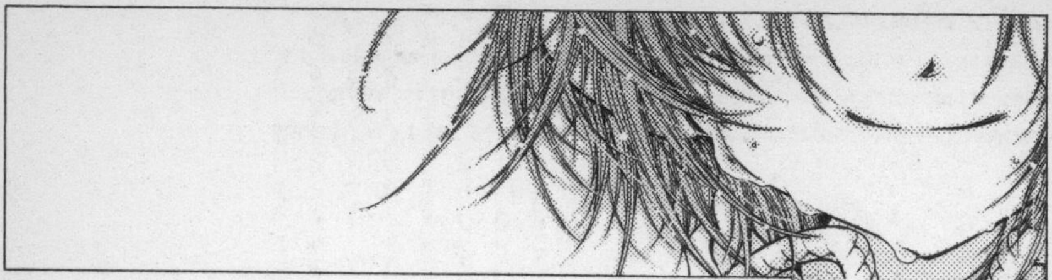

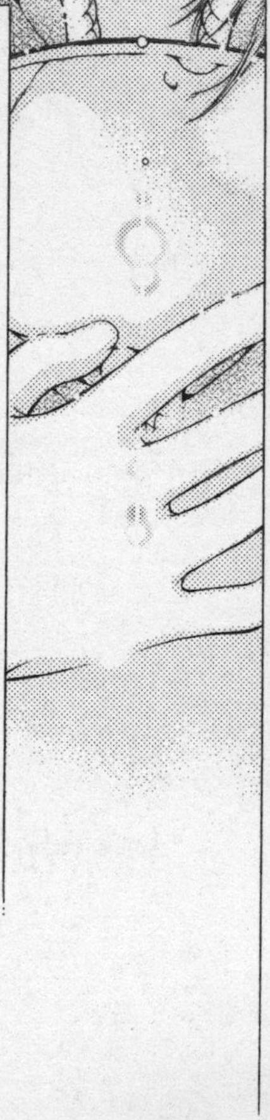

THESE WARM TEARS STREAMING DOWN MY FACE...

AND THE STABBING PAIN IN MY HEART...

AFTER A THOUSAND NIGHTS, THEY WILL BE NO MORE THAN A MEMORY.

PLEASE GIVE ME THE STRENGTH TO BELIEVE.

Aventura 1

Aventura 1

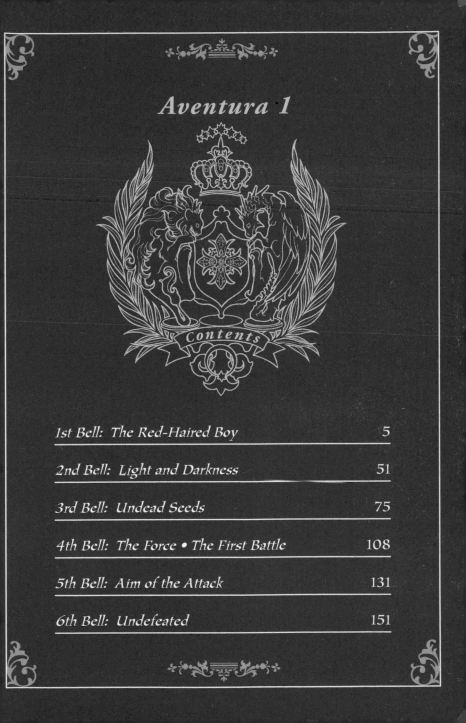

Contents

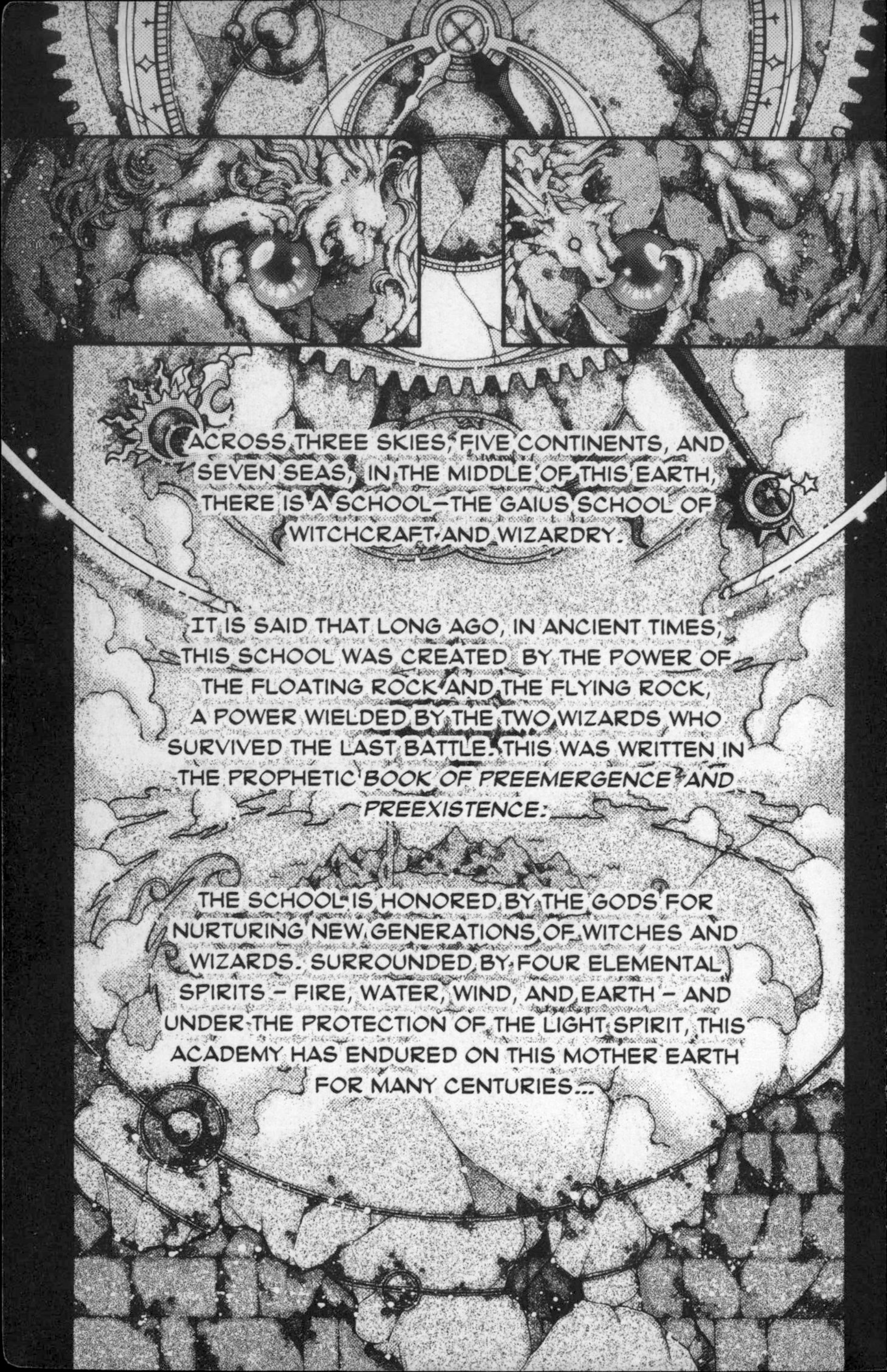
ACROSS THREE SKIES, FIVE CONTINENTS, AND SEVEN SEAS, IN THE MIDDLE OF THIS EARTH, THERE IS A SCHOOL—THE GAIUS SCHOOL OF WITCHCRAFT AND WIZARDRY.
IT IS SAID THAT LONG AGO, IN ANCIENT TIMES, THIS SCHOOL WAS CREATED BY THE POWER OF THE FLOATING ROCK AND THE FLYING ROCK, A POWER WIELDED BY THE TWO WIZARDS WHO SURVIVED THE LAST BATTLE. THIS WAS WRITTEN IN THE PROPHETIC *BOOK OF PREEMERGENCE AND PREEXISTENCE:*
THE SCHOOL IS HONORED BY THE GODS FOR NURTURING NEW GENERATIONS OF WITCHES AND WIZARDS. SURROUNDED BY FOUR ELEMENTAL SPIRITS – FIRE, WATER, WIND, AND EARTH – AND UNDER THE PROTECTION OF THE LIGHT SPIRIT, THIS ACADEMY HAS ENDURED ON THIS MOTHER EARTH FOR MANY CENTURIES...

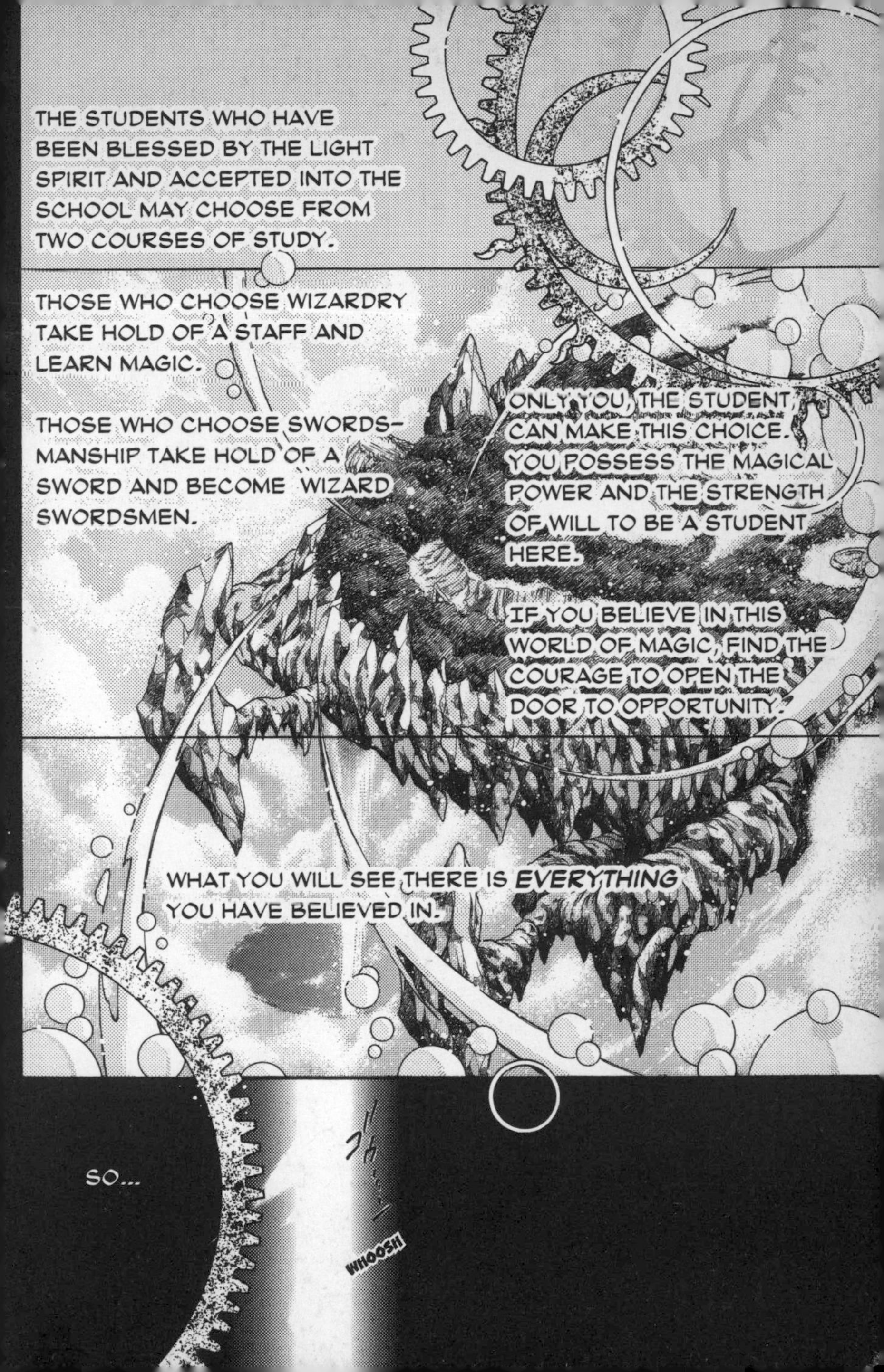
THE STUDENTS WHO HAVE BEEN BLESSED BY THE LIGHT SPIRIT AND ACCEPTED INTO THE SCHOOL MAY CHOOSE FROM TWO COURSES OF STUDY.
THOSE WHO CHOOSE WIZARDRY TAKE HOLD OF A STAFF AND LEARN MAGIC.
THOSE WHO CHOOSE SWORDS-MANSHIP TAKE HOLD OF A SWORD AND BECOME WIZARD SWORDSMEN.
ONLY YOU, THE STUDENT, CAN MAKE THIS CHOICE. YOU POSSESS THE MAGICAL POWER AND THE STRENGTH OF WILL TO BE A STUDENT HERE.
IF YOU BELIEVE IN THIS WORLD OF MAGIC, FIND THE COURAGE TO OPEN THE DOOR TO OPPORTUNITY.
WHAT YOU WILL SEE THERE IS *EVERYTHING* YOU HAVE BELIEVED IN.
SO...
WHOOSH

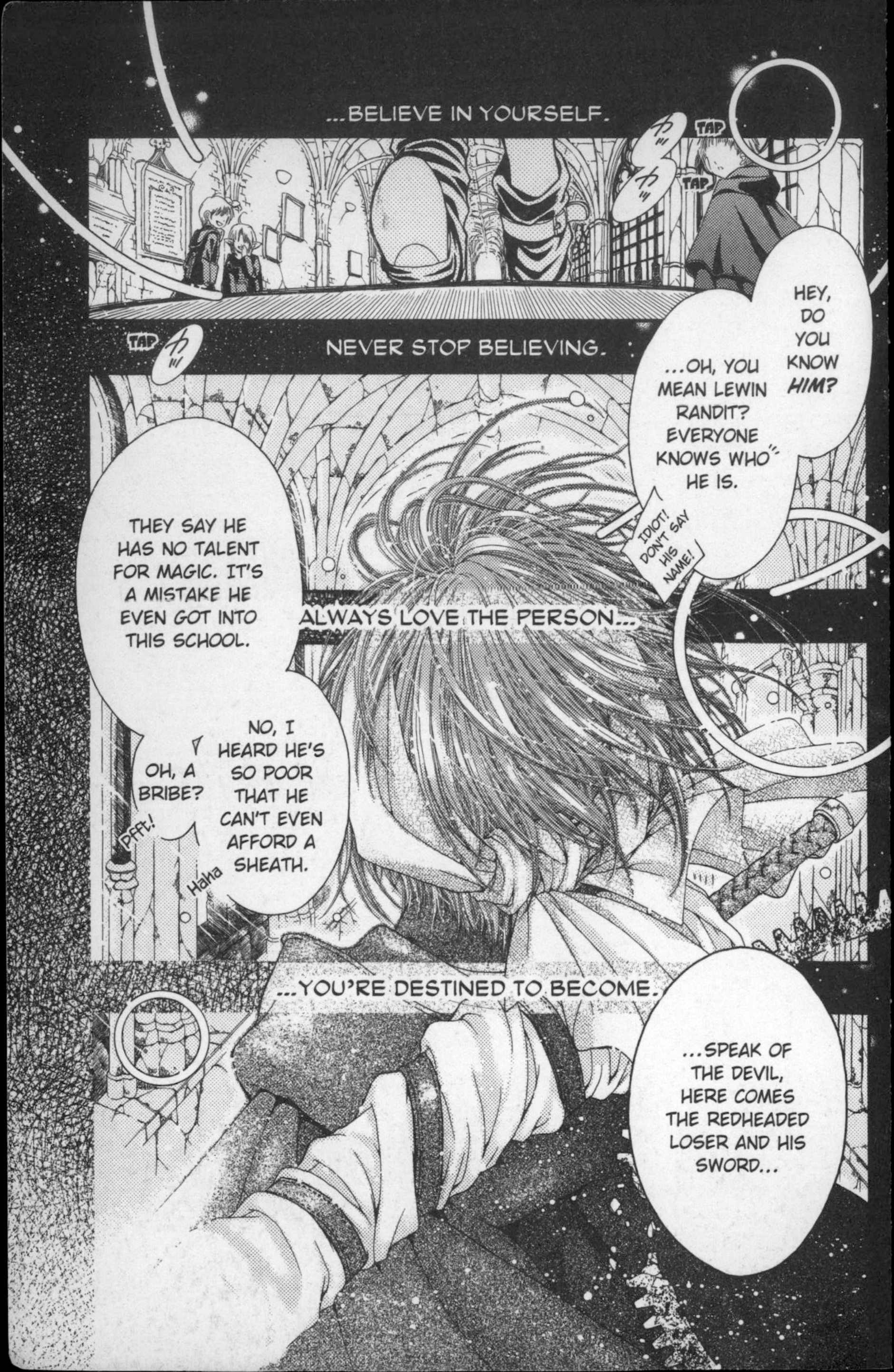
...BELIEVE IN YOURSELF.
TAP
TAP
TAP
NEVER STOP BELIEVING.
HEY, DO YOU KNOW HIM?
...OH, YOU MEAN LEWIN RANDIT? EVERYONE KNOWS WHO HE IS.
IDIOT! DON'T SAY HIS NAME!
THEY SAY HE HAS NO TALENT FOR MAGIC. IT'S A MISTAKE HE EVEN GOT INTO THIS SCHOOL.
ALWAYS LOVE THE PERSON...
OH, A BRIBE?
NO, I HEARD HE'S SO POOR THAT HE CAN'T EVEN AFFORD A SHEATH.
PFFt!
Haha
...YOU'RE DESTINED TO BECOME.
...SPEAK OF THE DEVIL, HERE COMES THE REDHEADED LOSER AND HIS SWORD...

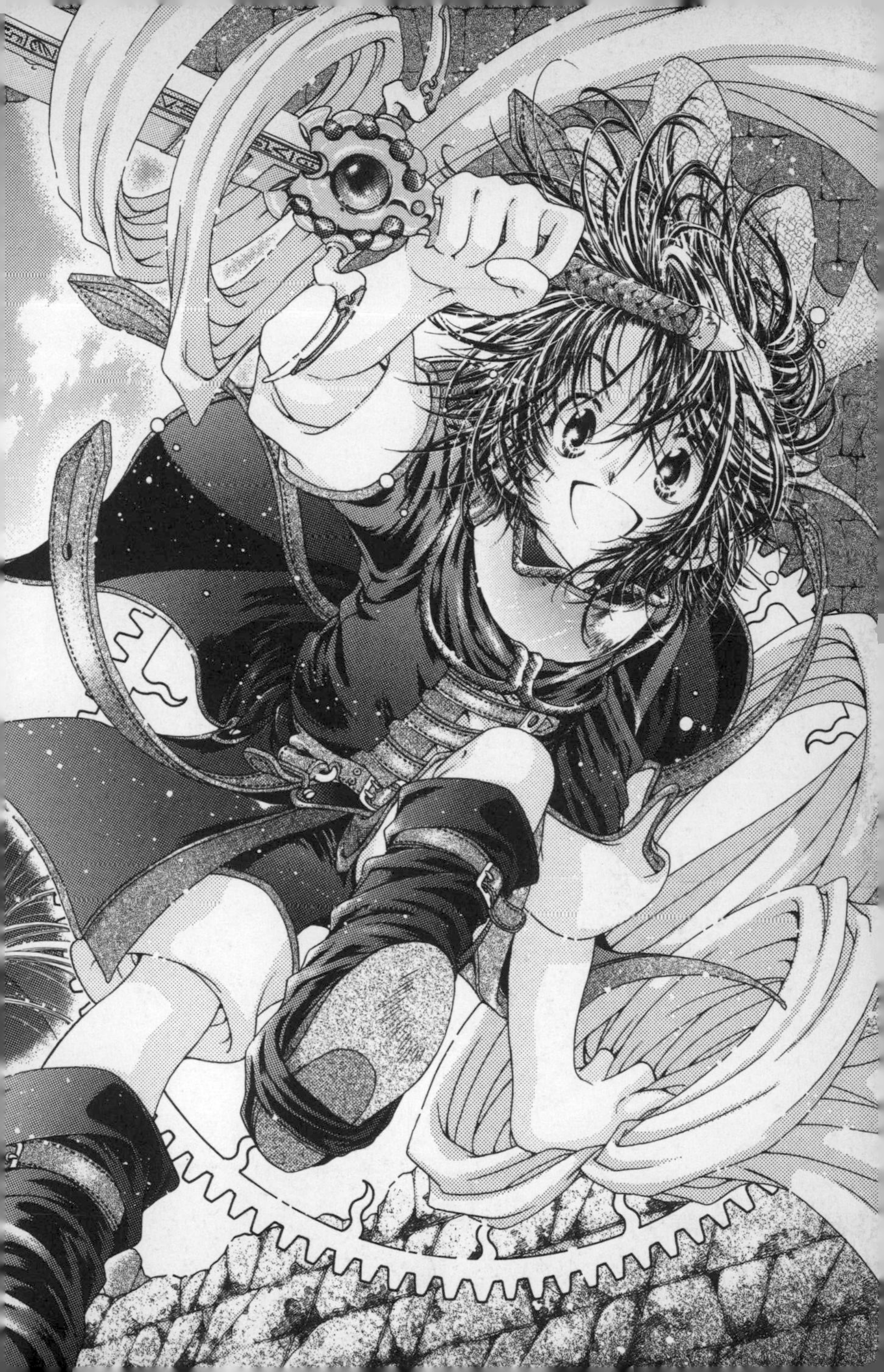

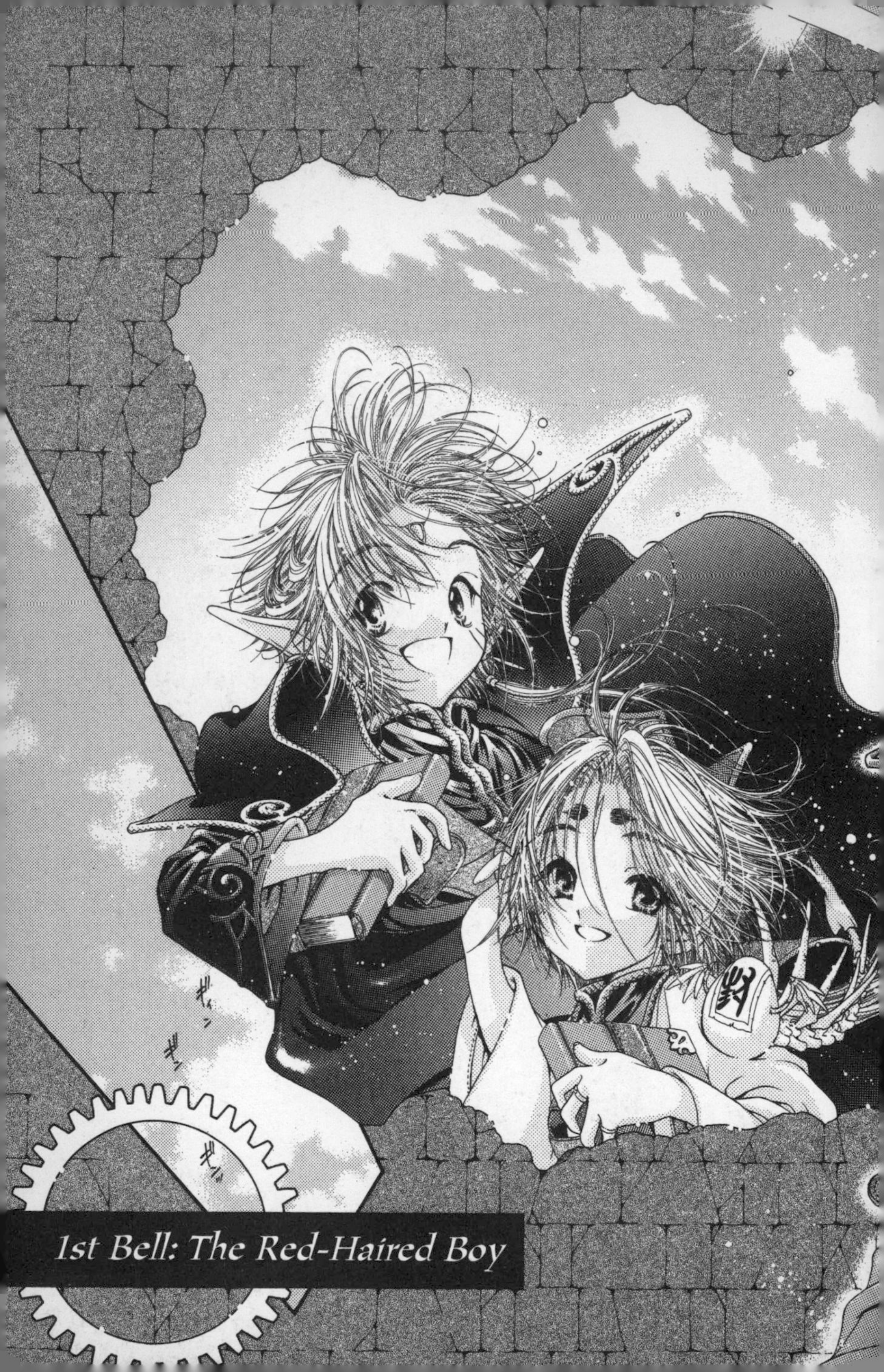
1st Bell: The Red-Haired Boy

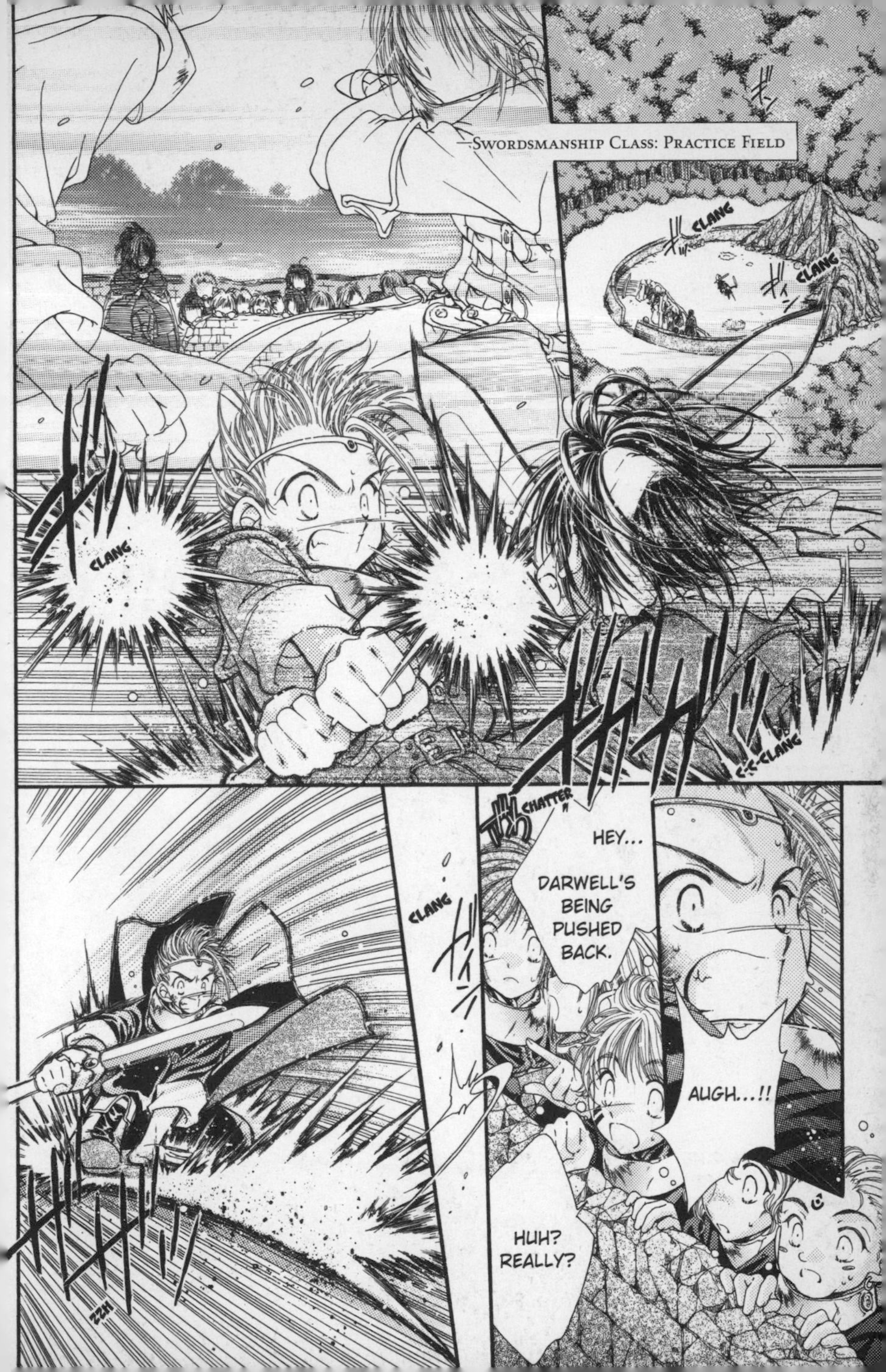
—Swordsmanship Class: Practice Field
CLANG
CLANG
CLANG
C-C-CLANG
CHATTER
HEY...
DARWELL'S BEING PUSHED BACK.
AUGH...!!
HUH? REALLY?
CLANG

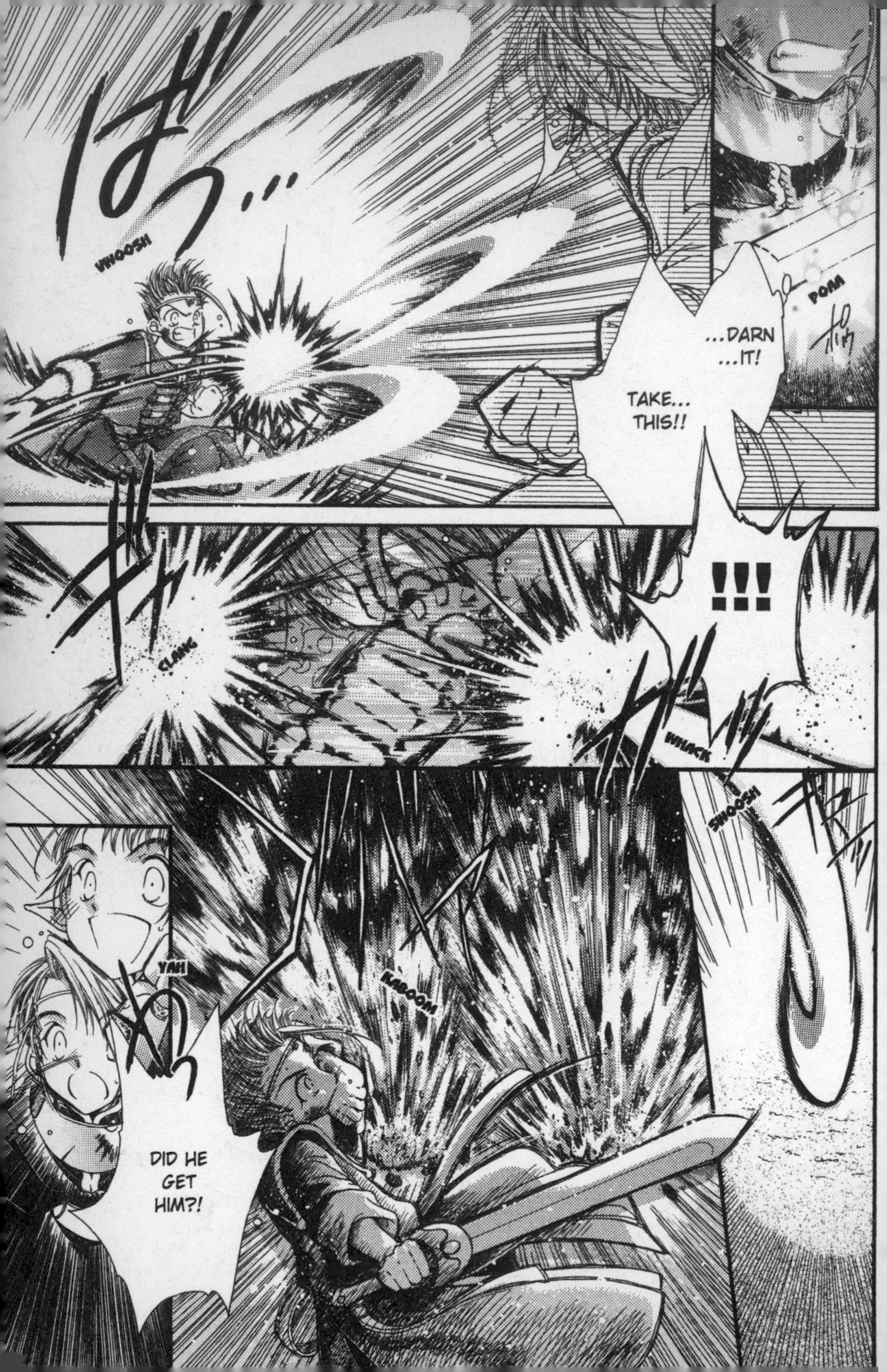
POAA
...DARN ...IT!
TAKE... THIS!!
WHOOSH
!!!
WHACK
CLANG
SHOOSH
KABOOM
YAH
DID HE GET HIM?!

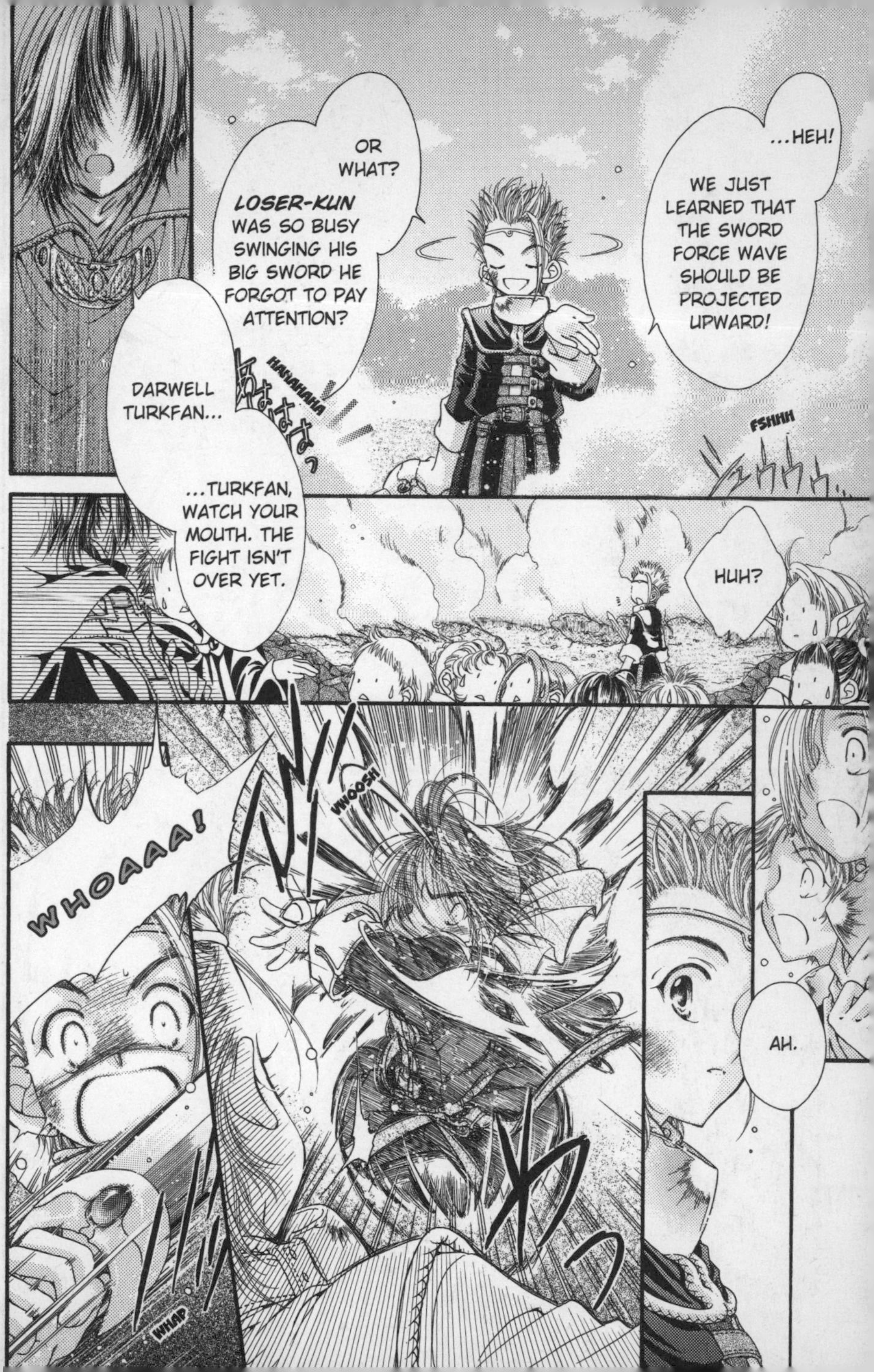
...HEH!
WE JUST LEARNED THAT THE SWORD FORCE WAVE SHOULD BE PROJECTED UPWARD!
OR WHAT? LOSER-KUN WAS SO BUSY SWINGING HIS BIG SWORD HE FORGOT TO PAY ATTENTION?
HAHAHAHA
FSHHH
DARWELL TURKFAN...
...TURKFAN, WATCH YOUR MOUTH. THE FIGHT ISN'T OVER YET.
HUH?
AH.
WHOOSH
WHOAAA!
WHAP

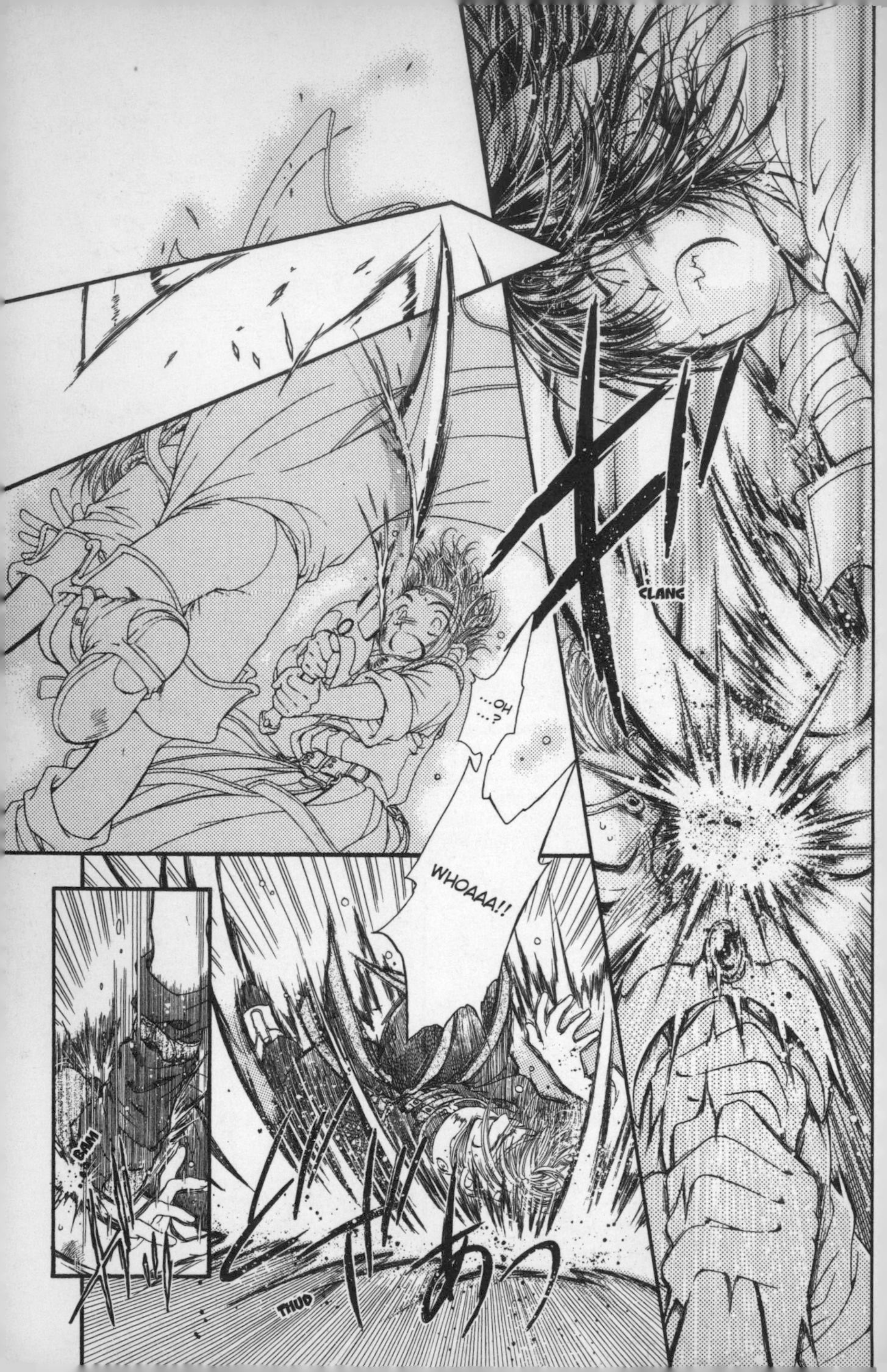
CLANG
...OH
...?
WHOAAA!!
THUD
BAM

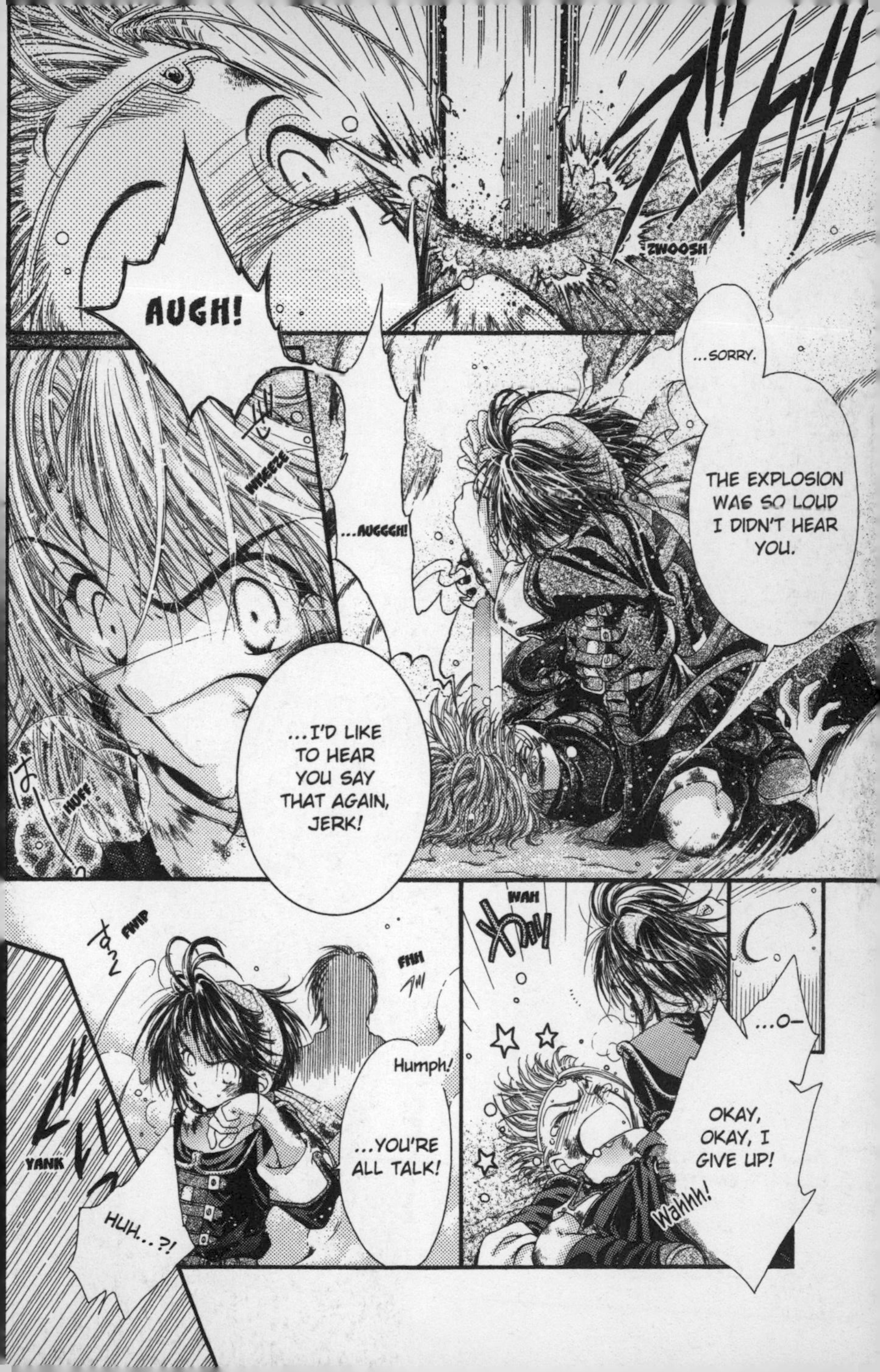
ZWOOSH
AUGH!
...SORRY.
THE EXPLOSION WAS SO LOUD I DIDN'T HEAR YOU.
WHEEZE
...AUGGGH!
...I'D LIKE TO HEAR YOU SAY THAT AGAIN, JERK!
HUFF
WAH
...O–
OKAY, OKAY, I GIVE UP!
Wahhh!
FHH
FWIP
Humph!
...YOU'RE ALL TALK!
YANK
HUH...?!

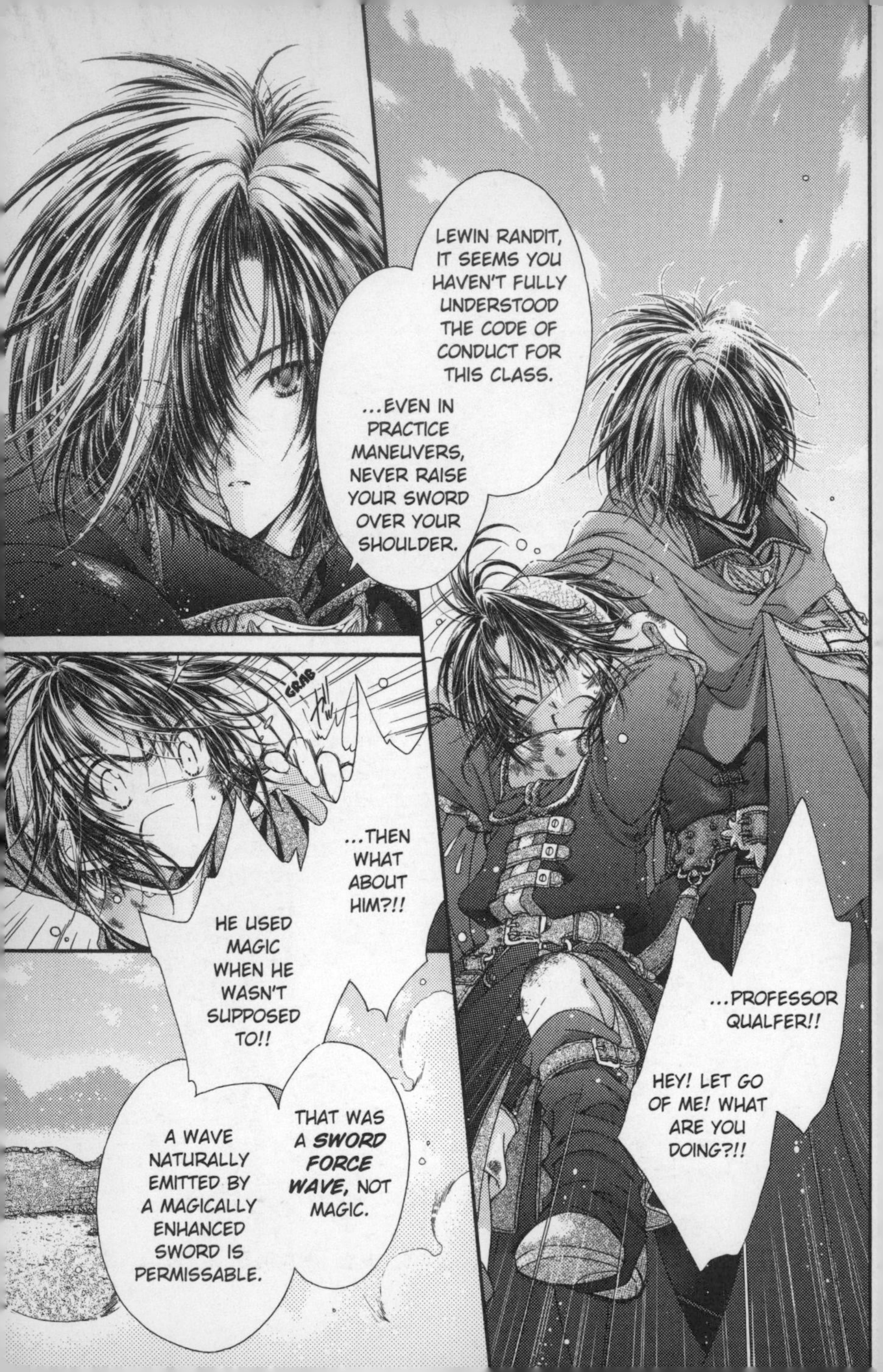
HEY! LET GO OF ME! WHAT ARE YOU DOING?!!
...PROFESSOR QUALFER!!
LEWIN RANDIT, IT SEEMS YOU HAVEN'T FULLY UNDERSTOOD THE CODE OF CONDUCT FOR THIS CLASS.
...EVEN IN PRACTICE MANEUVERS, NEVER RAISE YOUR SWORD OVER YOUR SHOULDER.
GRAB
...THEN WHAT ABOUT HIM?!!
HE USED MAGIC WHEN HE WASN'T SUPPOSED TO!!
THAT WAS A ***SWORD FORCE WAVE,*** NOT MAGIC.
A WAVE NATURALLY EMITTED BY A MAGICALLY ENHANCED SWORD IS PERMISSABLE.

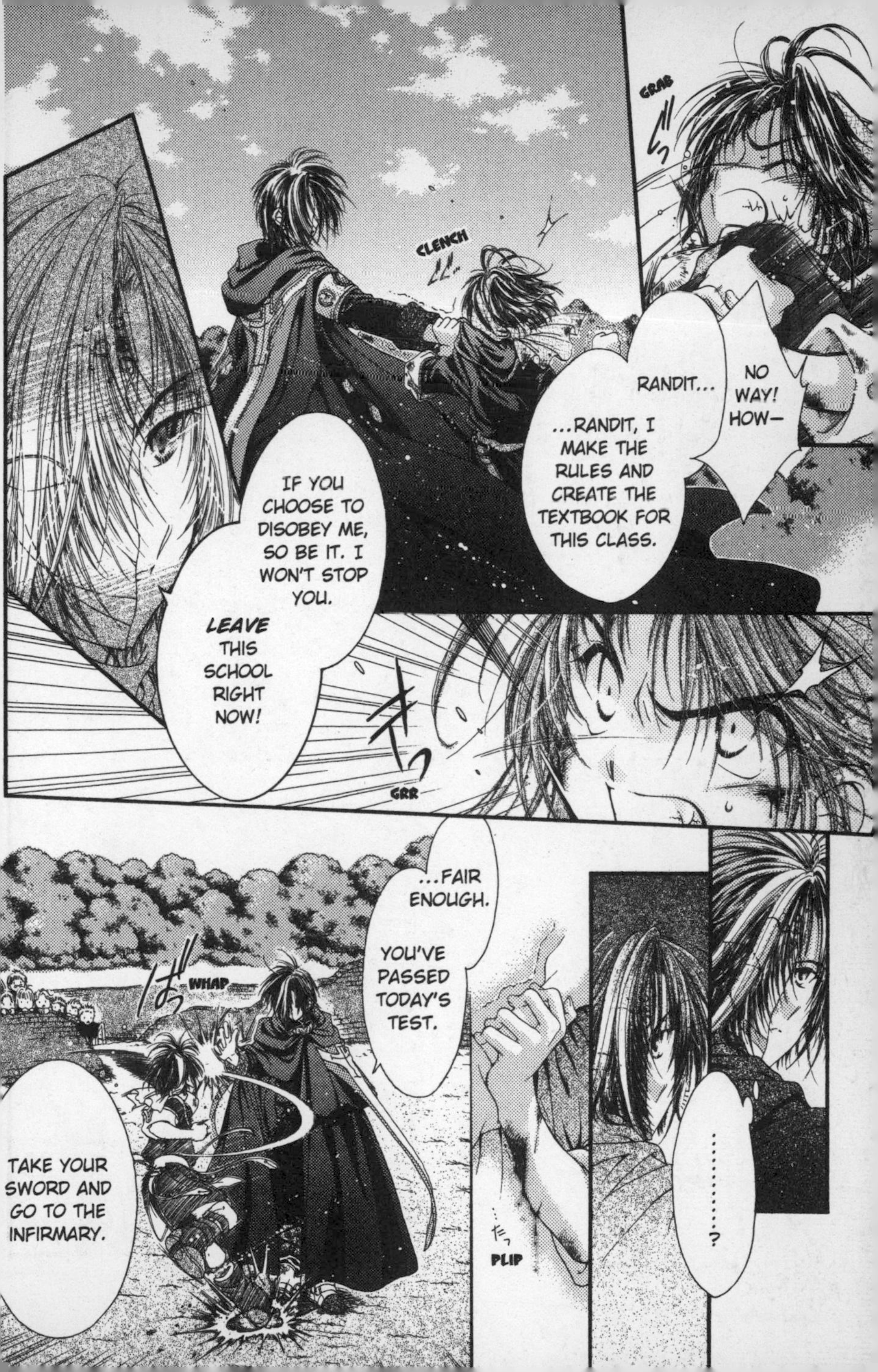
GRAB
NO WAY! HOW—
RANDIT...
...RANDIT, I MAKE THE RULES AND CREATE THE TEXTBOOK FOR THIS CLASS.
CLENCH
IF YOU CHOOSE TO DISOBEY ME, SO BE IT. I WON'T STOP YOU.
LEAVE THIS SCHOOL RIGHT NOW!
GRR
.......?
PLIP
...FAIR ENOUGH.
YOU'VE PASSED TODAY'S TEST.
WHAP
TAKE YOUR SWORD AND GO TO THE INFIRMARY.

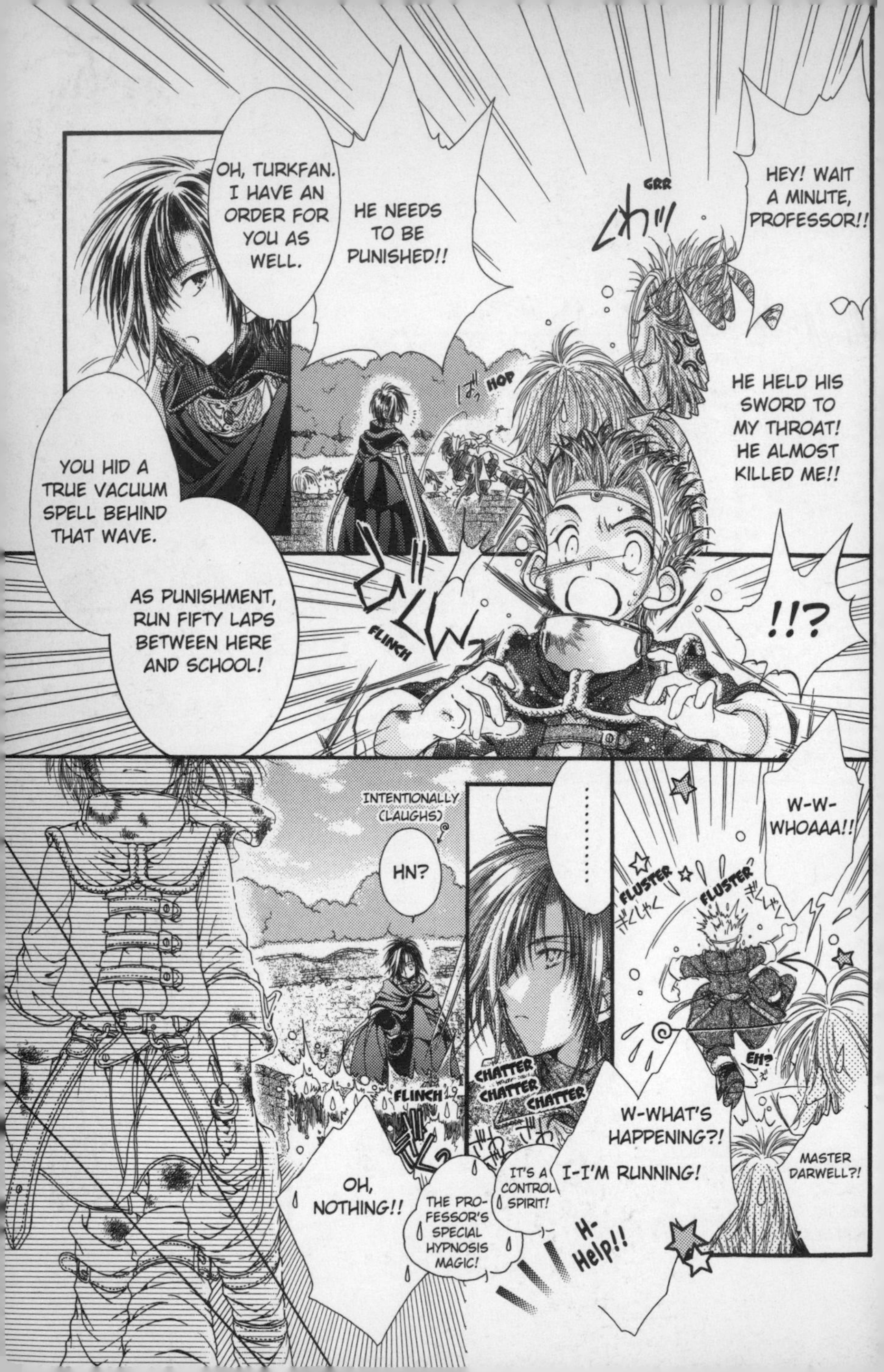
HEY! WAIT A MINUTE, PROFESSOR!!
GRR
HE NEEDS TO BE PUNISHED!!
HE HELD HIS SWORD TO MY THROAT! HE ALMOST KILLED ME!!
HOP
OH, TURKFAN. I HAVE AN ORDER FOR YOU AS WELL.
YOU HID A TRUE VACUUM SPELL BEHIND THAT WAVE.
!!?
FLINCH
AS PUNISHMENT, RUN FIFTY LAPS BETWEEN HERE AND SCHOOL!
W-W-WHOAAA!!
FLUSTER
FLUSTER
EH?
MASTER DARWELL?!
W-WHAT'S HAPPENING?!
I-I'M RUNNING!
H-Help!!
......
CHATTER
CHATTER
CHATTER
IT'S A CONTROL SPIRIT!
THE PRO-FESSOR'S SPECIAL HYPNOSIS MAGIC!
INTENTIONALLY (LAUGHS)
HN?
FLINCH
OH, NOTHING!!

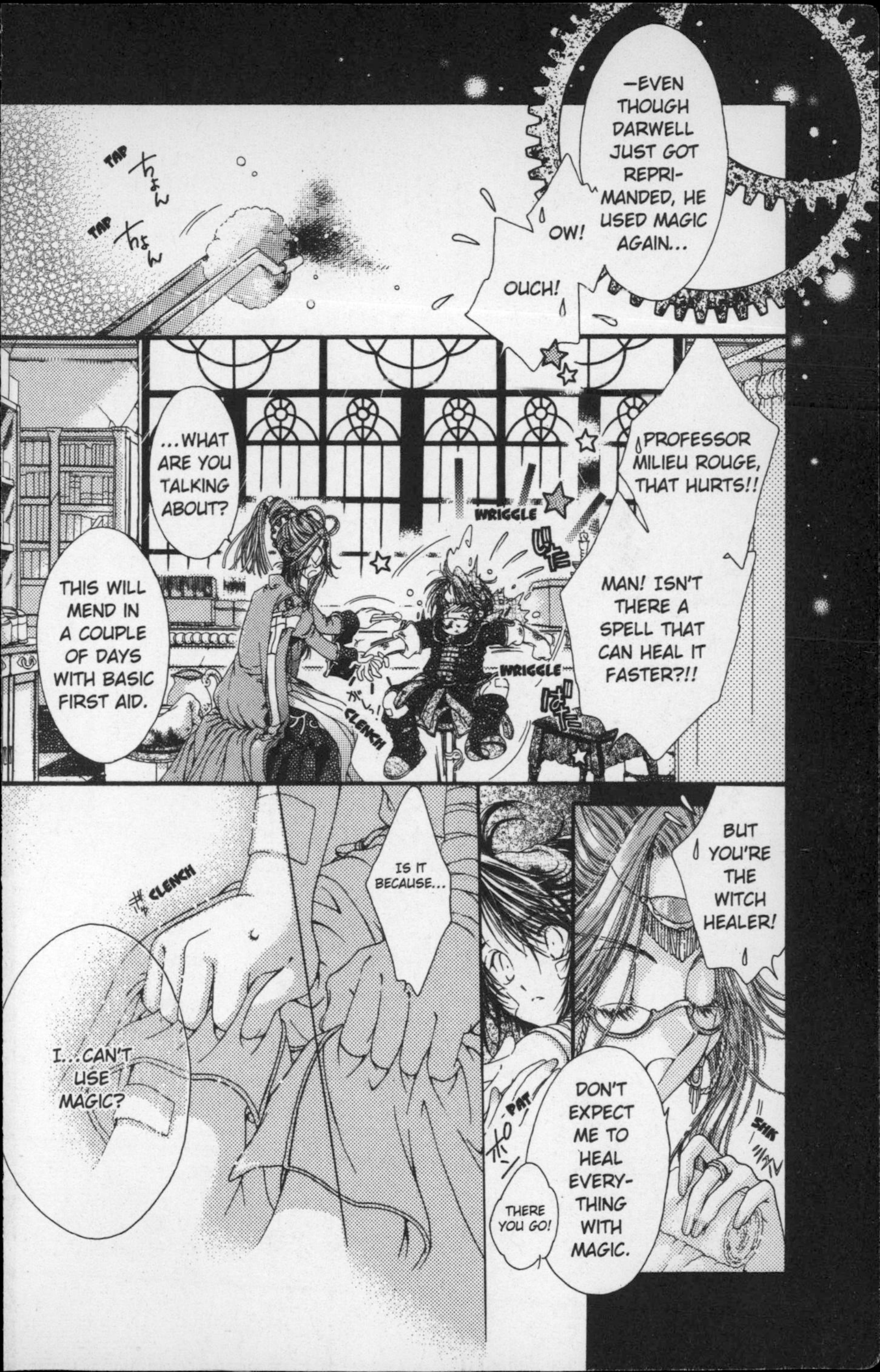
—EVEN THOUGH DARWELL JUST GOT REPRIMANDED, HE USED MAGIC AGAIN...
OW!
OUCH!
TAP
ちょん
TAP
ちょん
PROFESSOR MILIEU ROUGE, THAT HURTS!!
MAN! ISN'T THERE A SPELL THAT CAN HEAL IT FASTER?!!
WRIGGLE
WRIGGLE
...WHAT ARE YOU TALKING ABOUT?
THIS WILL MEND IN A COUPLE OF DAYS WITH BASIC FIRST AID.
CLENCH
BUT YOU'RE THE WITCH HEALER!
DON'T EXPECT ME TO HEAL EVERY-THING WITH MAGIC.
SHK
PAT
THERE YOU GO!
IS IT BECAUSE...
CLENCH
I...CAN'T USE MAGIC?

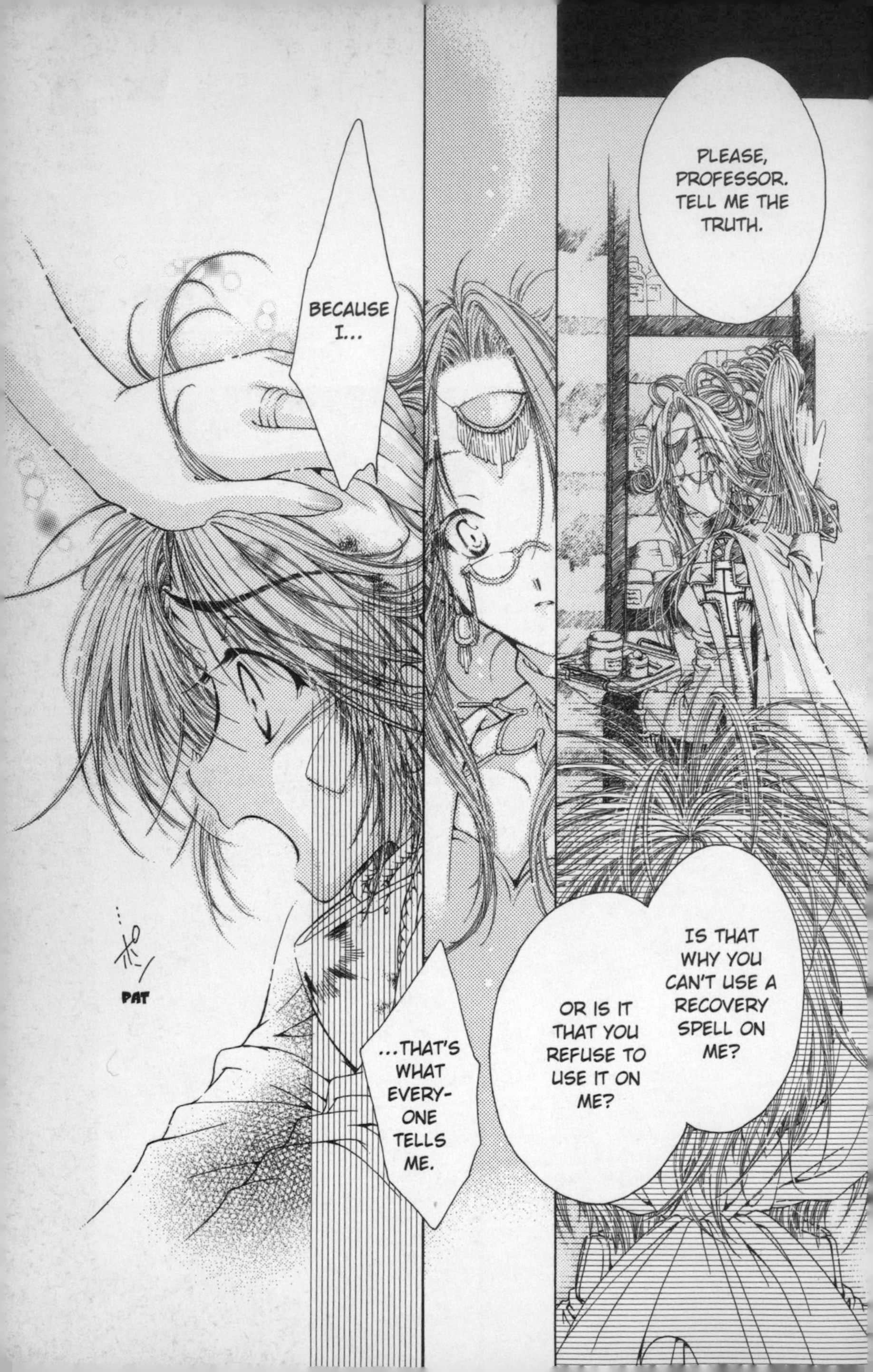
PLEASE, PROFESSOR. TELL ME THE TRUTH.
IS THAT WHY YOU CAN'T USE A RECOVERY SPELL ON ME?
OR IS IT THAT YOU REFUSE TO USE IT ON ME?
BECAUSE I...
...THAT'S WHAT EVERY-ONE TELLS ME.
PAT

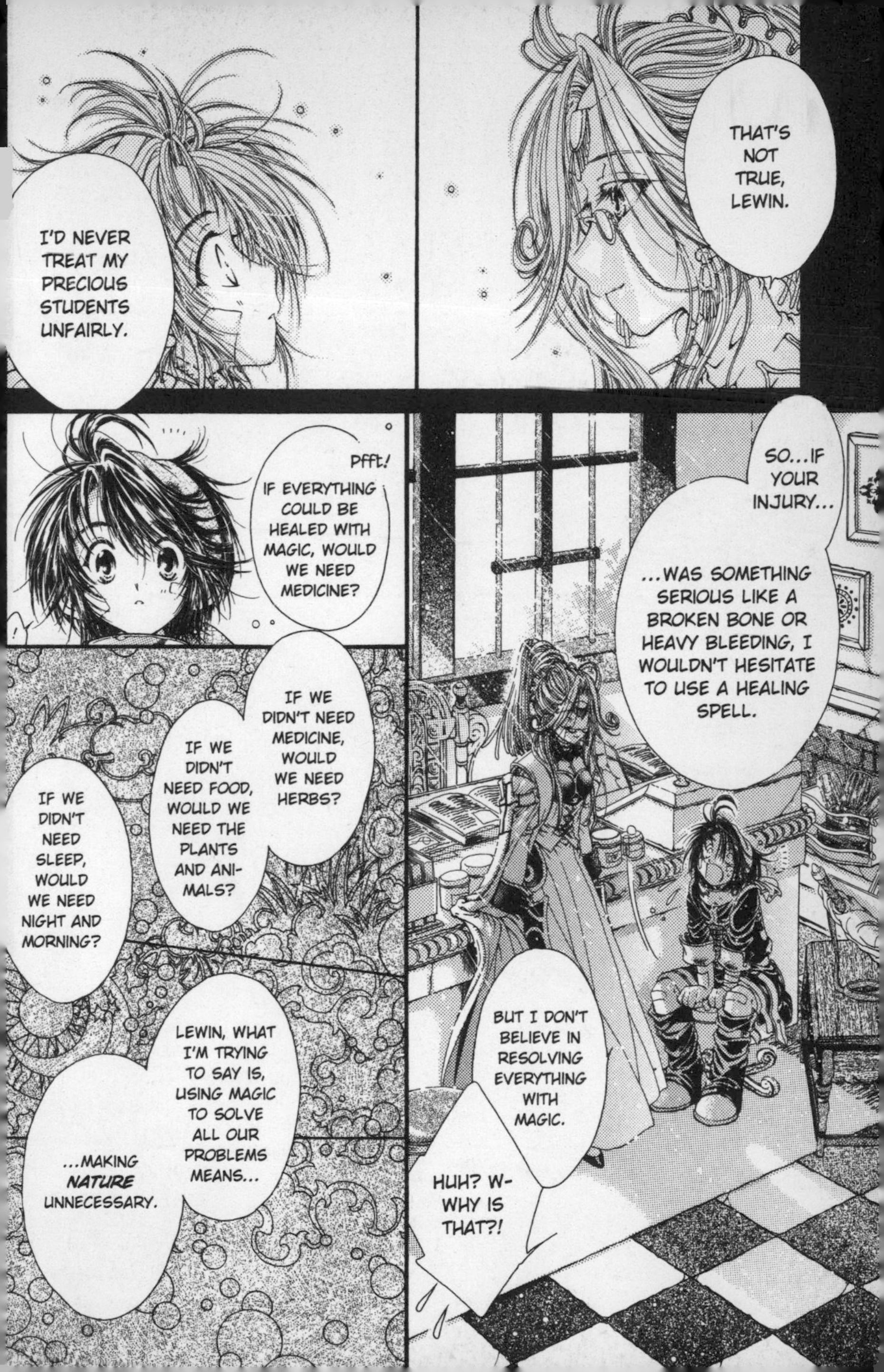
THAT'S NOT TRUE, LEWIN.
I'D NEVER TREAT MY PRECIOUS STUDENTS UNFAIRLY.
SO...IF YOUR INJURY...
...WAS SOMETHING SERIOUS LIKE A BROKEN BONE OR HEAVY BLEEDING, I WOULDN'T HESITATE TO USE A HEALING SPELL.
BUT I DON'T BELIEVE IN RESOLVING EVERYTHING WITH MAGIC.
HUH? W-WHY IS THAT?!
Pfft!
IF EVERYTHING COULD BE HEALED WITH MAGIC, WOULD WE NEED MEDICINE?
IF WE DIDN'T NEED MEDICINE, WOULD WE NEED HERBS?
IF WE DIDN'T NEED FOOD, WOULD WE NEED THE PLANTS AND ANI-MALS?
IF WE DIDN'T NEED SLEEP, WOULD WE NEED NIGHT AND MORNING?
LEWIN, WHAT I'M TRYING TO SAY IS, USING MAGIC TO SOLVE ALL OUR PROBLEMS MEANS...
...MAKING *NATURE* UNNECESSARY.

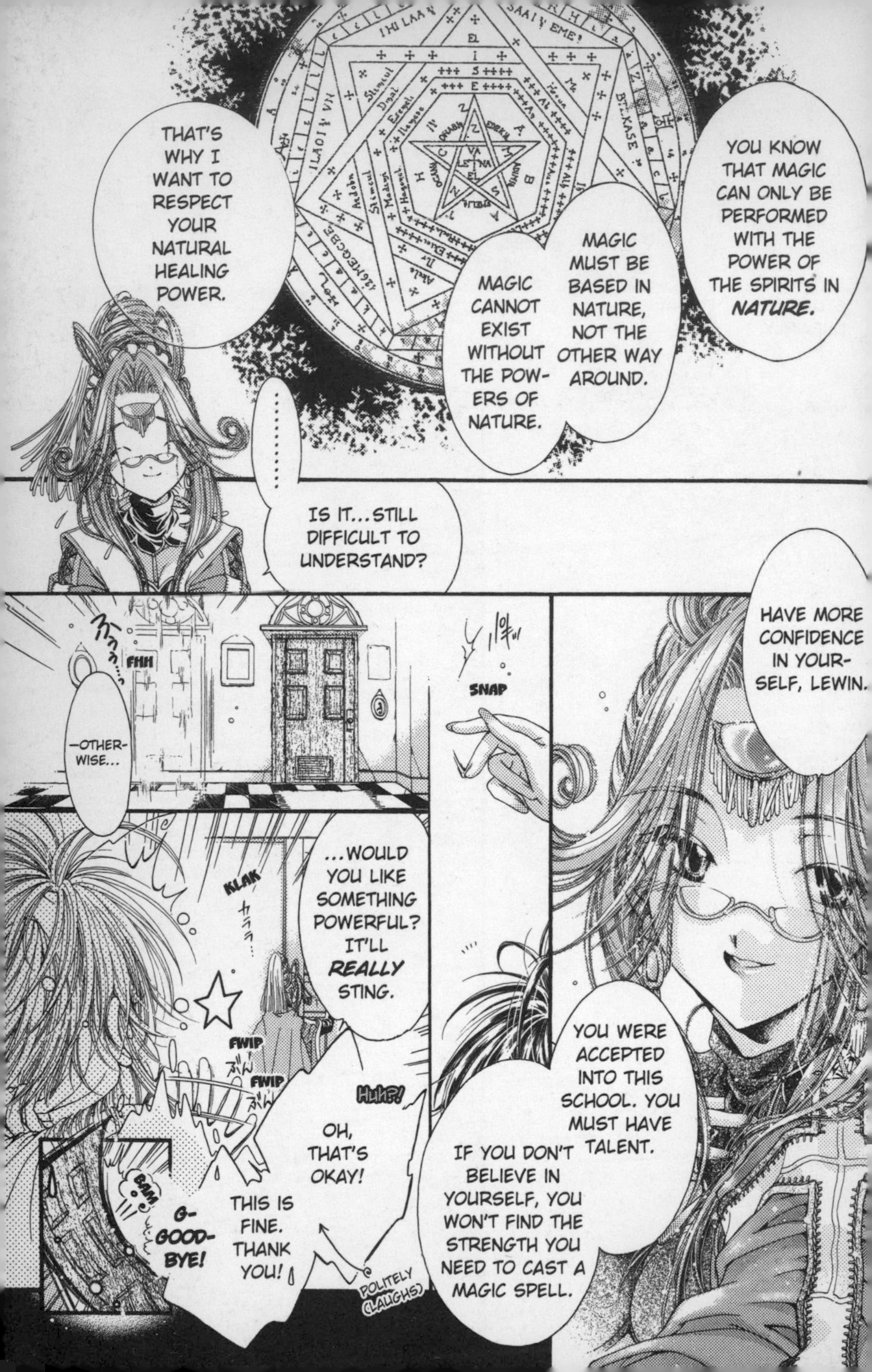
YOU KNOW THAT MAGIC CAN ONLY BE PERFORMED WITH THE POWER OF THE SPIRITS IN *NATURE.*
MAGIC MUST BE BASED IN NATURE, NOT THE OTHER WAY AROUND.
MAGIC CANNOT EXIST WITHOUT THE POWERS OF NATURE.
THAT'S WHY I WANT TO RESPECT YOUR NATURAL HEALING POWER.
......
IS IT...STILL DIFFICULT TO UNDERSTAND?
HAVE MORE CONFIDENCE IN YOURSELF, LEWIN.
YOU WERE ACCEPTED INTO THIS SCHOOL. YOU MUST HAVE TALENT.
IF YOU DON'T BELIEVE IN YOURSELF, YOU WON'T FIND THE STRENGTH YOU NEED TO CAST A MAGIC SPELL.
SNAP
...WOULD YOU LIKE SOMETHING POWERFUL? IT'LL *REALLY* STING.
HUH?!
OH, THAT'S OKAY!
THIS IS FINE. THANK YOU!
POLITELY (LAUGHS)
FHH
—OTHERWISE...
KLAK
FWIP
FWIP
BAM
G-GOODBYE!

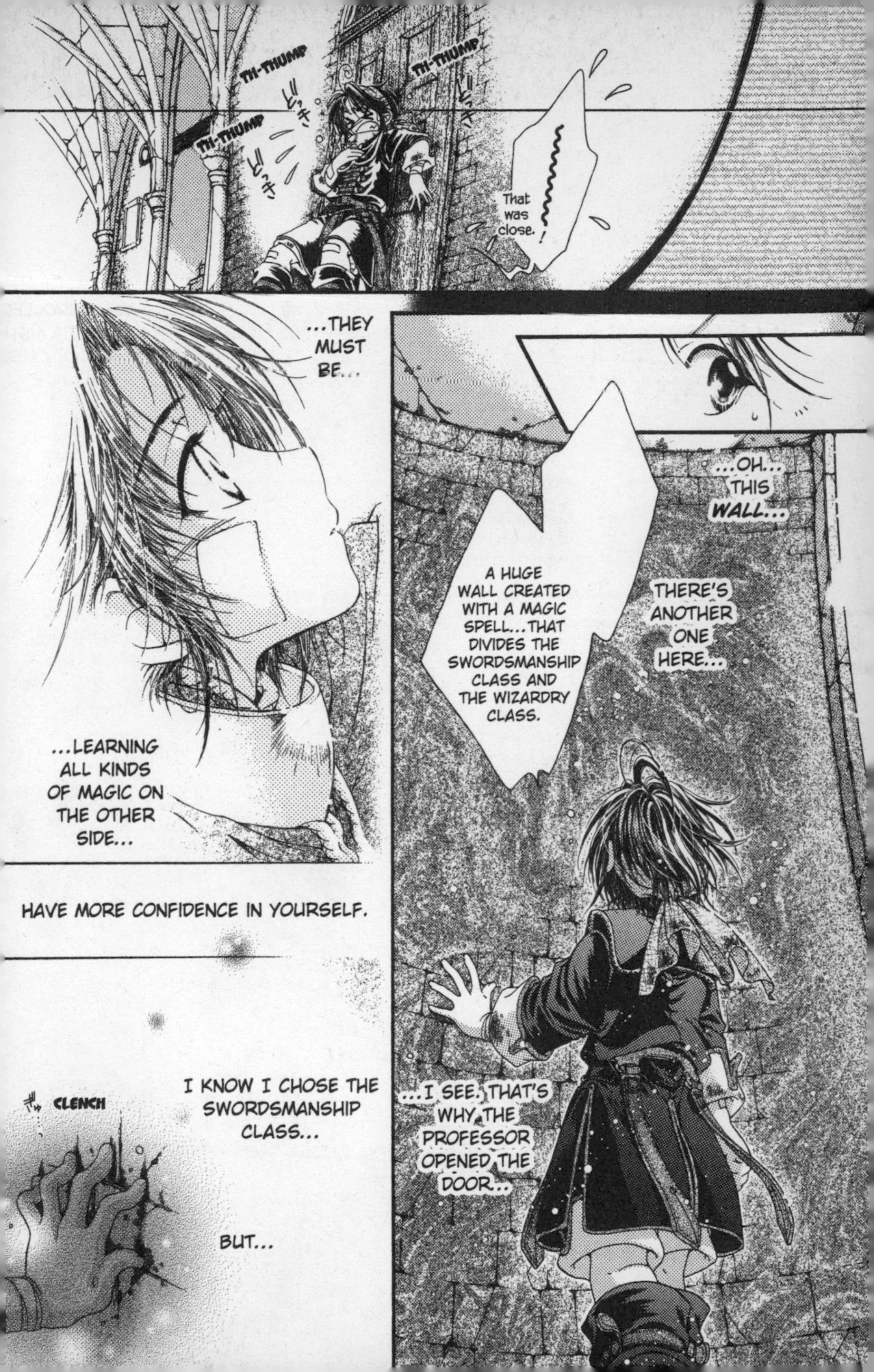
That was close.
TH-THUMP
TH-THUMP
TH-THUMP
...OH... THIS WALL...
A HUGE WALL CREATED WITH A MAGIC SPELL...THAT DIVIDES THE SWORDSMANSHIP CLASS AND THE WIZARDRY CLASS.
THERE'S ANOTHER ONE HERE...
...I SEE. THAT'S WHY THE PROFESSOR OPENED THE DOOR...
...THEY MUST BE...
...LEARNING ALL KINDS OF MAGIC ON THE OTHER SIDE...
HAVE MORE CONFIDENCE IN YOURSELF.
I KNOW I CHOSE THE SWORDSMANSHIP CLASS...
CLENCH
BUT...

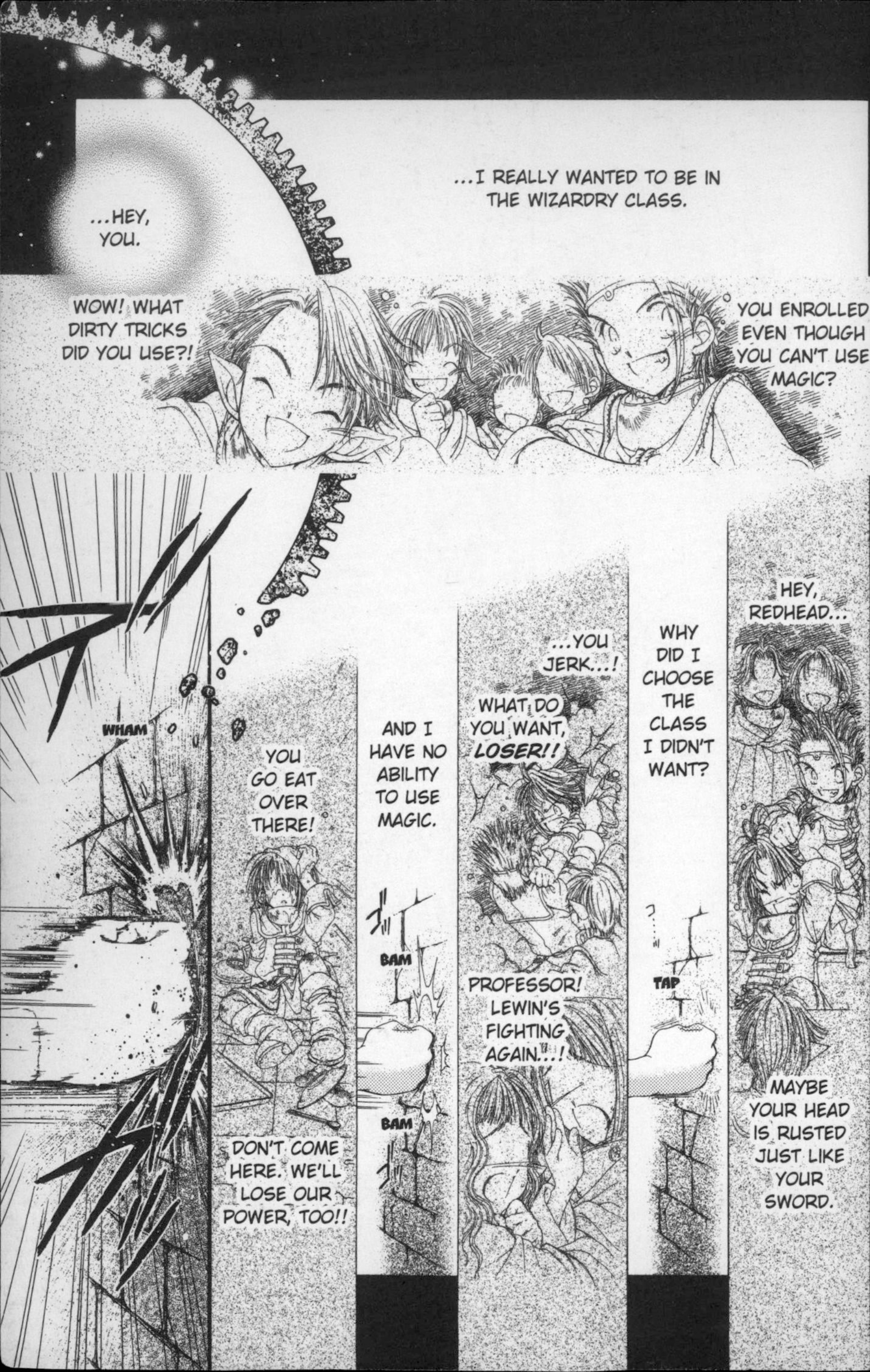
...I REALLY WANTED TO BE IN THE WIZARDRY CLASS.
...HEY, YOU.
YOU ENROLLED EVEN THOUGH YOU CAN'T USE MAGIC?
WOW! WHAT DIRTY TRICKS DID YOU USE?!
HEY, REDHEAD...
MAYBE YOUR HEAD IS RUSTED JUST LIKE YOUR SWORD.
WHY DID I CHOOSE THE CLASS I DIDN'T WANT?
TAP
...YOU JERK...!
WHAT DO YOU WANT, LOSER!!
PROFESSOR! LEWIN'S FIGHTING AGAIN...!
AND I HAVE NO ABILITY TO USE MAGIC.
BAM
BAM
YOU GO EAT OVER THERE!
DON'T COME HERE. WE'LL LOSE OUR POWER, TOO!!
WHAM

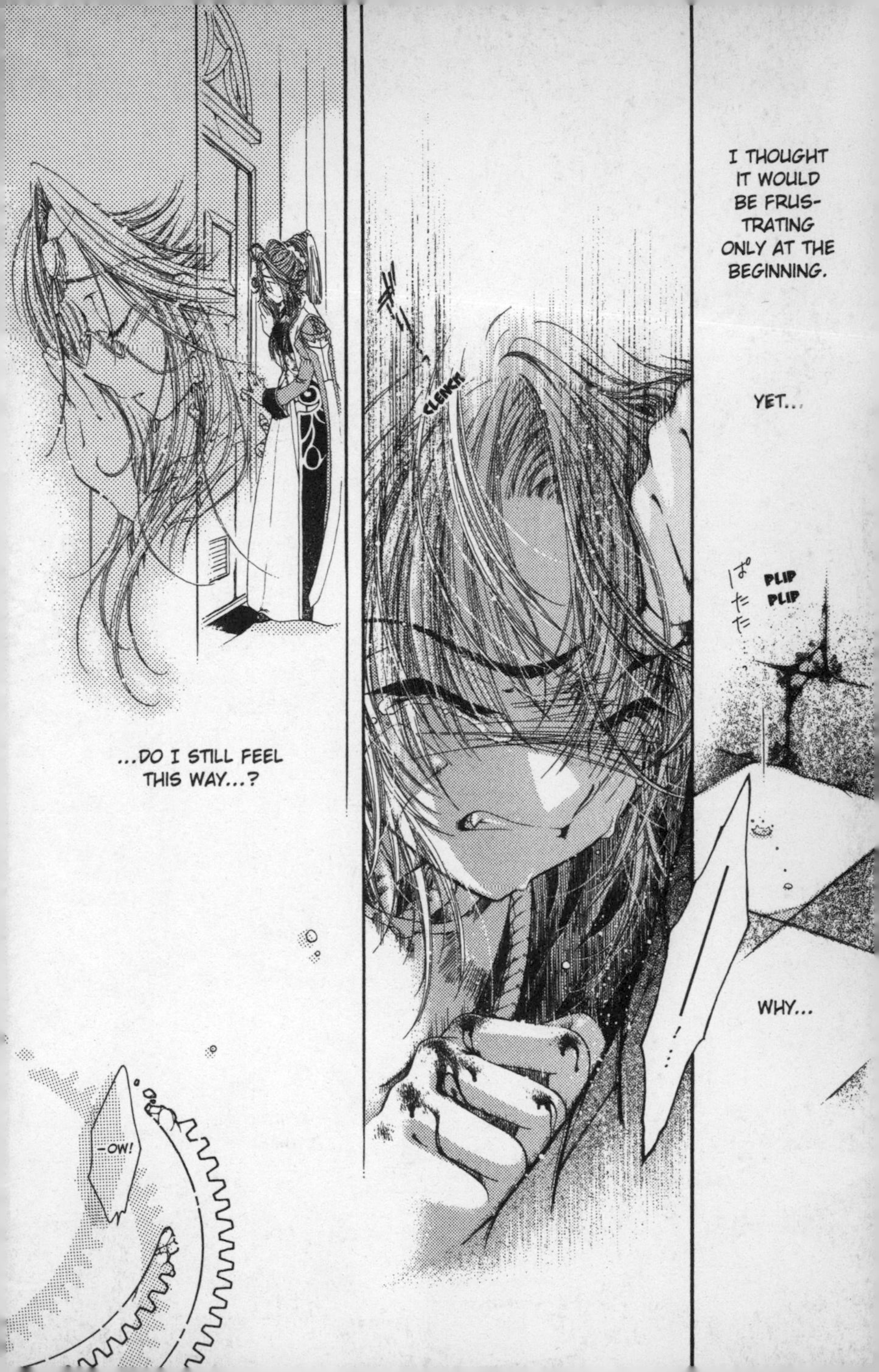
I THOUGHT IT WOULD BE FRUS-TRATING ONLY AT THE BEGINNING.
YET...
ぱたた
PLIP PLIP
WHY...
...!
CLENCH
...DO I STILL FEEL THIS WAY...?
-OW!

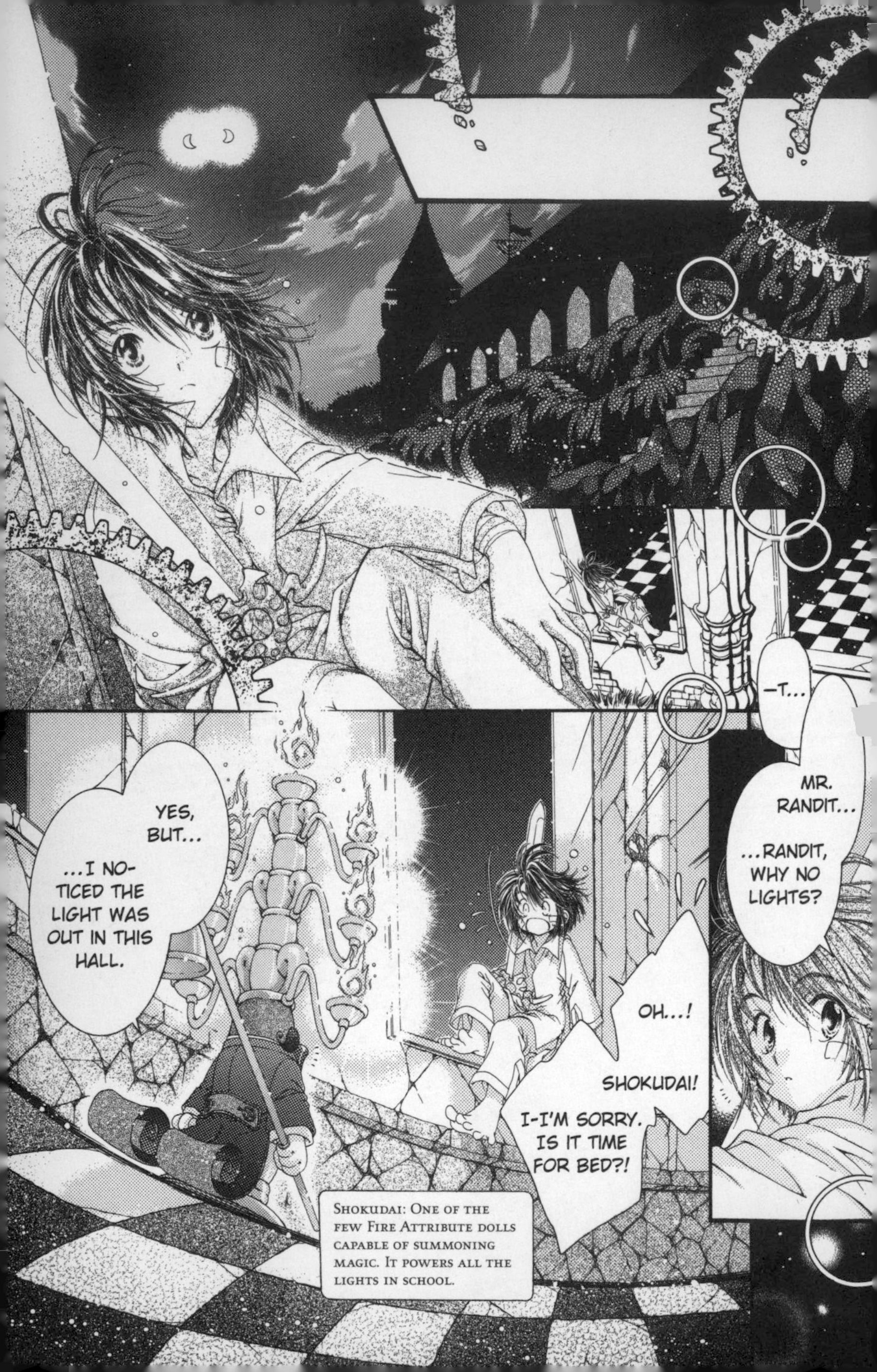
—T...
MR. RANDIT...
...RANDIT, WHY NO LIGHTS?
OH...!
SHOKUDAI!
I-I'M SORRY. IS IT TIME FOR BED?!
YES, BUT...
...I NOTICED THE LIGHT WAS OUT IN THIS HALL.
Shokudai: One of the few Fire Attribute dolls capable of summoning magic. It powers all the lights in school.

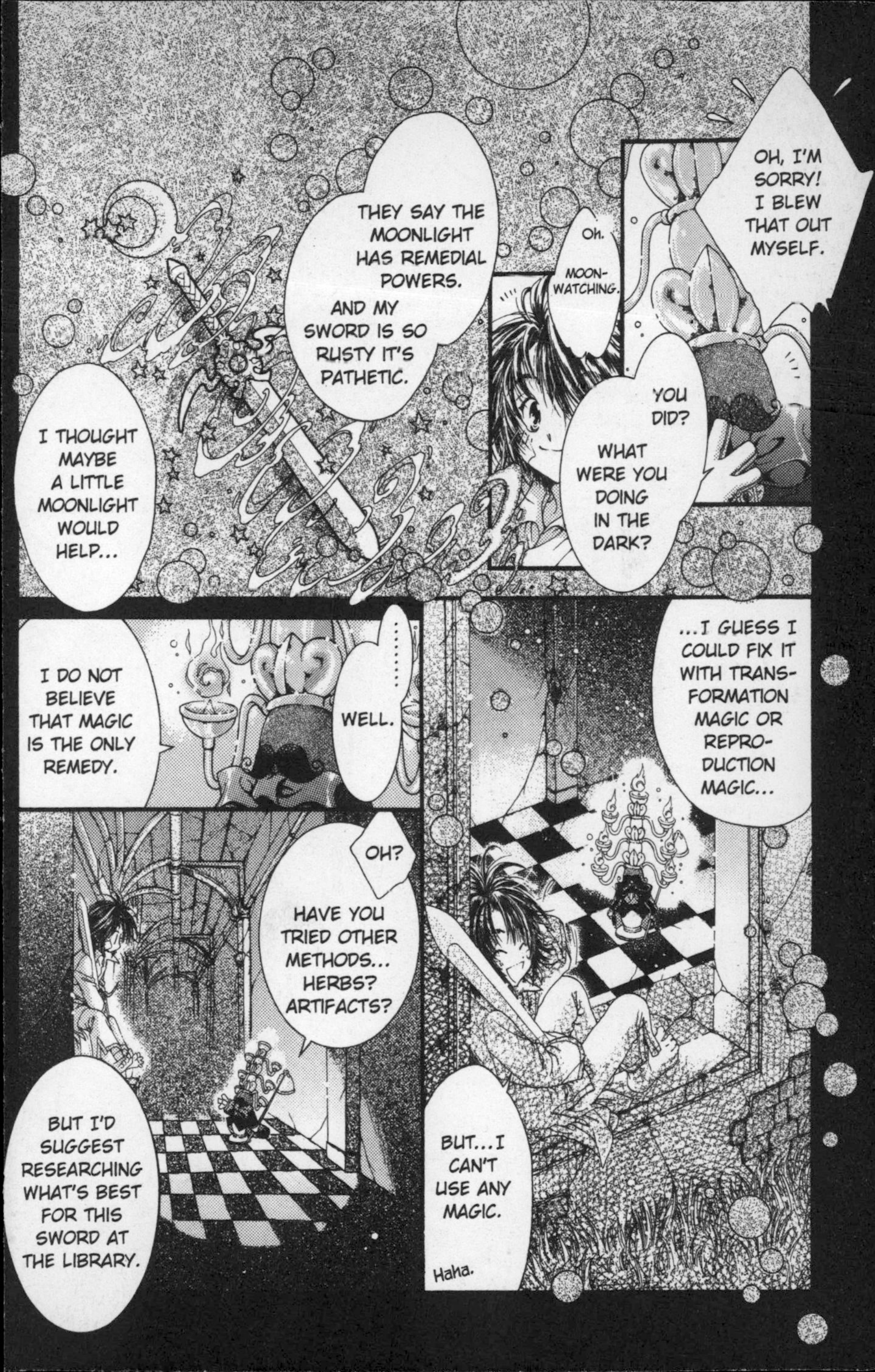
OH, I'M SORRY! I BLEW THAT OUT MYSELF.
YOU DID?
WHAT WERE YOU DOING IN THE DARK?
Oh.
MOON-WATCHING.
THEY SAY THE MOONLIGHT HAS REMEDIAL POWERS.
AND MY SWORD IS SO RUSTY IT'S PATHETIC.
I THOUGHT MAYBE A LITTLE MOONLIGHT WOULD HELP...
...I GUESS I COULD FIX IT WITH TRANS-FORMATION MAGIC OR REPRO-DUCTION MAGIC...
BUT...I CAN'T USE ANY MAGIC.
Haha.
......
WELL.
I DO NOT BELIEVE THAT MAGIC IS THE ONLY REMEDY.
OH?
HAVE YOU TRIED OTHER METHODS... HERBS? ARTIFACTS?
BUT I'D SUGGEST RESEARCHING WHAT'S BEST FOR THIS SWORD AT THE LIBRARY.

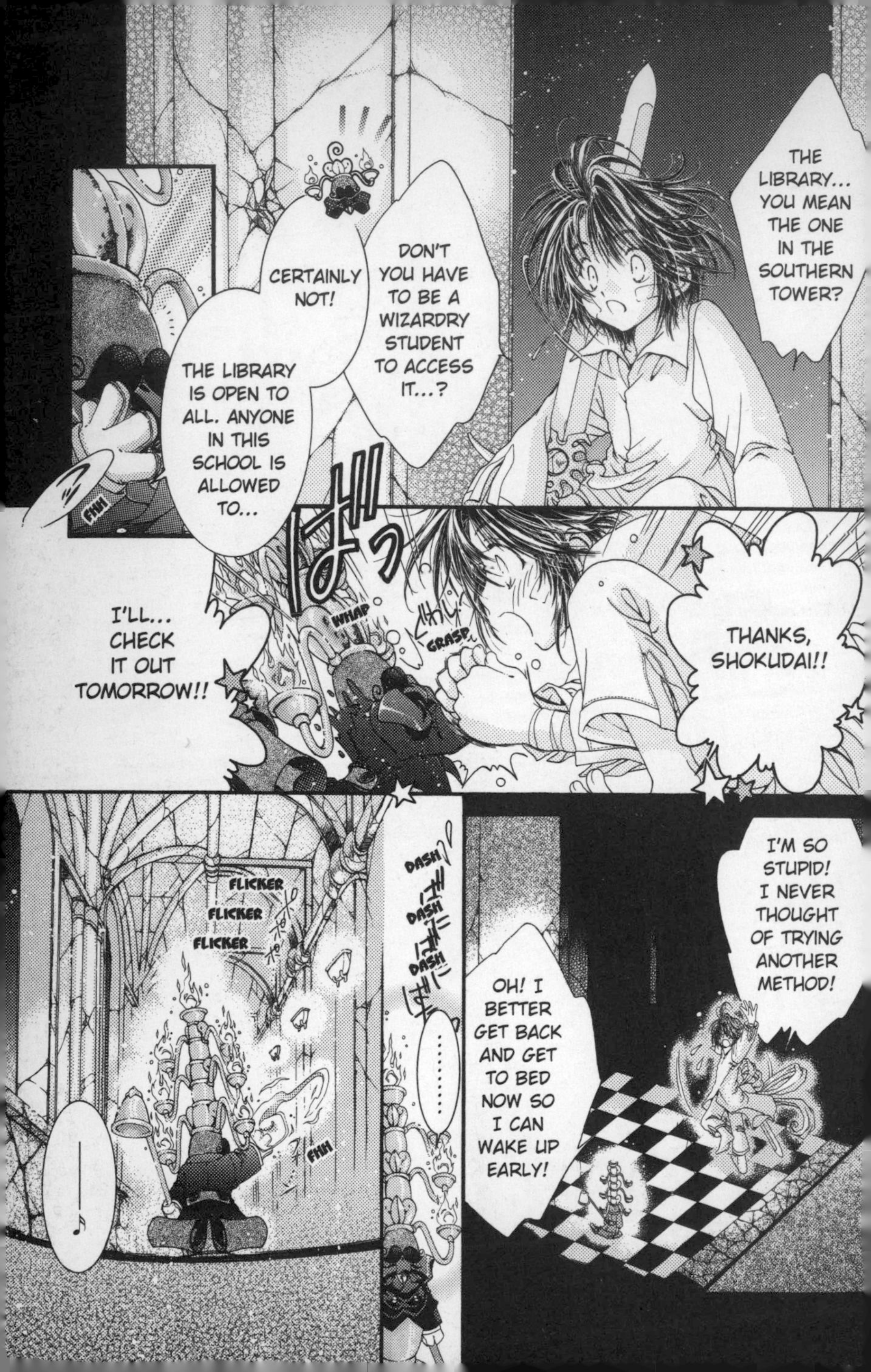
THE LIBRARY... YOU MEAN THE ONE IN THE SOUTHERN TOWER?
DON'T YOU HAVE TO BE A WIZARDRY STUDENT TO ACCESS IT...?
CERTAINLY NOT!
THE LIBRARY IS OPEN TO ALL. ANYONE IN THIS SCHOOL IS ALLOWED TO...
FHH
THANKS, SHOKUDAI!!
GRASP
WHAP
I'LL... CHECK IT OUT TOMORROW!!
I'M SO STUPID! I NEVER THOUGHT OF TRYING ANOTHER METHOD!
OH! I BETTER GET BACK AND GET TO BED NOW SO I CAN WAKE UP EARLY!
DASH
DASH
DASH
......
FLICKER
FLICKER
FLICKER
FHH
!

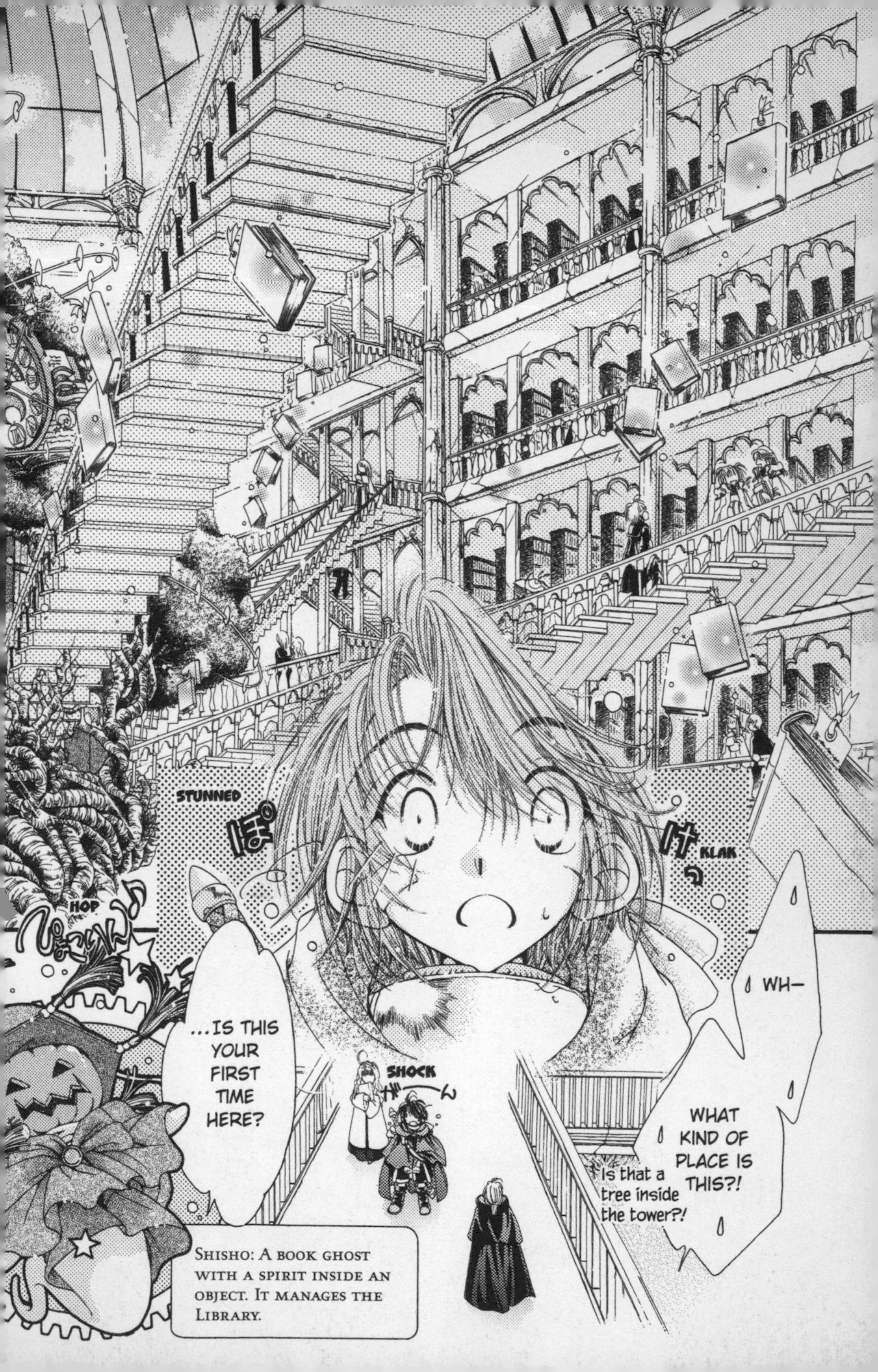
KLAK
STUNNED
WH—
WHAT KIND OF PLACE IS THIS?!
Is that a tree inside the tower?!
SHOCK
...IS THIS YOUR FIRST TIME HERE?
HOP
SHISHO: A BOOK GHOST WITH A SPIRIT INSIDE AN OBJECT. IT MANAGES THE LIBRARY.

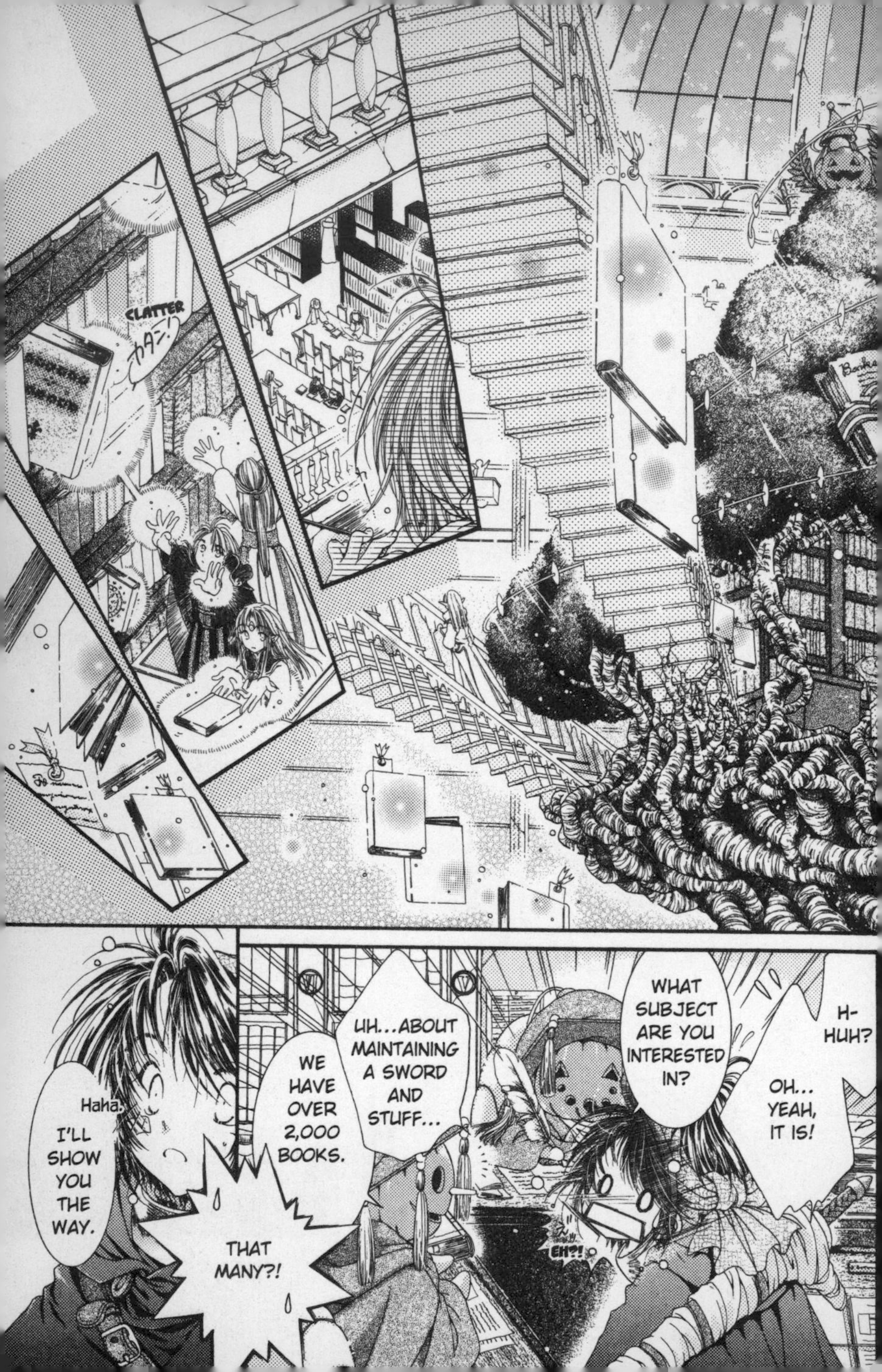
CLATTER
カタン!
H-HUH?
WHAT SUBJECT ARE YOU INTERESTED IN?
OH... YEAH, IT IS!
UH...ABOUT MAINTAINING A SWORD AND STUFF...
WE HAVE OVER 2,000 BOOKS.
EH?!
THAT MANY?!
Haha.
I'LL SHOW YOU THE WAY.

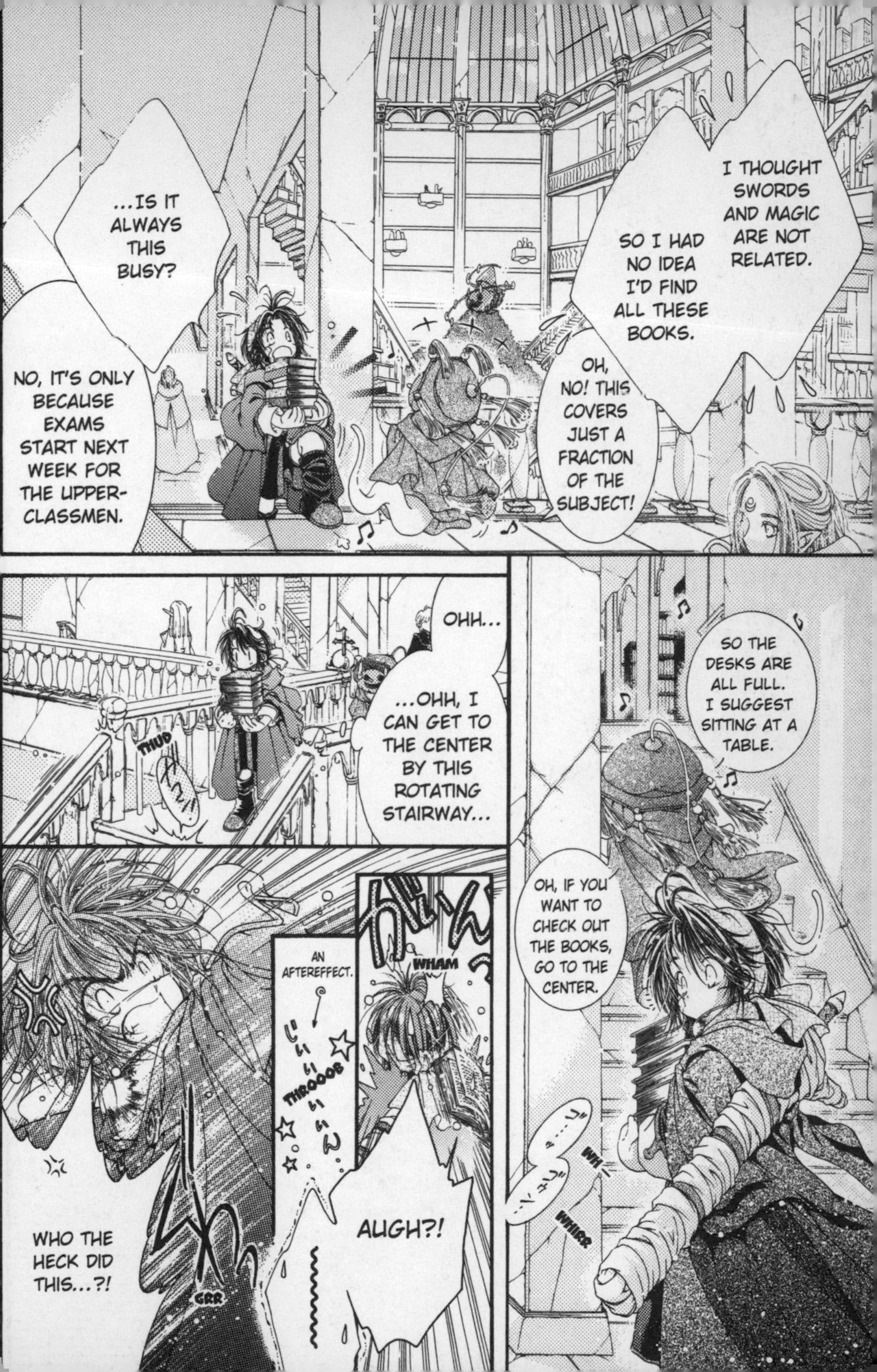
I THOUGHT SWORDS AND MAGIC ARE NOT RELATED.
SO I HAD NO IDEA I'D FIND ALL THESE BOOKS.
OH, NO! THIS COVERS JUST A FRACTION OF THE SUBJECT!
...IS IT ALWAYS THIS BUSY?
NO, IT'S ONLY BECAUSE EXAMS START NEXT WEEK FOR THE UPPER-CLASSMEN.
SO THE DESKS ARE ALL FULL. I SUGGEST SITTING AT A TABLE.
OH, IF YOU WANT TO CHECK OUT THE BOOKS, GO TO THE CENTER.
WH
WHIRR
OHH...
...OHH, I CAN GET TO THE CENTER BY THIS ROTATING STAIRWAY...
THUD
WHAM
AN AFTEREFFECT.
THROOOB
AUGH?!
WHO THE HECK DID THIS...?!
GRR

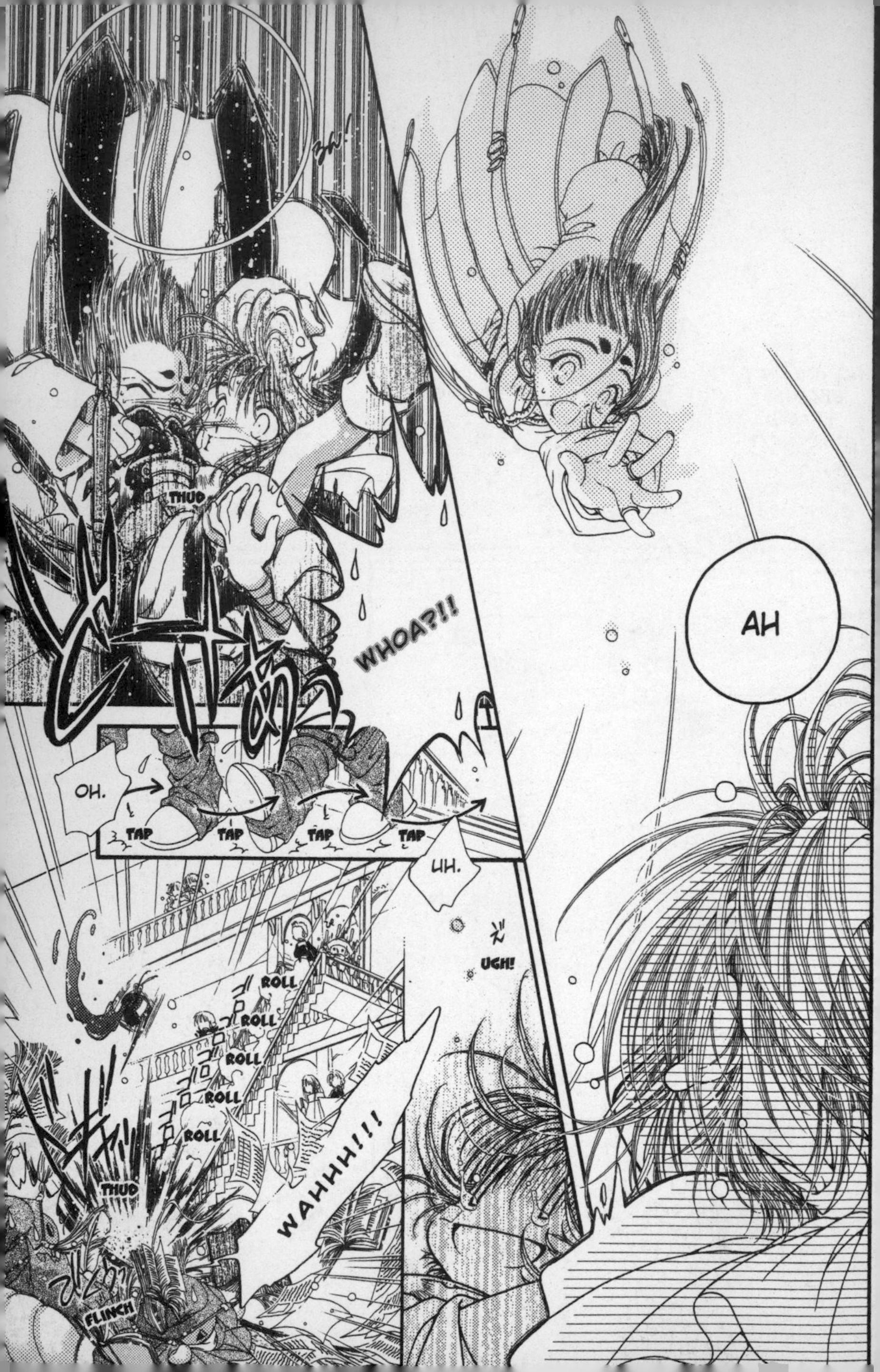

AH
THUD
WHOA?!!
OH.
TAP
TAP
TAP
TAP
UH.
UGH!
ROLL
ROLL
ROLL
ROLL
ROLL
WAHHH!!!
THUD
FLINCH

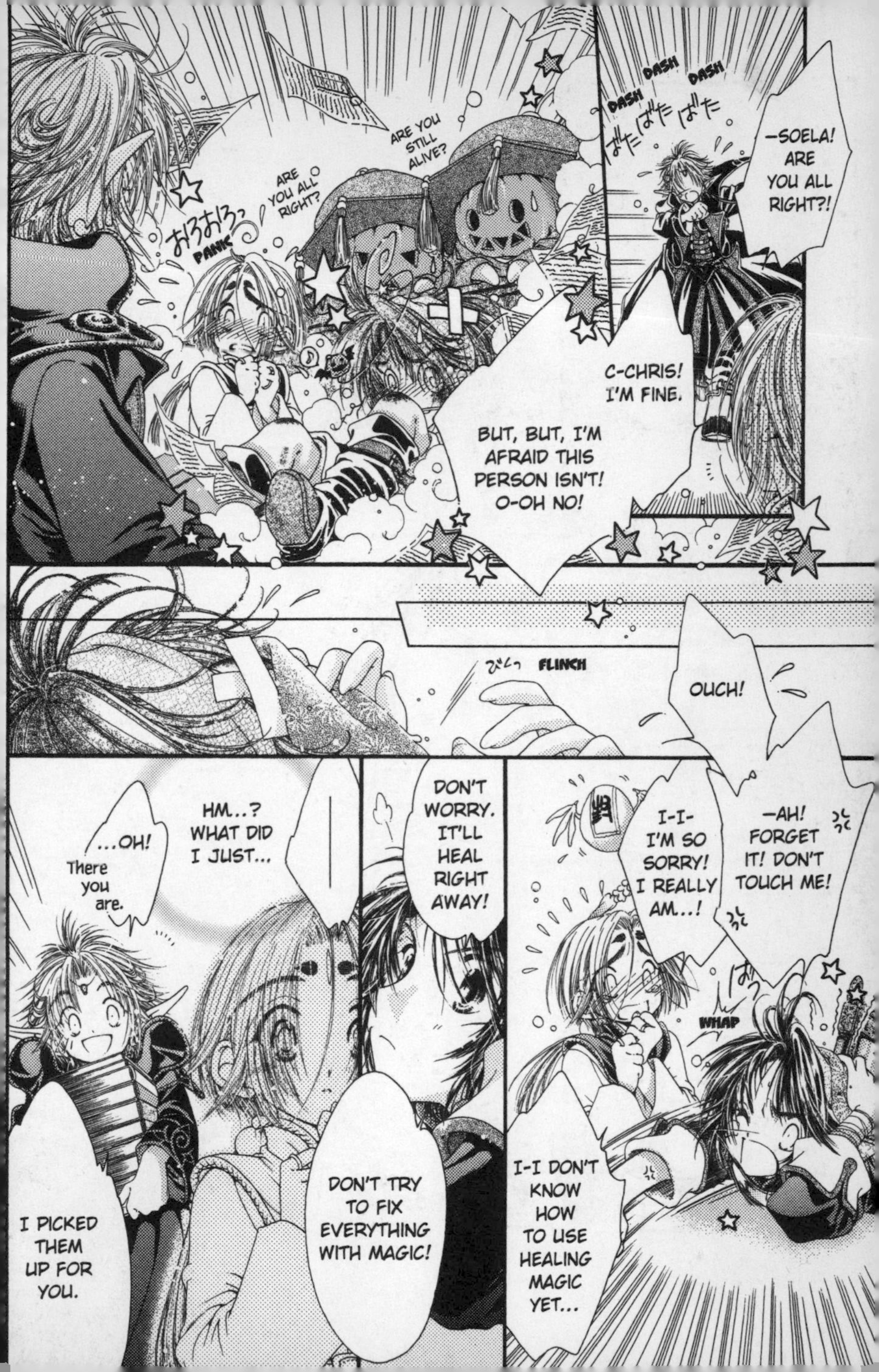

DASH DASH DASH
ばたばた
—SOELA! ARE YOU ALL RIGHT?!
ARE YOU STILL ALIVE?
ARE YOU ALL RIGHT?
おろおろ
PANIK
C-CHRIS! I'M FINE.
BUT, BUT, I'M AFRAID THIS PERSON ISN'T! O-OH NO!
OUCH!
びくっ
FLINCH
—AH! FORGET IT! DON'T TOUCH ME!
I-I- I'M SO SORRY! I REALLY AM...!
WHAP
I-I DON'T KNOW HOW TO USE HEALING MAGIC YET...
DON'T WORRY. IT'LL HEAL RIGHT AWAY!
DON'T TRY TO FIX EVERYTHING WITH MAGIC!
HM...? WHAT DID I JUST...
...OH!
There you are.
I PICKED THEM UP FOR YOU.

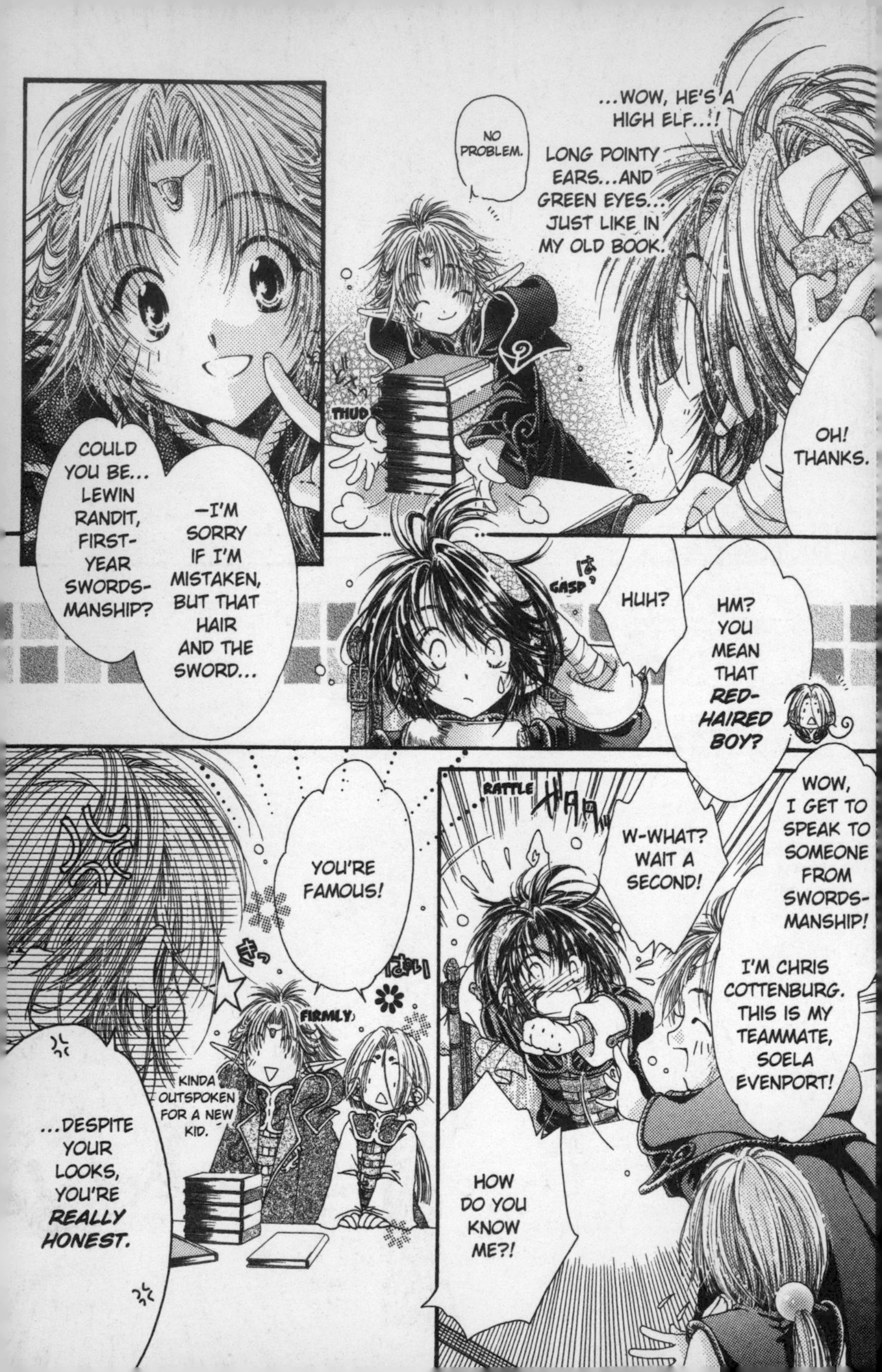

OH! THANKS.
NO PROBLEM.
...WOW, HE'S A HIGH ELF...!
LONG POINTY EARS...AND GREEN EYES... JUST LIKE IN MY OLD BOOK.
THUD
—I'M SORRY IF I'M MISTAKEN, BUT THAT HAIR AND THE SWORD...
COULD YOU BE... LEWIN RANDIT, FIRST-YEAR SWORDSMANSHIP?
HM? YOU MEAN THAT ***RED-HAIRED BOY?***
HUH?
GASP
WOW, I GET TO SPEAK TO SOMEONE FROM SWORDSMANSHIP!
I'M CHRIS COTTENBURG. THIS IS MY TEAMMATE, SOELA EVENPORT!
RATTLE
W-WHAT? WAIT A SECOND!
HOW DO YOU KNOW ME?!
YOU'RE FAMOUS!
FIRMLY
KINDA OUTSPOKEN FOR A NEW KID.
...DESPITE YOUR LOOKS, YOU'RE ***REALLY HONEST.***

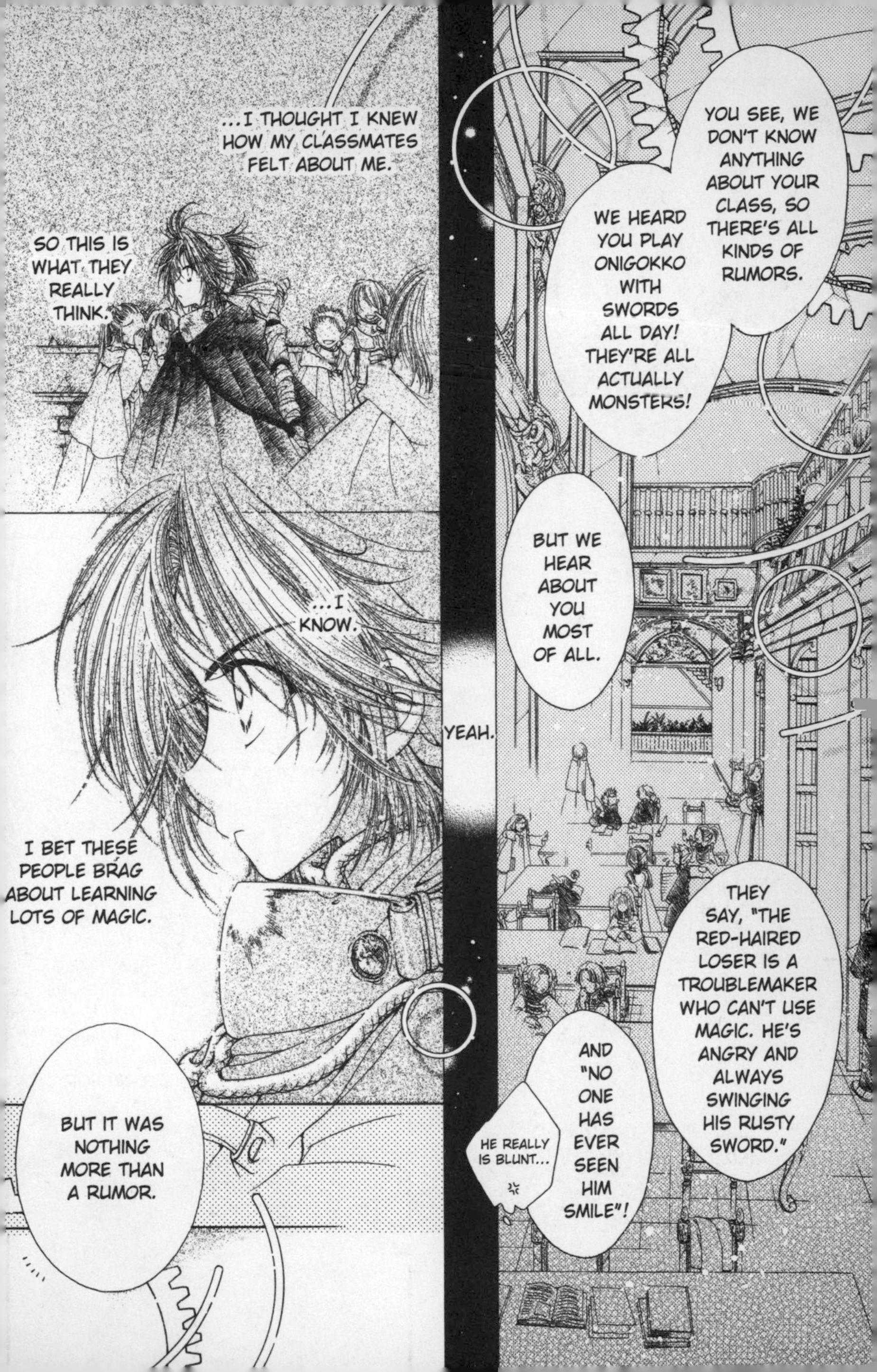
YOU SEE, WE DON'T KNOW ANYTHING ABOUT YOUR CLASS, SO THERE'S ALL KINDS OF RUMORS.
WE HEARD YOU PLAY ONIGOKKO WITH SWORDS ALL DAY! THEY'RE ALL ACTUALLY MONSTERS!
BUT WE HEAR ABOUT YOU MOST OF ALL.
THEY SAY, "THE RED-HAIRED LOSER IS A TROUBLEMAKER WHO CAN'T USE MAGIC. HE'S ANGRY AND ALWAYS SWINGING HIS RUSTY SWORD."
AND "NO ONE HAS EVER SEEN HIM SMILE"!
HE REALLY IS BLUNT...
YEAH.
...I THOUGHT I KNEW HOW MY CLASSMATES FELT ABOUT ME.
SO THIS IS WHAT THEY REALLY THINK.
...I KNOW.
I BET THESE PEOPLE BRAG ABOUT LEARNING LOTS OF MAGIC.
BUT IT WAS NOTHING MORE THAN A RUMOR.

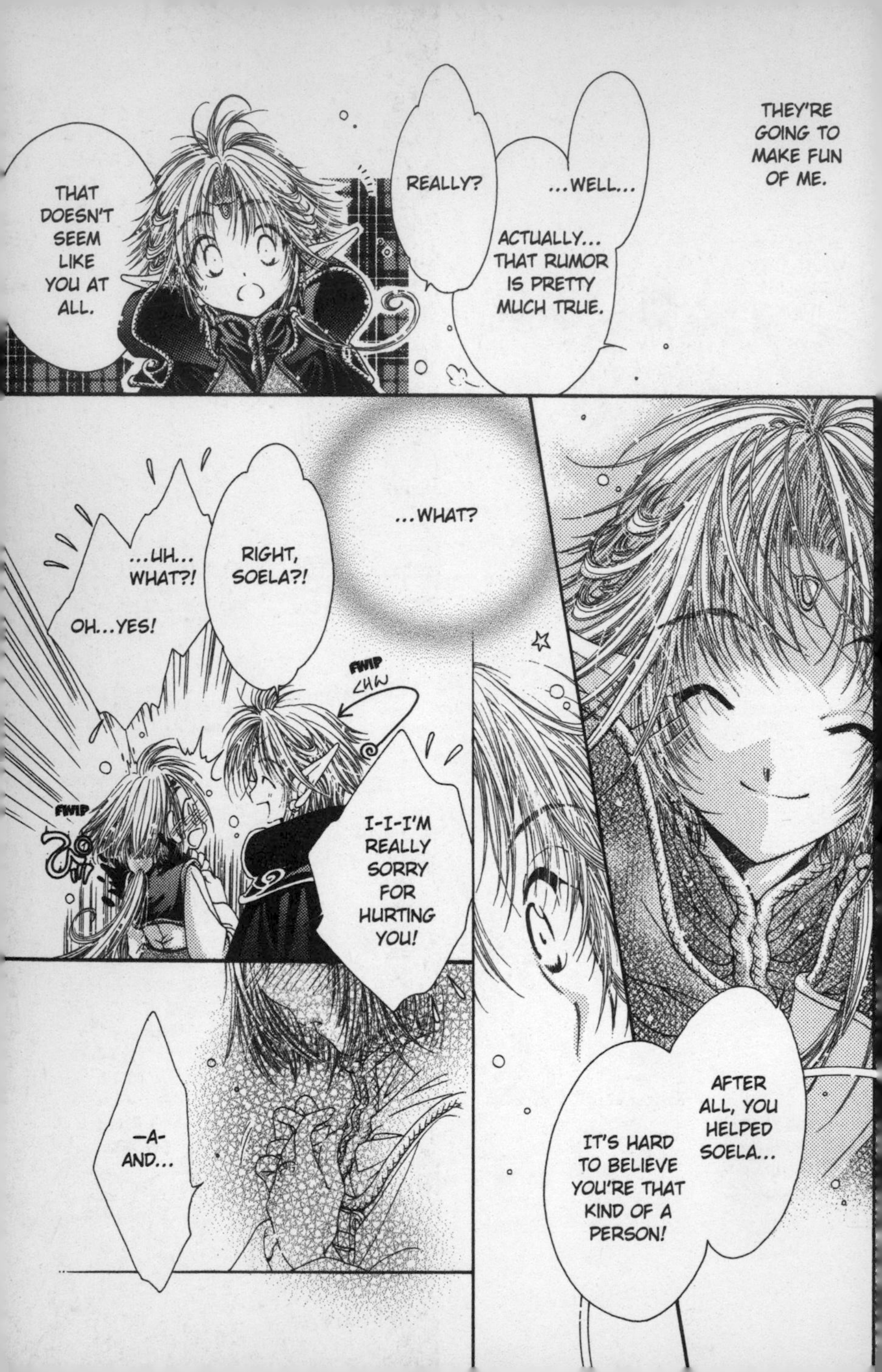
THEY'RE GOING TO MAKE FUN OF ME.
...WELL...
ACTUALLY... THAT RUMOR IS PRETTY MUCH TRUE.
REALLY?
THAT DOESN'T SEEM LIKE YOU AT ALL.
AFTER ALL, YOU HELPED SOELA...
IT'S HARD TO BELIEVE YOU'RE THAT KIND OF A PERSON!
...WHAT?
RIGHT, SOELA?!
...UH... WHAT?!
OH...YES!
FWIP
FWIP
I-I-I'M REALLY SORRY FOR HURTING YOU!
—A- AND...

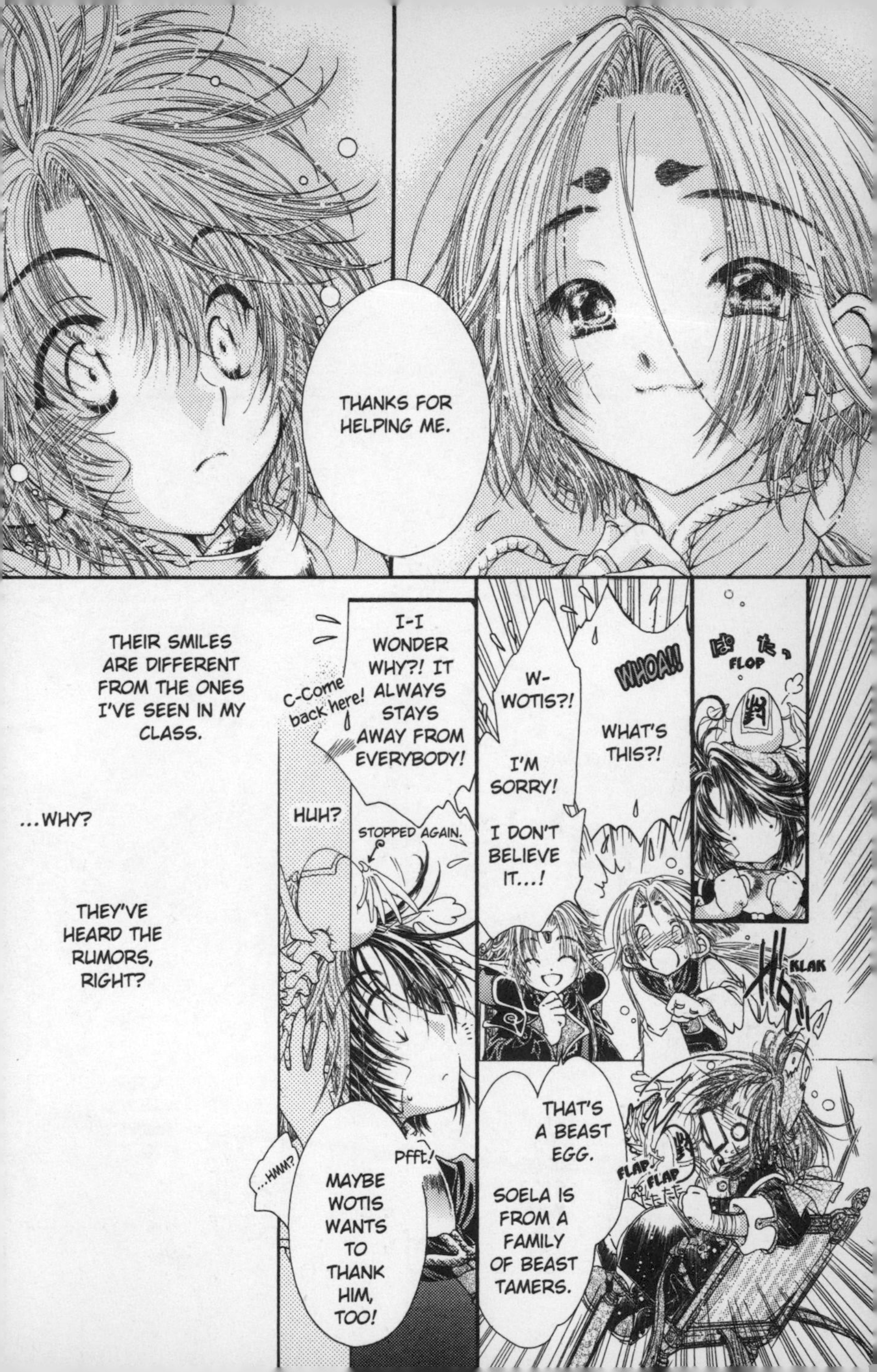
THANKS FOR HELPING ME.
FLOP
WHOA!!
WHAT'S THIS?!
W-WOTIS?!
I'M SORRY!
I DON'T BELIEVE IT...!
KLAK
THAT'S A BEAST EGG.
SOELA IS FROM A FAMILY OF BEAST TAMERS.
FLAP FLAP
I-I WONDER WHY?! IT ALWAYS STAYS AWAY FROM EVERYBODY!
C-Come back here!
HUH?
STOPPED AGAIN.
Pfft!
MAYBE WOTIS WANTS TO THANK HIM, TOO!
...HMM?
THEIR SMILES ARE DIFFERENT FROM THE ONES I'VE SEEN IN MY CLASS.
...WHY?
THEY'VE HEARD THE RUMORS, RIGHT?

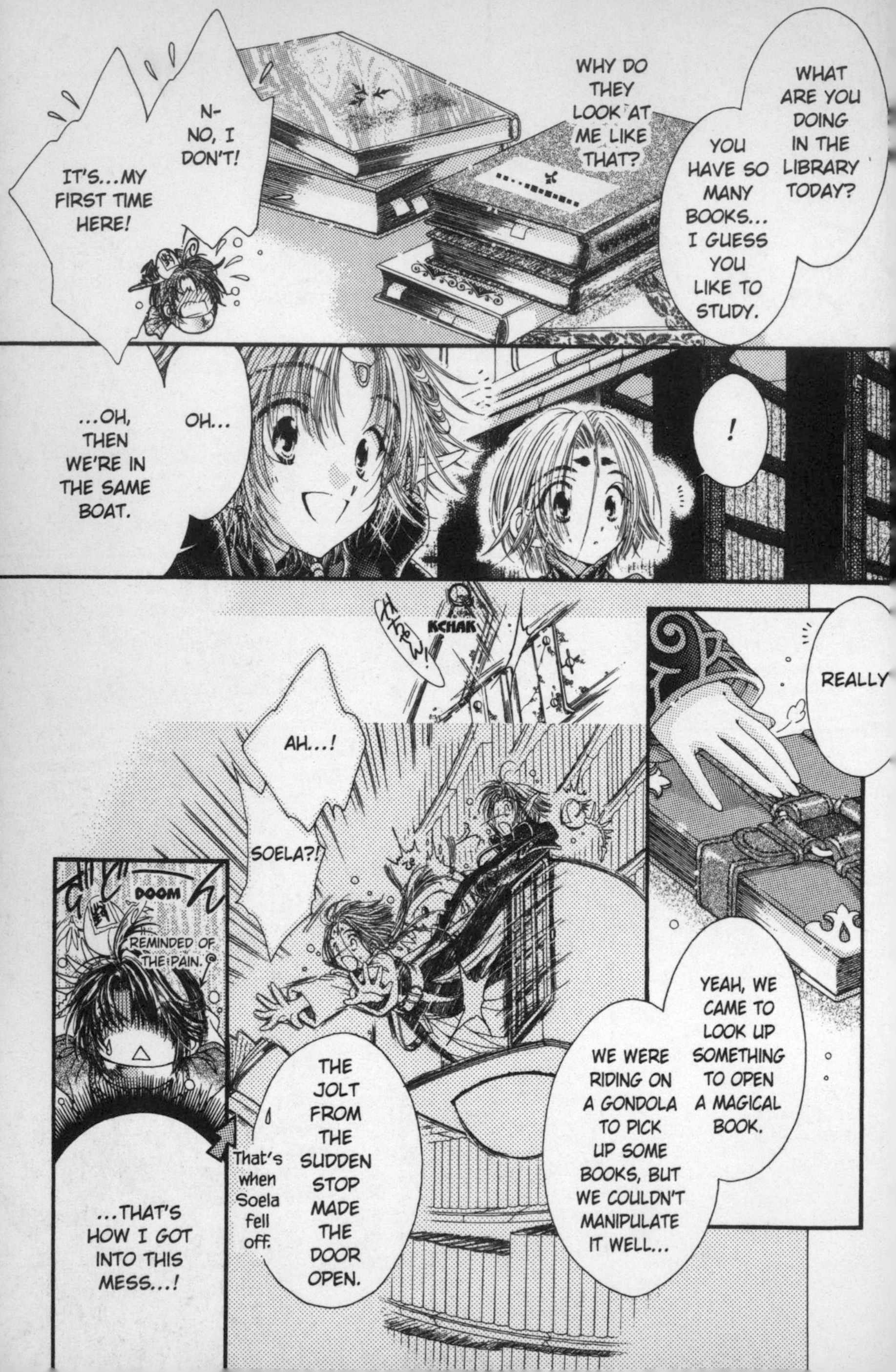
WHAT ARE YOU DOING IN THE LIBRARY TODAY?
YOU HAVE SO MANY BOOKS... I GUESS YOU LIKE TO STUDY.
WHY DO THEY LOOK AT ME LIKE THAT?
N-NO, I DON'T!
IT'S...MY FIRST TIME HERE!
!
OH...
...OH, THEN WE'RE IN THE SAME BOAT.
REALLY
YEAH, WE CAME TO LOOK UP SOMETHING TO OPEN A MAGICAL BOOK.
WE WERE RIDING ON A GONDOLA TO PICK UP SOME BOOKS, BUT WE COULDN'T MANIPULATE IT WELL...
KCHAK
AH...!
SOELA?!
THE JOLT FROM THE SUDDEN STOP MADE THE DOOR OPEN.
That's when Soela fell off.
DOOM
REMINDED OF THE PAIN.
...THAT'S HOW I GOT INTO THIS MESS...!

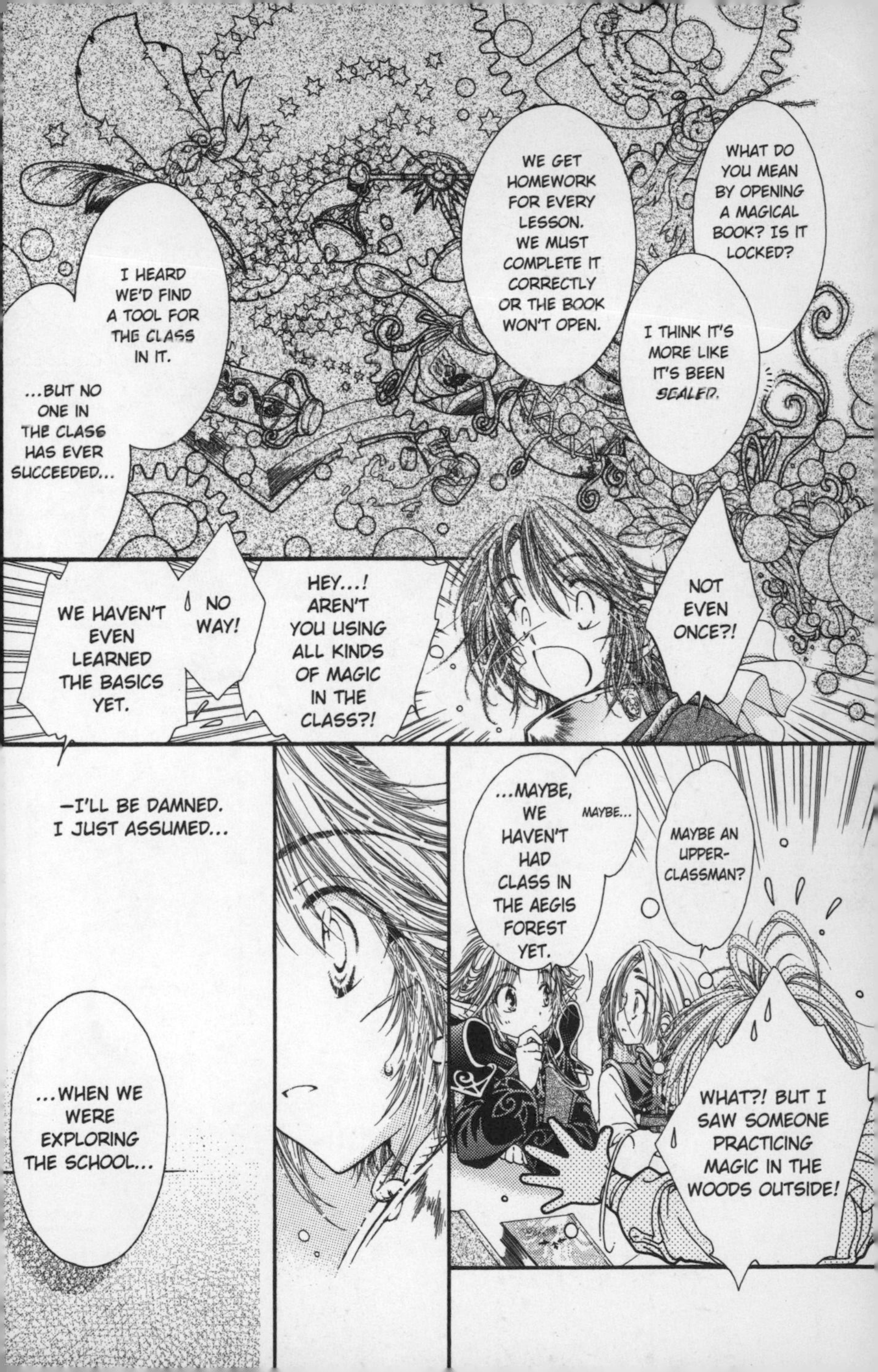
WHAT DO YOU MEAN BY OPENING A MAGICAL BOOK? IS IT LOCKED?
I THINK IT'S MORE LIKE IT'S BEEN SEALED.
WE GET HOMEWORK FOR EVERY LESSON. WE MUST COMPLETE IT CORRECTLY OR THE BOOK WON'T OPEN.
I HEARD WE'D FIND A TOOL FOR THE CLASS IN IT.
...BUT NO ONE IN THE CLASS HAS EVER SUCCEEDED...
NOT EVEN ONCE?!
HEY...! AREN'T YOU USING ALL KINDS OF MAGIC IN THE CLASS?!
NO WAY!
WE HAVEN'T EVEN LEARNED THE BASICS YET.
WHAT?! BUT I SAW SOMEONE PRACTICING MAGIC IN THE WOODS OUTSIDE!
MAYBE AN UPPER-CLASSMAN?
MAYBE...
...MAYBE, WE HAVEN'T HAD CLASS IN THE AEGIS FOREST YET.
—I'LL BE DAMNED. I JUST ASSUMED...
...WHEN WE WERE EXPLORING THE SCHOOL...

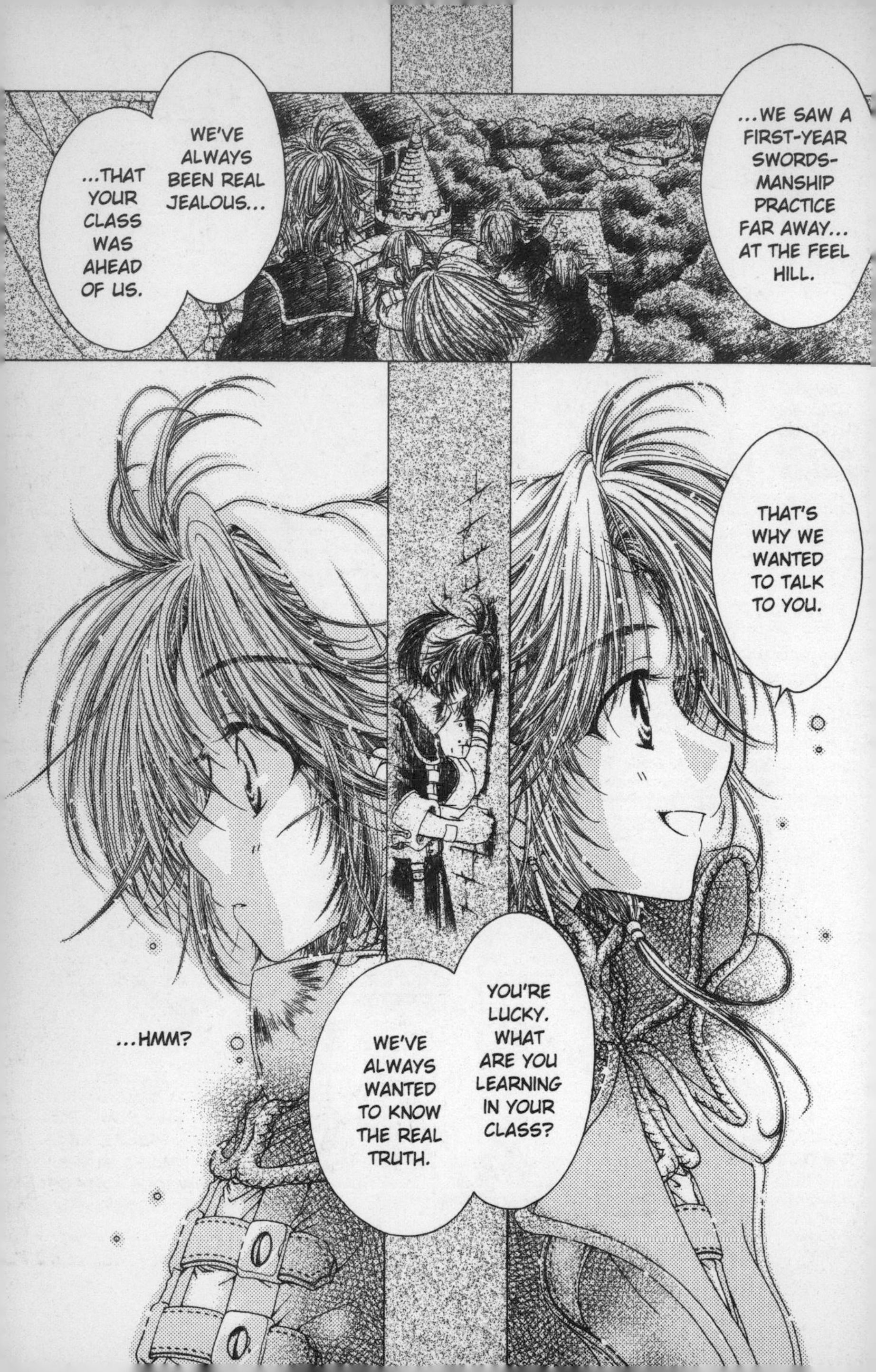
...WE SAW A FIRST-YEAR SWORDS-MANSHIP PRACTICE FAR AWAY... AT THE FEEL HILL.
WE'VE ALWAYS BEEN REAL JEALOUS...
...THAT YOUR CLASS WAS AHEAD OF US.
THAT'S WHY WE WANTED TO TALK TO YOU.
YOU'RE LUCKY. WHAT ARE YOU LEARNING IN YOUR CLASS?
WE'VE ALWAYS WANTED TO KNOW THE REAL TRUTH.
...HMM?

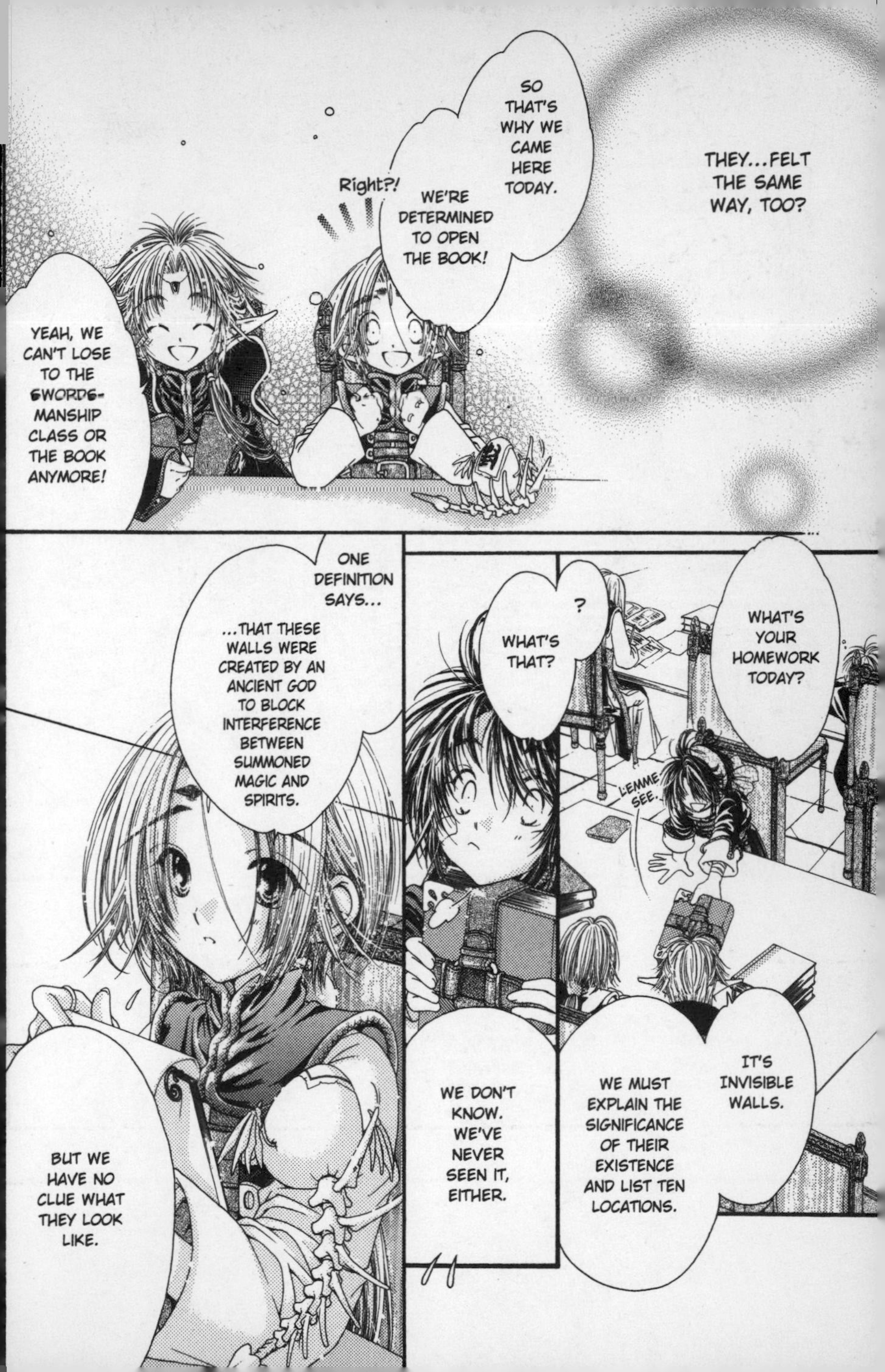
THEY...FELT THE SAME WAY, TOO?
SO THAT'S WHY WE CAME HERE TODAY.
WE'RE DETERMINED TO OPEN THE BOOK!
Right?!
YEAH, WE CAN'T LOSE TO THE SWORDSMANSHIP CLASS OR THE BOOK ANYMORE!
WHAT'S YOUR HOMEWORK TODAY?
LEMME SEE.
IT'S INVISIBLE WALLS.
WE MUST EXPLAIN THE SIGNIFICANCE OF THEIR EXISTENCE AND LIST TEN LOCATIONS.
?
WHAT'S THAT?
WE DON'T KNOW. WE'VE NEVER SEEN IT, EITHER.
ONE DEFINITION SAYS...
...THAT THESE WALLS WERE CREATED BY AN ANCIENT GOD TO BLOCK INTERFERENCE BETWEEN SUMMONED MAGIC AND SPIRITS.
BUT WE HAVE NO CLUE WHAT THEY LOOK LIKE.

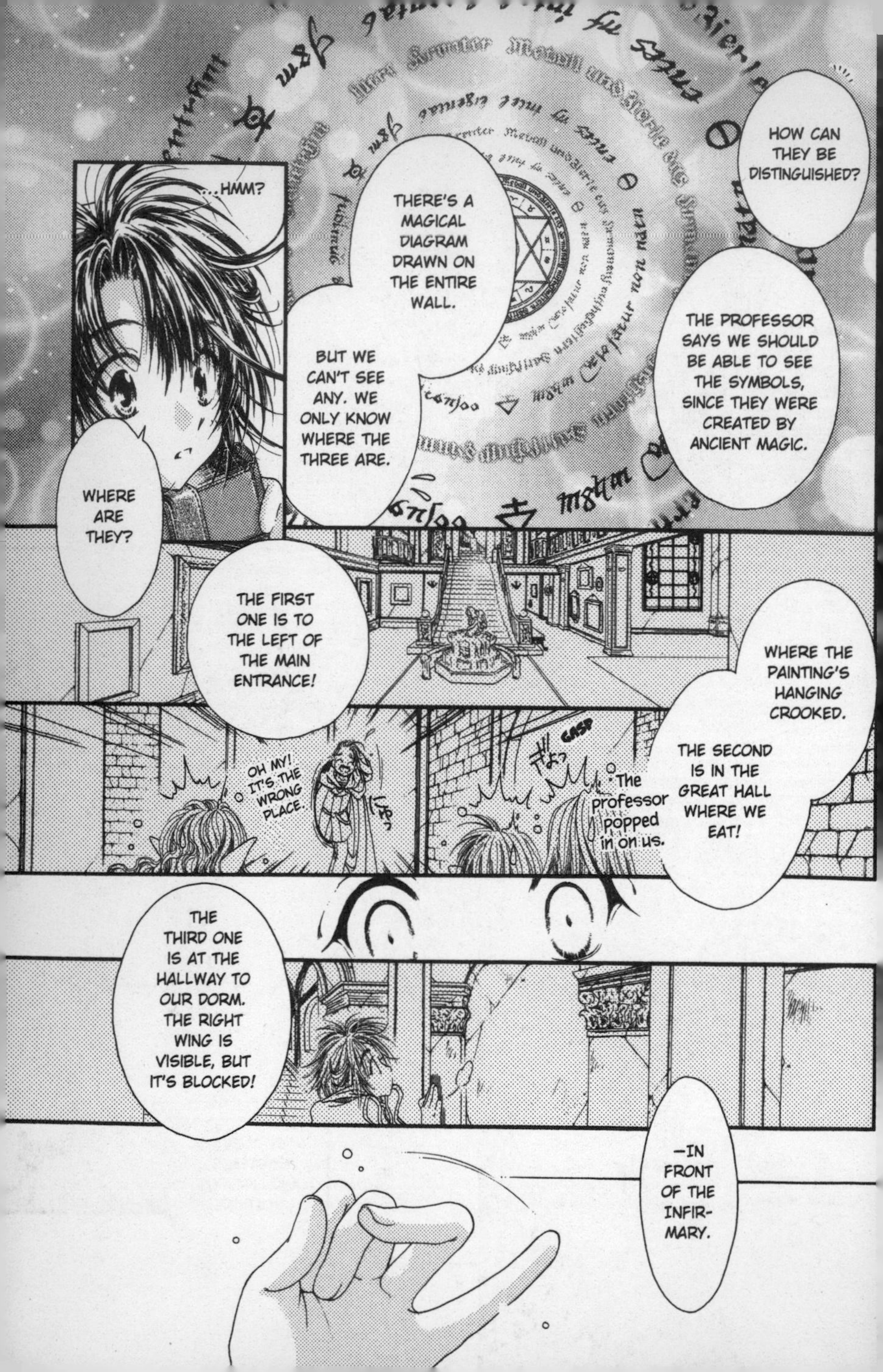
HOW CAN THEY BE DISTINGUISHED?
THE PROFESSOR SAYS WE SHOULD BE ABLE TO SEE THE SYMBOLS, SINCE THEY WERE CREATED BY ANCIENT MAGIC.
THERE'S A MAGICAL DIAGRAM DRAWN ON THE ENTIRE WALL.
BUT WE CAN'T SEE ANY. WE ONLY KNOW WHERE THE THREE ARE.
...HMM?
WHERE ARE THEY?
THE FIRST ONE IS TO THE LEFT OF THE MAIN ENTRANCE!
WHERE THE PAINTING'S HANGING CROOKED.
THE SECOND IS IN THE GREAT HALL WHERE WE EAT!
GASP
The professor popped in on us.
OH MY! IT'S THE WRONG PLACE.
THE THIRD ONE IS AT THE HALLWAY TO OUR DORM. THE RIGHT WING IS VISIBLE, BUT IT'S BLOCKED!
—IN FRONT OF THE INFIRMARY.

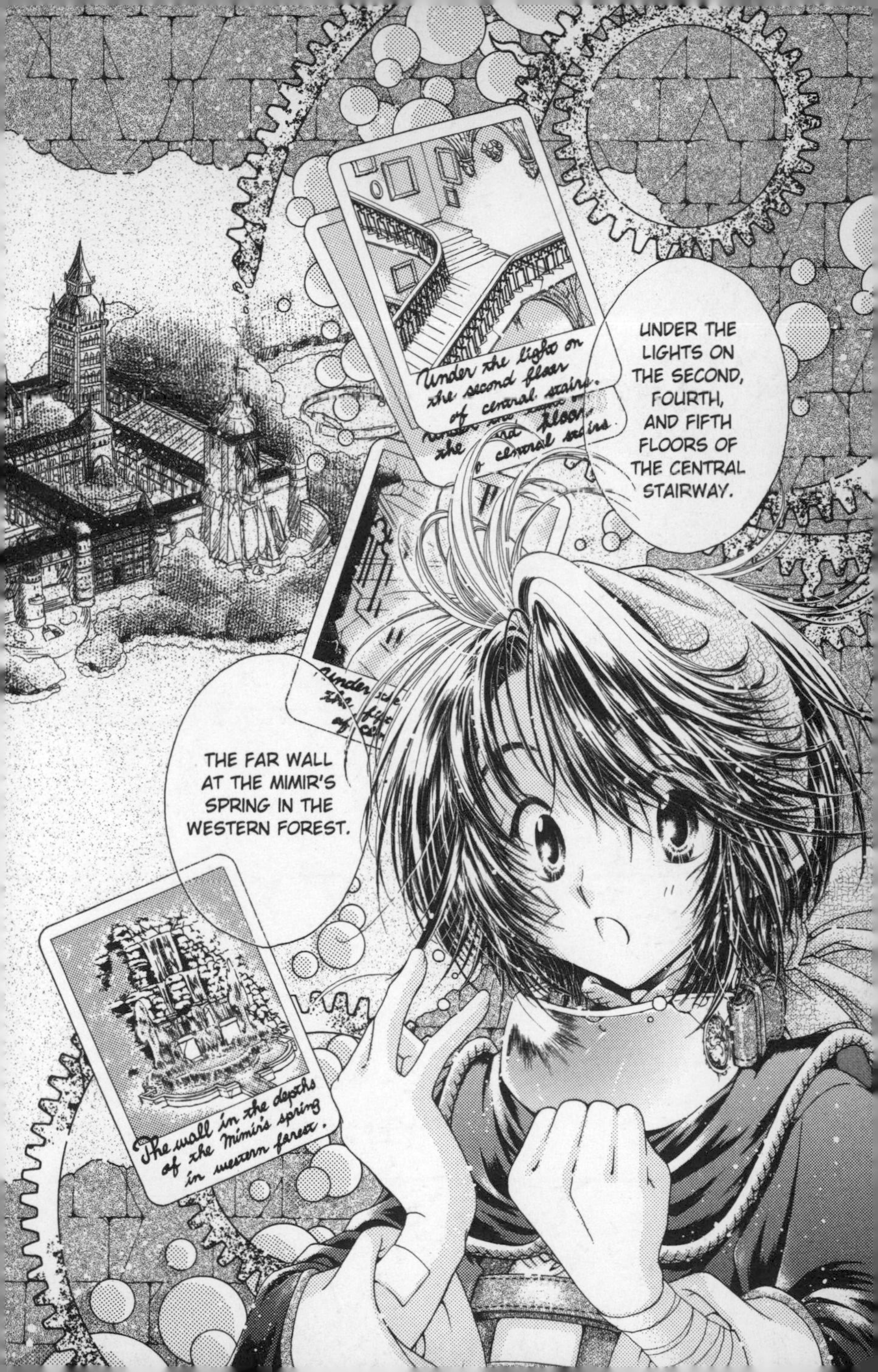
UNDER THE LIGHTS ON THE SECOND, FOURTH, AND FIFTH FLOORS OF THE CENTRAL STAIRWAY.
Under the lights on the second floor of central stairs.
THE FAR WALL AT THE MIMIR'S SPRING IN THE WESTERN FOREST.
The wall in the depths of the Mimir's spring in western forest.

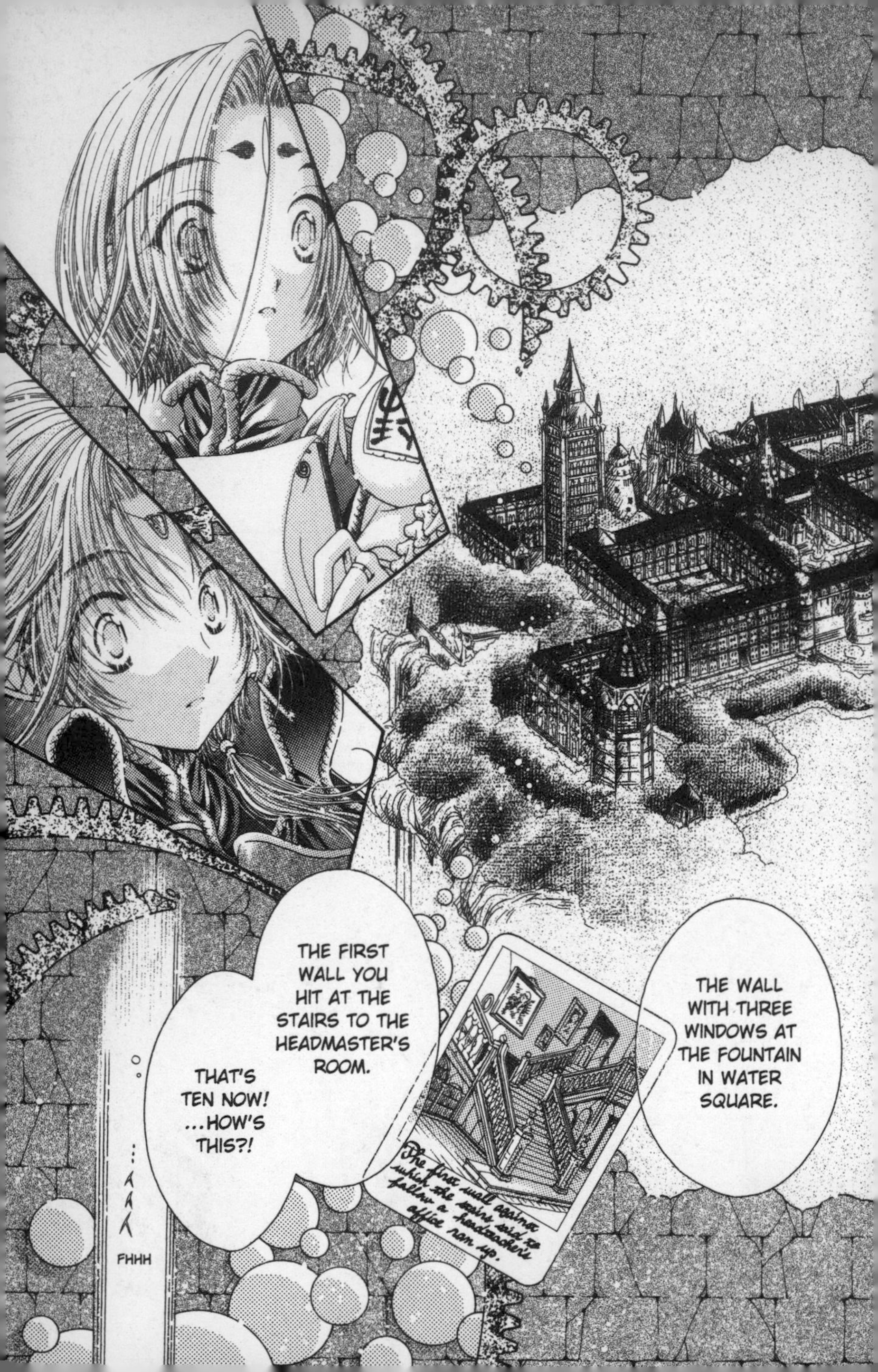
THE WALL WITH THREE WINDOWS AT THE FOUNTAIN IN WATER SQUARE.
The first wall against which the stairs said to follow a headteacher's office ran up.
THE FIRST WALL YOU HIT AT THE STAIRS TO THE HEADMASTER'S ROOM.
THAT'S TEN NOW! ...HOW'S THIS?!
FHHH

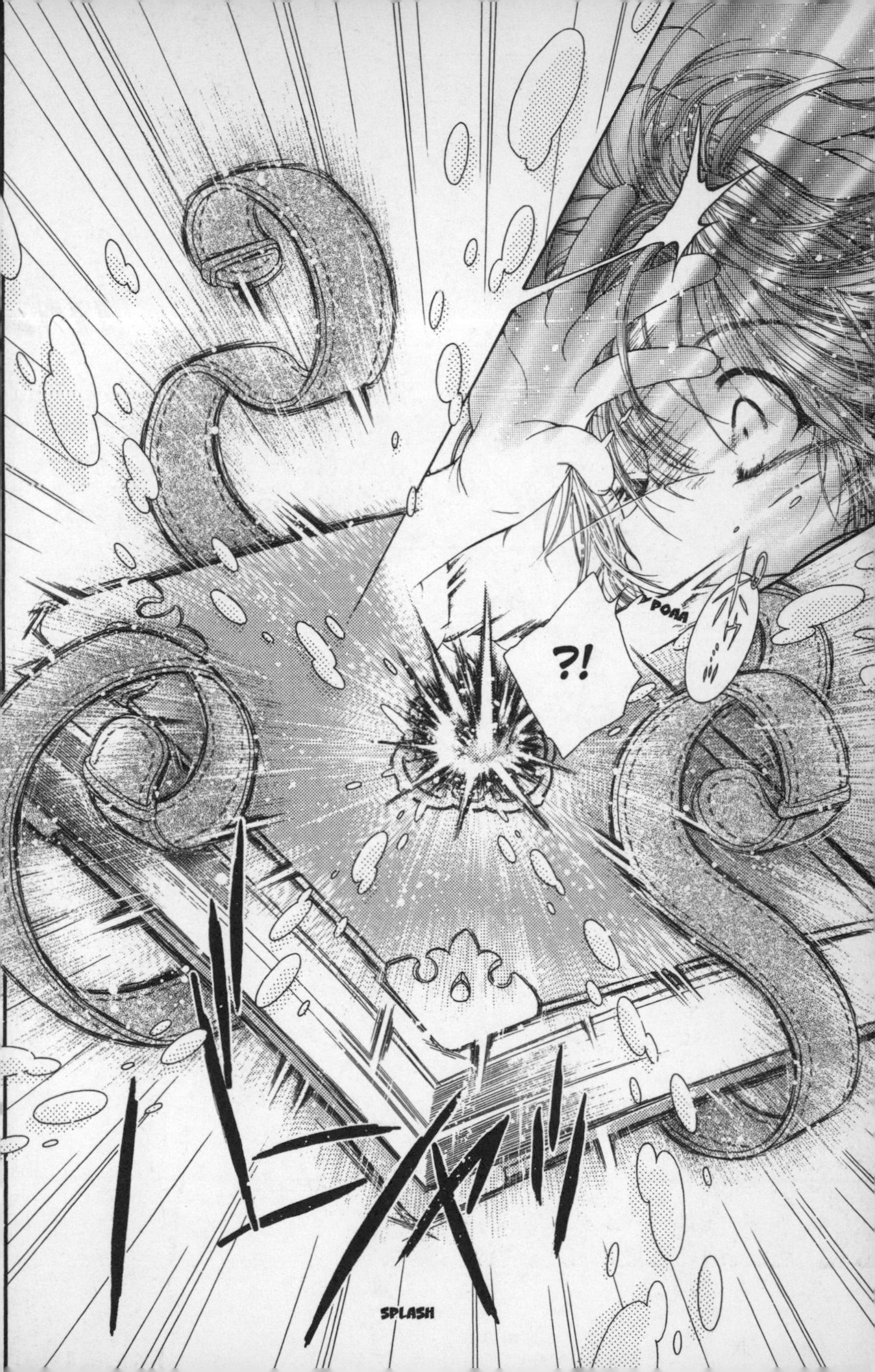
POAA
?!
SPLASH

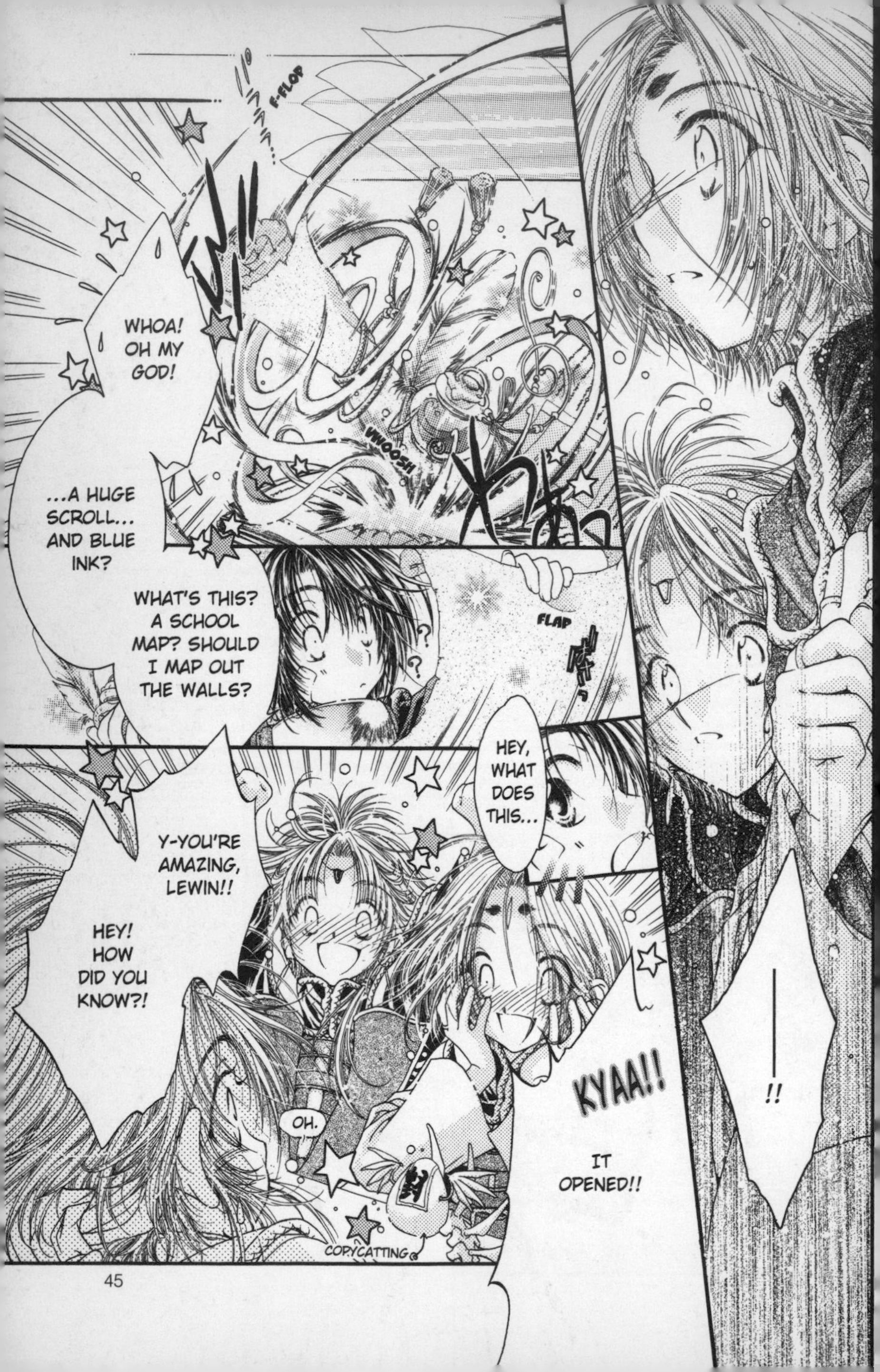
—!!
F-FLOP
WHOA! OH MY GOD!
WHOOSH
...A HUGE SCROLL... AND BLUE INK?
FLAP
WHAT'S THIS? A SCHOOL MAP? SHOULD I MAP OUT THE WALLS?
HEY, WHAT DOES THIS...
KYAA!!
IT OPENED!!
Y-YOU'RE AMAZING, LEWIN!!
HEY! HOW DID YOU KNOW?!
OH.
COPYCATTING

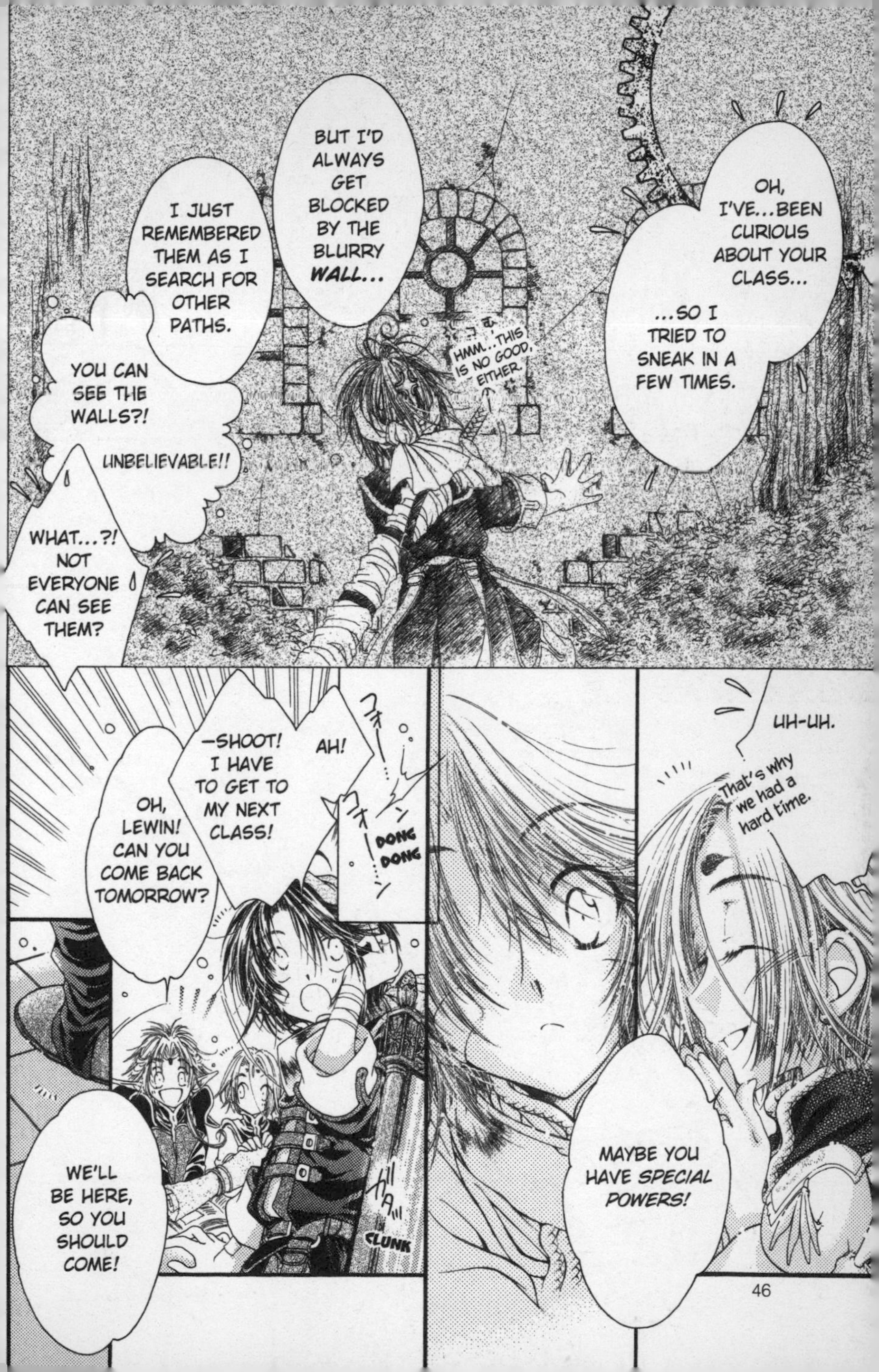
OH, I'VE...BEEN CURIOUS ABOUT YOUR CLASS...
...SO I TRIED TO SNEAK IN A FEW TIMES.
BUT I'D ALWAYS GET BLOCKED BY THE BLURRY WALL...
HMM...THIS IS NO GOOD, EITHER.
I JUST REMEMBERED THEM AS I SEARCH FOR OTHER PATHS.
YOU CAN SEE THE WALLS?!
UNBELIEVABLE!!
WHAT...?! NOT EVERYONE CAN SEE THEM?
UH-UH.
That's why we had a hard time.
MAYBE YOU HAVE SPECIAL POWERS!
AH!
DONG DONG
—SHOOT! I HAVE TO GET TO MY NEXT CLASS!
OH, LEWIN! CAN YOU COME BACK TOMORROW?
CLUNK
WE'LL BE HERE, SO YOU SHOULD COME!

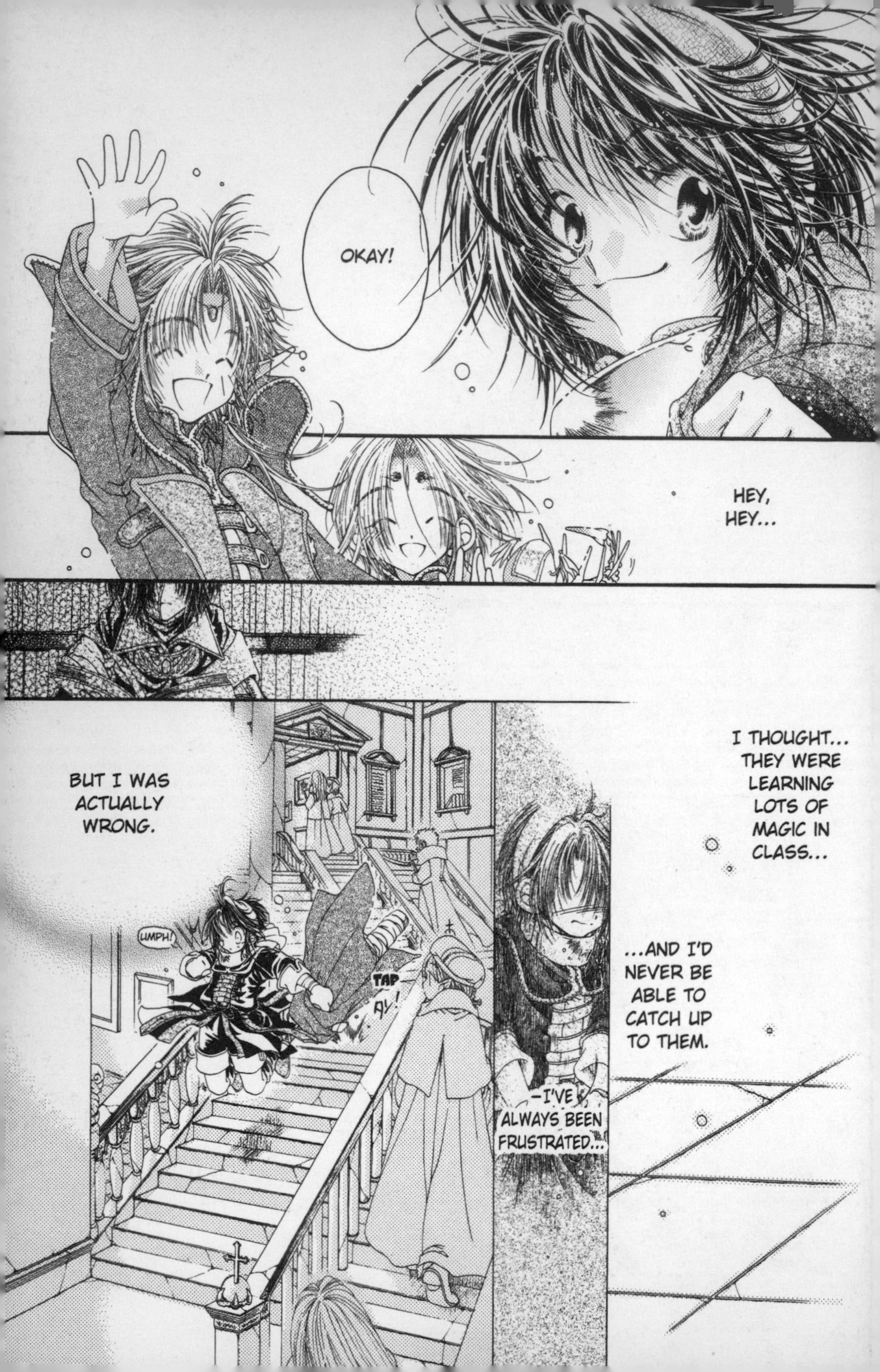
OKAY!
HEY, HEY...
I THOUGHT... THEY WERE LEARNING LOTS OF MAGIC IN CLASS...
...AND I'D NEVER BE ABLE TO CATCH UP TO THEM.
—I'VE ALWAYS BEEN FRUSTRATED...
BUT I WAS ACTUALLY WRONG.
UMPH!
TAP
AY!

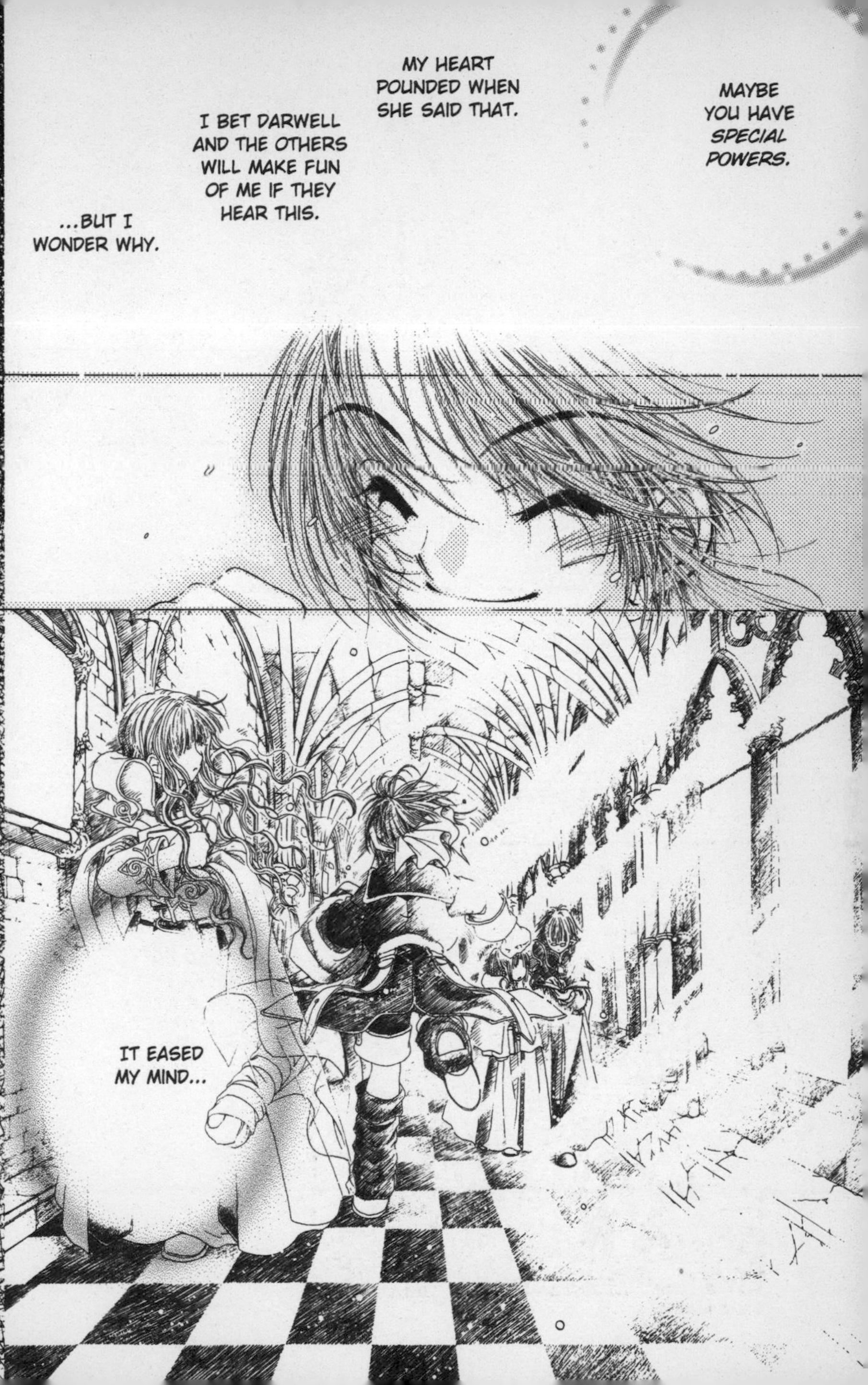
MAYBE YOU HAVE SPECIAL POWERS.
MY HEART POUNDED WHEN SHE SAID THAT.
I BET DARWELL AND THE OTHERS WILL MAKE FUN OF ME IF THEY HEAR THIS.
...BUT I WONDER WHY.
IT EASED MY MIND...

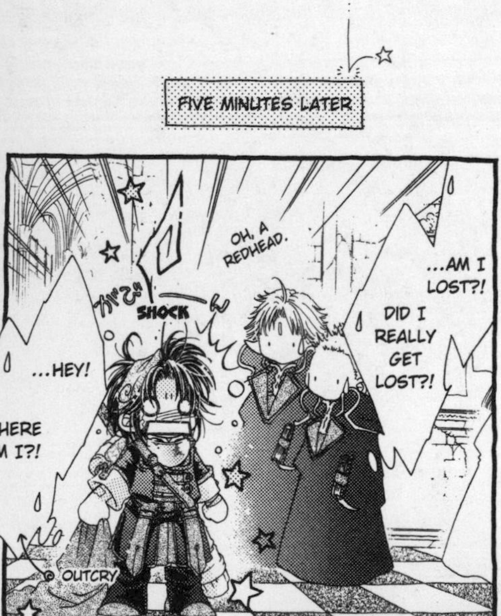
FIVE MINUTES LATER
...AM I LOST?!
DID I REALLY GET LOST?!
OH, A REDHEAD.
SHOCK
...HEY!
WHERE AM I?!
OUTCRY

GOT CARRIED AWAY.

AN ITEM PLACED BETWEEN PAGES OF A BOOK IN THE LIBRARY SCENE IN THE *1ST BELL*.

FLYING LABEL

WRITE THE ADDRESSEE'S NAME.
TITLE OF THE BOOK
YOUR EMBLEM OR SIGNATURE
PLACE IT BETWEEN THE PAGES AND LET IT GO!

UHH, THE MEETING IS AFTER THE AFTERNOON CLASS.
TWO RESEARCH ANNOUNCEMENTS AFTER THAT...
ARGH, I HAVE NO TIME TO RETURN MY BOOKS.
DASH
DASH
DASH
メモ
busy
...THE BOOKS ARE DUE TODAY...
TODAY, HUH...?
BOTHERSOME
lazy
THAT'S WHAT I ALWAYS SAY!
DON'T MISS THE DUE DATE!
MUST HONOR IT!
耳イタイっす
TOO LOUD.
あわわ
PANIC
......
RETURNING HIS BOOKS.

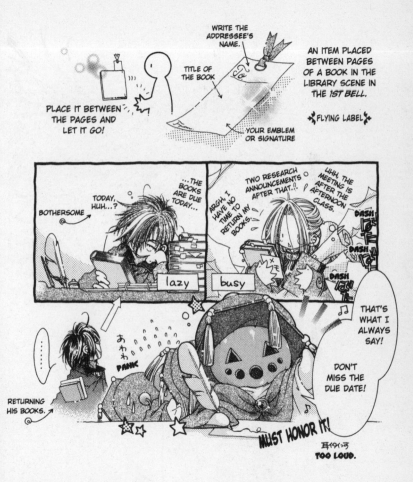

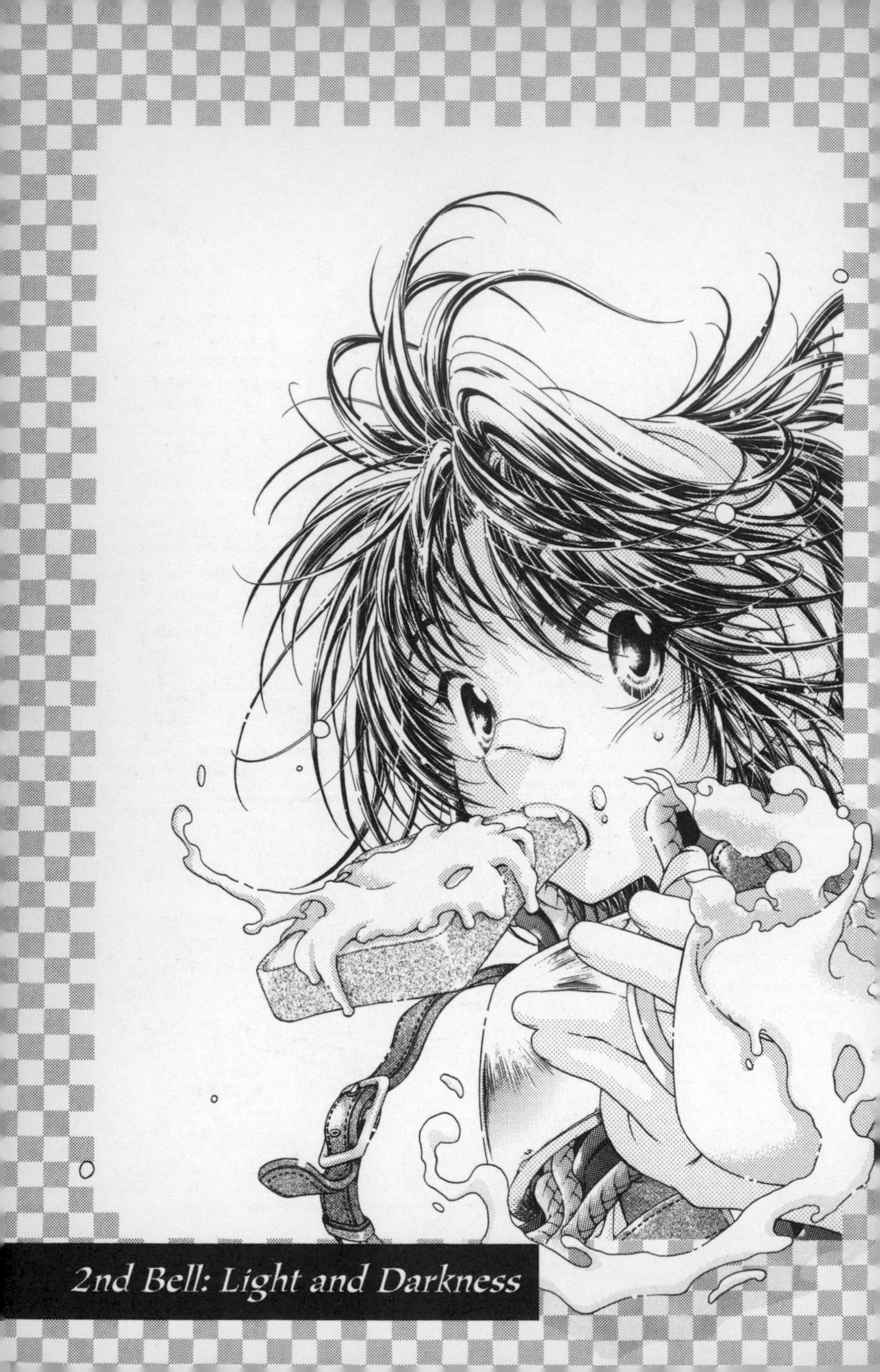

2nd Bell: Light and Darkness

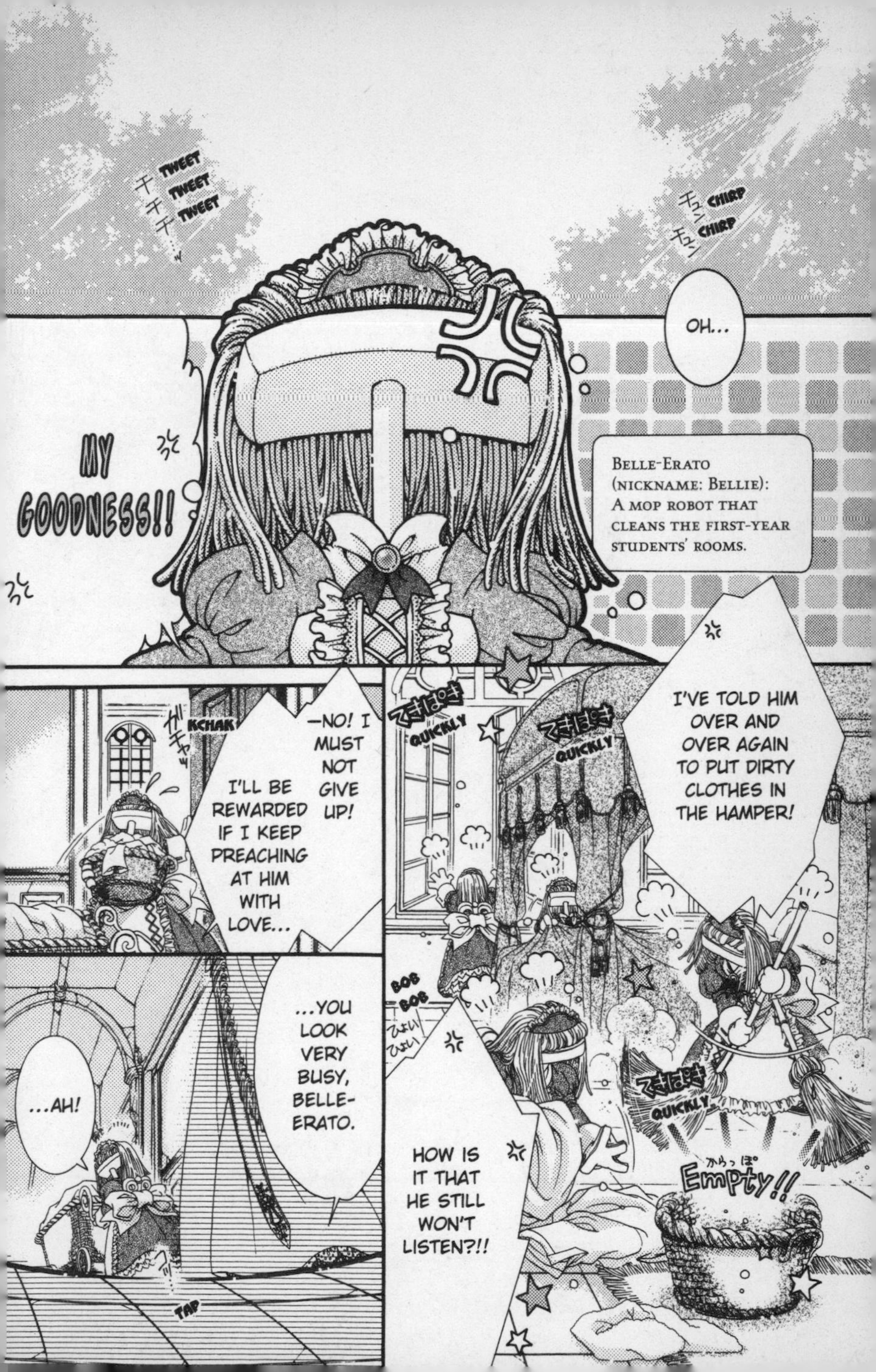
チュン CHIRP
チュン CHIRP
OH...
チチチ... TWEET TWEET TWEET
Belle-Erato (nickname: Bellie): A mop robot that cleans the first-year students' rooms.
MY GOODNESS!!
I'VE TOLD HIM OVER AND OVER AGAIN TO PUT DIRTY CLOTHES IN THE HAMPER!
てきぱき QUICKLY
てきぱき QUICKLY
BOB BOB
HOW IS IT THAT HE STILL WON'T LISTEN?!!
てきぱき QUICKLY
からっぽ Empty!!
—NO! I MUST NOT GIVE UP!
I'LL BE REWARDED IF I KEEP PREACHING AT HIM WITH LOVE...
ガチャッ KCHAK
...YOU LOOK VERY BUSY, BELLE-ERATO.
...AH!
TAP

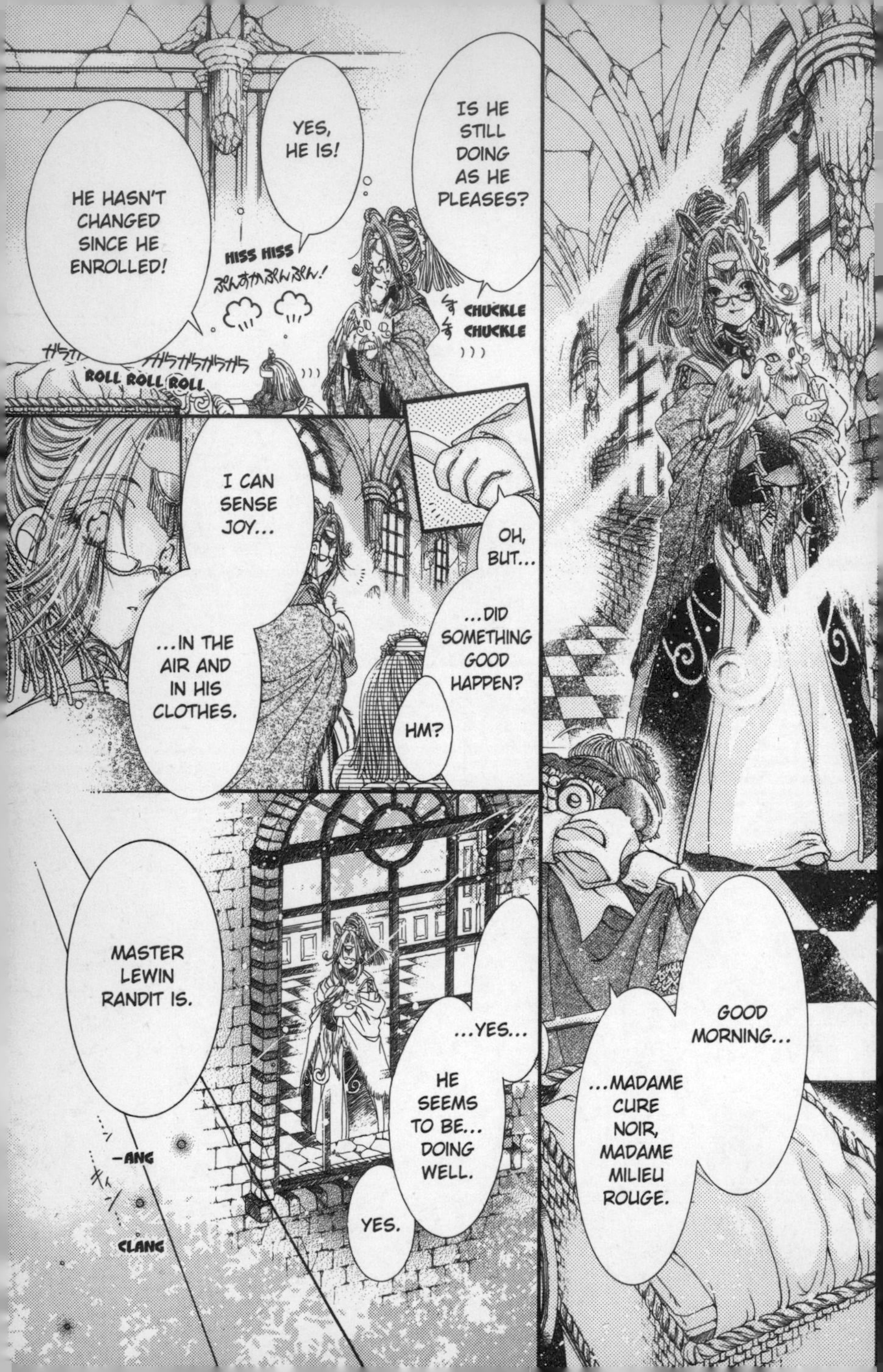
GOOD MORNING...
...MADAME CURE NOIR, MADAME MILIEU ROUGE.
IS HE STILL DOING AS HE PLEASES?
CHUCKLE CHUCKLE
YES, HE IS!
HISS HISS
HE HASN'T CHANGED SINCE HE ENROLLED!
ROLL ROLL ROLL
OH, BUT...
...DID SOMETHING GOOD HAPPEN?
HM?
I CAN SENSE JOY...
...IN THE AIR AND IN HIS CLOTHES.
...YES...
HE SEEMS TO BE... DOING WELL.
YES.
MASTER LEWIN RANDIT IS.
-ANG
CLANG

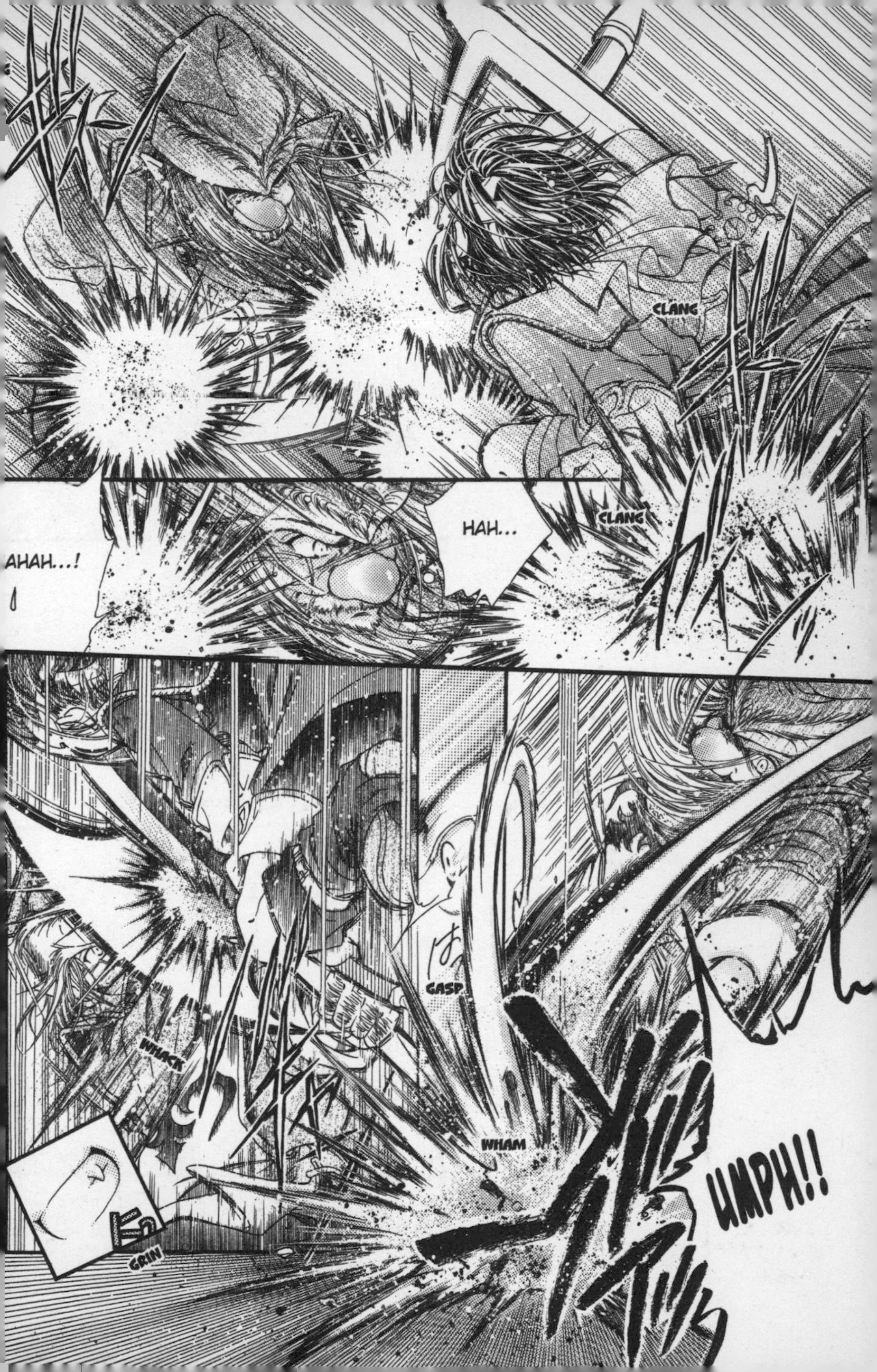
CLANG
CLANG
HAH...
AHAH...!
UMPH!!
WHAM
GASP
WHACK
GRIN

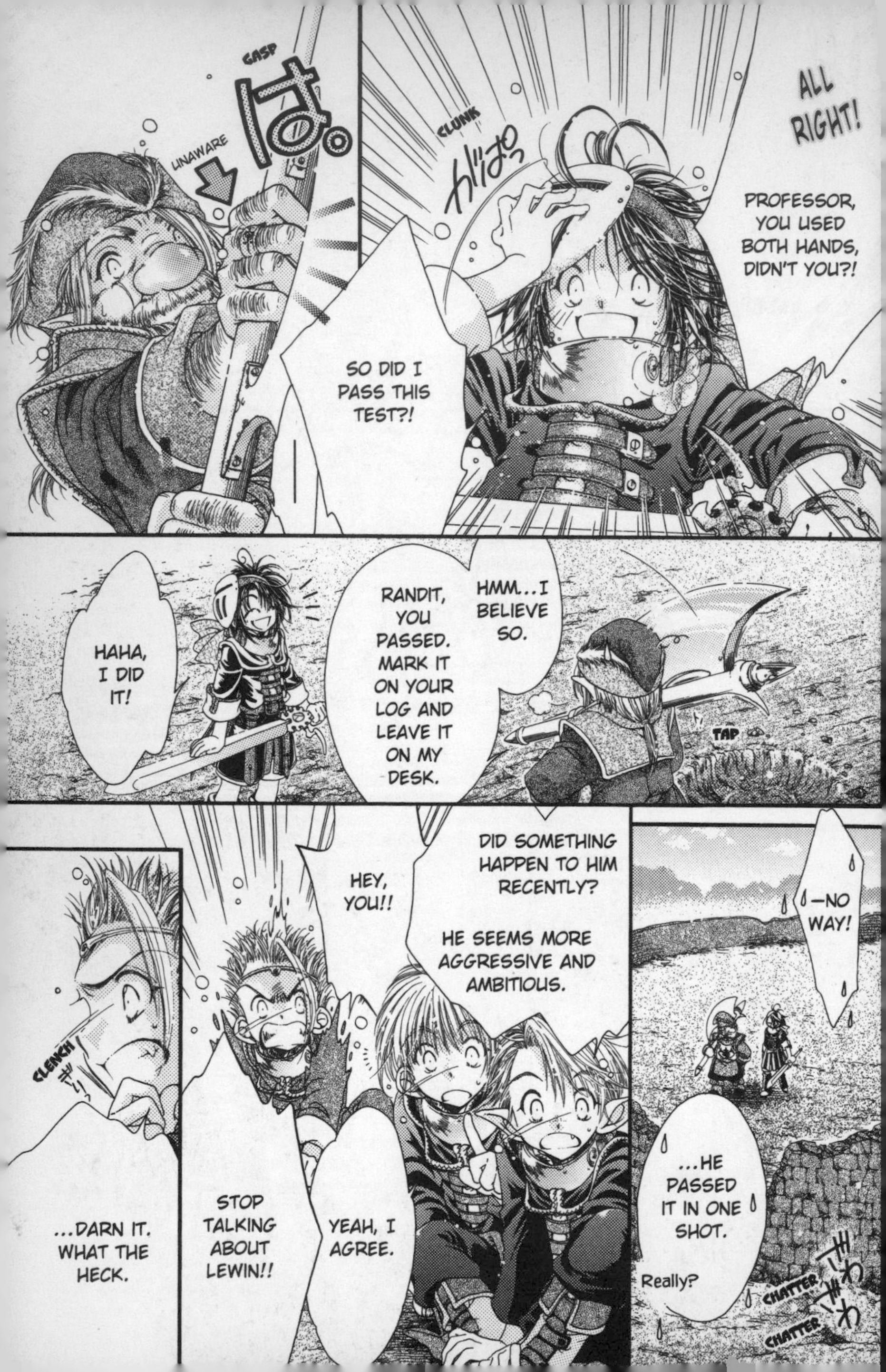
ALL RIGHT!
CLUNK
PROFESSOR, YOU USED BOTH HANDS, DIDN'T YOU?!
SO DID I PASS THIS TEST?!
GASP
は。
UNAWARE
HMM...I BELIEVE SO.
RANDIT, YOU PASSED. MARK IT ON YOUR LOG AND LEAVE IT ON MY DESK.
TAP
HAHA, I DID IT!
—NO WAY!
...HE PASSED IT IN ONE SHOT.
Really?
CHATTER
CHATTER
DID SOMETHING HAPPEN TO HIM RECENTLY?
HE SEEMS MORE AGGRESSIVE AND AMBITIOUS.
HEY, YOU!!
YEAH, I AGREE.
STOP TALKING ABOUT LEWIN!!
CLENCH
...DARN IT. WHAT THE HECK.

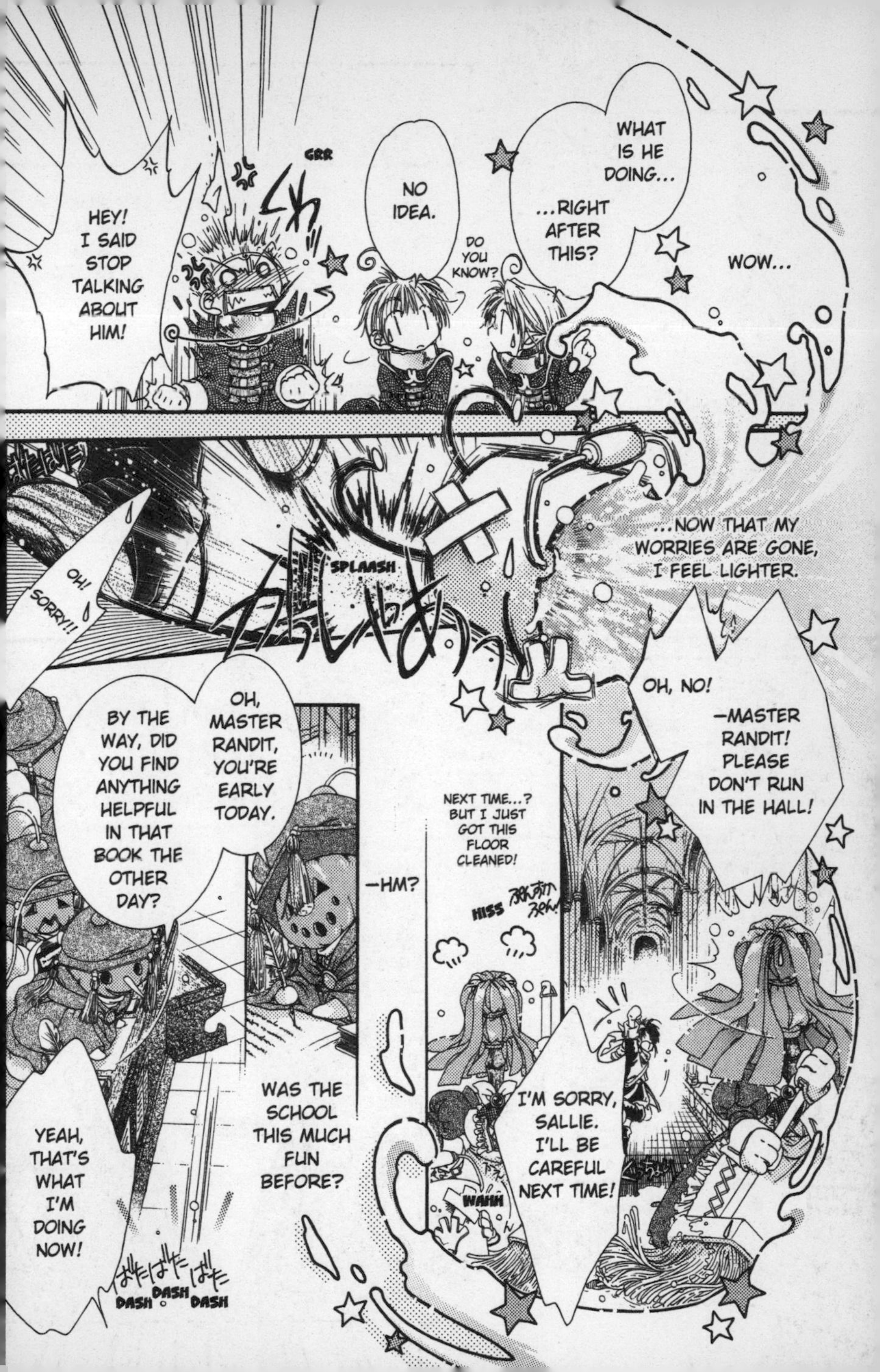
WOW...
WHAT IS HE DOING...
...RIGHT AFTER THIS?
DO YOU KNOW?
NO IDEA.
GRR
HEY! I SAID STOP TALKING ABOUT HIM!
...NOW THAT MY WORRIES ARE GONE, I FEEL LIGHTER.
SPLAASH
OH! SORRY!!
OH, NO!
—MASTER RANDIT! PLEASE DON'T RUN IN THE HALL!
I'M SORRY, SALLIE. I'LL BE CAREFUL NEXT TIME!
HISS
NEXT TIME...? BUT I JUST GOT THIS FLOOR CLEANED!
WAHH
—HM?
WAS THE SCHOOL THIS MUCH FUN BEFORE?
OH, MASTER RANDIT, YOU'RE EARLY TODAY.
BY THE WAY, DID YOU FIND ANYTHING HELPFUL IN THAT BOOK THE OTHER DAY?
YEAH, THAT'S WHAT I'M DOING NOW!
DASH DASH DASH

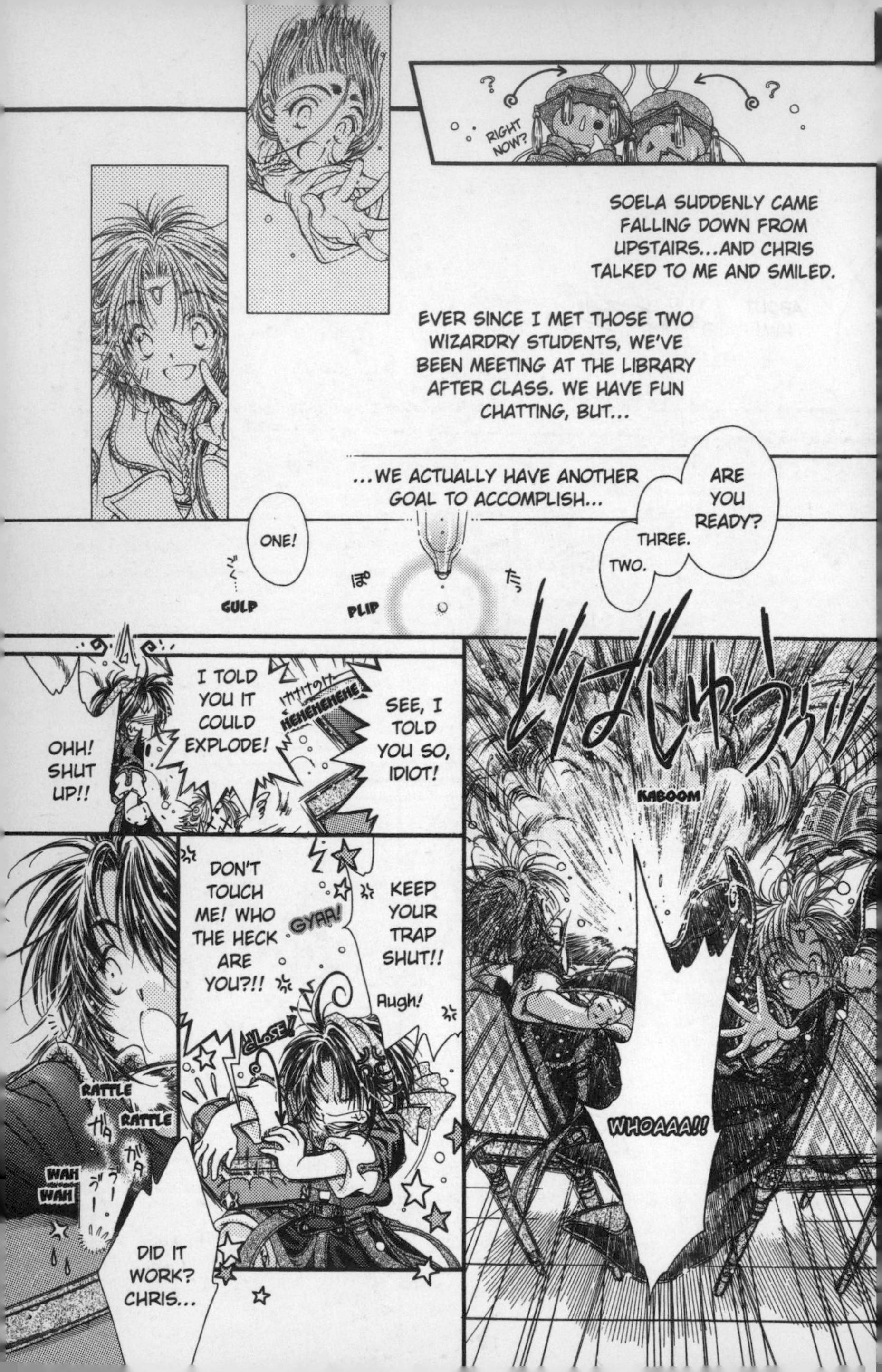
RIGHT NOW?
SOELA SUDDENLY CAME FALLING DOWN FROM UPSTAIRS...AND CHRIS TALKED TO ME AND SMILED.
EVER SINCE I MET THOSE TWO WIZARDRY STUDENTS, WE'VE BEEN MEETING AT THE LIBRARY AFTER CLASS. WE HAVE FUN CHATTING, BUT...
...WE ACTUALLY HAVE ANOTHER GOAL TO ACCOMPLISH...
ARE YOU READY?
THREE.
TWO.
ONE!
PLIP
GULP
KABOOM
WHOAAA!!
SEE, I TOLD YOU SO, IDIOT!
HEHEHEHEHE
I TOLD YOU IT COULD EXPLODE!
OHH! SHUT UP!!
KEEP YOUR TRAP SHUT!!
Augh!
GYAA!
DON'T TOUCH ME! WHO THE HECK ARE YOU?!!
CLOSE!
RATTLE
RATTLE
WAH
WAH
DID IT WORK? CHRIS...

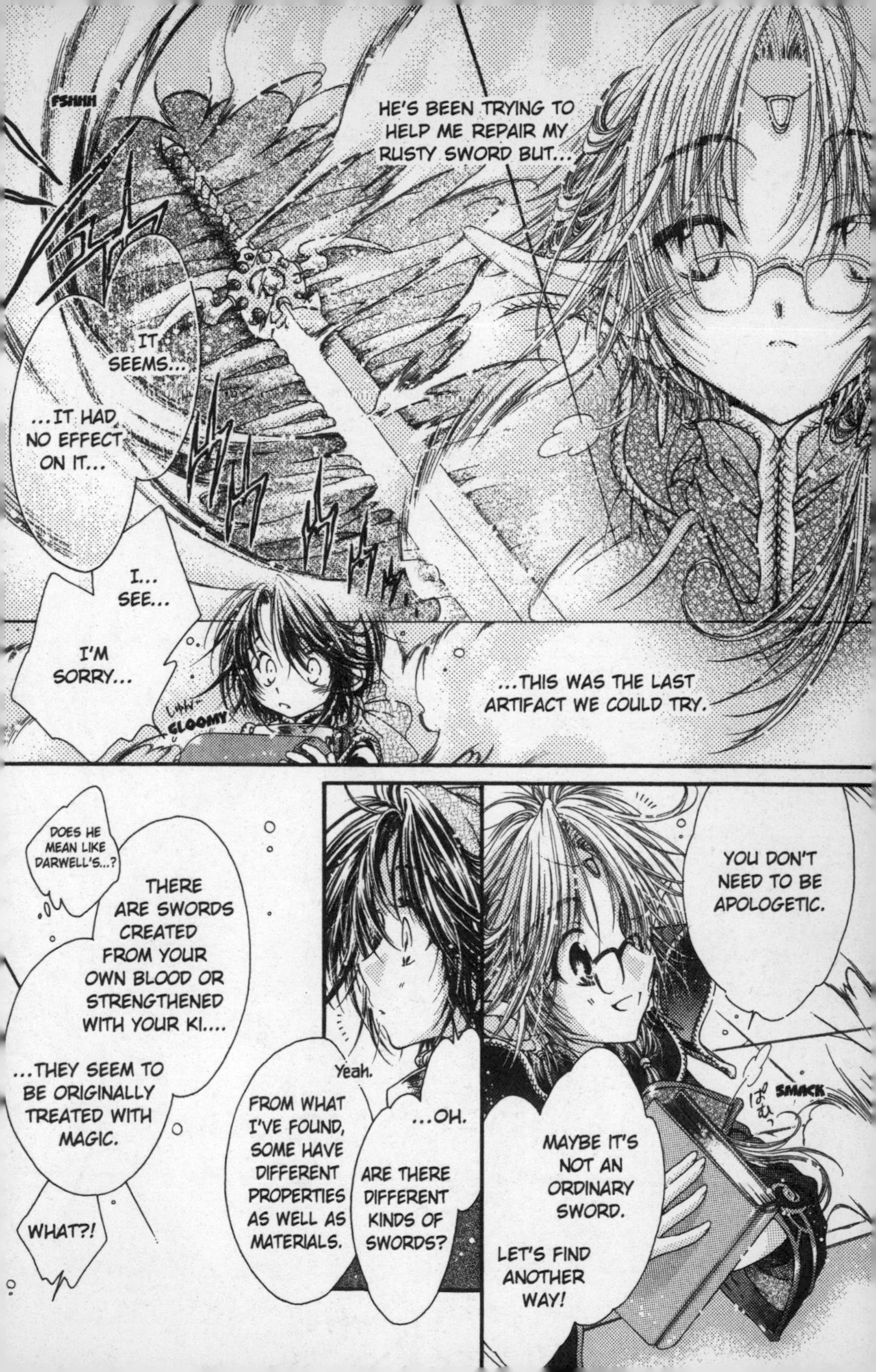
HE'S BEEN TRYING TO HELP ME REPAIR MY RUSTY SWORD BUT...
FSHHH
IT SEEMS...
...IT HAD NO EFFECT ON IT...
...THIS WAS THE LAST ARTIFACT WE COULD TRY.
I... SEE...
I'M SORRY...
GLOOMY
YOU DON'T NEED TO BE APOLOGETIC.
SMACK
MAYBE IT'S NOT AN ORDINARY SWORD.
LET'S FIND ANOTHER WAY!
...OH.
ARE THERE DIFFERENT KINDS OF SWORDS?
Yeah.
FROM WHAT I'VE FOUND, SOME HAVE DIFFERENT PROPERTIES AS WELL AS MATERIALS.
DOES HE MEAN LIKE DARWELL'S...?
THERE ARE SWORDS CREATED FROM YOUR OWN BLOOD OR STRENGTHENED WITH YOUR KI....
...THEY SEEM TO BE ORIGINALLY TREATED WITH MAGIC.
WHAT?!

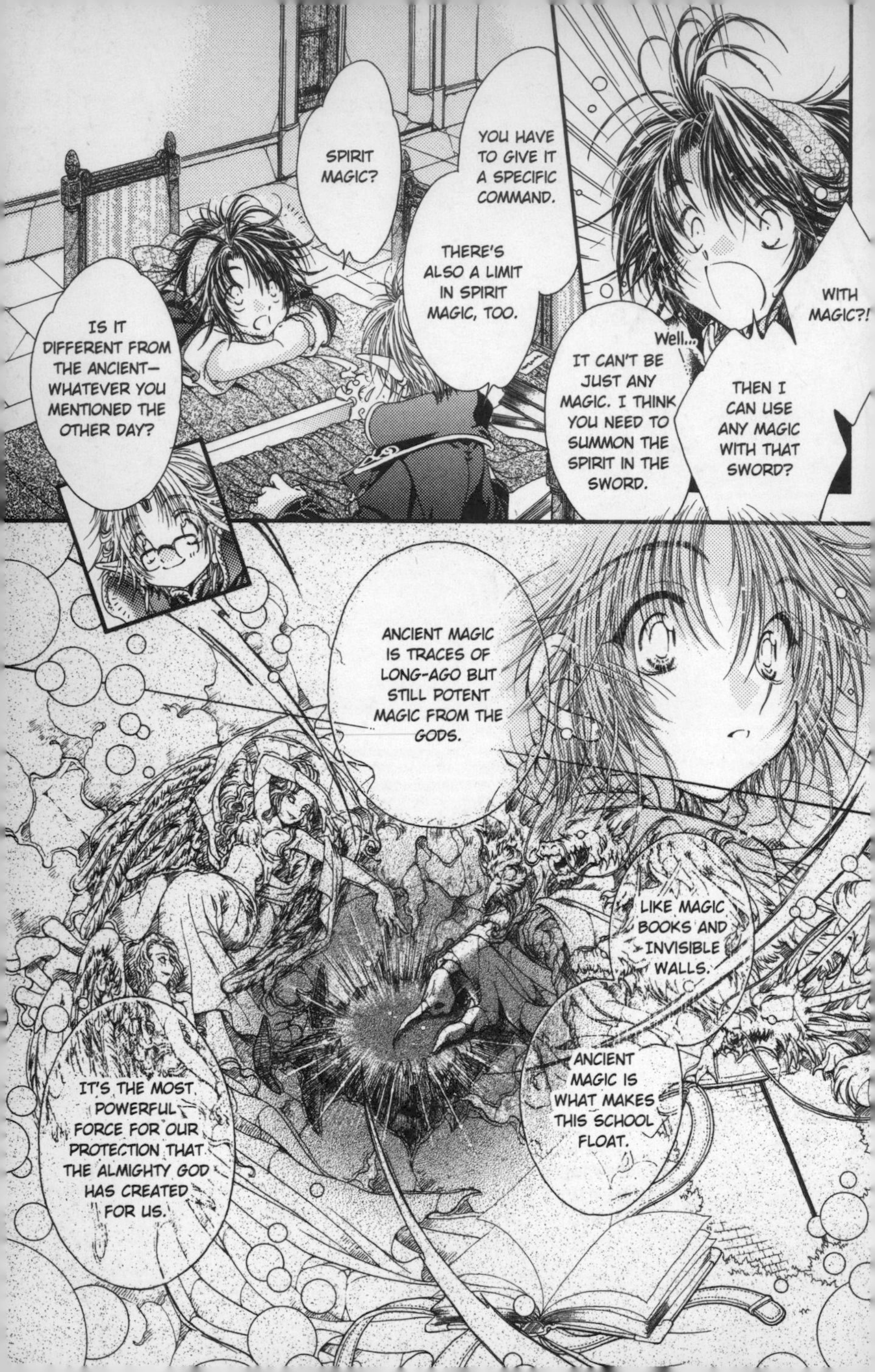
WITH MAGIC?!
THEN I CAN USE ANY MAGIC WITH THAT SWORD?
Well...
IT CAN'T BE JUST ANY MAGIC. I THINK YOU NEED TO SUMMON THE SPIRIT IN THE SWORD.
YOU HAVE TO GIVE IT A SPECIFIC COMMAND.
THERE'S ALSO A LIMIT IN SPIRIT MAGIC, TOO.
SPIRIT MAGIC?
IS IT DIFFERENT FROM THE ANCIENT—WHATEVER YOU MENTIONED THE OTHER DAY?
ANCIENT MAGIC IS TRACES OF LONG-AGO BUT STILL POTENT MAGIC FROM THE GODS.
LIKE MAGIC BOOKS AND INVISIBLE WALLS.
ANCIENT MAGIC IS WHAT MAKES THIS SCHOOL FLOAT.
IT'S THE MOST POWERFUL FORCE FOR OUR PROTECTION THAT THE ALMIGHTY GOD HAS CREATED FOR US.

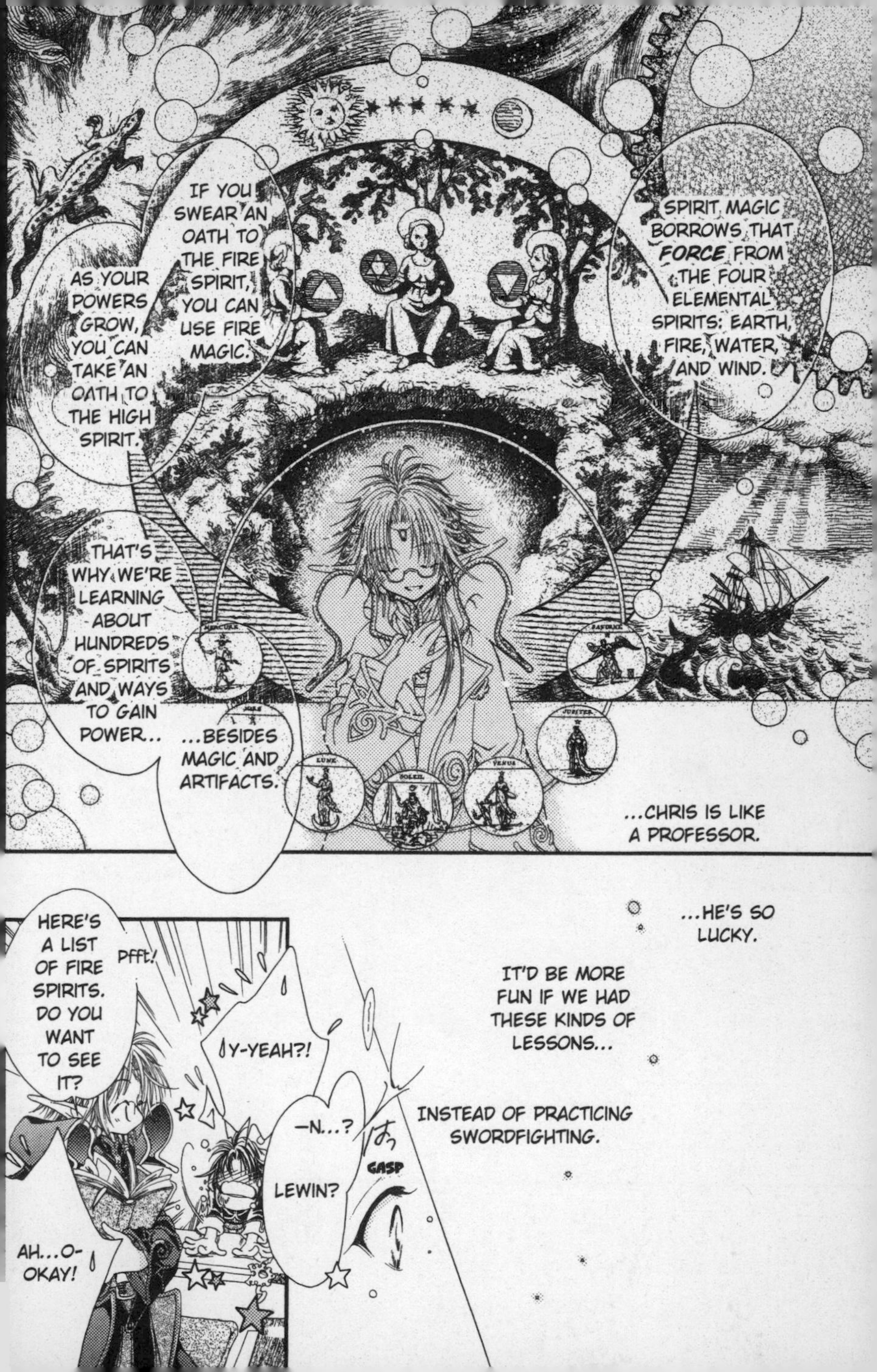
SPIRIT MAGIC BORROWS THAT FORCE FROM THE FOUR ELEMENTAL SPIRITS: EARTH, FIRE, WATER, AND WIND.
IF YOU SWEAR AN OATH TO THE FIRE SPIRIT, YOU CAN USE FIRE MAGIC.
AS YOUR POWERS GROW, YOU CAN TAKE AN OATH TO THE HIGH SPIRIT.
THAT'S WHY WE'RE LEARNING ABOUT HUNDREDS OF SPIRITS AND WAYS TO GAIN POWER...
...BESIDES MAGIC AND ARTIFACTS.
...CHRIS IS LIKE A PROFESSOR.
...HE'S SO LUCKY.
IT'D BE MORE FUN IF WE HAD THESE KINDS OF LESSONS...
INSTEAD OF PRACTICING SWORDFIGHTING.
HERE'S A LIST OF FIRE SPIRITS. DO YOU WANT TO SEE IT?
—N...?
はっ
GASP
LEWIN?
Y-YEAH?!
Pfft!
AH...O-OKAY!

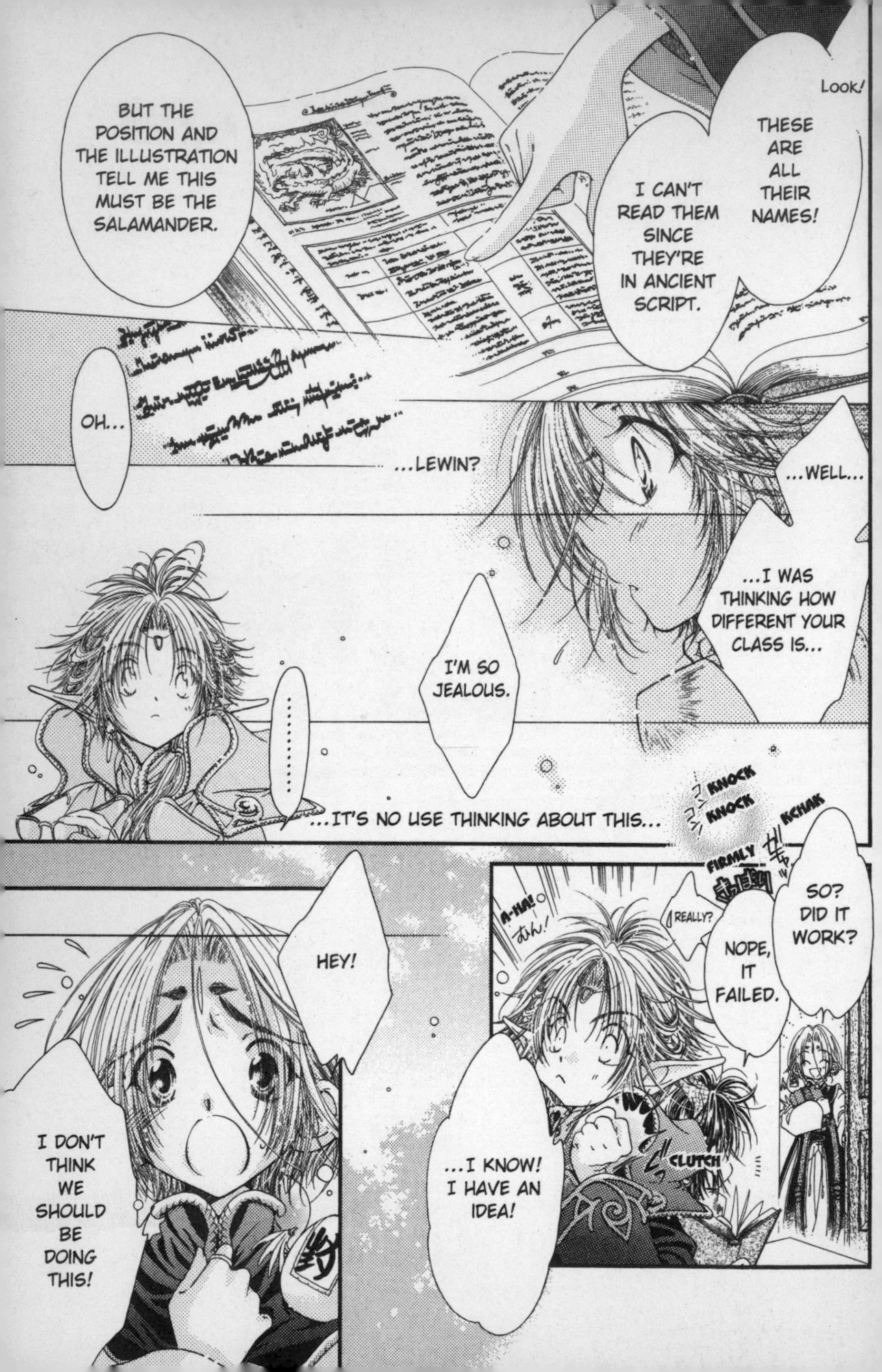

Look!
THESE ARE ALL THEIR NAMES!
I CAN'T READ THEM SINCE THEY'RE IN ANCIENT SCRIPT.
BUT THE POSITION AND THE ILLUSTRATION TELL ME THIS MUST BE THE SALAMANDER.
OH...
...LEWIN?
...WELL...
...I WAS THINKING HOW DIFFERENT YOUR CLASS IS...
I'M SO JEALOUS.
......
...IT'S NO USE THINKING ABOUT THIS...
KNOCK
KNOCK
KCHAK
FIRMLY
SO? DID IT WORK?
NOPE, IT FAILED.
REALLY?
A-HA!
CLUTCH
...I KNOW! I HAVE AN IDEA!
HEY!
I DON'T THINK WE SHOULD BE DOING THIS!

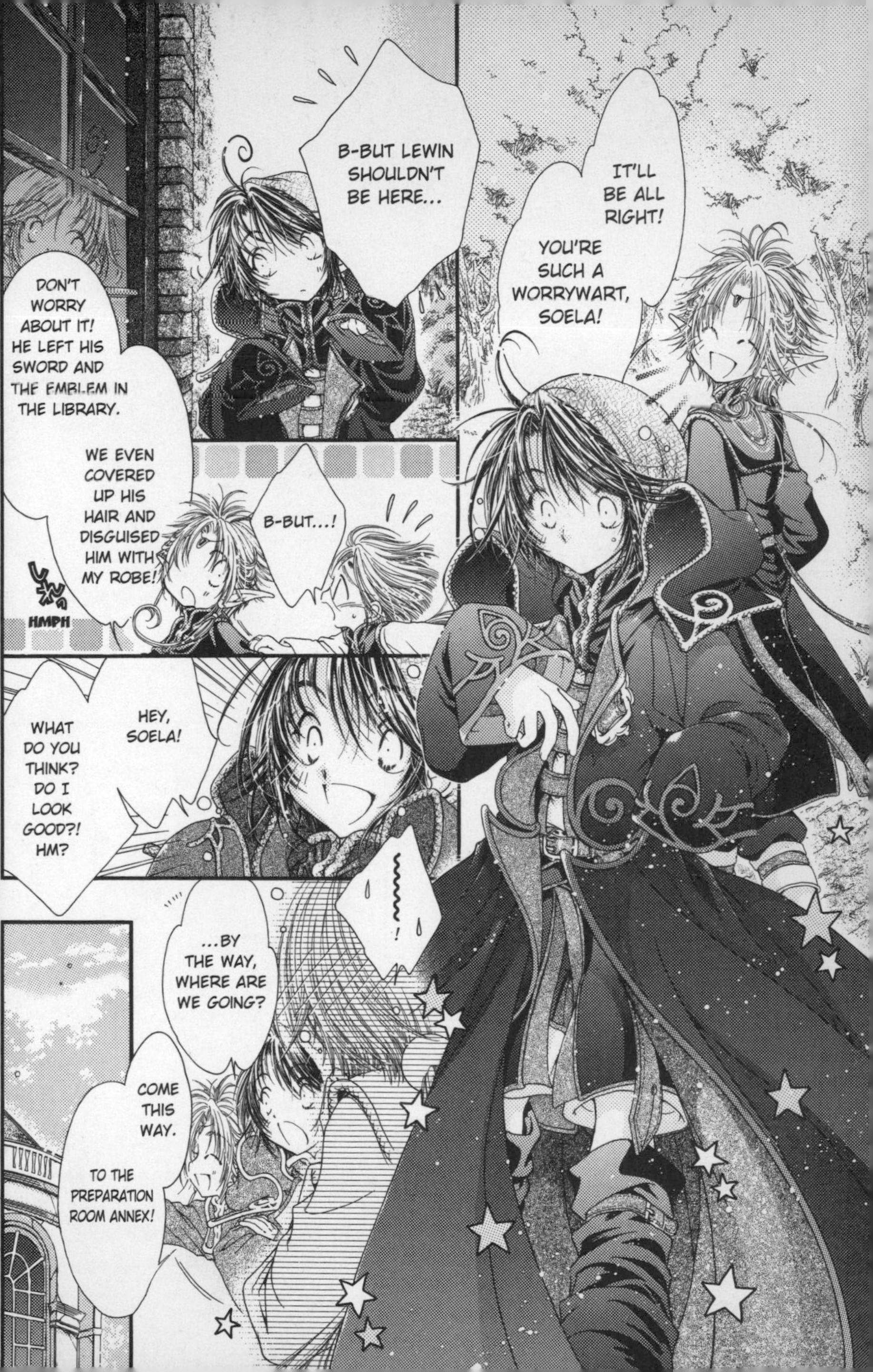
IT'LL BE ALL RIGHT!
YOU'RE SUCH A WORRYWART, SOELA!
B-BUT LEWIN SHOULDN'T BE HERE...
DON'T WORRY ABOUT IT! HE LEFT HIS SWORD AND THE EMBLEM IN THE LIBRARY.
B-BUT...!
WE EVEN COVERED UP HIS HAIR AND DISGUISED HIM WITH MY ROBE!
HMPH
HEY, SOELA!
WHAT DO YOU THINK? DO I LOOK GOOD?! HM?
~~~!
...BY THE WAY, WHERE ARE WE GOING?
COME THIS WAY.
TO THE PREPARATION ROOM ANNEX!
~~~

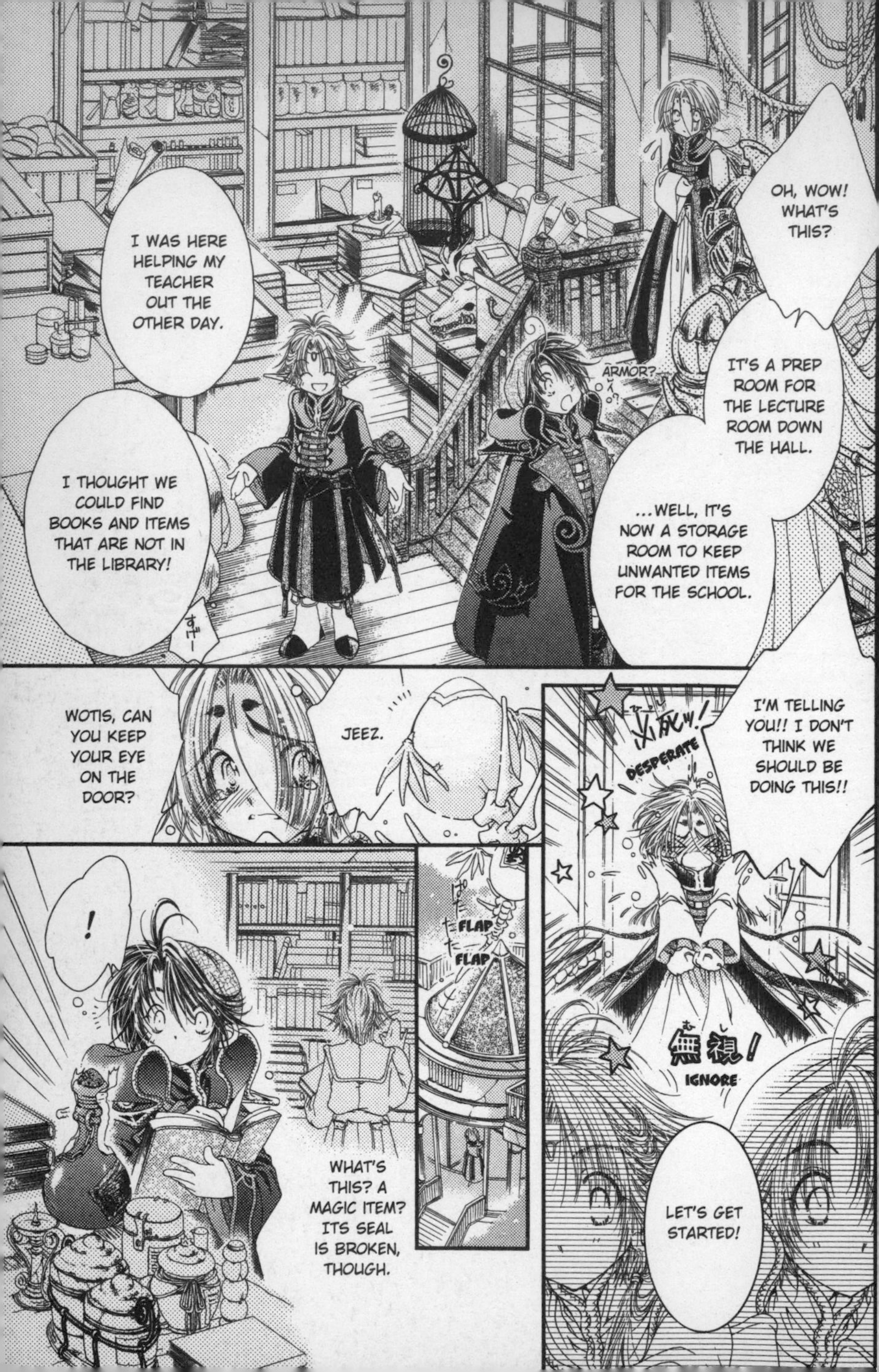

OH, WOW! WHAT'S THIS?
IT'S A PREP ROOM FOR THE LECTURE ROOM DOWN THE HALL.
...WELL, IT'S NOW A STORAGE ROOM TO KEEP UNWANTED ITEMS FOR THE SCHOOL.
ARMOR?
I WAS HERE HELPING MY TEACHER OUT THE OTHER DAY.
I THOUGHT WE COULD FIND BOOKS AND ITEMS THAT ARE NOT IN THE LIBRARY!
すげー
I'M TELLING YOU!! I DON'T THINK WE SHOULD BE DOING THIS!!
必死ッ!
DESPERATE
無視!
IGNORE
LET'S GET STARTED!
WOTIS, CAN YOU KEEP YOUR EYE ON THE DOOR?
JEEZ.
ぱたたた
FLAP
FLAP
!
WHAT'S THIS? A MAGIC ITEM? ITS SEAL IS BROKEN, THOUGH.

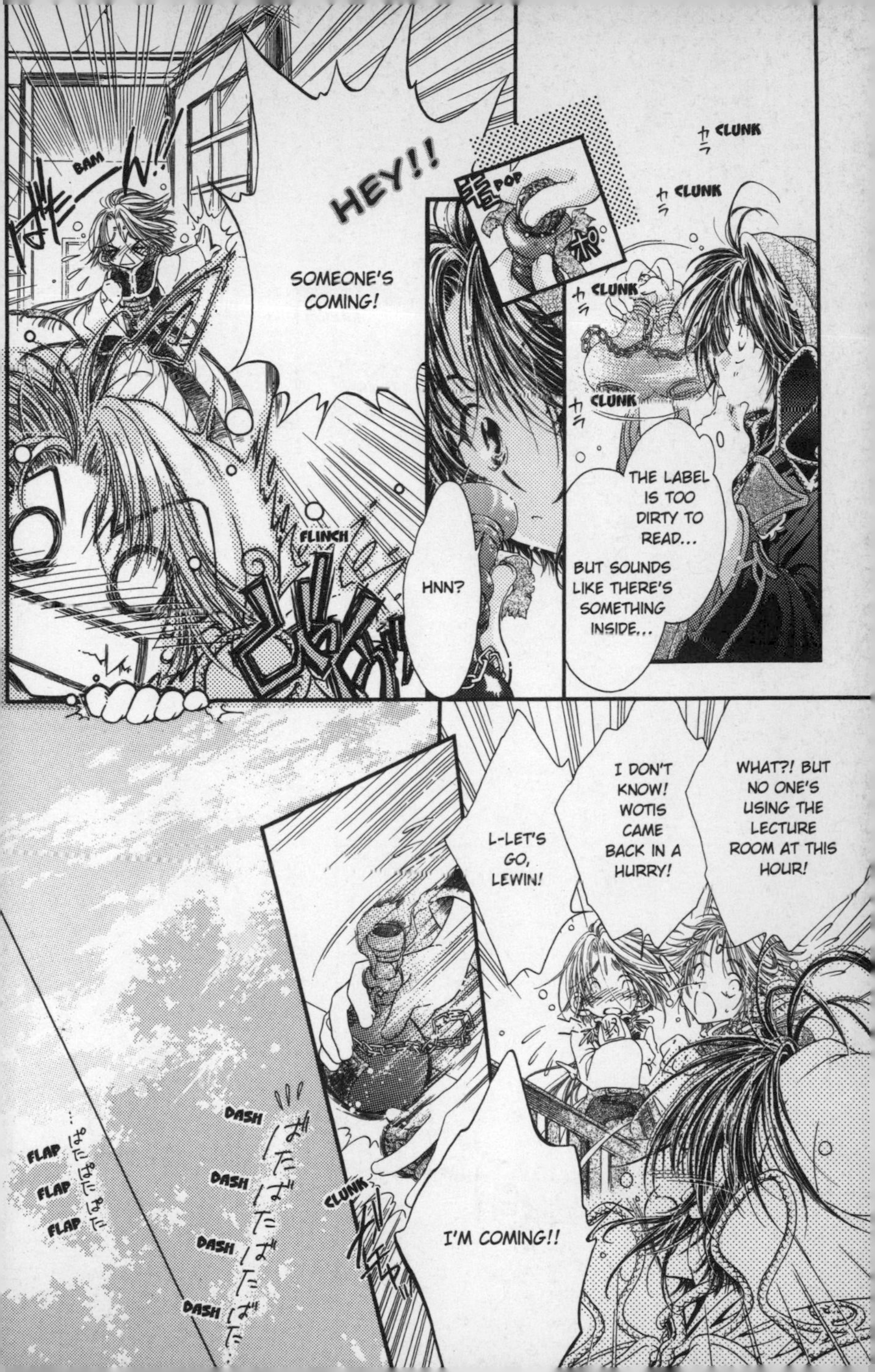
CLUNK
CLUNK
CLUNK
CLUNK
THE LABEL IS TOO DIRTY TO READ...
BUT SOUNDS LIKE THERE'S SOMETHING INSIDE...
POP
HNN?
HEY!!
BAM
SOMEONE'S COMING!
FLINCH
WHAT?! BUT NO ONE'S USING THE LECTURE ROOM AT THIS HOUR!
I DON'T KNOW! WOTIS CAME BACK IN A HURRY!
L-LET'S GO, LEWIN!
I'M COMING!!
CLUNK
DASH
DASH
DASH
DASH
FLAP
FLAP
FLAP

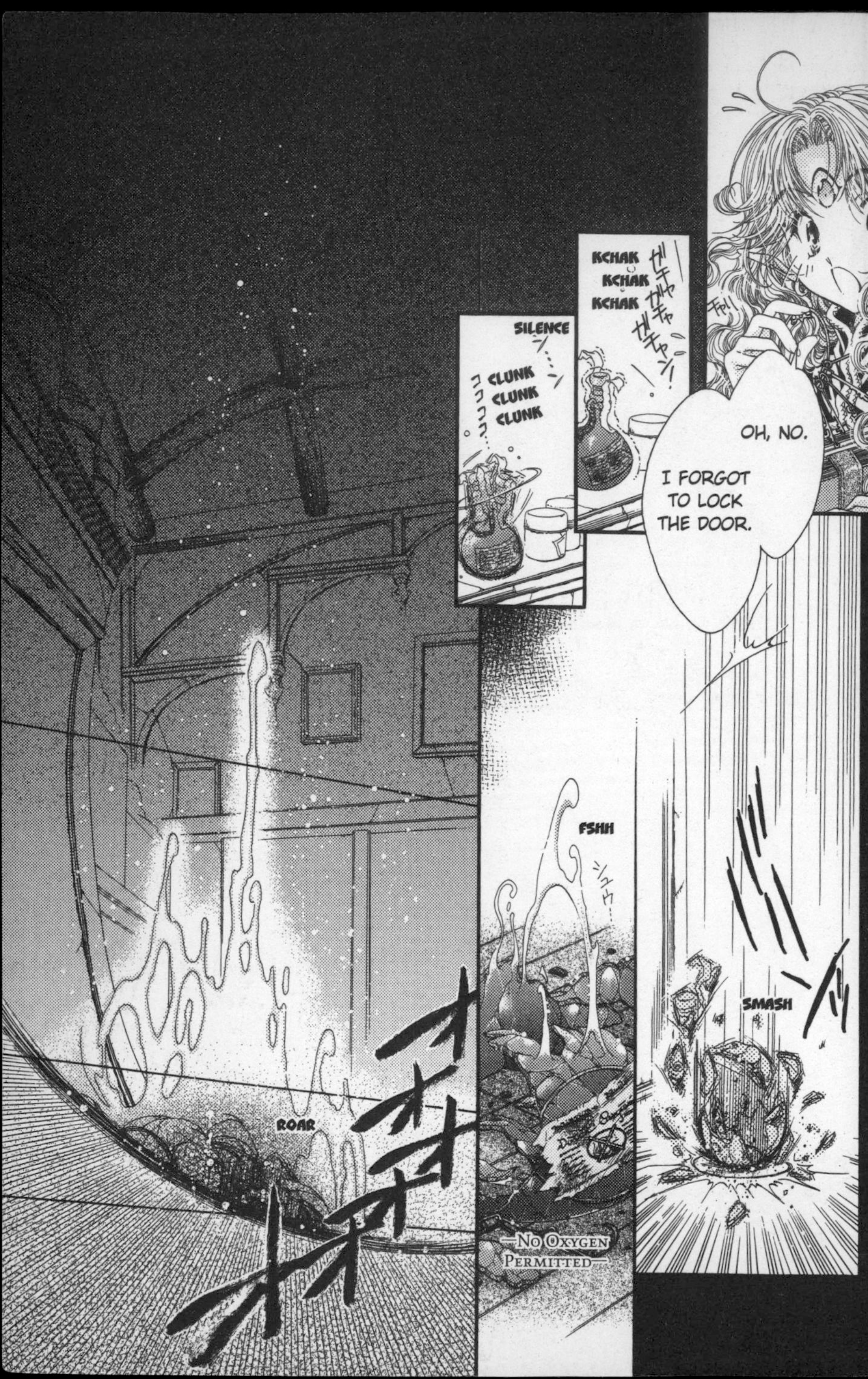
OH, NO.
I FORGOT TO LOCK THE DOOR.
KCHAK KCHAK KCHAK
SILENCE
CLUNK CLUNK CLUNK
SMASH
FSHH
—NO OXYGEN PERMITTED—
ROAR

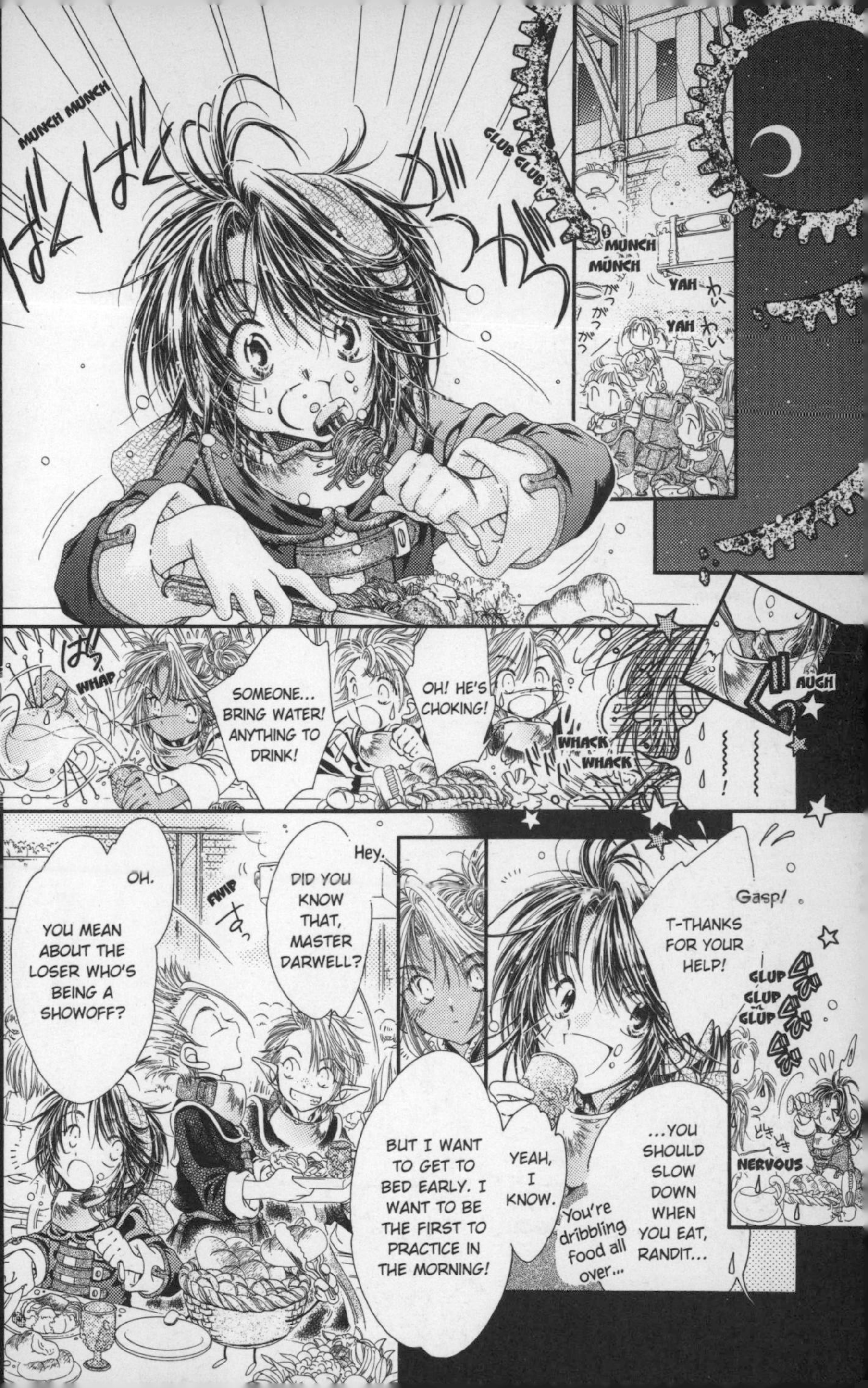

GLUB GLUB
MUNCH MUNCH
YAH YAH
MUNCH MUNCH
AUGH
WHACK WHACK
OH! HE'S CHOKING!
SOMEONE... BRING WATER! ANYTHING TO DRINK!
WHAP
Gasp!
T-THANKS FOR YOUR HELP!
GLUP GLUP GLUP
NERVOUS
...YOU SHOULD SLOW DOWN WHEN YOU EAT, RANDIT...
You're dribbling food all over...
YEAH, I KNOW.
BUT I WANT TO GET TO BED EARLY. I WANT TO BE THE FIRST TO PRACTICE IN THE MORNING!
Hey.
DID YOU KNOW THAT, MASTER DARWELL?
FWIP
OH.
YOU MEAN ABOUT THE LOSER WHO'S BEING A SHOWOFF?

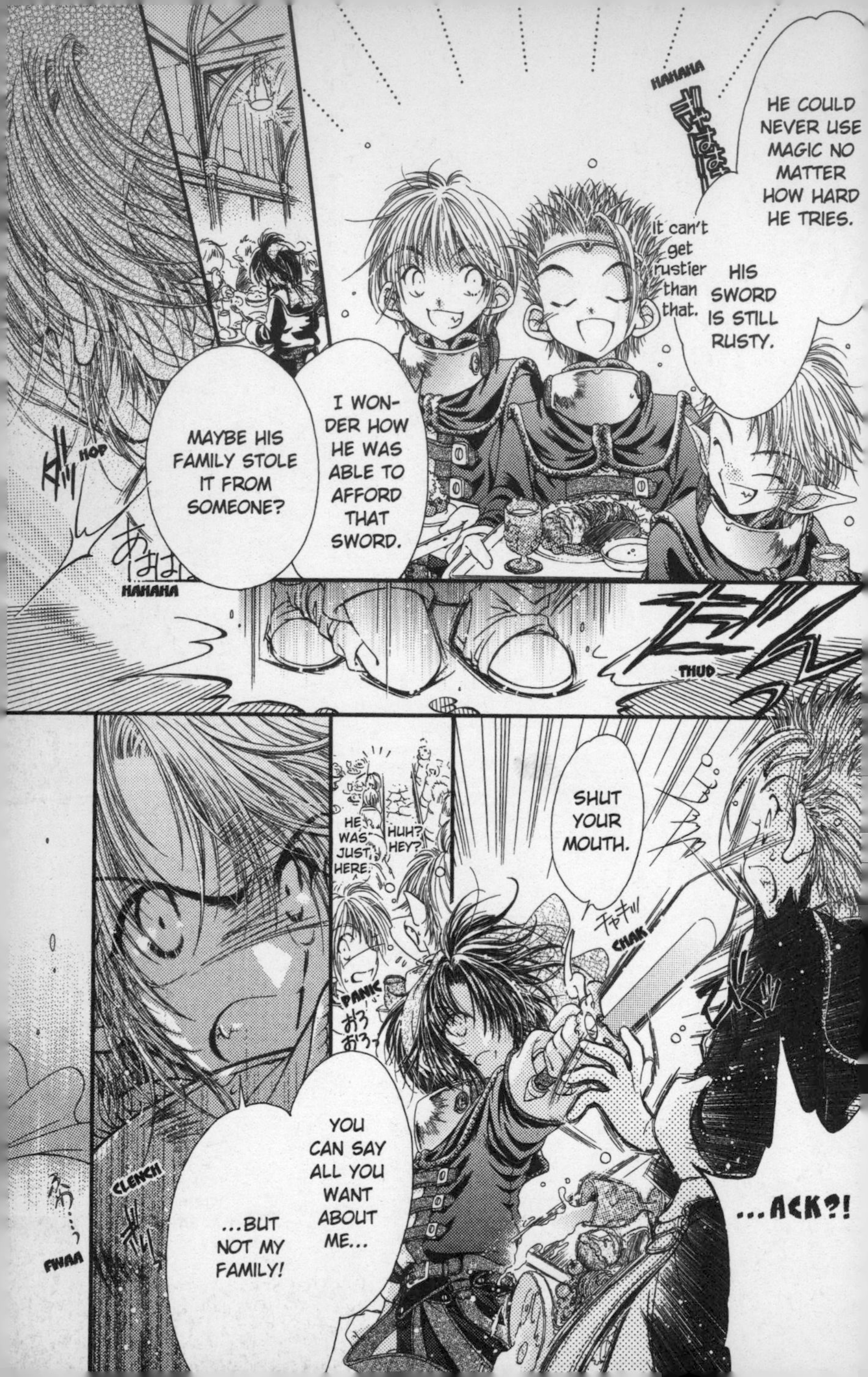
HAHAHA
HE COULD NEVER USE MAGIC NO MATTER HOW HARD HE TRIES.
HIS SWORD IS STILL RUSTY.
it can't get rustier than that.
I WONDER HOW HE WAS ABLE TO AFFORD THAT SWORD.
MAYBE HIS FAMILY STOLE IT FROM SOMEONE?
HOP
HAHAHA
THUD
SHUT YOUR MOUTH.
HUH? HEY?
HE WAS JUST HERE.
CHAK
PANIC
...ACK?!
YOU CAN SAY ALL YOU WANT ABOUT ME...
...BUT NOT MY FAMILY!
CLENCH
FWAA

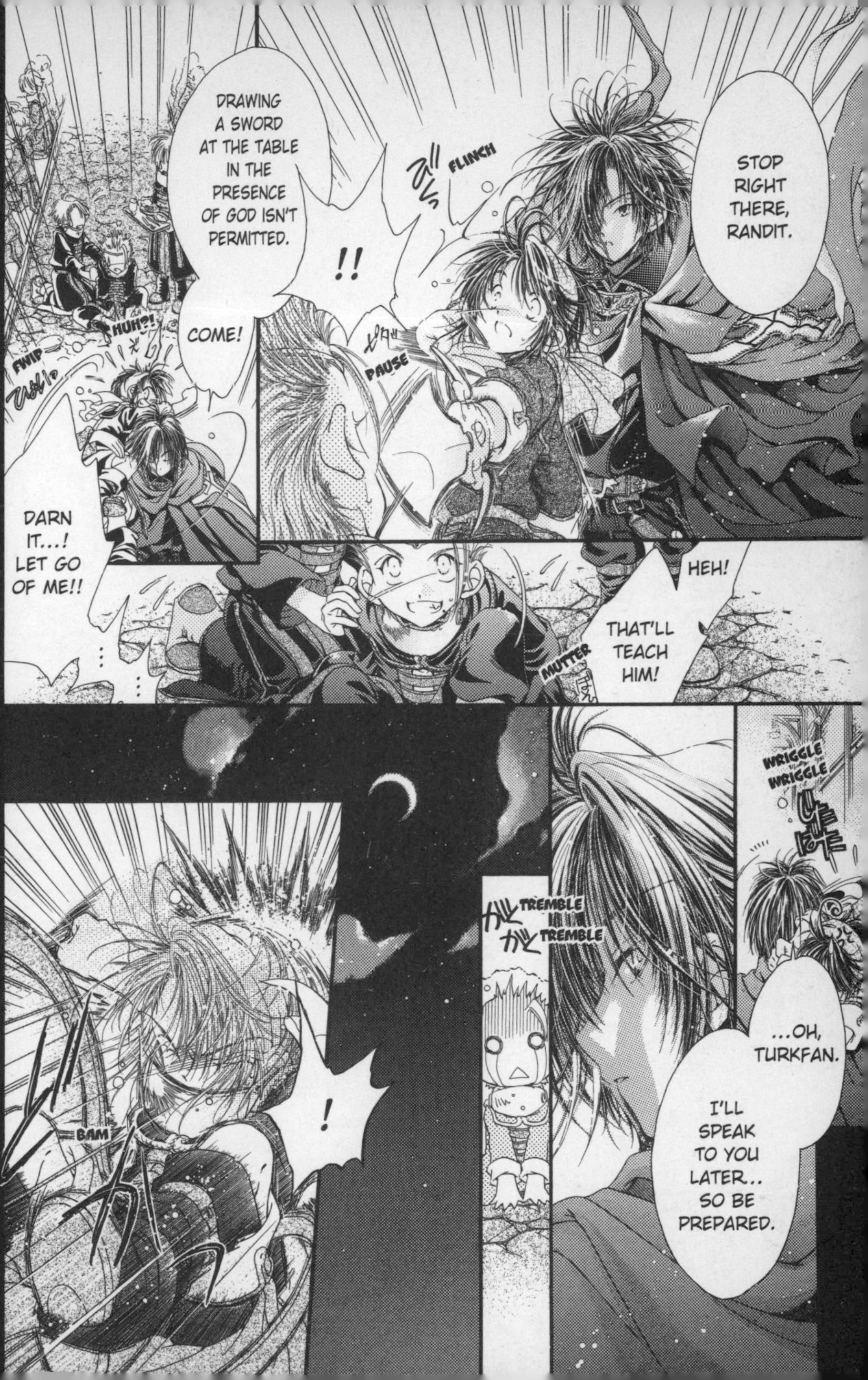
STOP RIGHT THERE, RANDIT.
FLINCH
!!
PAUSE
DRAWING A SWORD AT THE TABLE IN THE PRESENCE OF GOD ISN'T PERMITTED.
HUH?!
FWIP
COME!
DARN IT...! LET GO OF ME!!
HEH!
THAT'LL TEACH HIM!
MUTTER
...
...
WRIGGLE WRIGGLE
...OH, TURKFAN.
I'LL SPEAK TO YOU LATER.. SO BE PREPARED.
TREMBLE
TREMBLE
!
BAM

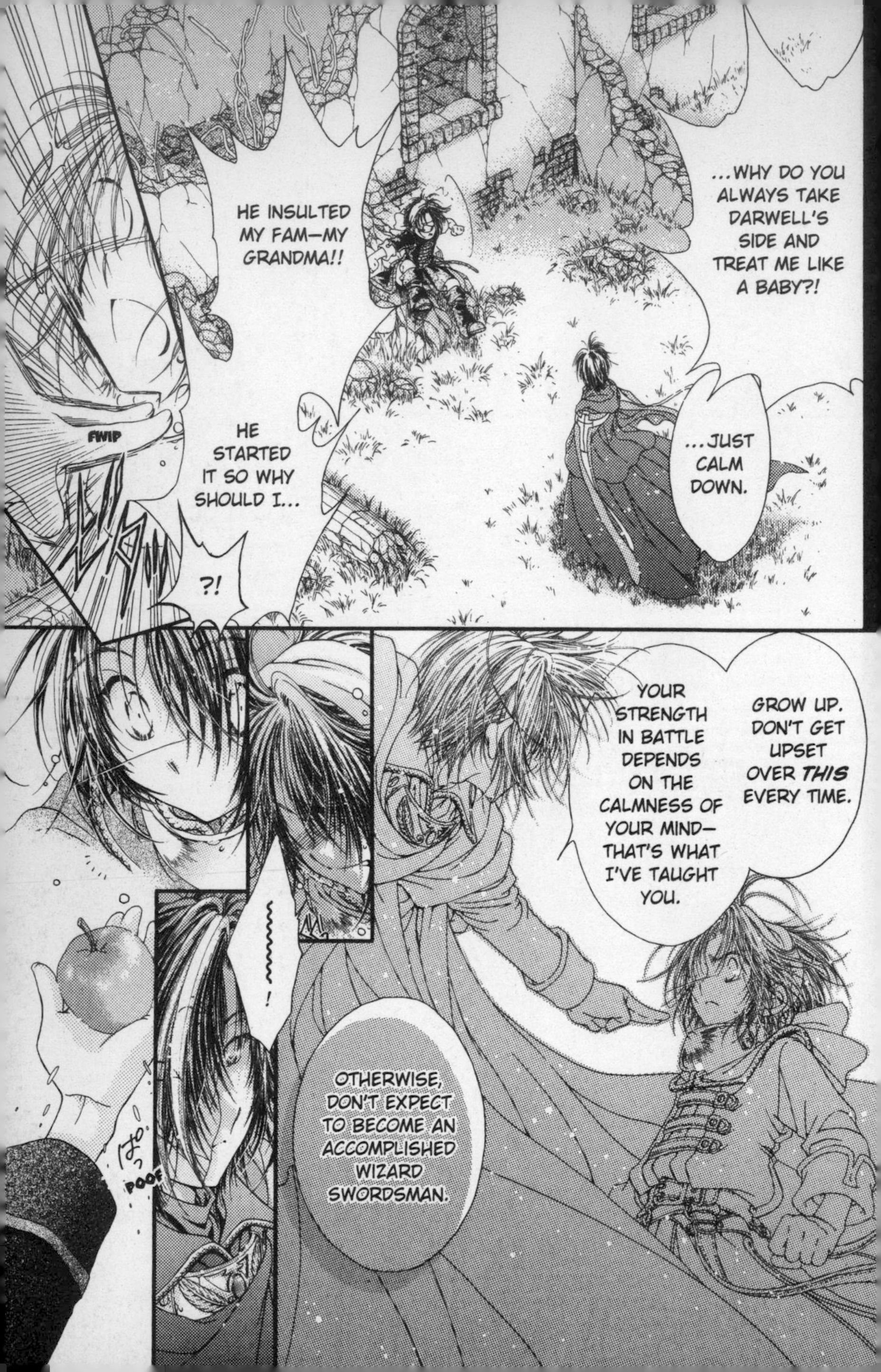
...WHY DO YOU ALWAYS TAKE DARWELL'S SIDE AND TREAT ME LIKE A BABY?!
HE INSULTED MY FAM—MY GRANDMA!!
...JUST CALM DOWN.
HE STARTED IT SO WHY SHOULD I...
FWIP
?!
GROW UP. DON'T GET UPSET OVER *THIS* EVERY TIME.
YOUR STRENGTH IN BATTLE DEPENDS ON THE CALMNESS OF YOUR MIND—THAT'S WHAT I'VE TAUGHT YOU.
OTHERWISE, DON'T EXPECT TO BECOME AN ACCOMPLISHED WIZARD SWORDSMAN.
......!
POOF

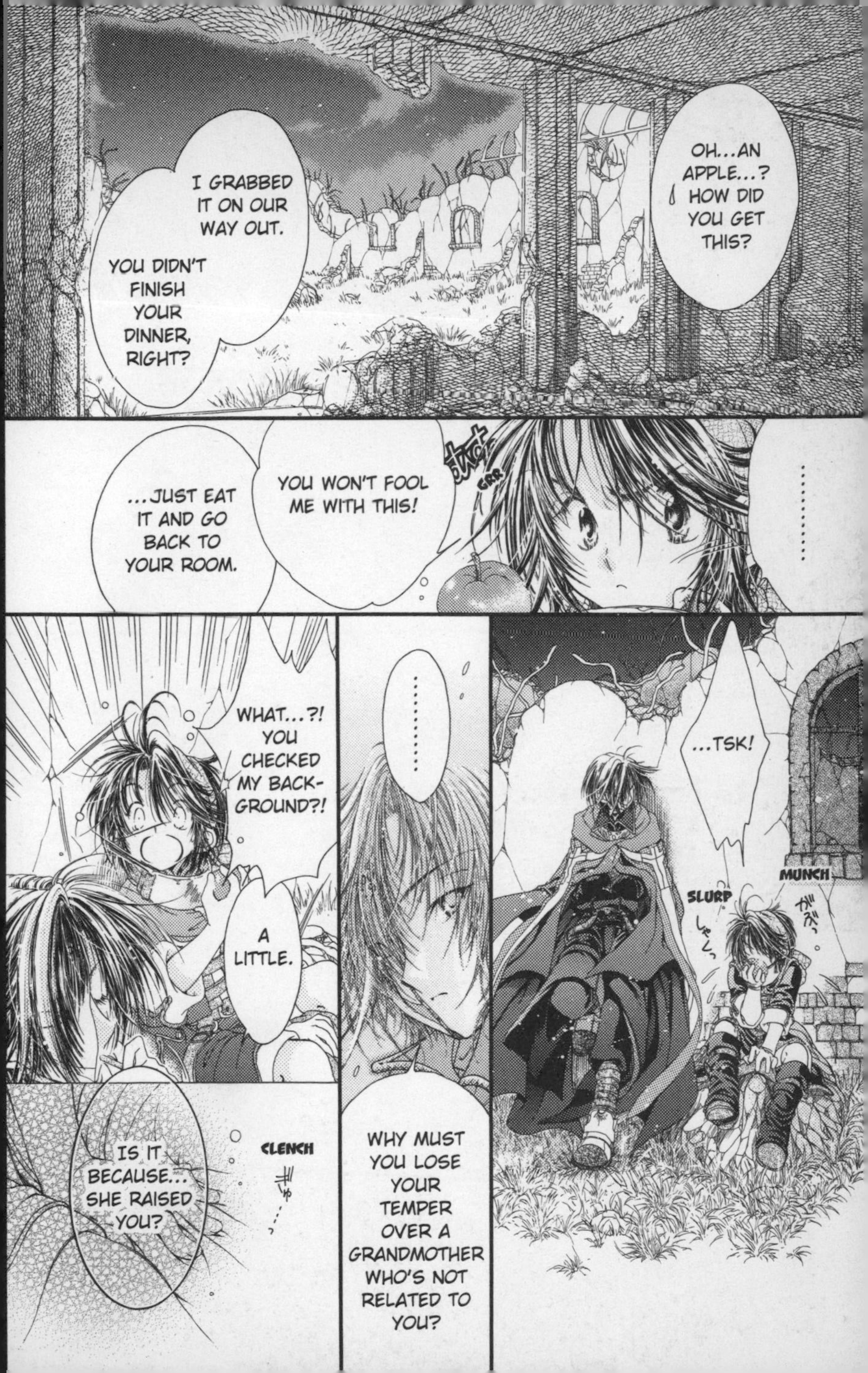
OH...AN APPLE...? HOW DID YOU GET THIS?
I GRABBED IT ON OUR WAY OUT.
YOU DIDN'T FINISH YOUR DINNER, RIGHT?
......
GRR
YOU WON'T FOOL ME WITH THIS!
...JUST EAT IT AND GO BACK TO YOUR ROOM.
...TSK!
MUNCH
SLURP
......
WHY MUST YOU LOSE YOUR TEMPER OVER A GRANDMOTHER WHO'S NOT RELATED TO YOU?
WHAT...?! YOU CHECKED MY BACK-GROUND?!
A LITTLE.
IS IT BECAUSE... SHE RAISED YOU?
CLENCH

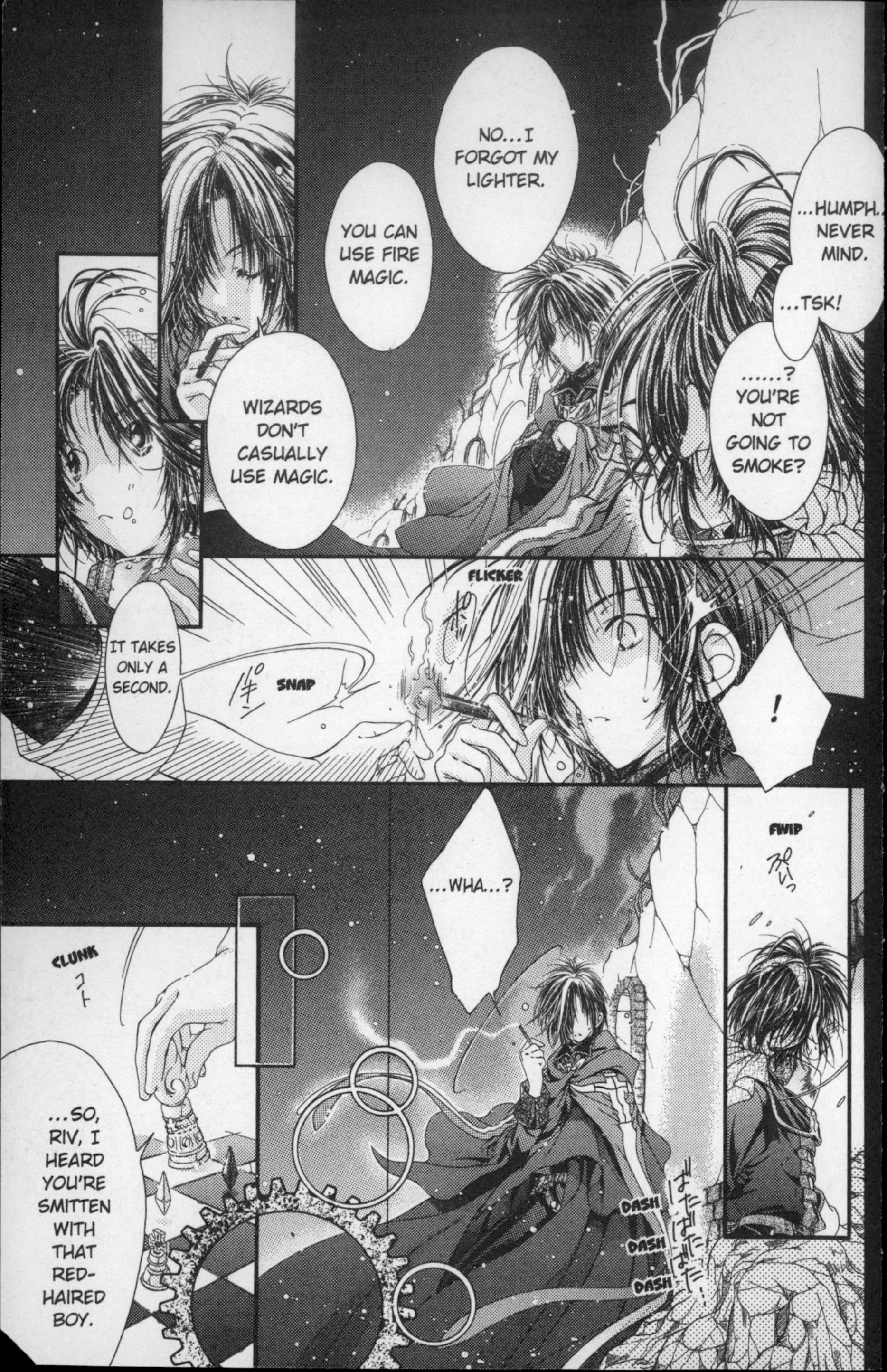
...HUMPH... NEVER MIND.
...TSK!
......? YOU'RE NOT GOING TO SMOKE?
NO...I FORGOT MY LIGHTER.
YOU CAN USE FIRE MAGIC.
WIZARDS DON'T CASUALLY USE MAGIC.
!
FLICKER
SNAP
IT TAKES ONLY A SECOND.
FWIP
...WHA...?
DASH
DASH
DASH
CLUNK
...SO, RIV, I HEARD YOU'RE SMITTEN WITH THAT RED-HAIRED BOY.

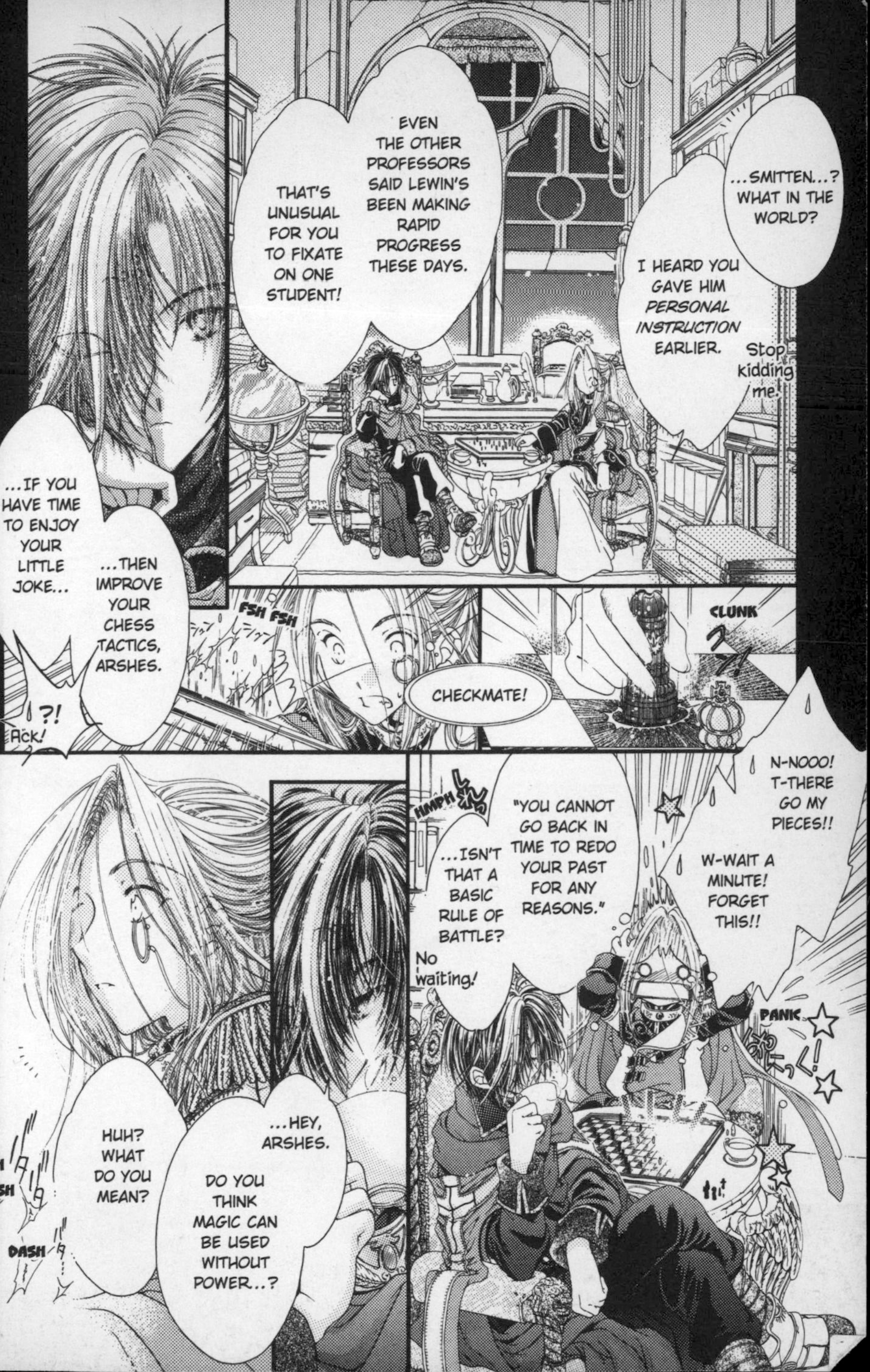
...SMITTEN...? WHAT IN THE WORLD?
I HEARD YOU GAVE HIM *PERSONAL INSTRUCTION* EARLIER.
Stop kidding me!
EVEN THE OTHER PROFESSORS SAID LEWIN'S BEEN MAKING RAPID PROGRESS THESE DAYS.
THAT'S UNUSUAL FOR YOU TO FIXATE ON ONE STUDENT!
CLUNK
CHECKMATE!
FSH FSH
?!
Ack!
...IF YOU HAVE TIME TO ENJOY YOUR LITTLE JOKE...
...THEN IMPROVE YOUR CHESS TACTICS, ARSHES.
N-NOOO! T-THERE GO MY PIECES!!
W-WAIT A MINUTE! FORGET THIS!!
PANIC
"YOU CANNOT GO BACK IN TIME TO REDO YOUR PAST FOR ANY REASONS."
HMPH
...ISN'T THAT A BASIC RULE OF BATTLE?
No waiting!
...HEY, ARSHES.
DO YOU THINK MAGIC CAN BE USED WITHOUT POWER...?
HUH? WHAT DO YOU MEAN?
DASH

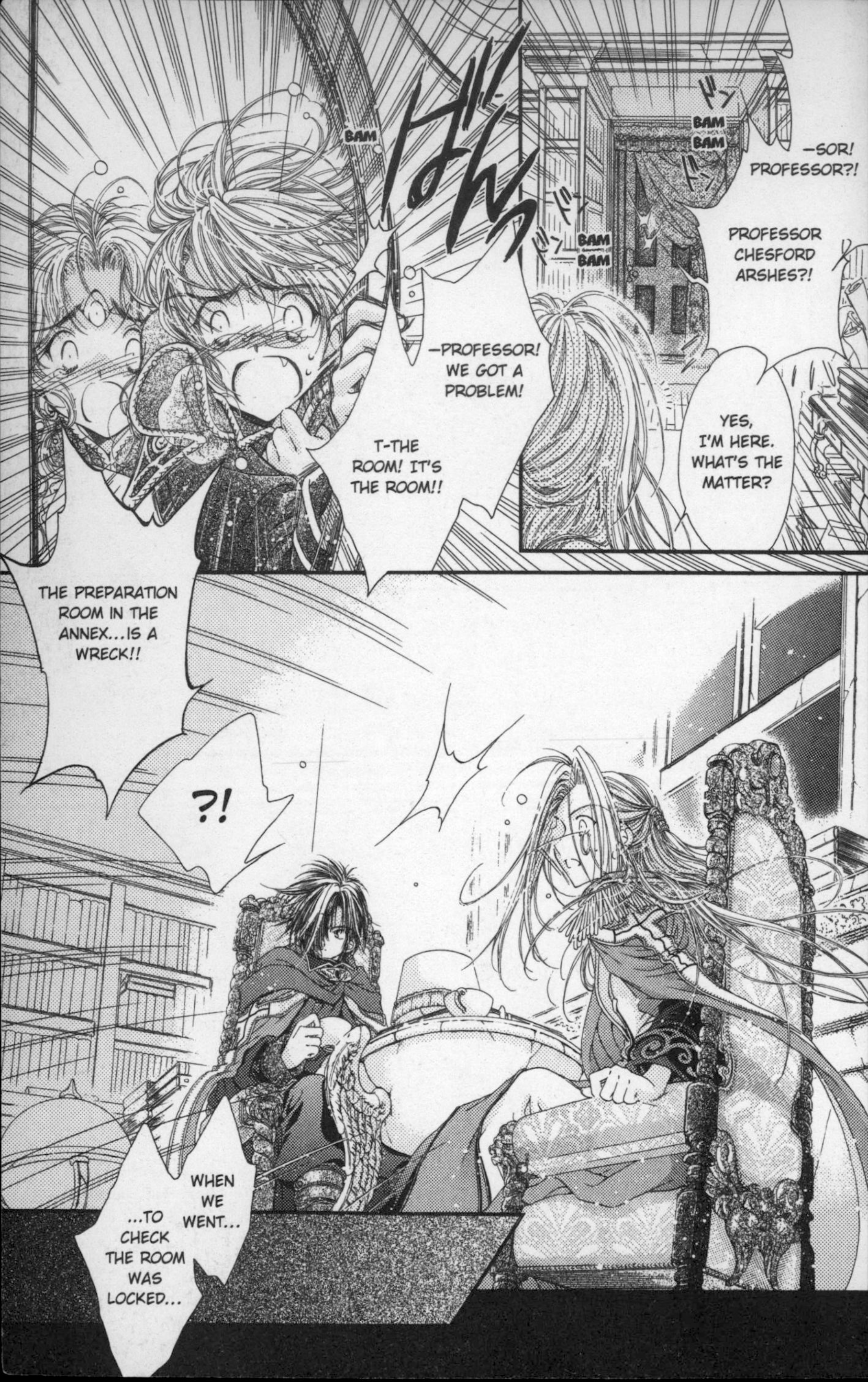

BAM
BAM
BAM
BAM
—SOR! PROFESSOR?!
PROFESSOR CHESFORD ARSHES?!
YES, I'M HERE. WHAT'S THE MATTER?
ばん
BAM
—PROFESSOR! WE GOT A PROBLEM!
T-THE ROOM! IT'S THE ROOM!!
THE PREPARATION ROOM IN THE ANNEX...IS A WRECK!!
?!
WHEN WE WENT...
...TO CHECK THE ROOM WAS LOCKED...

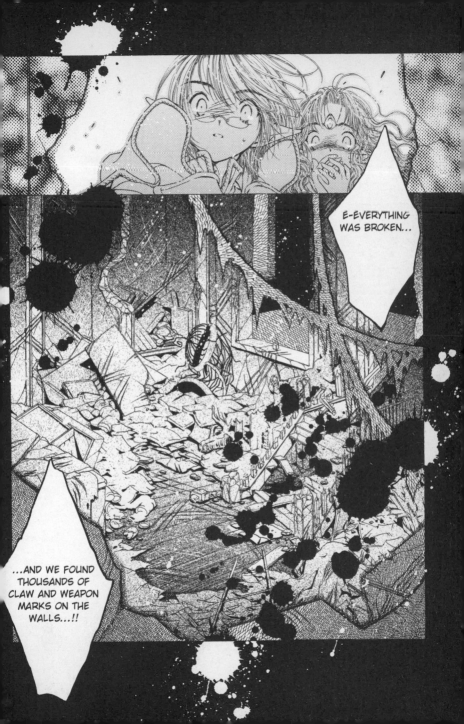

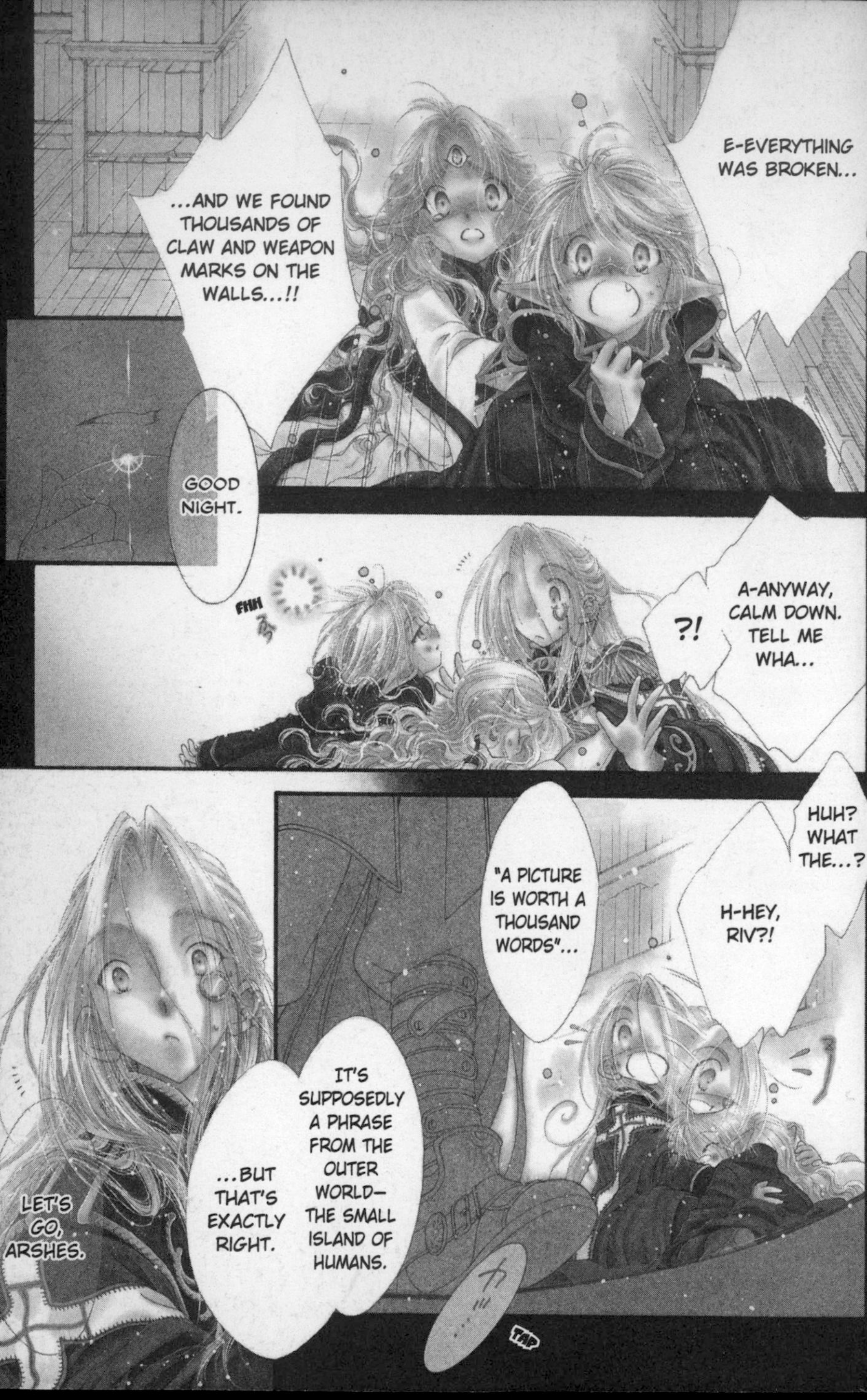
E-EVERYTHING WAS BROKEN...
...AND WE FOUND THOUSANDS OF CLAW AND WEAPON MARKS ON THE WALLS...!!
GOOD NIGHT.
A-ANYWAY, CALM DOWN. TELL ME WHA...
?!
FHH
HUH? WHAT THE...?
H-HEY, RIV?!
"A PICTURE IS WORTH A THOUSAND WORDS"...
IT'S SUPPOSEDLY A PHRASE FROM THE OUTER WORLD— THE SMALL ISLAND OF HUMANS.
...BUT THAT'S EXACTLY RIGHT.
TAP
LET'S GO, ARSHES.

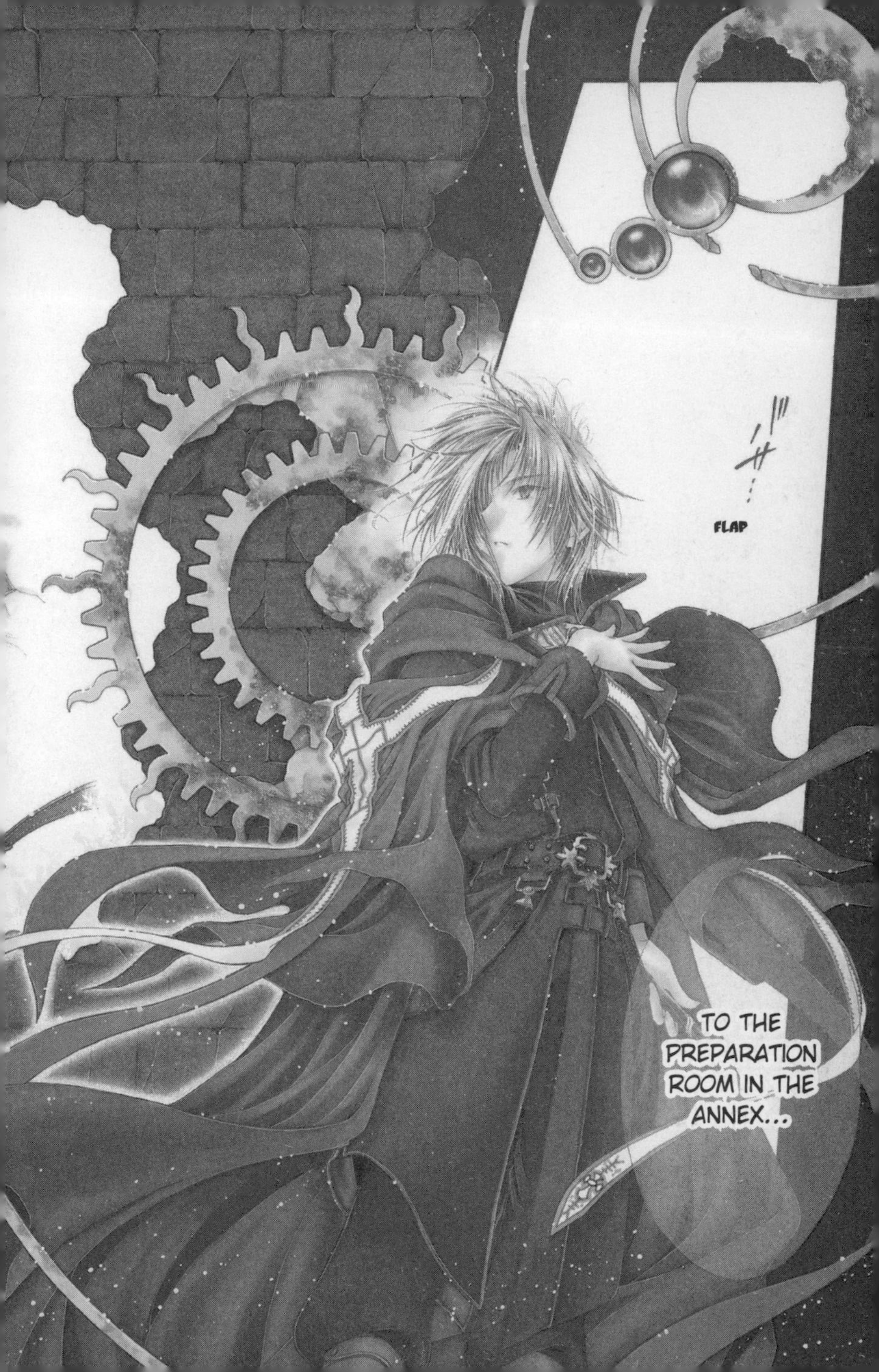

バサ…
FLAP
TO THE PREPARATION ROOM IN THE ANNEX...

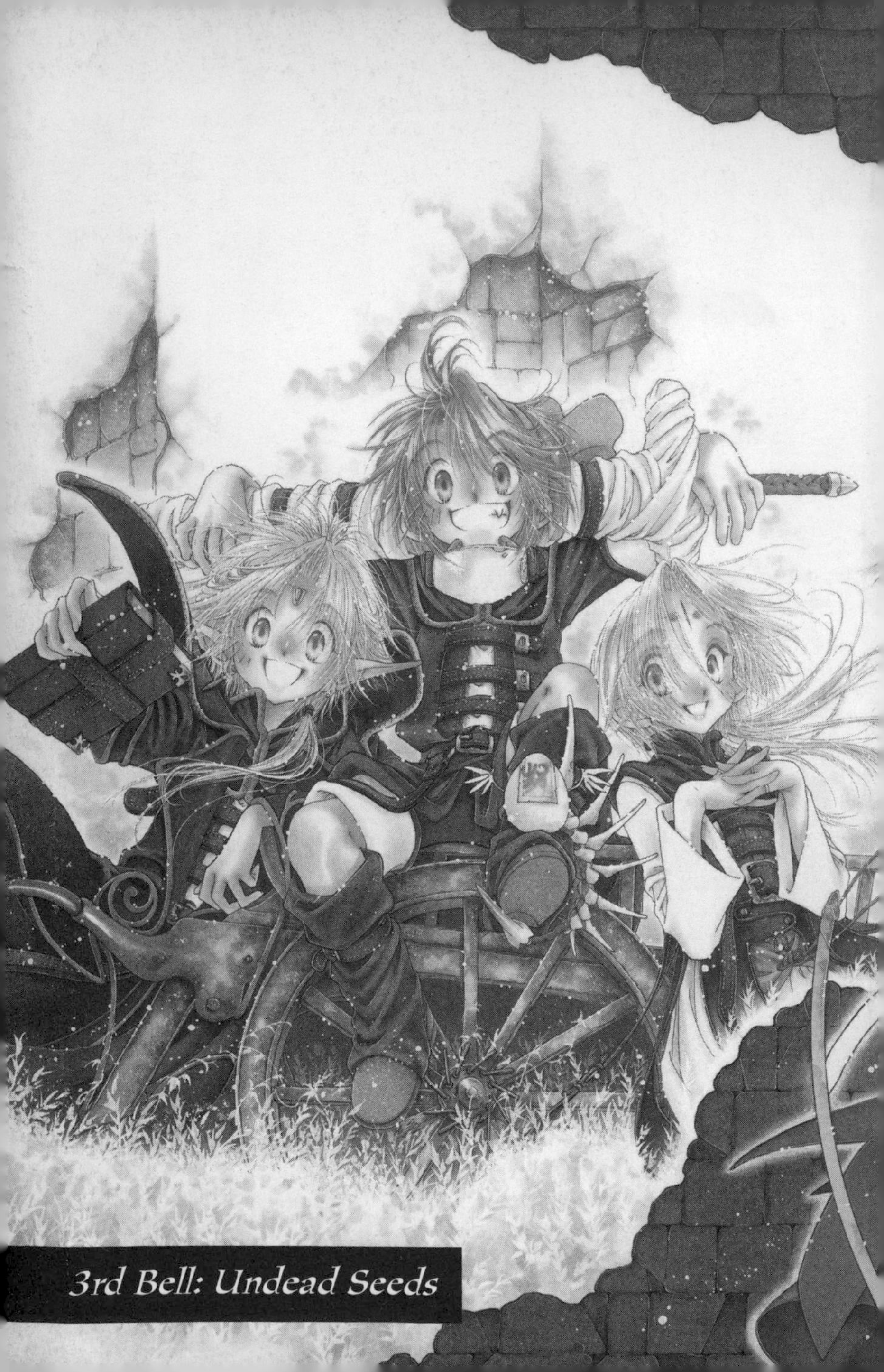

3rd Bell: Undead Seeds

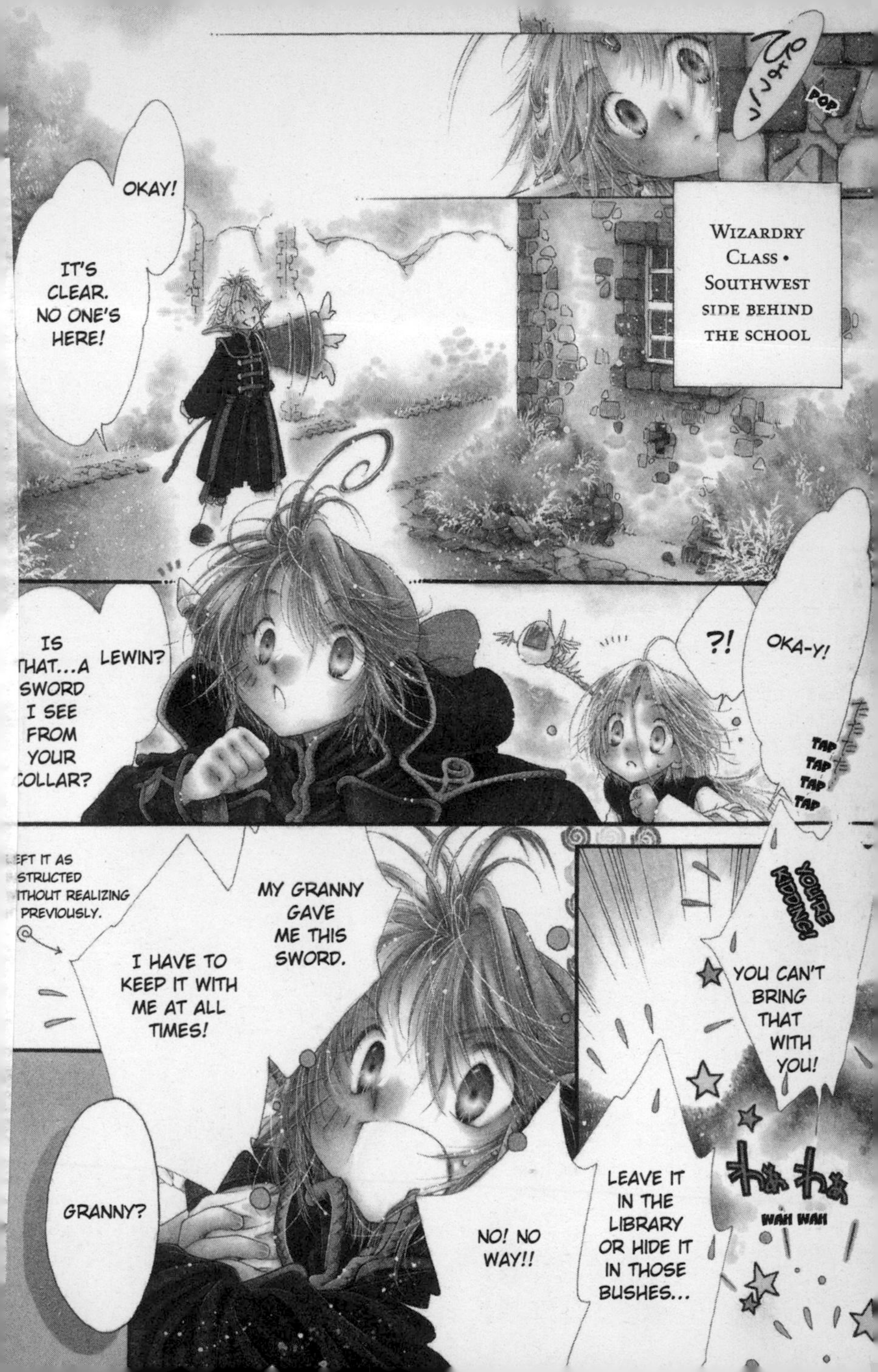
POP!
Wizardry Class • Southwest side behind the school
OKAY!
IT'S CLEAR. NO ONE'S HERE!
OKA-Y!
?!
TAP TAP TAP TAP
LEWIN?
IS THAT...A SWORD I SEE FROM YOUR COLLAR?
YOU'RE KIDDING!
YOU CAN'T BRING THAT WITH YOU!
LEAVE IT IN THE LIBRARY OR HIDE IT IN THOSE BUSHES...
WAH WAH
NO! NO WAY!!
MY GRANNY GAVE ME THIS SWORD.
I HAVE TO KEEP IT WITH ME AT ALL TIMES!
EFT IT AS STRUCTED WITHOUT REALIZING PREVIOUSLY.
GRANNY?

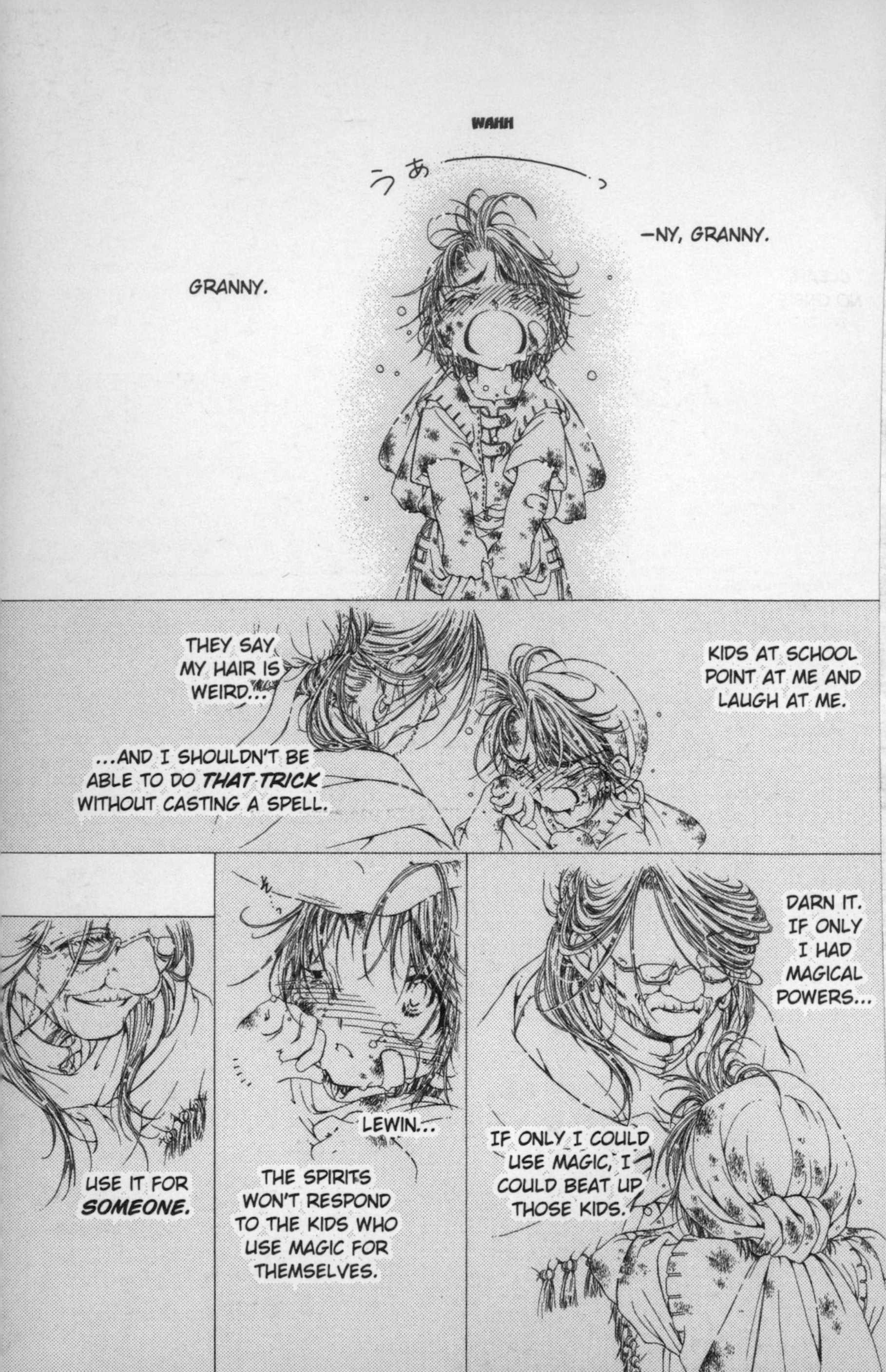
WAHH
うあ―っ
—NY, GRANNY.
GRANNY.
KIDS AT SCHOOL POINT AT ME AND LAUGH AT ME.
THEY SAY MY HAIR IS WEIRD...
...AND I SHOULDN'T BE ABLE TO DO *THAT TRICK* WITHOUT CASTING A SPELL.
DARN IT. IF ONLY I HAD MAGICAL POWERS...
IF ONLY I COULD USE MAGIC, I COULD BEAT UP THOSE KIDS.
LEWIN...
THE SPIRITS WON'T RESPOND TO THE KIDS WHO USE MAGIC FOR THEMSELVES.
USE IT FOR *SOMEONE.*

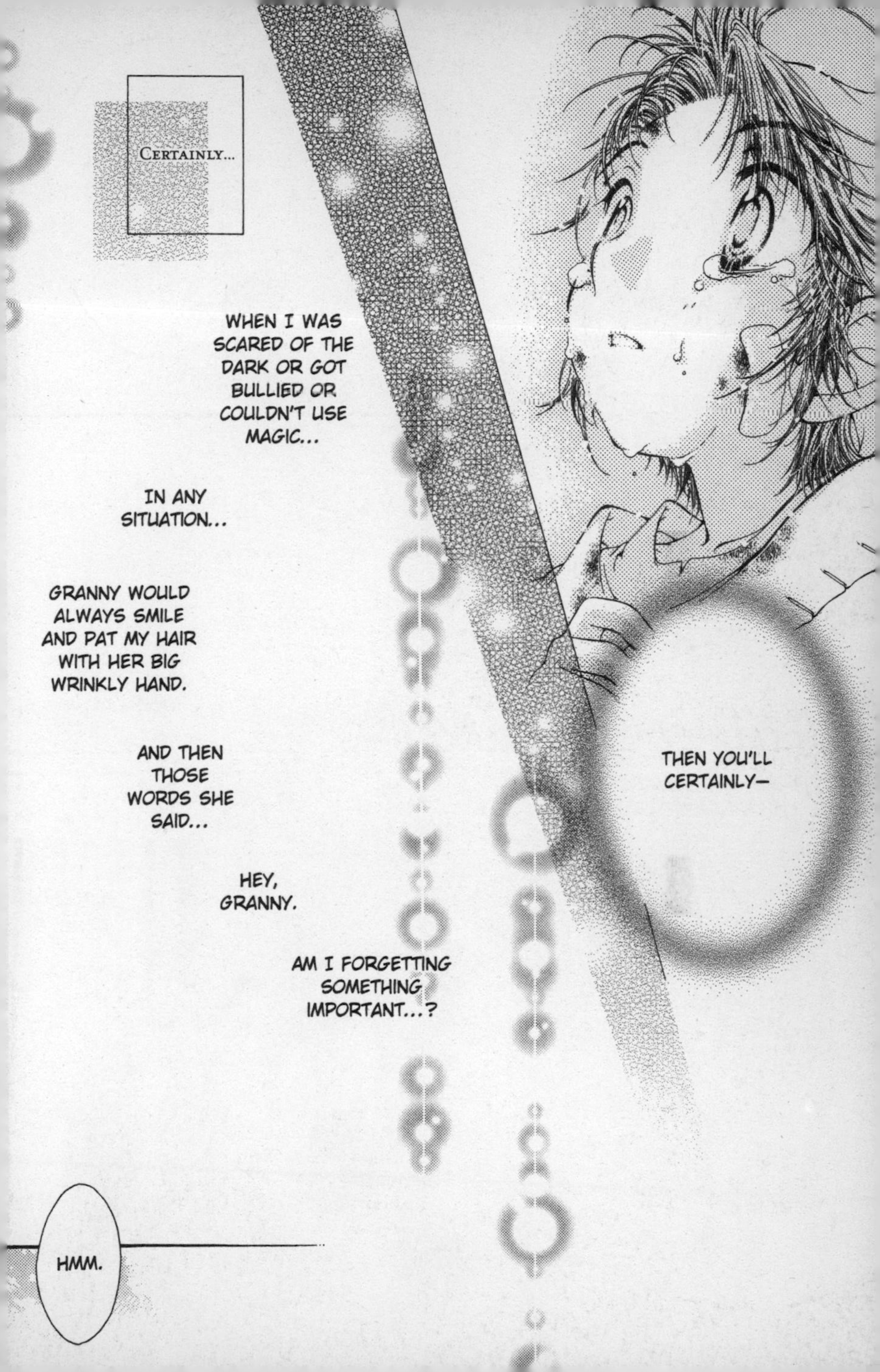
Certainly...
WHEN I WAS SCARED OF THE DARK OR GOT BULLIED OR COULDN'T USE MAGIC...
IN ANY SITUATION...
GRANNY WOULD ALWAYS SMILE AND PAT MY HAIR WITH HER BIG WRINKLY HAND.
AND THEN THOSE WORDS SHE SAID...
THEN YOU'LL CERTAINLY—
HEY, GRANNY.
AM I FORGETTING SOMETHING IMPORTANT...?
HMM.

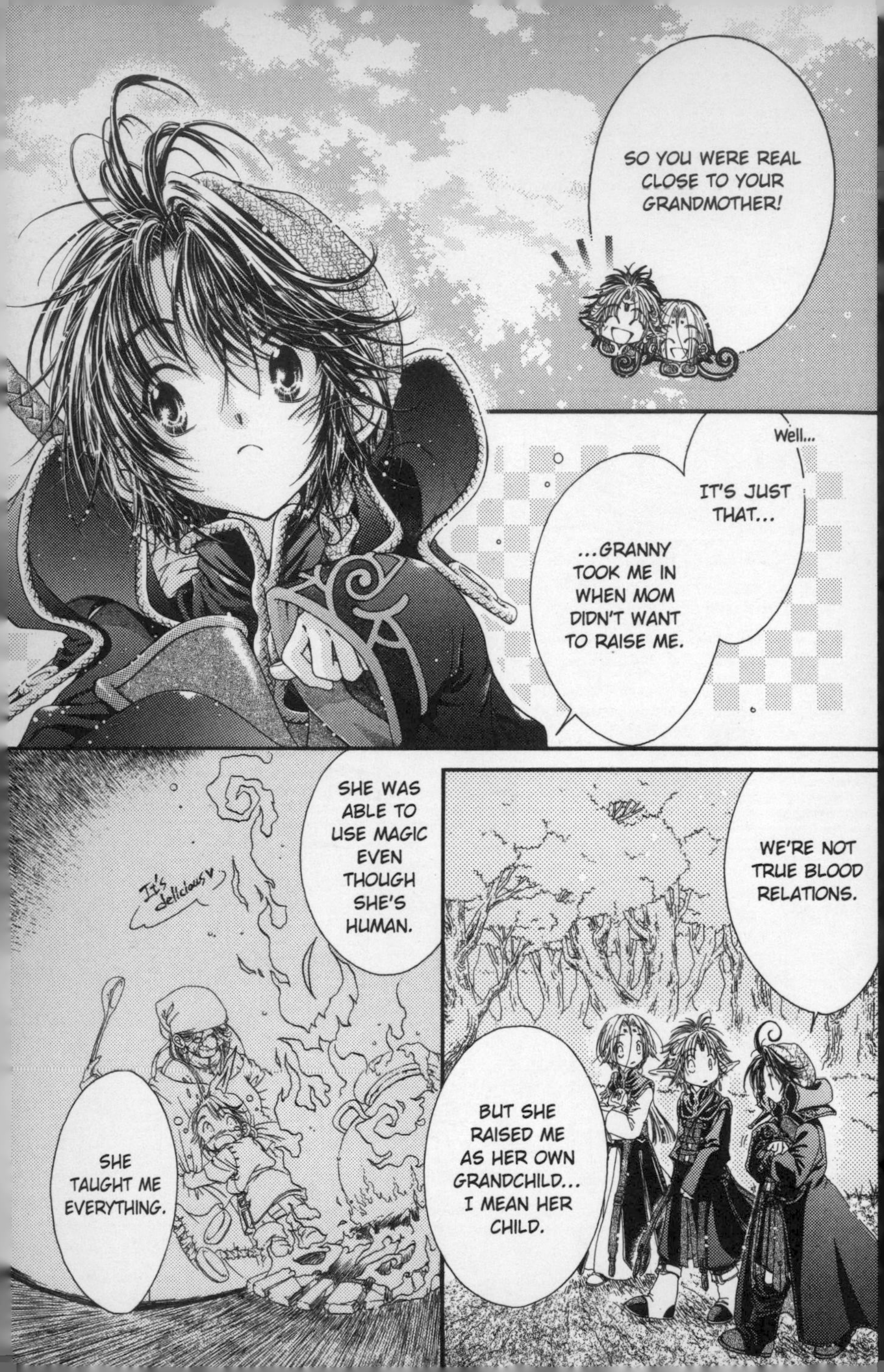
SO YOU WERE REAL CLOSE TO YOUR GRANDMOTHER!
Well...
IT'S JUST THAT...
...GRANNY TOOK ME IN WHEN MOM DIDN'T WANT TO RAISE ME.
WE'RE NOT TRUE BLOOD RELATIONS.
BUT SHE RAISED ME AS HER OWN GRANDCHILD... I MEAN HER CHILD.
SHE WAS ABLE TO USE MAGIC EVEN THOUGH SHE'S HUMAN.
It's delicious♥
SHE TAUGHT ME EVERYTHING.

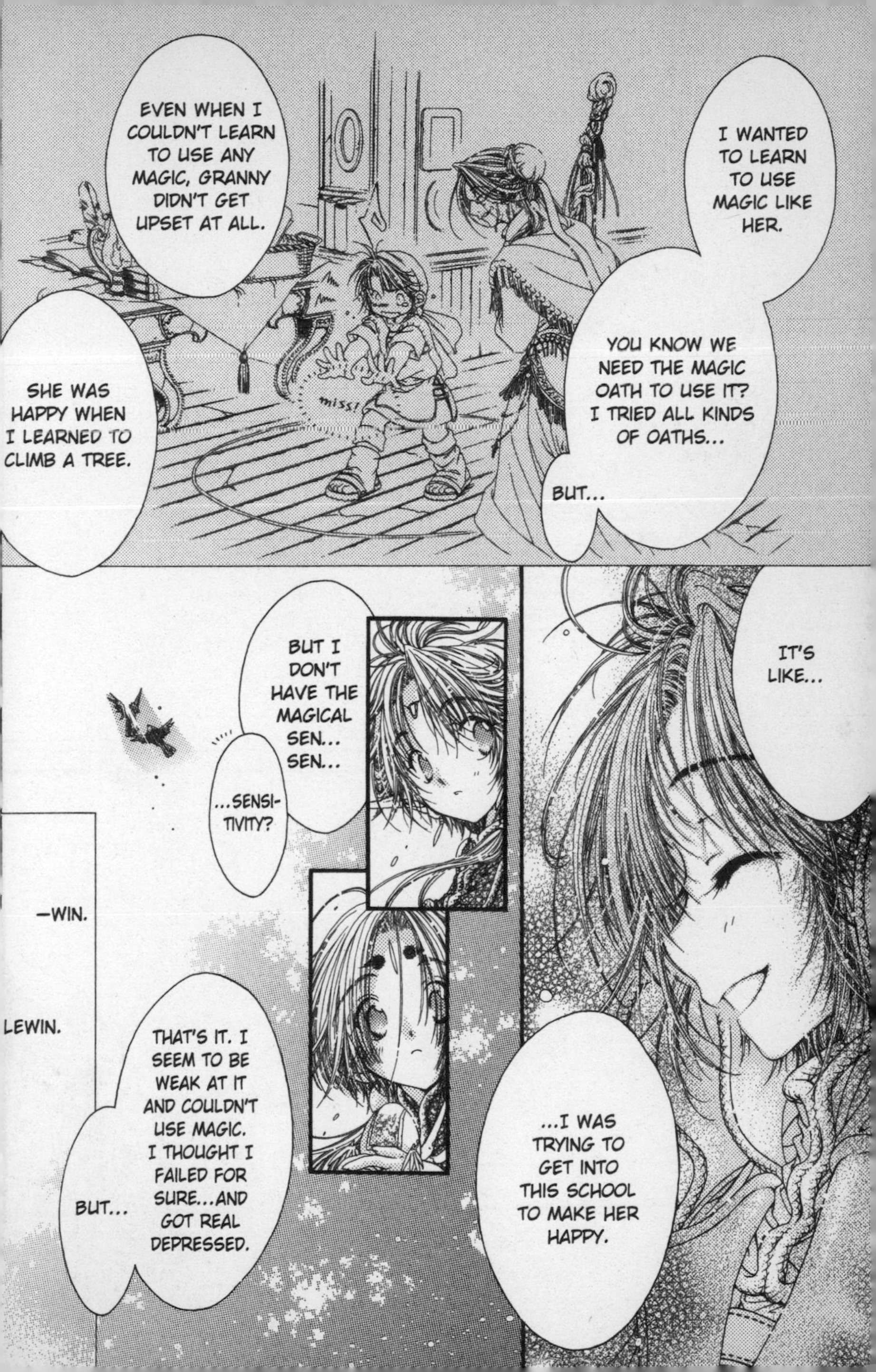
I WANTED TO LEARN TO USE MAGIC LIKE HER.
YOU KNOW WE NEED THE MAGIC OATH TO USE IT? I TRIED ALL KINDS OF OATHS...
BUT...
EVEN WHEN I COULDN'T LEARN TO USE ANY MAGIC, GRANNY DIDN'T GET UPSET AT ALL.
miss!
SHE WAS HAPPY WHEN I LEARNED TO CLIMB A TREE.
IT'S LIKE...
...I WAS TRYING TO GET INTO THIS SCHOOL TO MAKE HER HAPPY.
BUT I DON'T HAVE THE MAGICAL SEN... SEN...
...SENSI-TIVITY?
THAT'S IT. I SEEM TO BE WEAK AT IT AND COULDN'T USE MAGIC. I THOUGHT I FAILED FOR SURE...AND GOT REAL DEPRESSED.
BUT...
—WIN.
LEWIN.

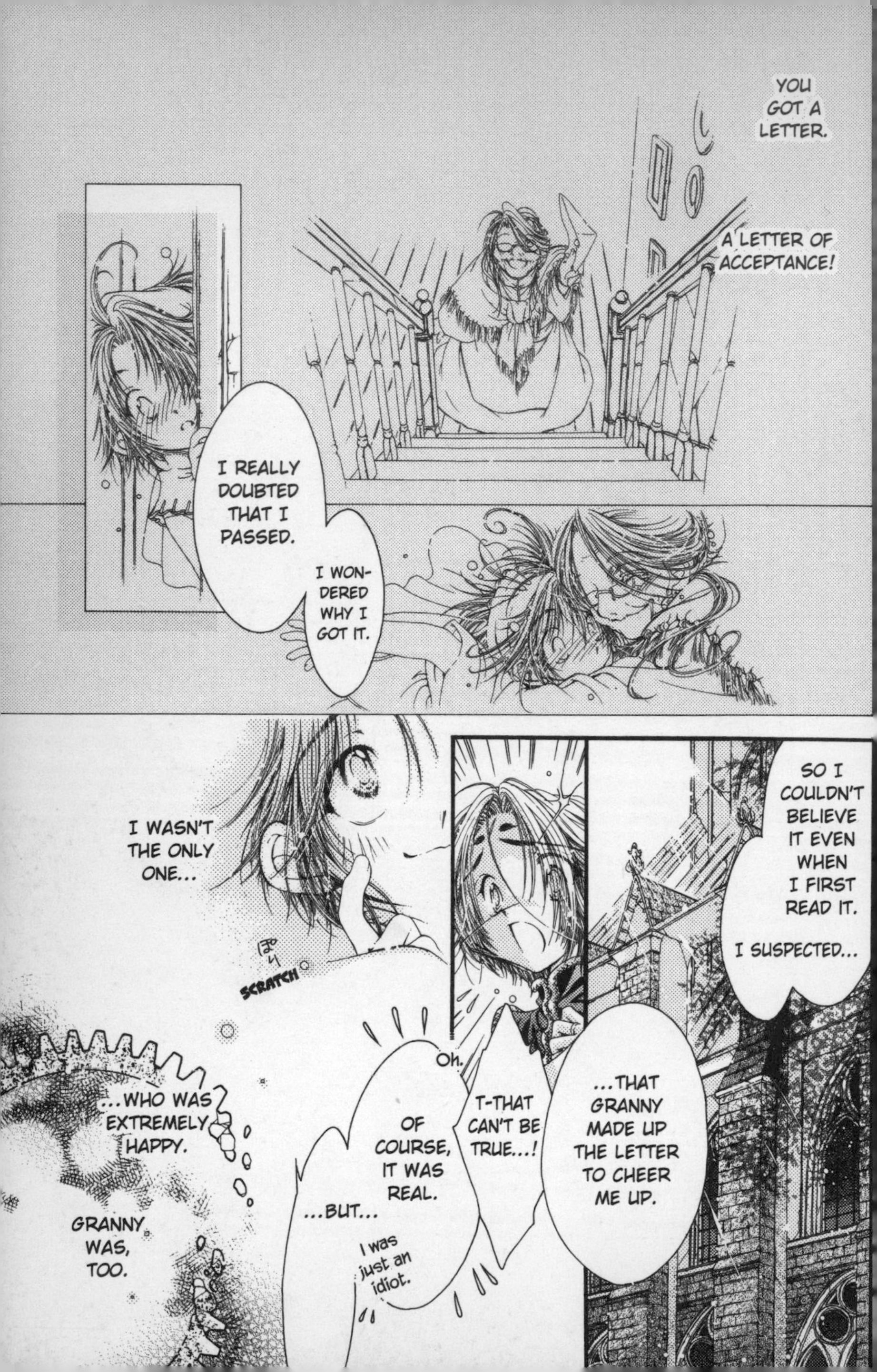
YOU GOT A LETTER.
A LETTER OF ACCEPTANCE!
I REALLY DOUBTED THAT I PASSED.
I WONDERED WHY I GOT IT.
SO I COULDN'T BELIEVE IT EVEN WHEN I FIRST READ IT.
I SUSPECTED...
...THAT GRANNY MADE UP THE LETTER TO CHEER ME UP.
T-THAT CAN'T BE TRUE...!
Oh.
OF COURSE, IT WAS REAL.
...BUT...
I was just an idiot.
I WASN'T THE ONLY ONE...
SCRATCH
...WHO WAS EXTREMELY HAPPY.
GRANNY WAS, TOO.

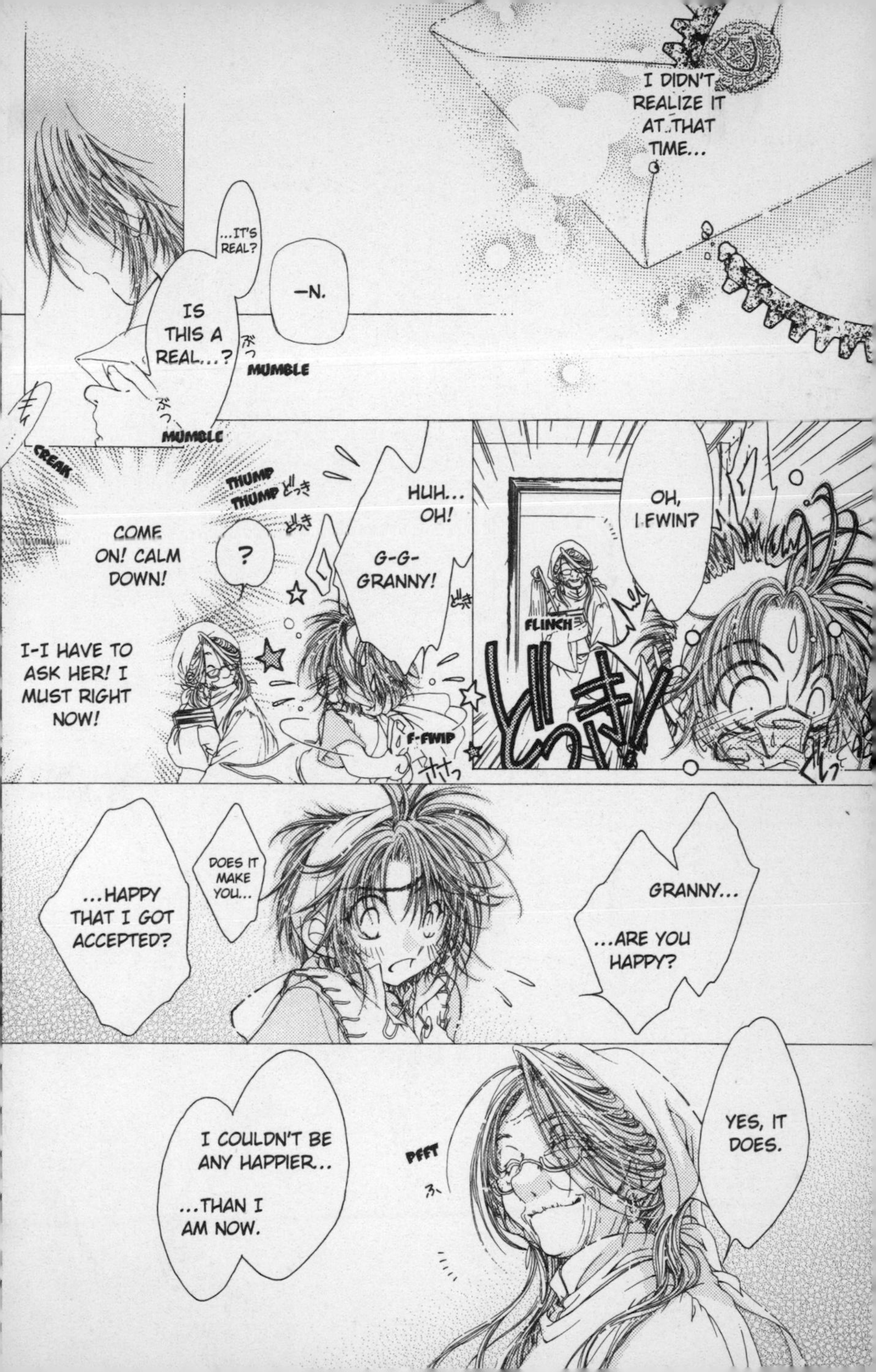
I DIDN'T REALIZE IT AT THAT TIME...
—N.
...IT'S REAL?
IS THIS A REAL...?
ぶっ
MUMBLE
ぶっ
MUMBLE
OH, LEFWIN?
FLINCH
どっき!
HUH... OH!
G-G-GRANNY!
THUMP THUMP どっき どっき
?
COME ON! CALM DOWN!
I-I HAVE TO ASK HER! I MUST RIGHT NOW!
F-FWIP
CREAK
GRANNY...
...ARE YOU HAPPY?
DOES IT MAKE YOU...
...HAPPY THAT I GOT ACCEPTED?
YES, IT DOES.
PFFT
ふ
I COULDN'T BE ANY HAPPIER...
...THAN I AM NOW.

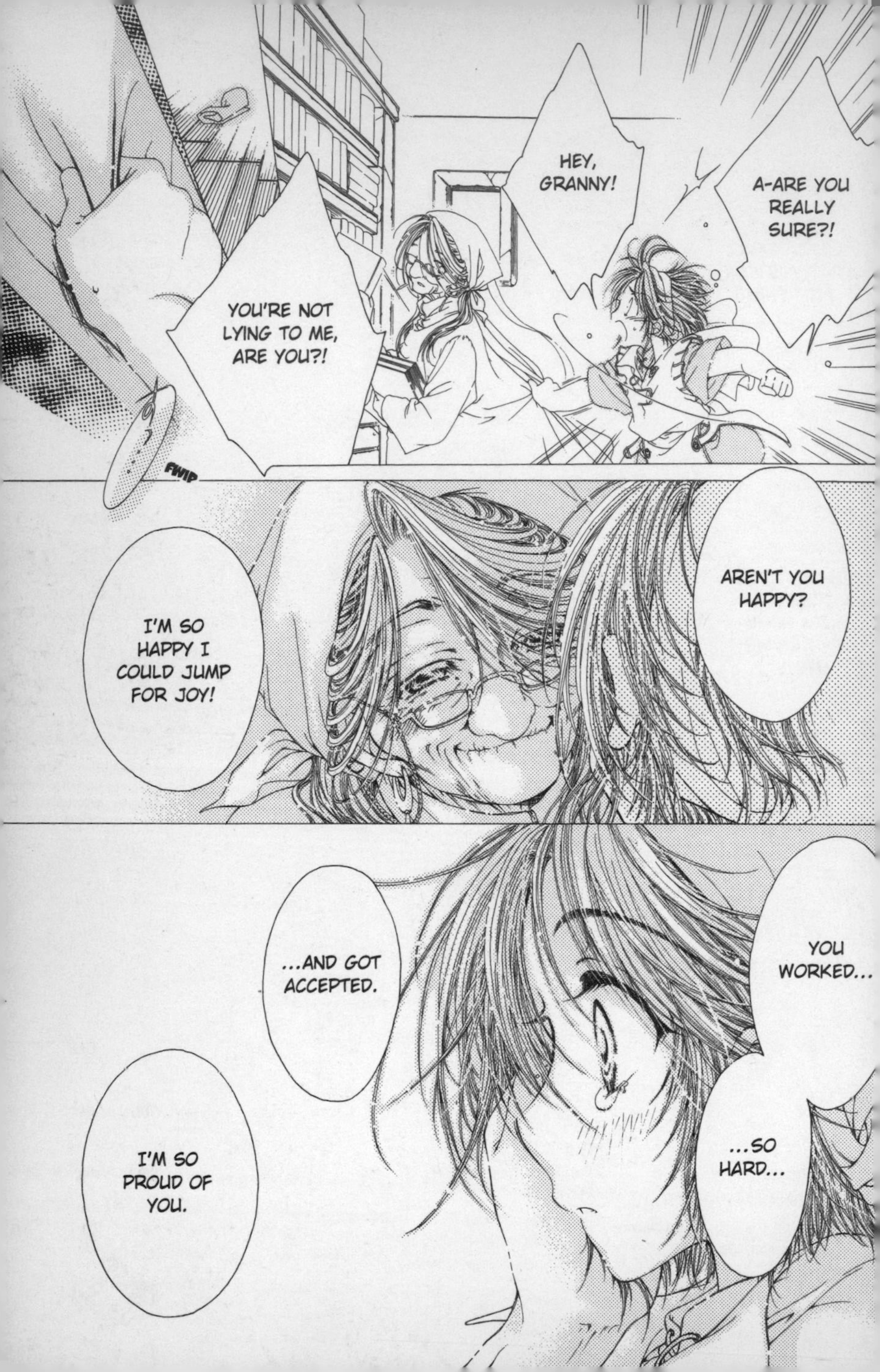
A-ARE YOU REALLY SURE?!
HEY, GRANNY!
YOU'RE NOT LYING TO ME, ARE YOU?!
FWIP
AREN'T YOU HAPPY?
I'M SO HAPPY I COULD JUMP FOR JOY!
YOU WORKED...
...SO HARD...
...AND GOT ACCEPTED.
I'M SO PROUD OF YOU.

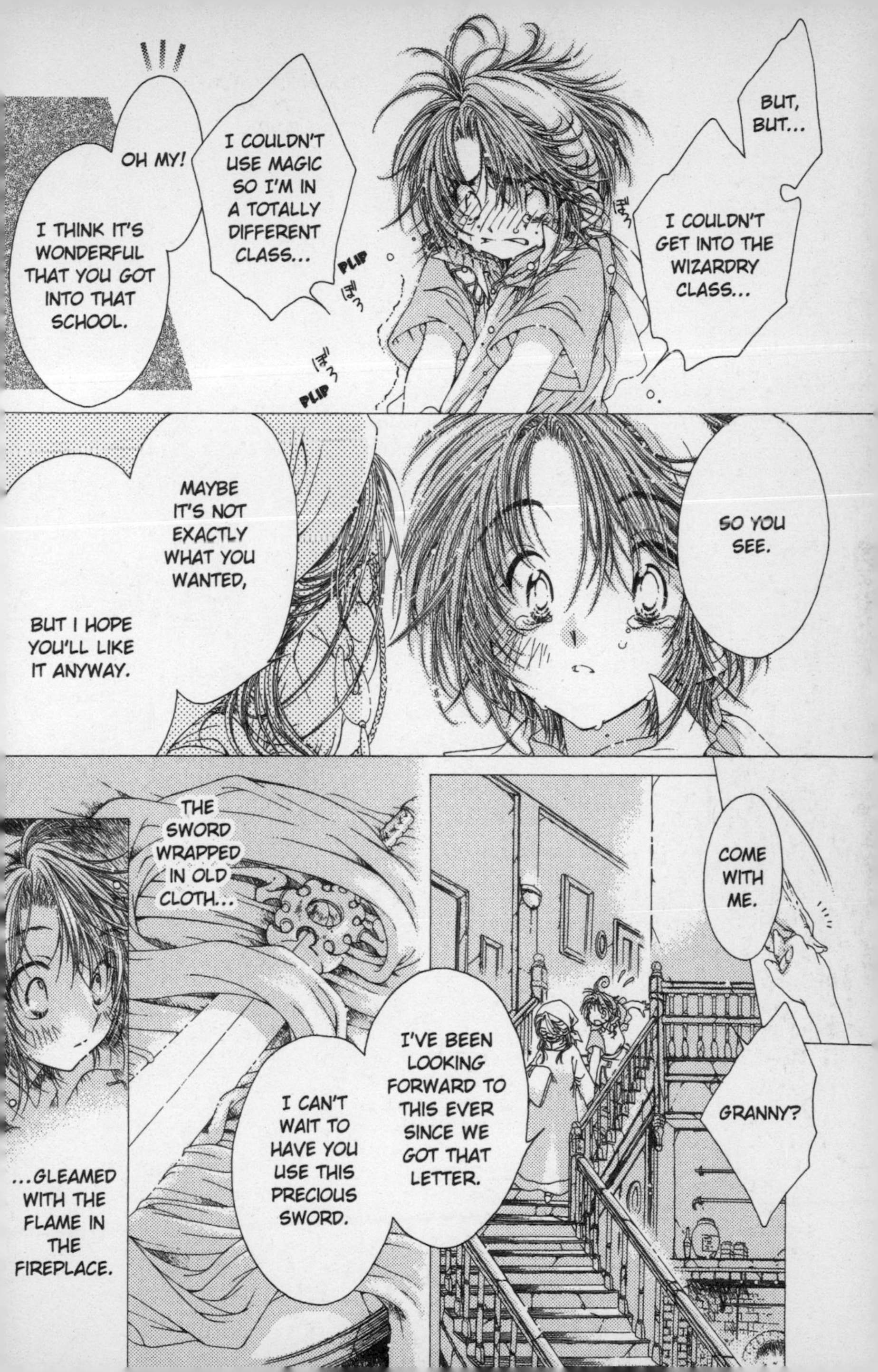
BUT, BUT...
I COULDN'T GET INTO THE WIZARDRY CLASS...
I COULDN'T USE MAGIC SO I'M IN A TOTALLY DIFFERENT CLASS...
PLIP
PLIP
OH MY!
I THINK IT'S WONDERFUL THAT YOU GOT INTO THAT SCHOOL.
SO YOU SEE.
MAYBE IT'S NOT EXACTLY WHAT YOU WANTED,
BUT I HOPE YOU'LL LIKE IT ANYWAY.
COME WITH ME.
GRANNY?
I'VE BEEN LOOKING FORWARD TO THIS EVER SINCE WE GOT THAT LETTER.
I CAN'T WAIT TO HAVE YOU USE THIS PRECIOUS SWORD.
THE SWORD WRAPPED IN OLD CLOTH...
...GLEAMED WITH THE FLAME IN THE FIREPLACE.

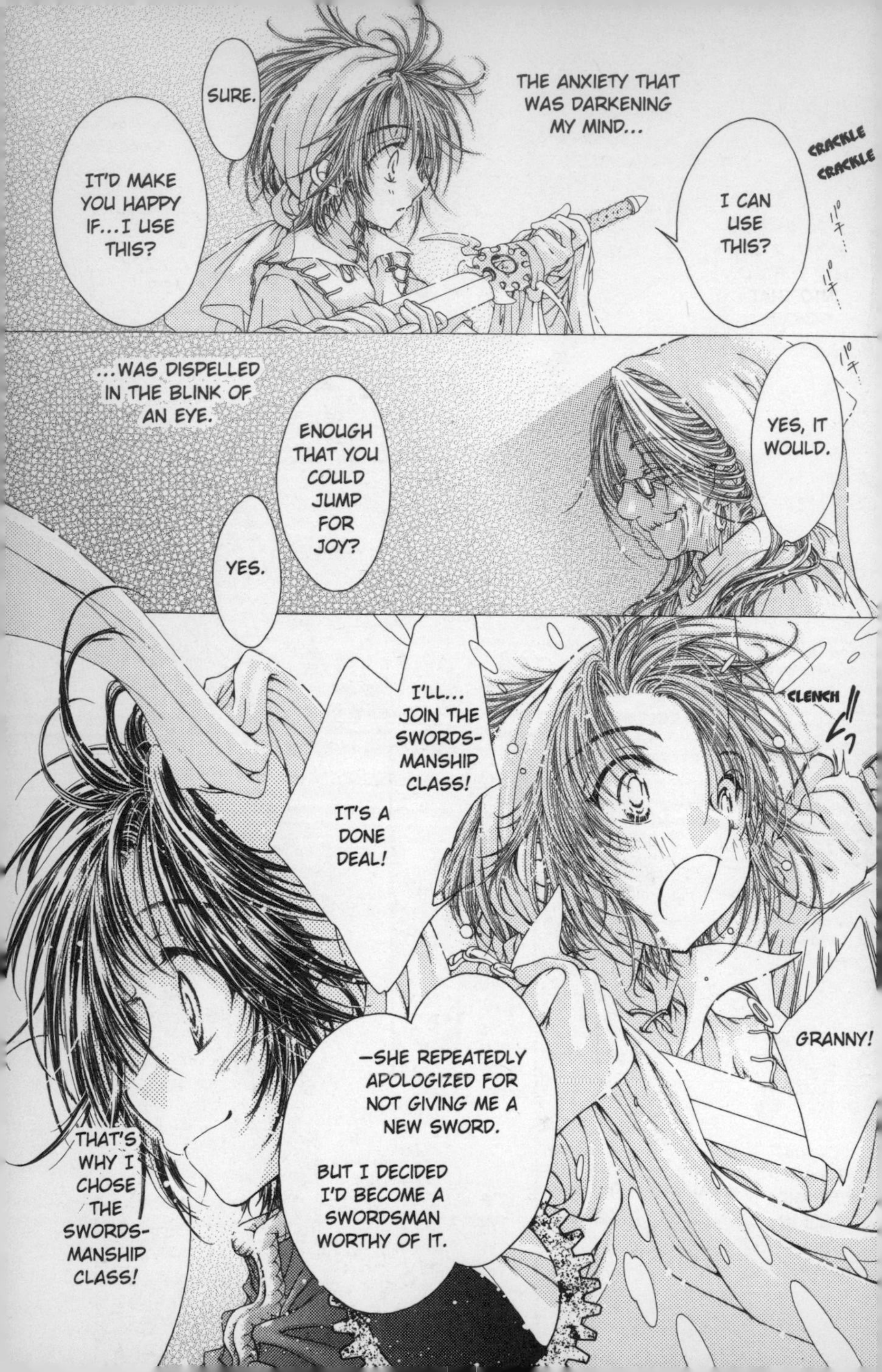
I CAN USE THIS?
CRACKLE CRACKLE
THE ANXIETY THAT WAS DARKENING MY MIND...
SURE.
IT'D MAKE YOU HAPPY IF...I USE THIS?
YES, IT WOULD.
...WAS DISPELLED IN THE BLINK OF AN EYE.
ENOUGH THAT YOU COULD JUMP FOR JOY?
YES.
CLENCH
GRANNY!
I'LL... JOIN THE SWORDS-MANSHIP CLASS!
IT'S A DONE DEAL!
—SHE REPEATEDLY APOLOGIZED FOR NOT GIVING ME A NEW SWORD.
BUT I DECIDED I'D BECOME A SWORDSMAN WORTHY OF IT.
THAT'S WHY I CHOSE THE SWORDS-MANSHIP CLASS!

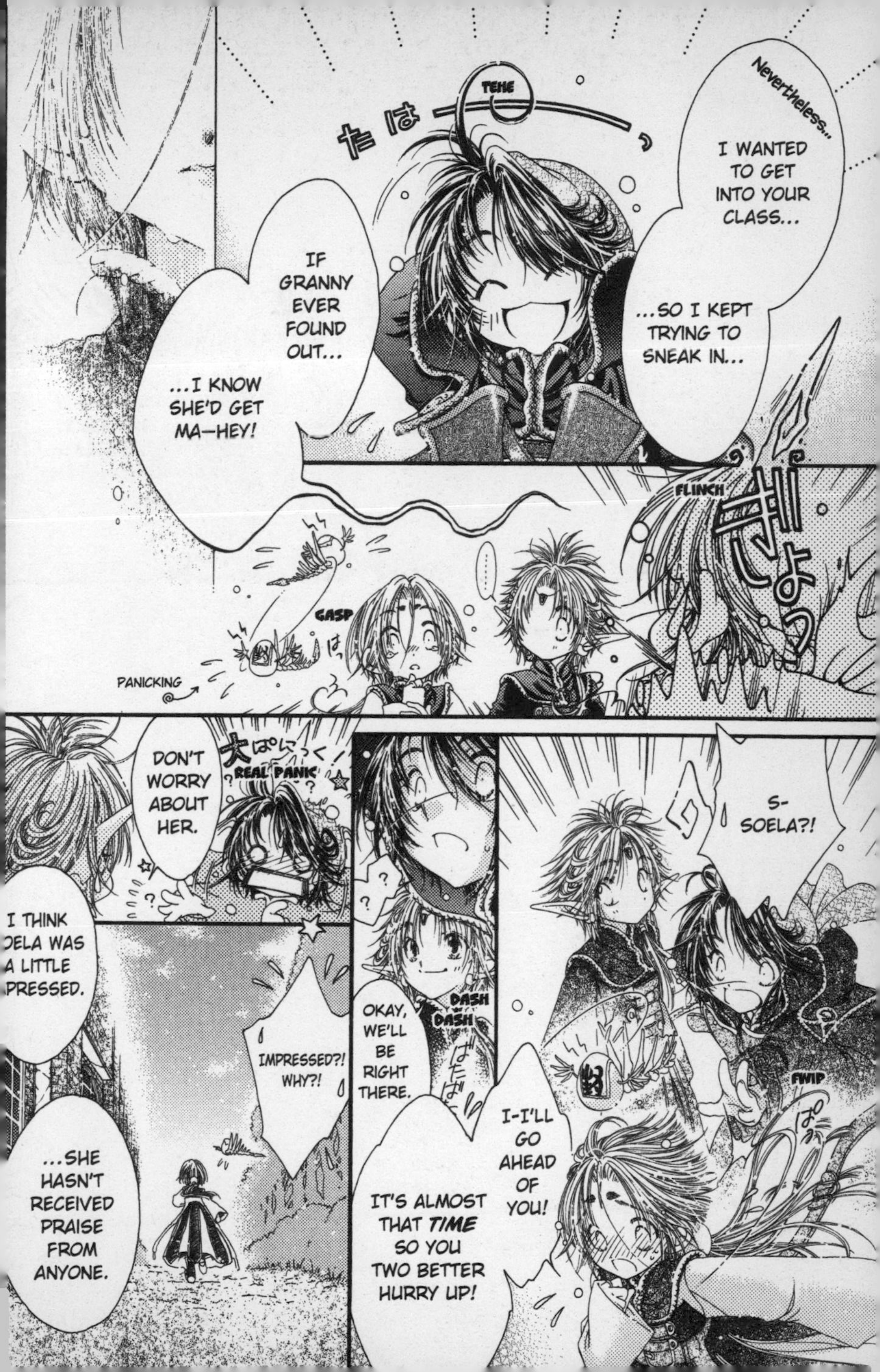
Nevertheless...
I WANTED TO GET INTO YOUR CLASS...
...SO I KEPT TRYING TO SNEAK IN...
たはー
TEHE
IF GRANNY EVER FOUND OUT...
...I KNOW SHE'D GET MA—HEY!
ぎょっ
FLINCH
GASP
PANICKING
S-SOELA?!
FWIP
I-I'LL GO AHEAD OF YOU!
DASH
DASH
OKAY, WE'LL BE RIGHT THERE.
IT'S ALMOST THAT TIME SO YOU TWO BETTER HURRY UP!
DON'T WORRY ABOUT HER.
REAL PANIC
I THINK OELA WAS A LITTLE PRESSED.
IMPRESSED?! WHY?!
...SHE HASN'T RECEIVED PRAISE FROM ANYONE.

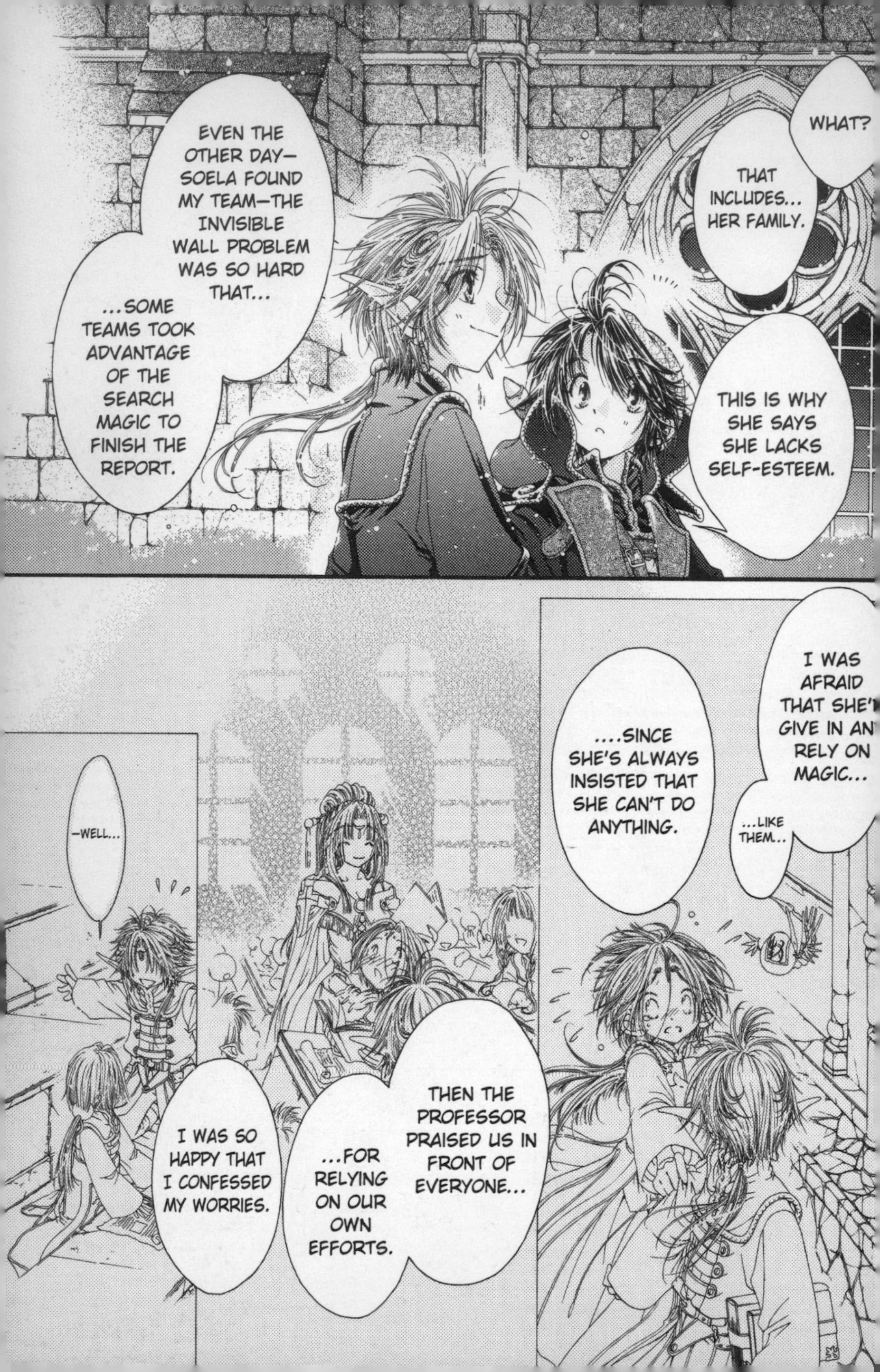
WHAT?
THAT INCLUDES... HER FAMILY.
THIS IS WHY SHE SAYS SHE LACKS SELF-ESTEEM.
EVEN THE OTHER DAY—SOELA FOUND MY TEAM—THE INVISIBLE WALL PROBLEM WAS SO HARD THAT...
...SOME TEAMS TOOK ADVANTAGE OF THE SEARCH MAGIC TO FINISH THE REPORT.
I WAS AFRAID THAT SHE'D GIVE IN AND RELY ON MAGIC...
...LIKE THEM...
....SINCE SHE'S ALWAYS INSISTED THAT SHE CAN'T DO ANYTHING.
THEN THE PROFESSOR PRAISED US IN FRONT OF EVERYONE...
...FOR RELYING ON OUR OWN EFFORTS.
I WAS SO HAPPY THAT I CONFESSED MY WORRIES.
—WELL...

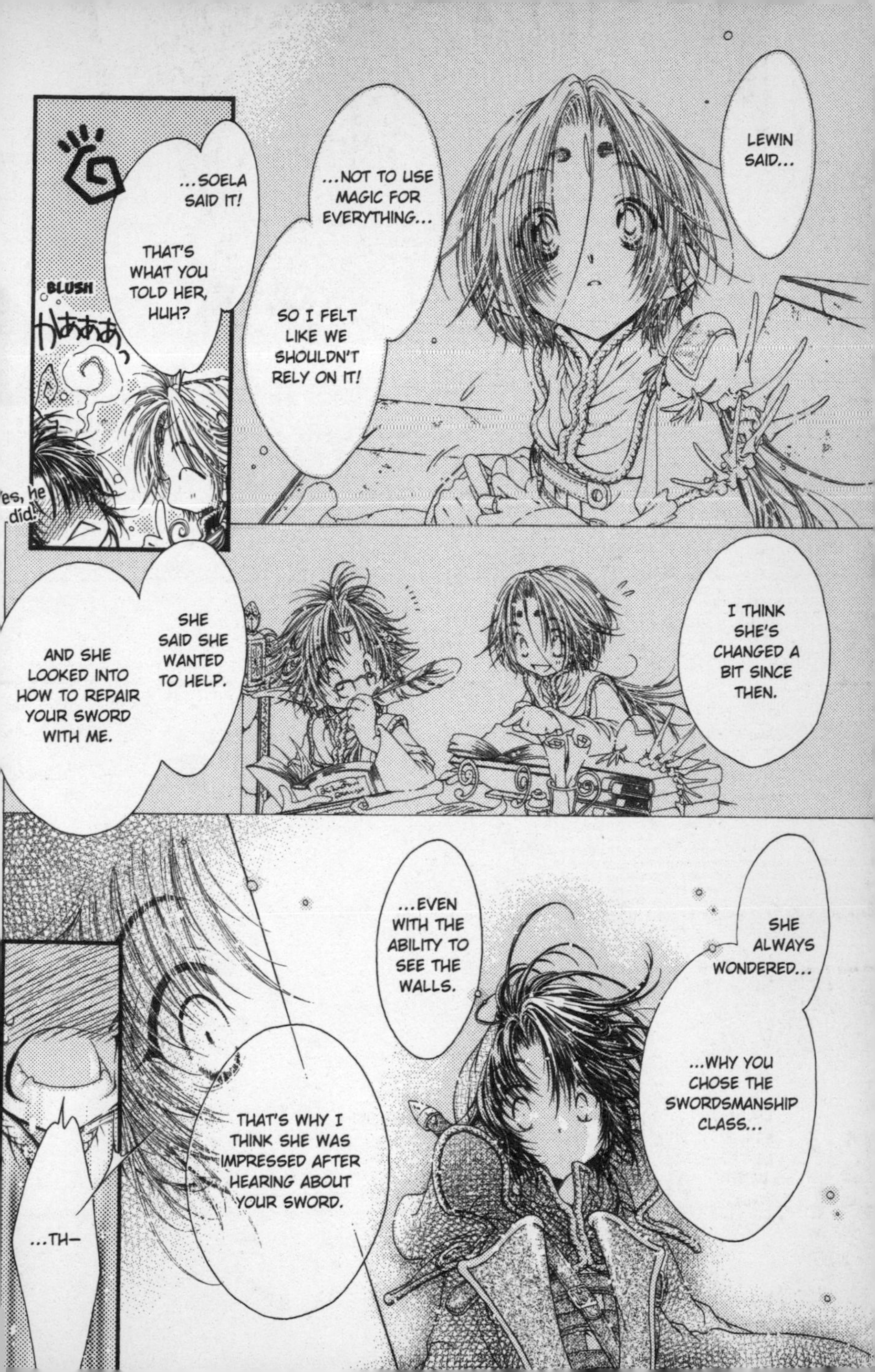
LEWIN SAID...
...NOT TO USE MAGIC FOR EVERYTHING...
SO I FELT LIKE WE SHOULDN'T RELY ON IT!
...SOELA SAID IT!
THAT'S WHAT YOU TOLD HER, HUH?
BLUSH
es, he did!
I THINK SHE'S CHANGED A BIT SINCE THEN.
SHE SAID SHE WANTED TO HELP.
AND SHE LOOKED INTO HOW TO REPAIR YOUR SWORD WITH ME.
SHE ALWAYS WONDERED...
...WHY YOU CHOSE THE SWORDSMANSHIP CLASS...
...EVEN WITH THE ABILITY TO SEE THE WALLS.
THAT'S WHY I THINK SHE WAS IMPRESSED AFTER HEARING ABOUT YOUR SWORD.
...TH—

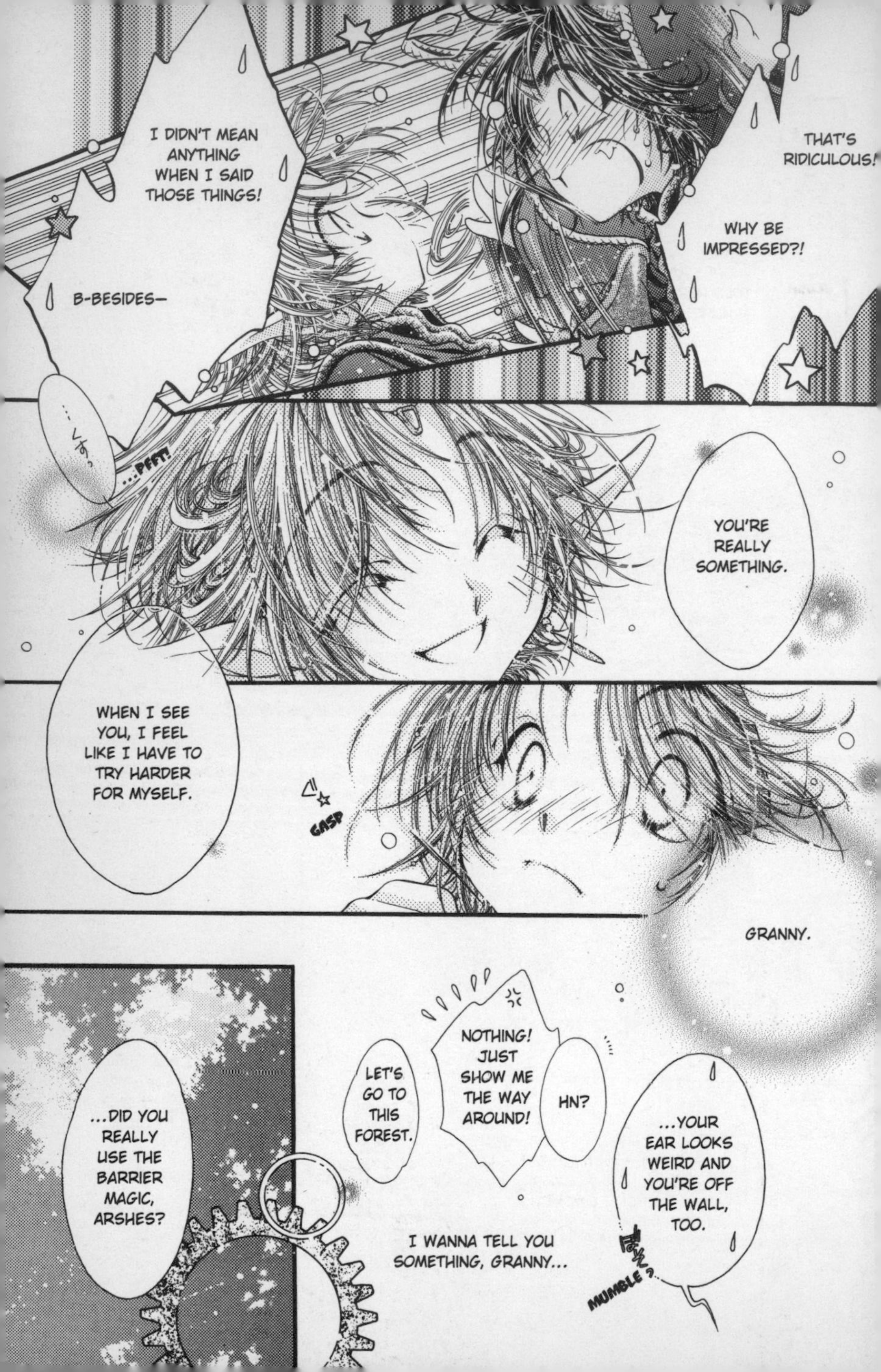
THAT'S RIDICULOUS!
WHY BE IMPRESSED?!
I DIDN'T MEAN ANYTHING WHEN I SAID THOSE THINGS!
B-BESIDES—
...くすっ
...PFFT!
YOU'RE REALLY SOMETHING.
WHEN I SEE YOU, I FEEL LIKE I HAVE TO TRY HARDER FOR MYSELF.
GASP
GRANNY.
...YOUR EAR LOOKS WEIRD AND YOU'RE OFF THE WALL, TOO.
MUMBLE
HN?
NOTHING! JUST SHOW ME THE WAY AROUND!
LET'S GO TO THIS FOREST.
I WANNA TELL YOU SOMETHING, GRANNY...
...DID YOU REALLY USE THE BARRIER MAGIC, ARSHES?

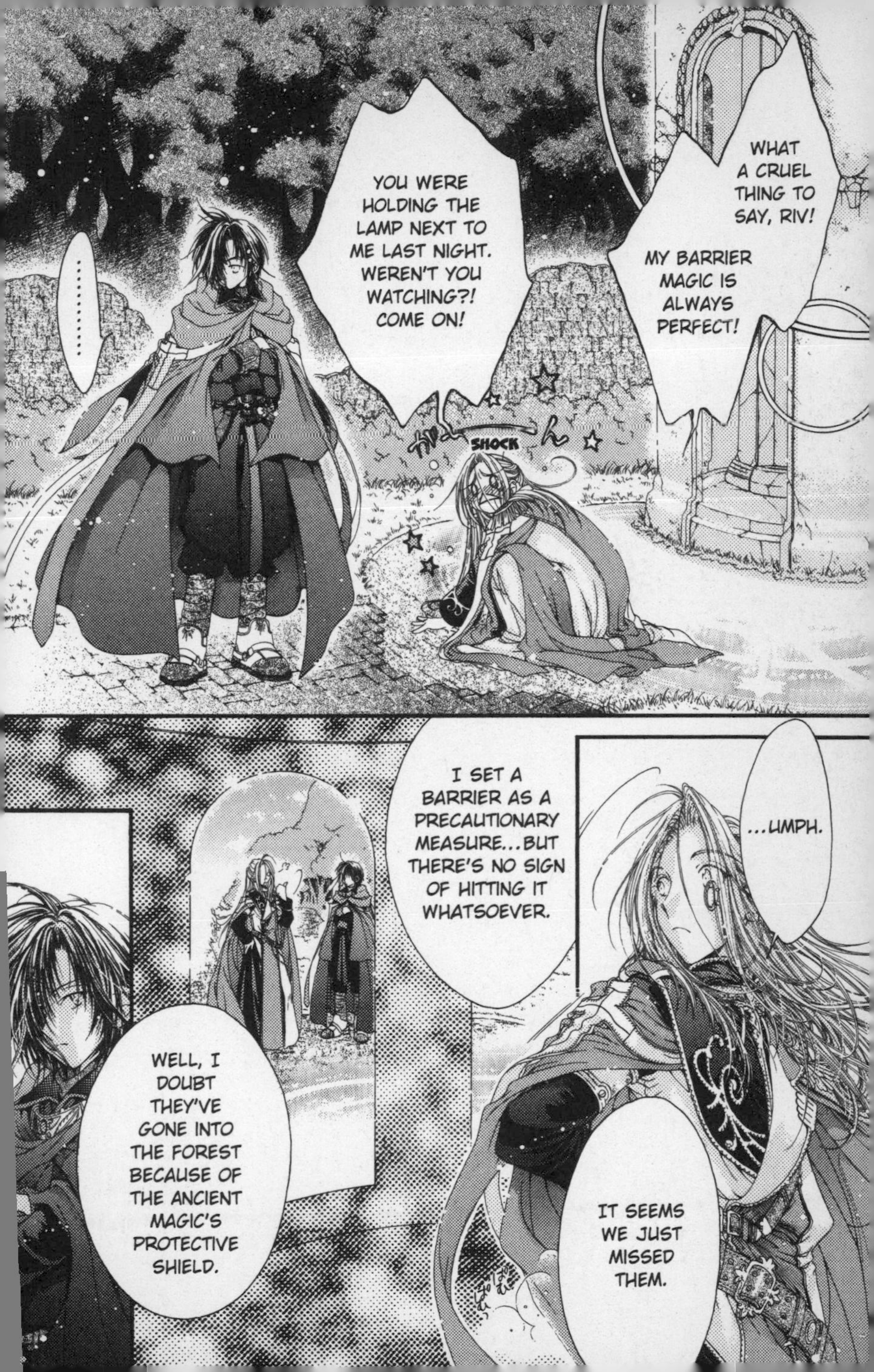
WHAT A CRUEL THING TO SAY, RIV!
MY BARRIER MAGIC IS ALWAYS PERFECT!
YOU WERE HOLDING THE LAMP NEXT TO ME LAST NIGHT. WEREN'T YOU WATCHING?! COME ON!
SHOCK
......
...UMPH.
I SET A BARRIER AS A PRECAUTIONARY MEASURE...BUT THERE'S NO SIGN OF HITTING IT WHATSOEVER.
IT SEEMS WE JUST MISSED THEM.
WELL, I DOUBT THEY'VE GONE INTO THE FOREST BECAUSE OF THE ANCIENT MAGIC'S PROTECTIVE SHIELD.

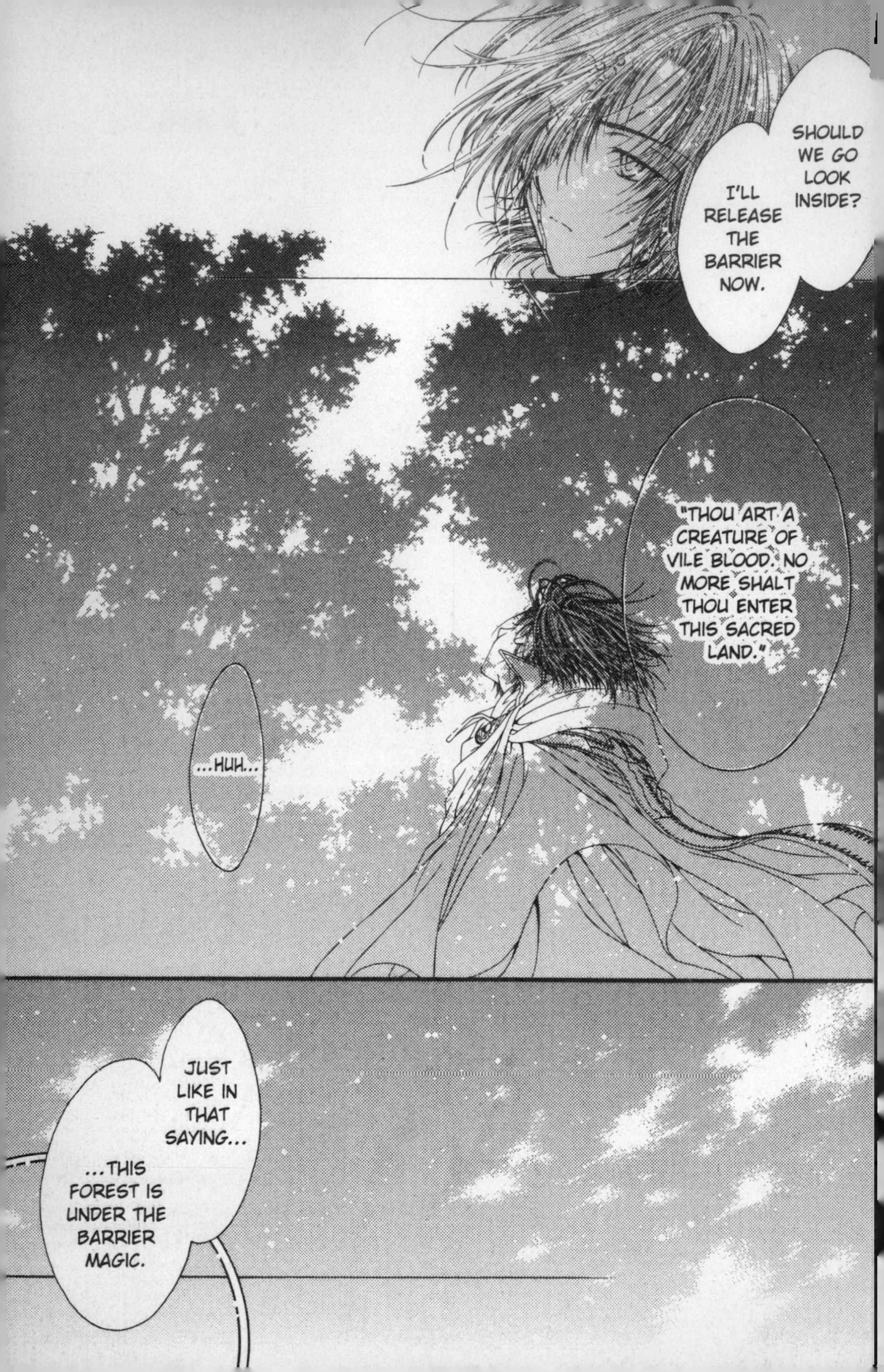
SHOULD WE GO LOOK INSIDE?
I'LL RELEASE THE BARRIER NOW.
"THOU ART A CREATURE OF VILE BLOOD. NO MORE SHALT THOU ENTER THIS SACRED LAND."
...HUH...
JUST LIKE IN THAT SAYING...
...THIS FOREST IS UNDER THE BARRIER MAGIC.

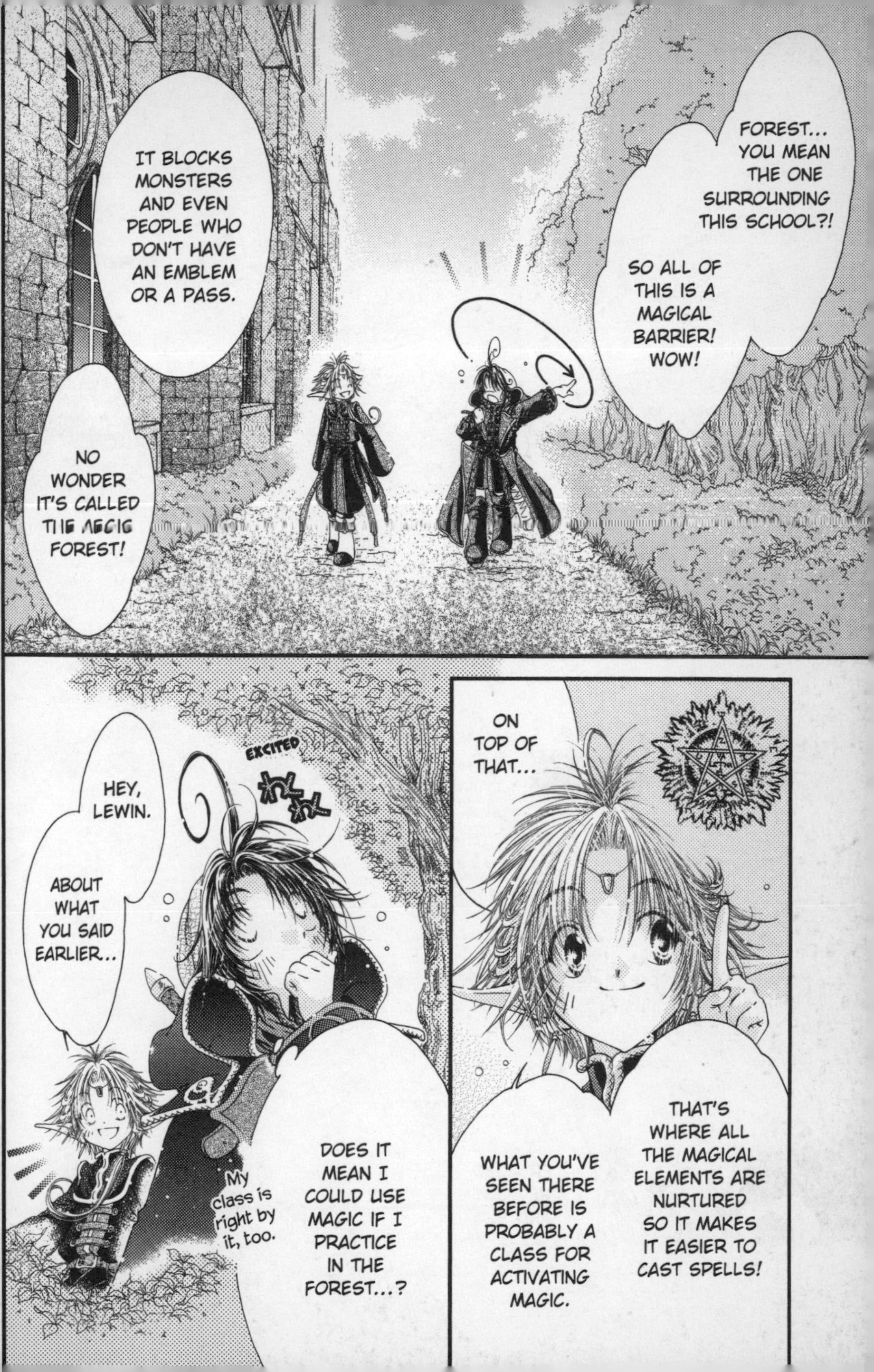
FOREST... YOU MEAN THE ONE SURROUNDING THIS SCHOOL?!
SO ALL OF THIS IS A MAGICAL BARRIER! WOW!
IT BLOCKS MONSTERS AND EVEN PEOPLE WHO DON'T HAVE AN EMBLEM OR A PASS.
NO WONDER IT'S CALLED THE MAGIC FOREST!
ON TOP OF THAT...
THAT'S WHERE ALL THE MAGICAL ELEMENTS ARE NURTURED SO IT MAKES IT EASIER TO CAST SPELLS!
WHAT YOU'VE SEEN THERE BEFORE IS PROBABLY A CLASS FOR ACTIVATING MAGIC.
EXCITED
HEY, LEWIN.
ABOUT WHAT YOU SAID EARLIER...
DOES IT MEAN I COULD USE MAGIC IF I PRACTICE IN THE FOREST...?
My class is right by it, too.

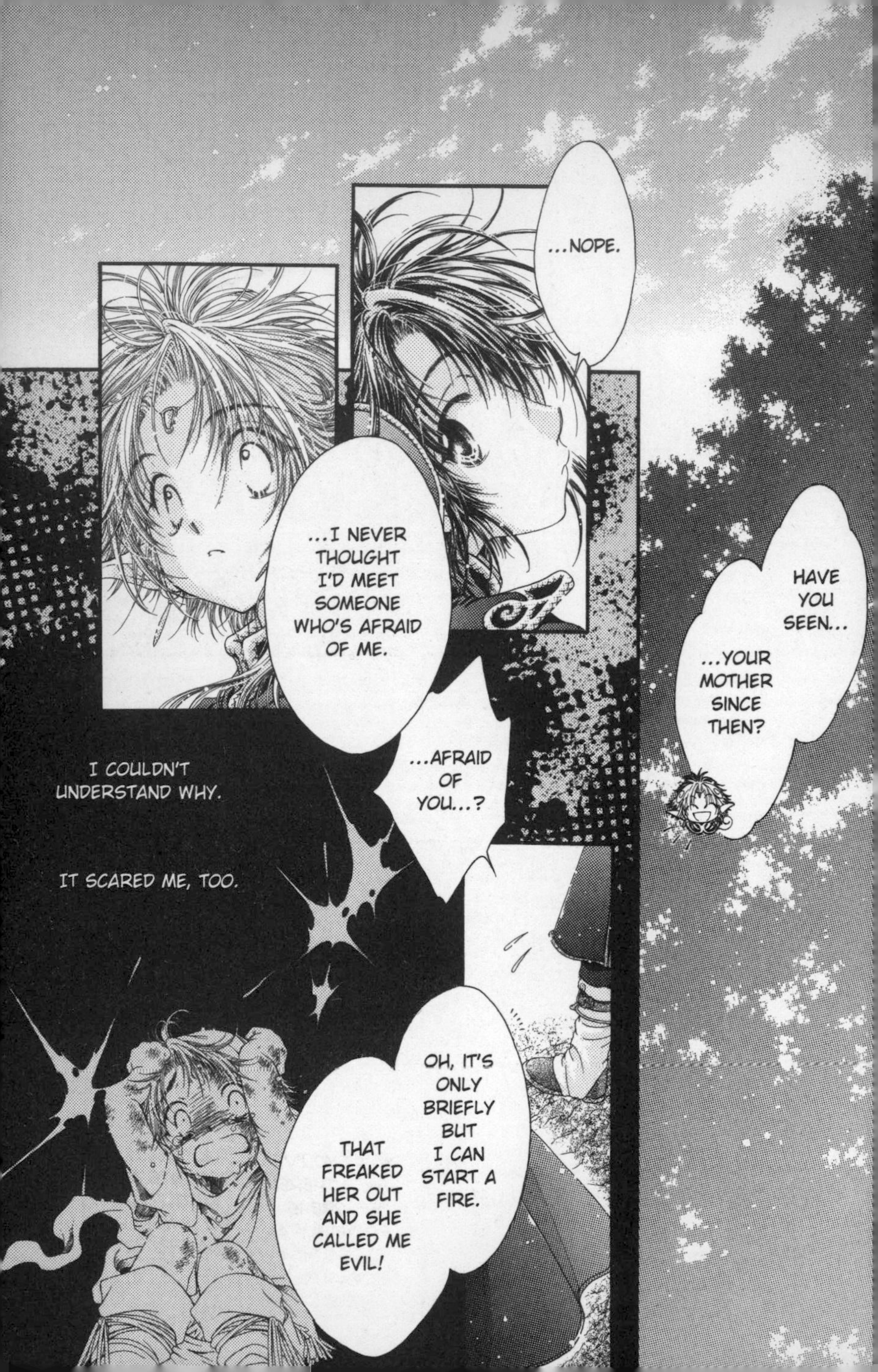
HAVE YOU SEEN... ...YOUR MOTHER SINCE THEN?
...NOPE.
...I NEVER THOUGHT I'D MEET SOMEONE WHO'S AFRAID OF ME.
...AFRAID OF YOU...?
I COULDN'T UNDERSTAND WHY.
IT SCARED ME, TOO.
OH, IT'S ONLY BRIEFLY BUT I CAN START A FIRE.
THAT FREAKED HER OUT AND SHE CALLED ME EVIL!

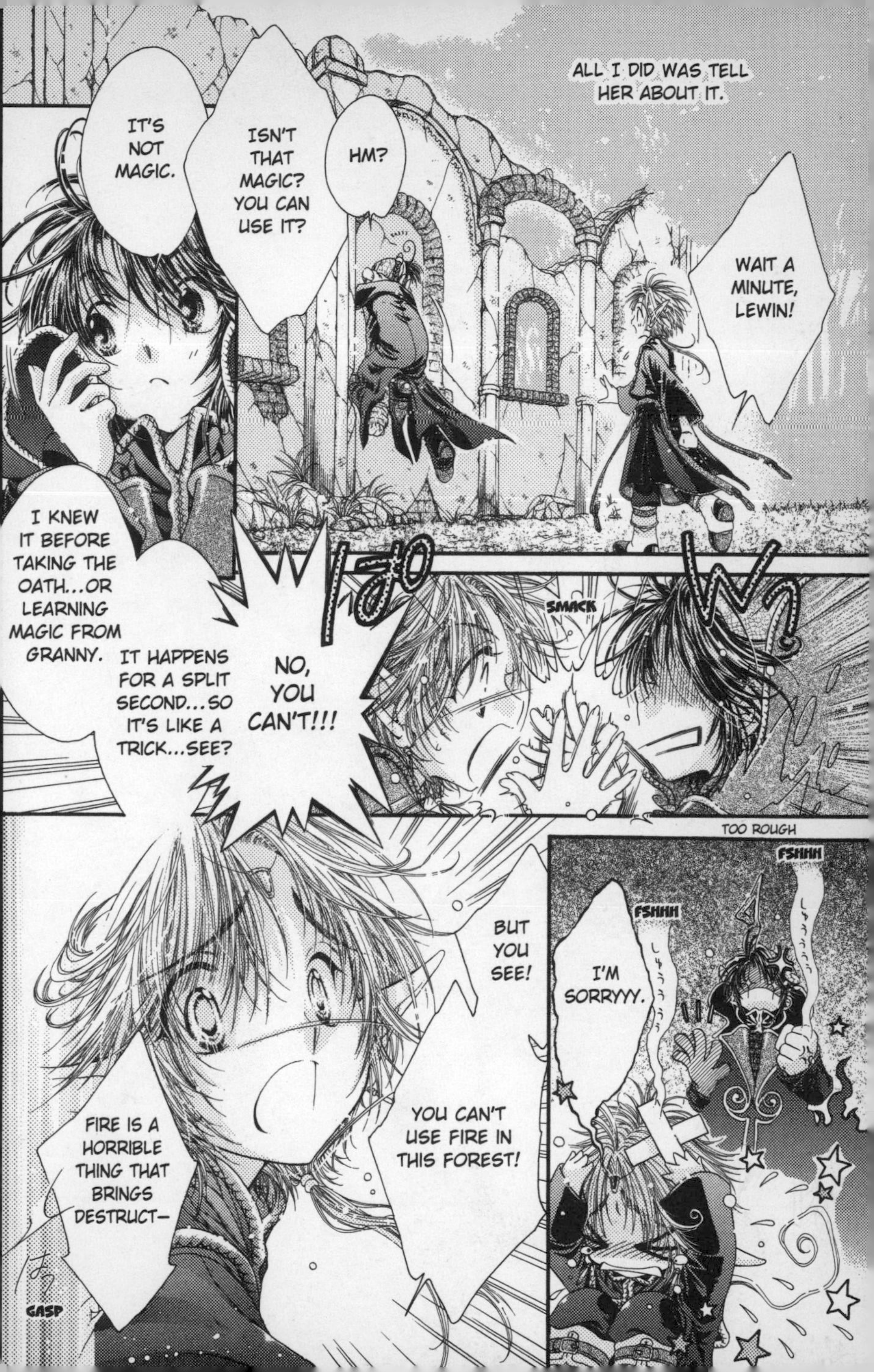
ALL I DID WAS TELL HER ABOUT IT.
WAIT A MINUTE, LEWIN!
HM?
ISN'T THAT MAGIC? YOU CAN USE IT?
IT'S NOT MAGIC.
I KNEW IT BEFORE TAKING THE OATH...OR LEARNING MAGIC FROM GRANNY.
IT HAPPENS FOR A SPLIT SECOND...SO IT'S LIKE A TRICK...SEE?
NO, YOU CAN'T!!!
SMACK
TOO ROUGH
FSHHH
FSHHH
しゅううう
しゅううう
I'M SORRYYY.
BUT YOU SEE!
YOU CAN'T USE FIRE IN THIS FOREST!
FIRE IS A HORRIBLE THING THAT BRINGS DESTRUCT—
GASP

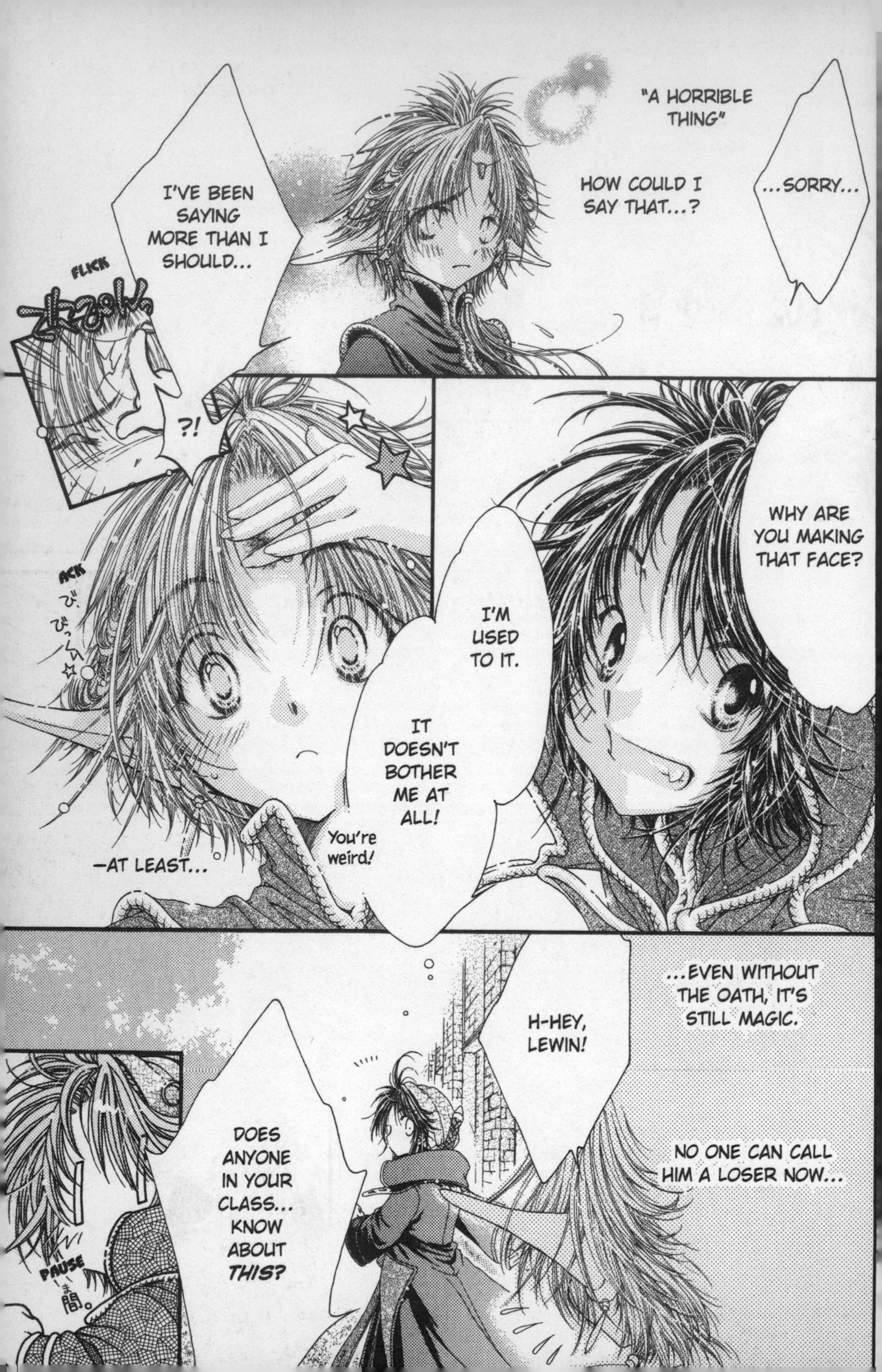
...SORRY...
"A HORRIBLE THING"
HOW COULD I SAY THAT...?
I'VE BEEN SAYING MORE THAN I SHOULD...
FLICK
WHY ARE YOU MAKING THAT FACE?
I'M USED TO IT.
IT DOESN'T BOTHER ME AT ALL!
?!
ACK
You're weird!
—AT LEAST...
...EVEN WITHOUT THE OATH, IT'S STILL MAGIC.
NO ONE CAN CALL HIM A LOSER NOW...
H-HEY, LEWIN!
DOES ANYONE IN YOUR CLASS... KNOW ABOUT *THIS?*
PAUSE

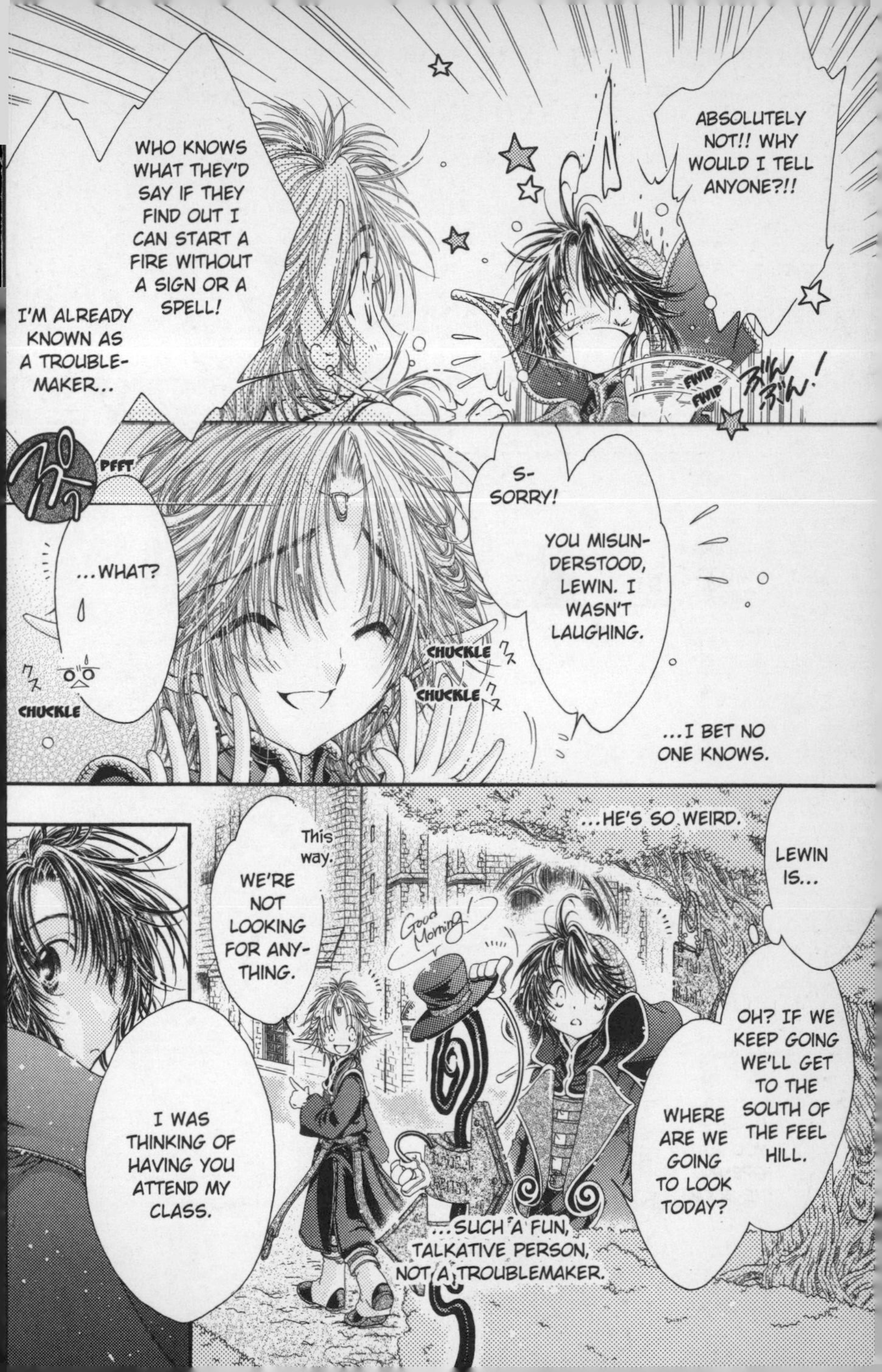
ABSOLUTELY NOT!! WHY WOULD I TELL ANYONE?!!
FWIP FWIP
ぶんぶん!
WHO KNOWS WHAT THEY'D SAY IF THEY FIND OUT I CAN START A FIRE WITHOUT A SIGN OR A SPELL!
I'M ALREADY KNOWN AS A TROUBLE-MAKER..
S-SORRY!
YOU MISUNDER-STOOD, LEWIN. I WASN'T LAUGHING.
...I BET NO ONE KNOWS.
CHUCKLE
CHUCKLE
PFFT
...WHAT?
CHUCKLE
LEWIN IS...
...HE'S SO WEIRD.
OH? IF WE KEEP GOING WE'LL GET TO THE SOUTH OF THE FEEL HILL.
WHERE ARE WE GOING TO LOOK TODAY?
Good Morning!
This way.
WE'RE NOT LOOKING FOR ANY-THING.
...SUCH A FUN, TALKATIVE PERSON, NOT A TROUBLEMAKER.
I WAS THINKING OF HAVING YOU ATTEND MY CLASS.

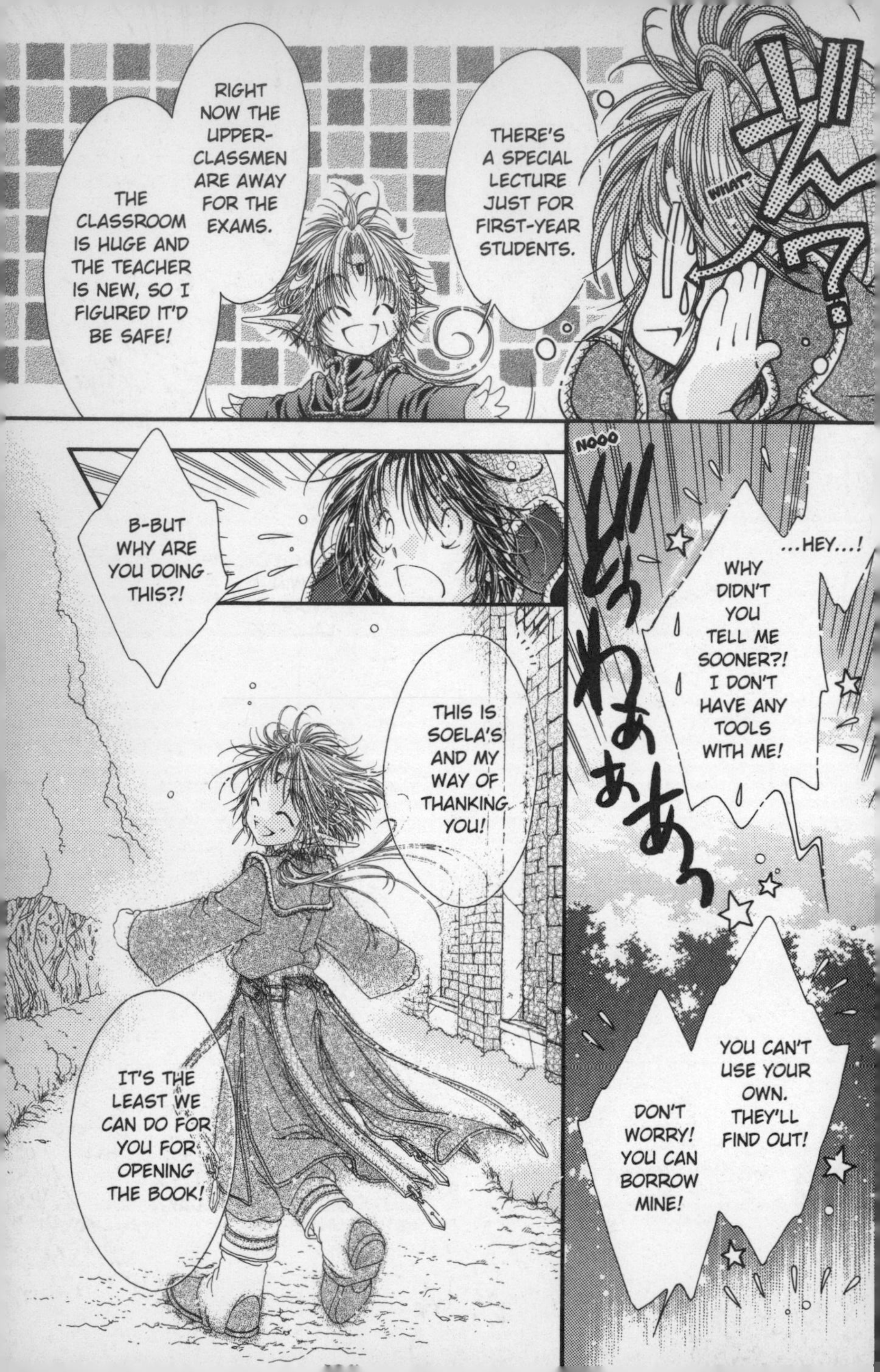
WHAT?
THERE'S A SPECIAL LECTURE JUST FOR FIRST-YEAR STUDENTS.
RIGHT NOW THE UPPER-CLASSMEN ARE AWAY FOR THE EXAMS.
THE CLASSROOM IS HUGE AND THE TEACHER IS NEW, SO I FIGURED IT'D BE SAFE!
NOOO
...HEY...!
WHY DIDN'T YOU TELL ME SOONER?! I DON'T HAVE ANY TOOLS WITH ME!
YOU CAN'T USE YOUR OWN. THEY'LL FIND OUT!
DON'T WORRY! YOU CAN BORROW MINE!
B-BUT WHY ARE YOU DOING THIS?!
THIS IS SOELA'S AND MY WAY OF THANKING YOU!
IT'S THE LEAST WE CAN DO FOR YOU FOR OPENING THE BOOK!

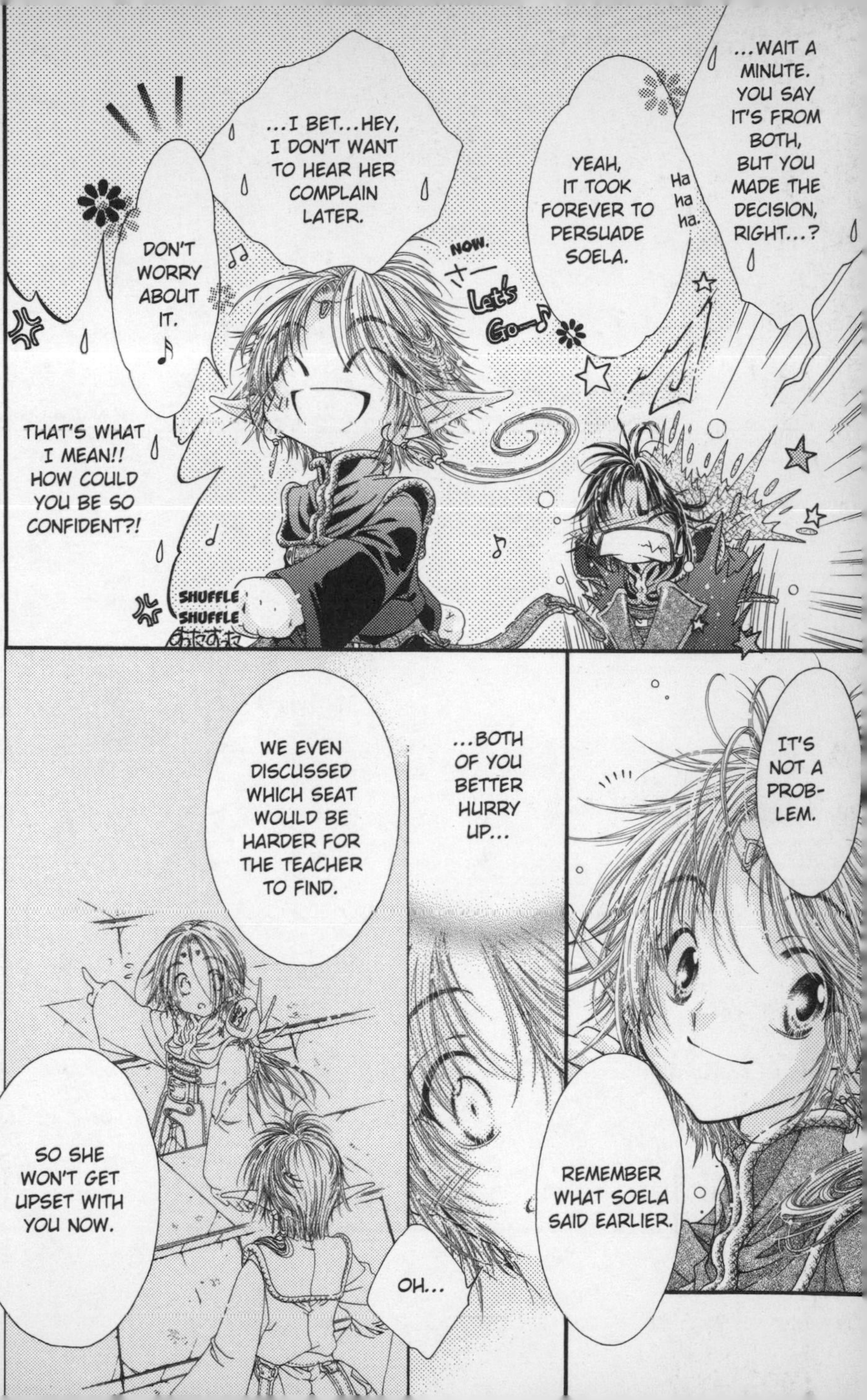
...WAIT A MINUTE. YOU SAY IT'S FROM BOTH, BUT YOU MADE THE DECISION, RIGHT...?
Ha ha ha.
YEAH, IT TOOK FOREVER TO PERSUADE SOELA.
NOW. Let's Go—
...I BET...HEY, I DON'T WANT TO HEAR HER COMPLAIN LATER.
DON'T WORRY ABOUT IT.
THAT'S WHAT I MEAN!! HOW COULD YOU BE SO CONFIDENT?!
SHUFFLE SHUFFLE
IT'S NOT A PROB-LEM.
REMEMBER WHAT SOELA SAID EARLIER.
...BOTH OF YOU BETTER HURRY UP...
OH...
WE EVEN DISCUSSED WHICH SEAT WOULD BE HARDER FOR THE TEACHER TO FIND.
SO SHE WON'T GET UPSET WITH YOU NOW.

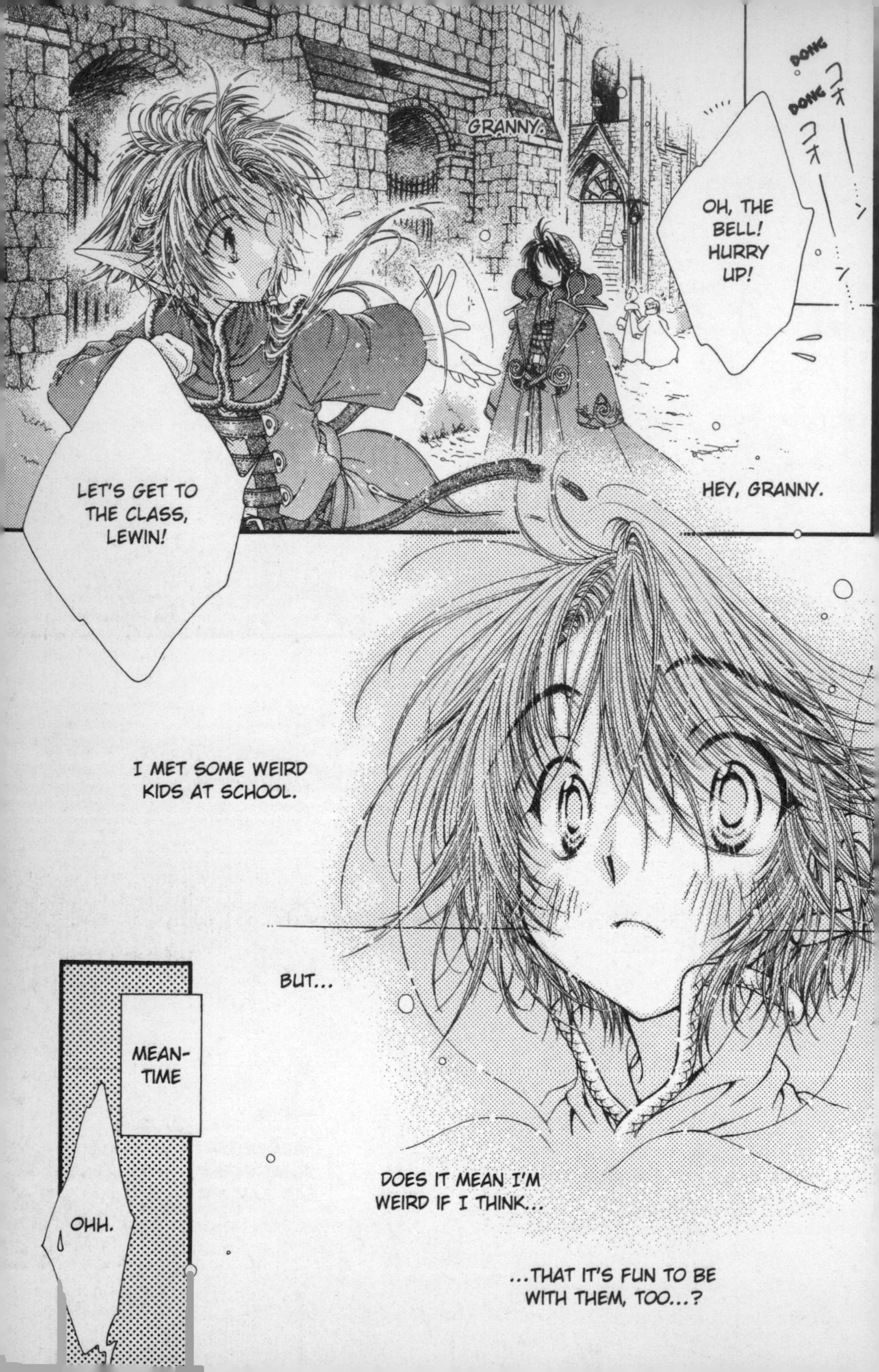
DONG
DONG
コォー…ン
コォー…ン
OH, THE BELL! HURRY UP!
GRANNY.
HEY, GRANNY.
LET'S GET TO THE CLASS, LEWIN!
I MET SOME WEIRD KIDS AT SCHOOL.
BUT...
DOES IT MEAN I'M WEIRD IF I THINK...
...THAT IT'S FUN TO BE WITH THEM, TOO...?
MEAN-TIME
OHH.

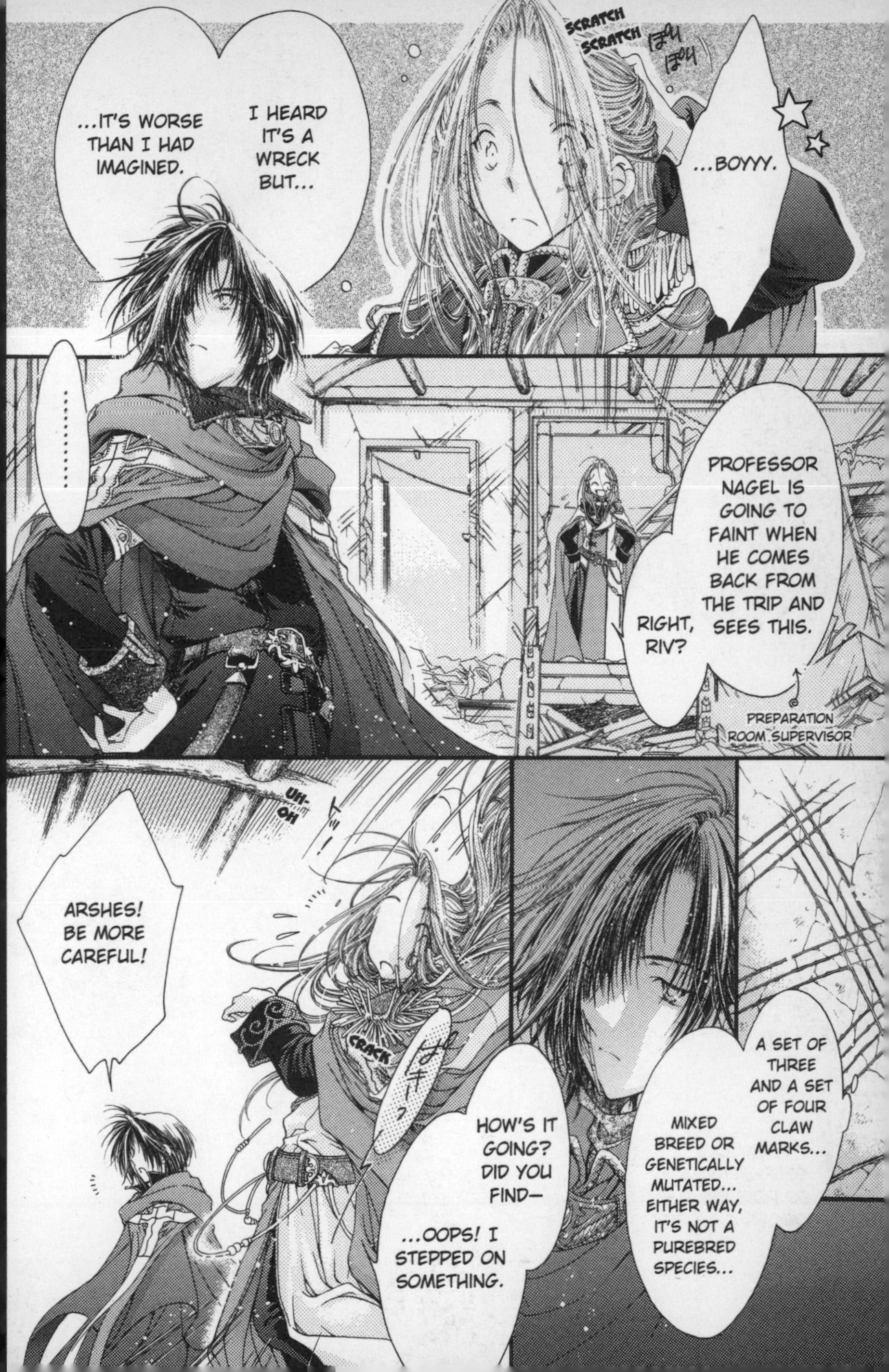
SCRATCH SCRATCH
ぽり ぽり
...BOYYY.
I HEARD IT'S A WRECK BUT...
...IT'S WORSE THAN I HAD IMAGINED.
PROFESSOR NAGEL IS GOING TO FAINT WHEN HE COMES BACK FROM THE TRIP AND SEES THIS.
RIGHT, RIV?
PREPARATION ROOM SUPERVISOR
......
A SET OF THREE AND A SET OF FOUR CLAW MARKS...
MIXED BREED OR GENETICALLY MUTATED... EITHER WAY, IT'S NOT A PUREBRED SPECIES...
HOW'S IT GOING? DID YOU FIND—
...OOPS! I STEPPED ON SOMETHING.
CRACK
UH-OH
ARSHES! BE MORE CAREFUL!

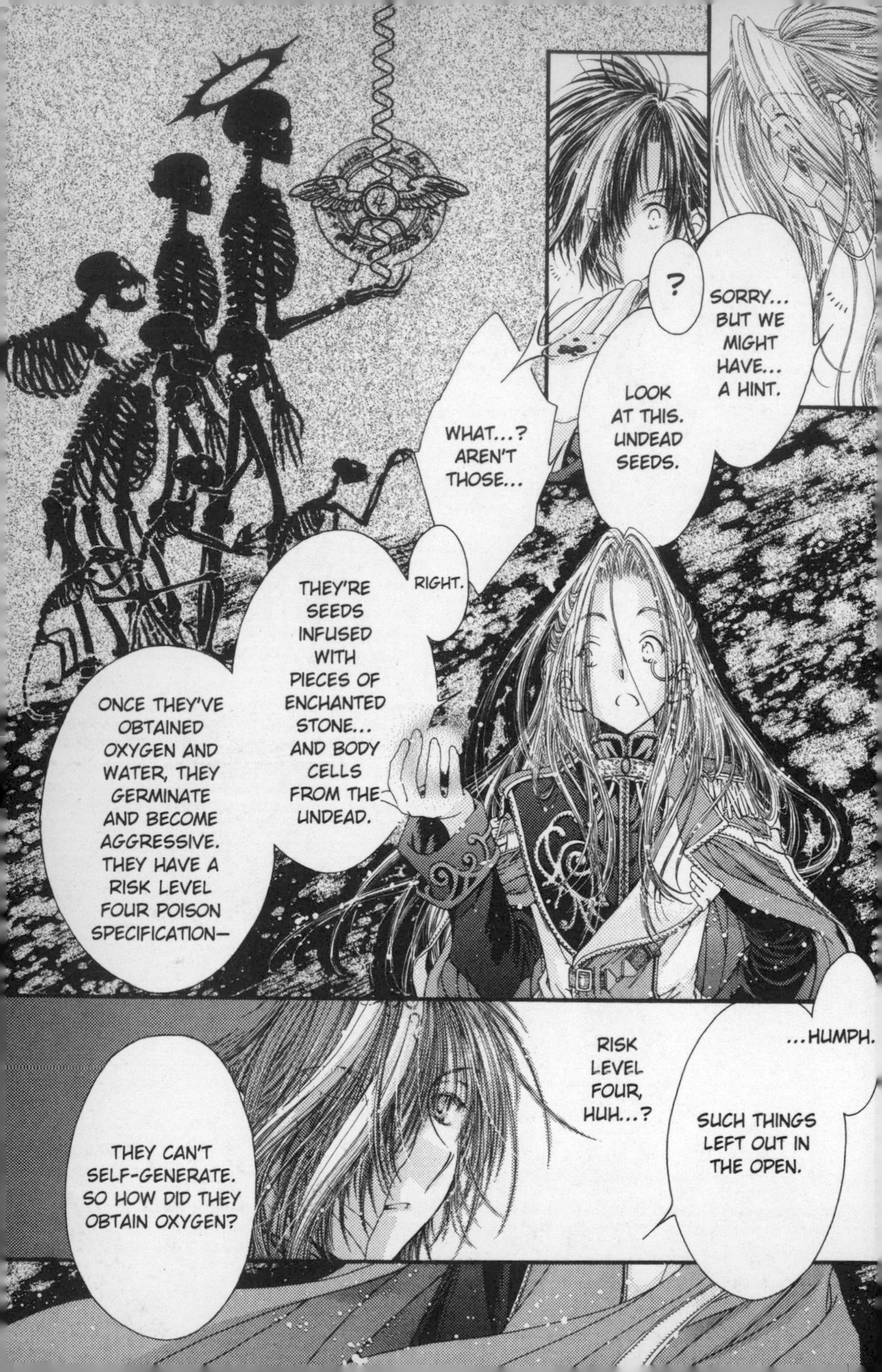
SORRY... BUT WE MIGHT HAVE... A HINT.
?
LOOK AT THIS. UNDEAD SEEDS.
WHAT...? AREN'T THOSE...
RIGHT.
THEY'RE SEEDS INFUSED WITH PIECES OF ENCHANTED STONE... AND BODY CELLS FROM THE UNDEAD.
ONCE THEY'VE OBTAINED OXYGEN AND WATER, THEY GERMINATE AND BECOME AGGRESSIVE. THEY HAVE A RISK LEVEL FOUR POISON SPECIFICATION—
...HUMPH.
SUCH THINGS LEFT OUT IN THE OPEN.
RISK LEVEL FOUR, HUH...?
THEY CAN'T SELF-GENERATE. SO HOW DID THEY OBTAIN OXYGEN?

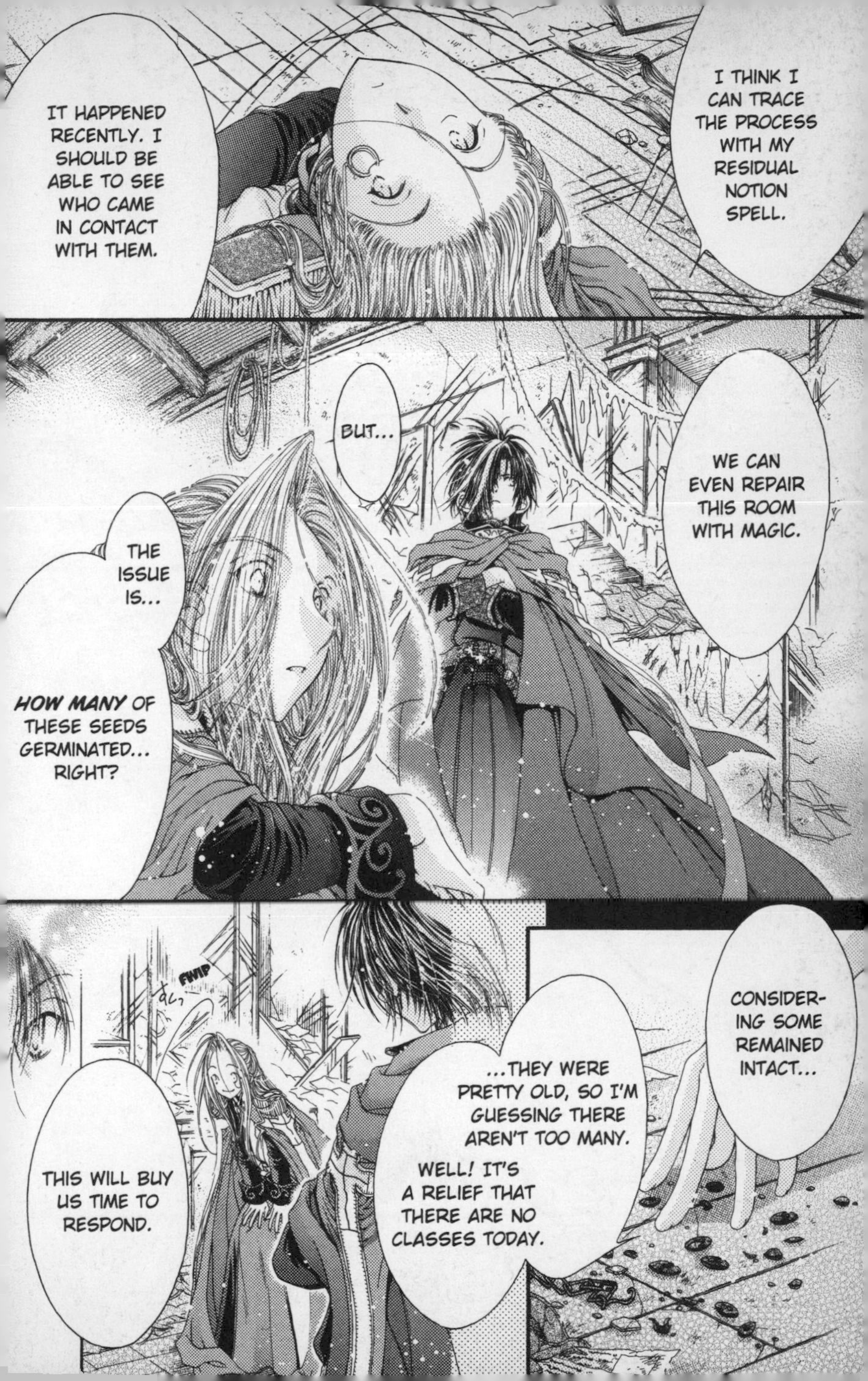
I THINK I CAN TRACE THE PROCESS WITH MY RESIDUAL NOTION SPELL.
IT HAPPENED RECENTLY. I SHOULD BE ABLE TO SEE WHO CAME IN CONTACT WITH THEM.
WE CAN EVEN REPAIR THIS ROOM WITH MAGIC.
BUT...
THE ISSUE IS...
HOW MANY OF THESE SEEDS GERMINATED... RIGHT?
CONSIDER-ING SOME REMAINED INTACT...
...THEY WERE PRETTY OLD, SO I'M GUESSING THERE AREN'T TOO MANY.
WELL! IT'S A RELIEF THAT THERE ARE NO CLASSES TODAY.
FWIP
THIS WILL BUY US TIME TO RESPOND.

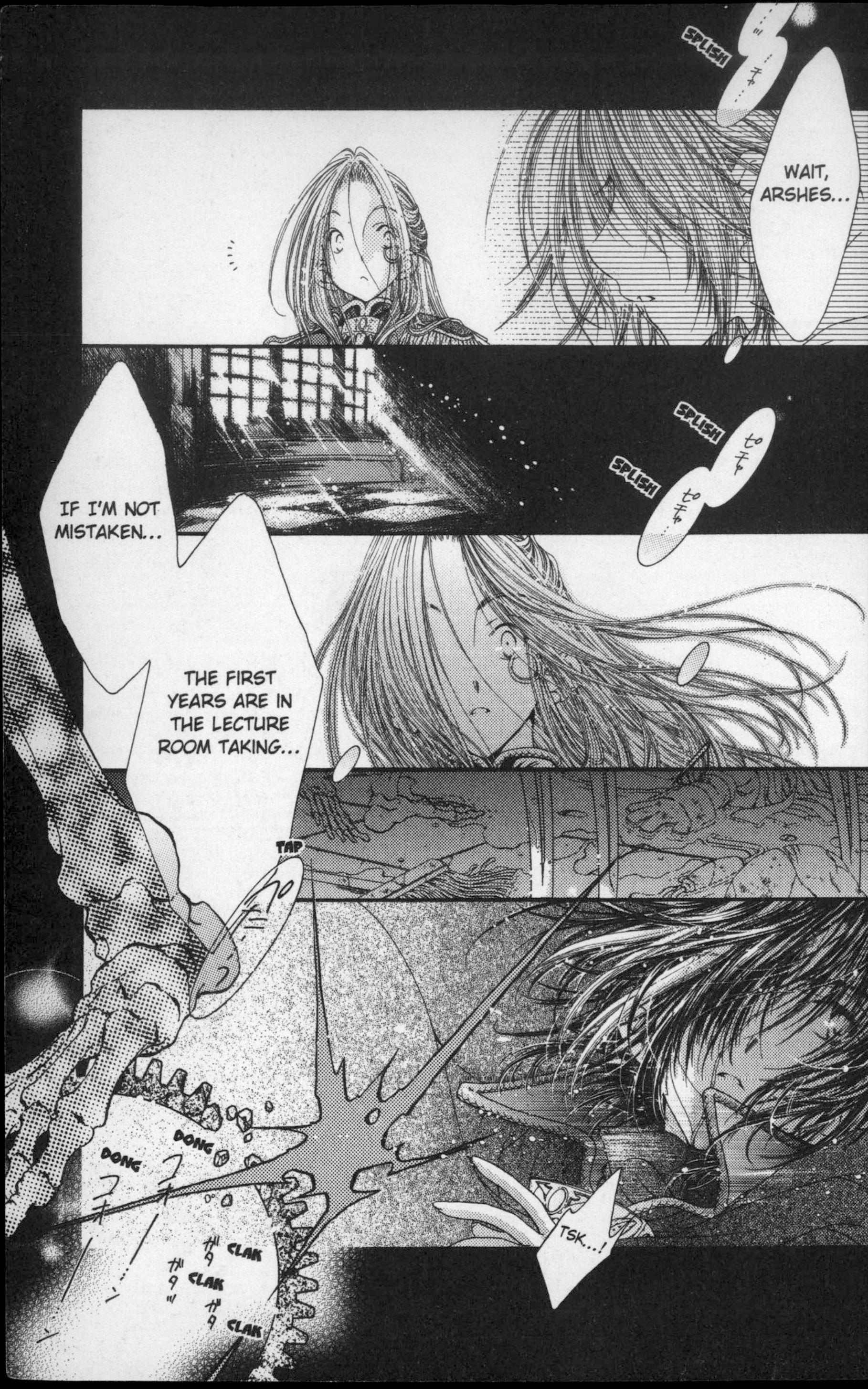
SPLISH
WAIT, ARSHES...
SPLISH
SPLISH
IF I'M NOT MISTAKEN...
THE FIRST YEARS ARE IN THE LECTURE ROOM TAKING...
TAP
TSK...!
DONG
DONG
CLAK
CLAK
CLAK

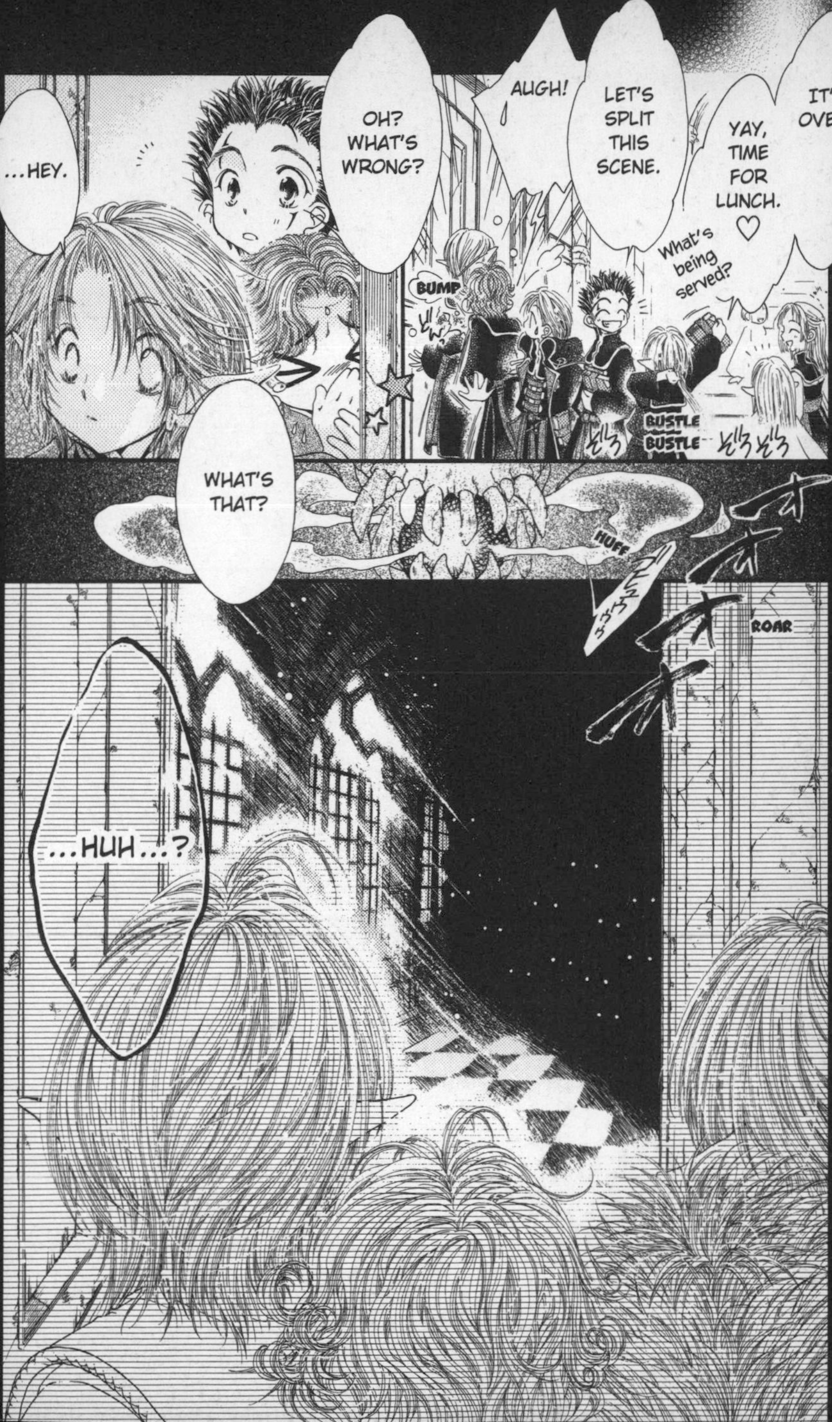
IT'S OVER.
YAY, TIME FOR LUNCH. ♡
What's being served?
LET'S SPLIT THIS SCENE.
AUGH!
BUMP
BUSTLE BUSTLE
OH? WHAT'S WRONG?
...HEY.
WHAT'S THAT?
HUFF
ROAR
...HUH...?

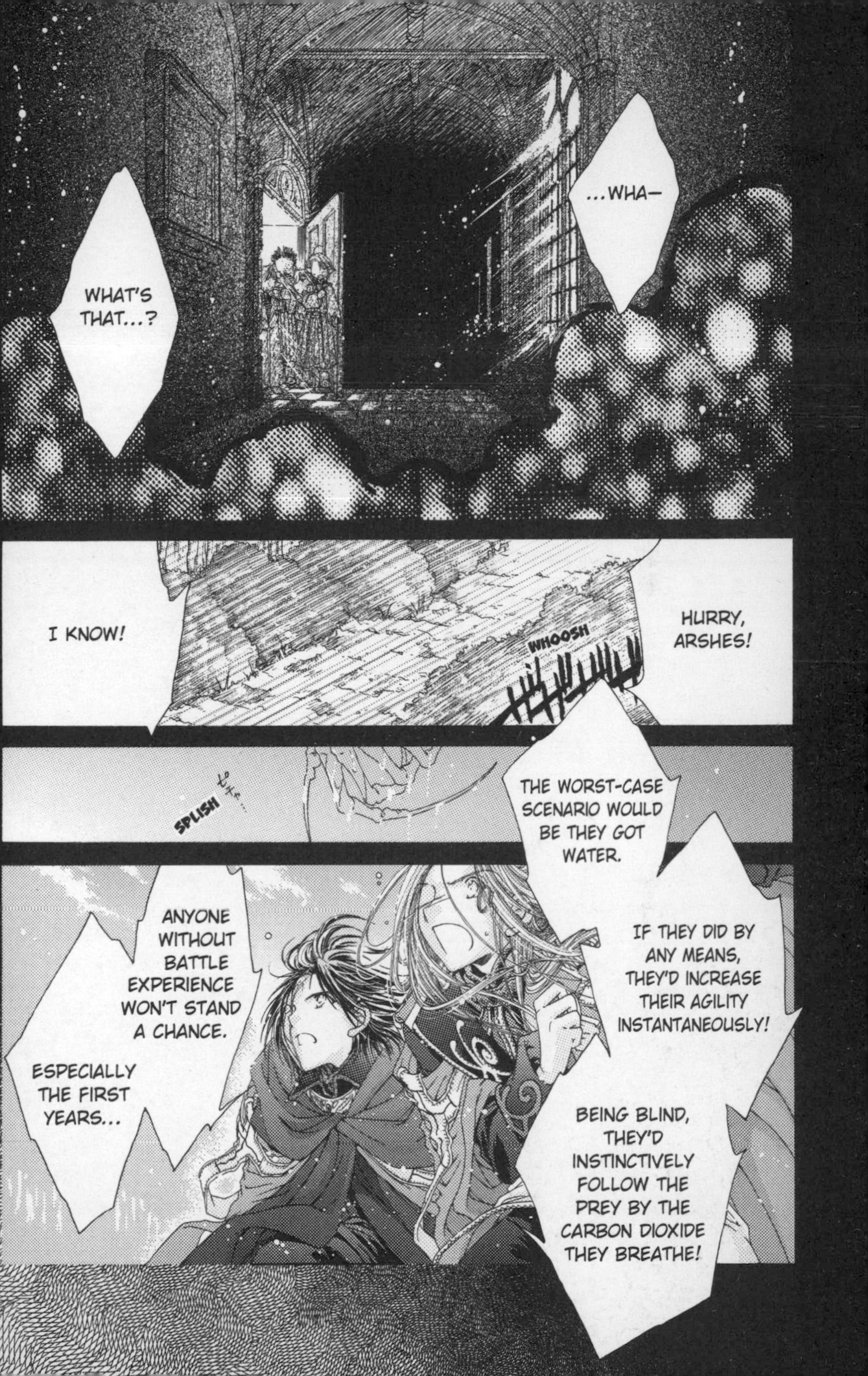
...WHA—
WHAT'S THAT...?
HURRY, ARSHES!
WHOOSH
I KNOW!
THE WORST-CASE SCENARIO WOULD BE THEY GOT WATER.
SPLISH
IF THEY DID BY ANY MEANS, THEY'D INCREASE THEIR AGILITY INSTANTANEOUSLY!
BEING BLIND, THEY'D INSTINCTIVELY FOLLOW THE PREY BY THE CARBON DIOXIDE THEY BREATHE!
ANYONE WITHOUT BATTLE EXPERIENCE WON'T STAND A CHANCE.
ESPECIALLY THE FIRST YEARS...

4th Bell: The Force • The First Battle

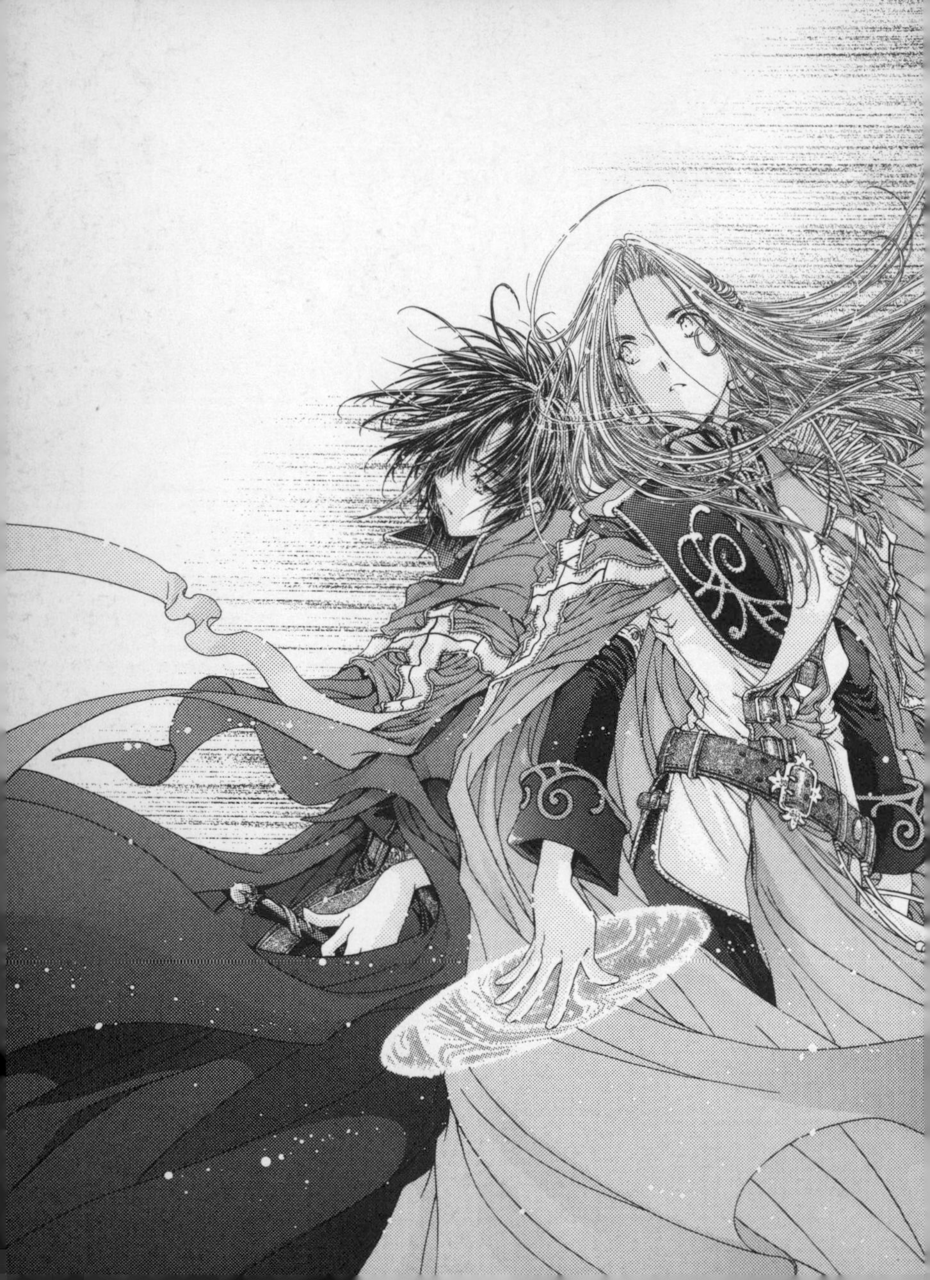

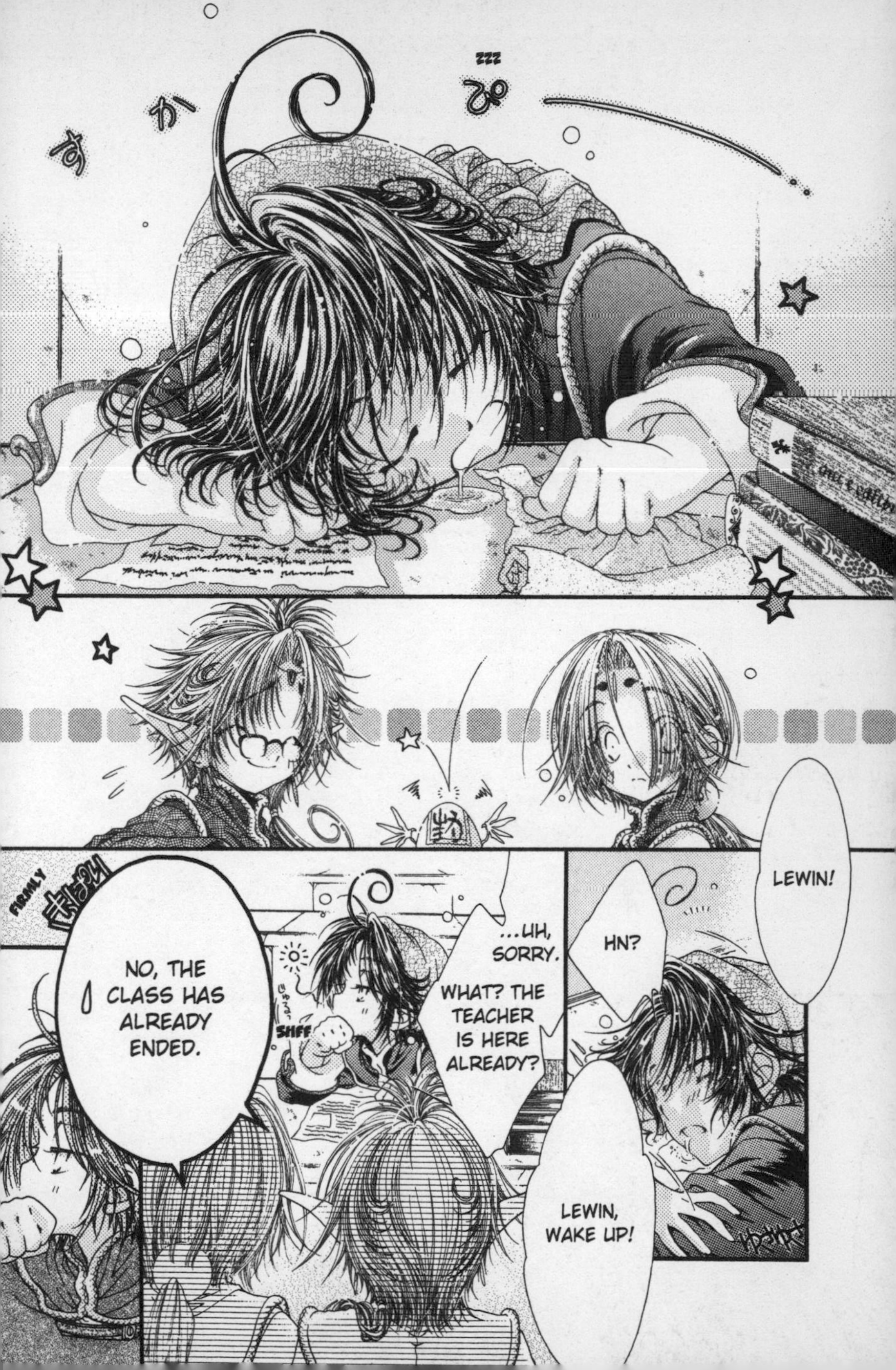
すかぴ
zzz
LEWIN!
HN?
LEWIN, WAKE UP!
...UH, SORRY.
WHAT? THE TEACHER IS HERE ALREADY?
SHIFF
NO, THE CLASS HAS ALREADY ENDED.
FIRMLY

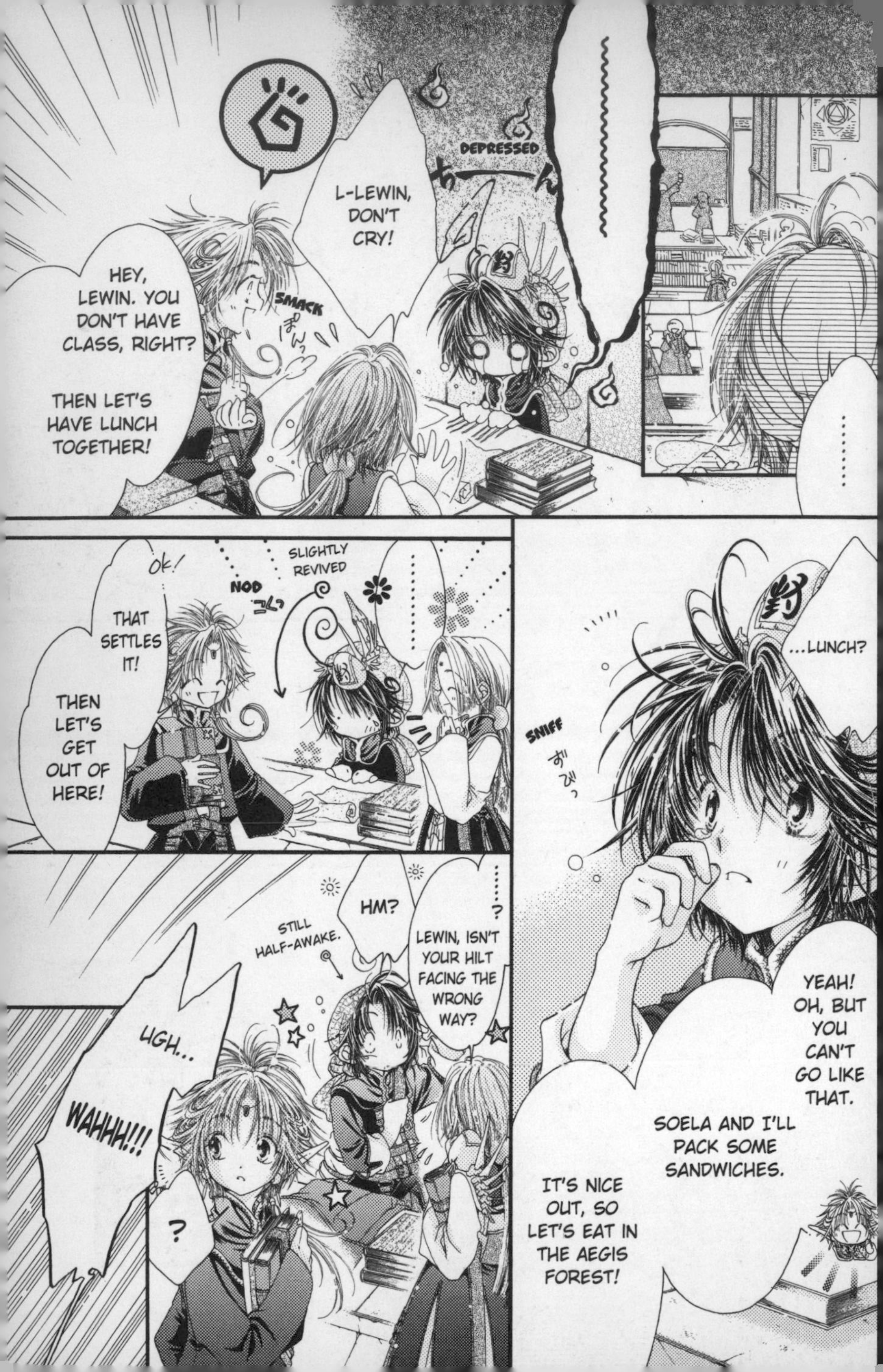
......
DEPRESSED
ちーん
L-LEWIN, DON'T CRY!
HEY, LEWIN. YOU DON'T HAVE CLASS, RIGHT?
SMACK
ぽんっ
THEN LET'S HAVE LUNCH TOGETHER!
...LUNCH?
SNIFF
ずびっ
YEAH! OH, BUT YOU CAN'T GO LIKE THAT.
SOELA AND I'LL PACK SOME SANDWICHES.
IT'S NICE OUT, SO LET'S EAT IN THE AEGIS FOREST!
...
SLIGHTLY REVIVED
NOD
こくっ
Ok!
THAT SETTLES IT!
THEN LET'S GET OUT OF HERE!
...?
LEWIN, ISN'T YOUR HILT FACING THE WRONG WAY?
HM?
STILL HALF-AWAKE.
UGH...
WAHHH!!!
?

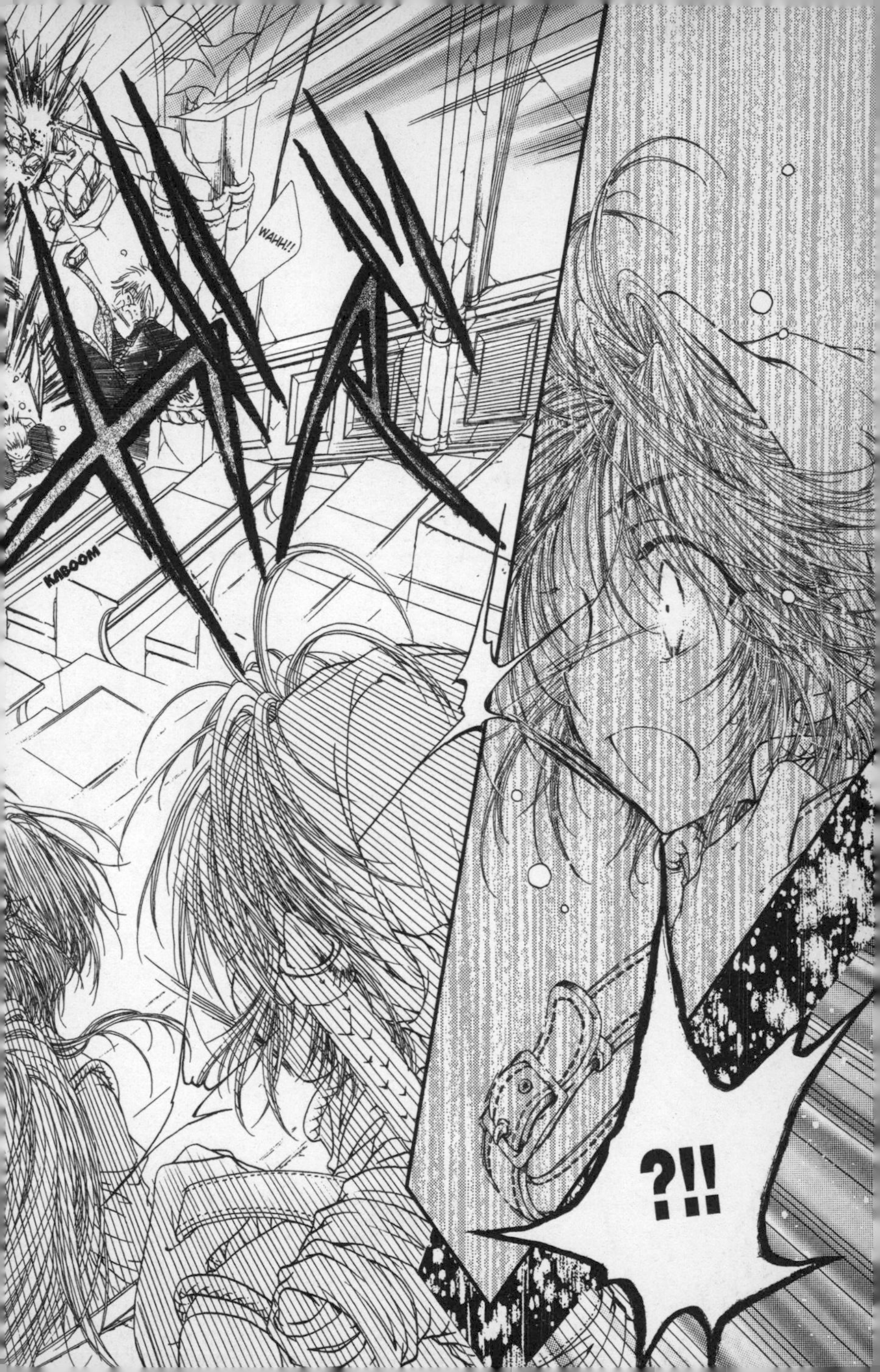
?!!
WAHH!!
KABOOM

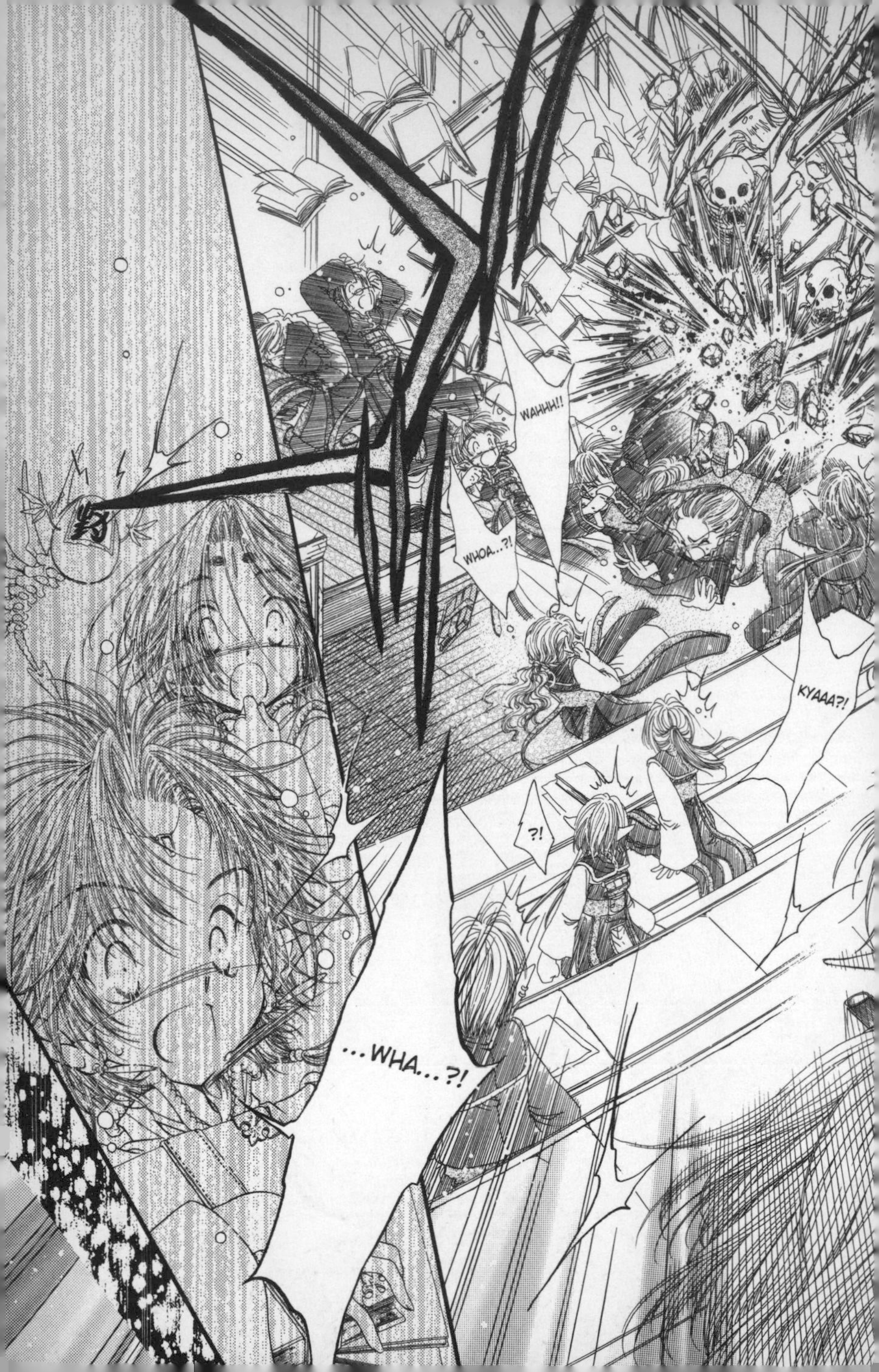
WAHHH!!
WHOA...?!
KYAAA?!
?!
...WHA...?!

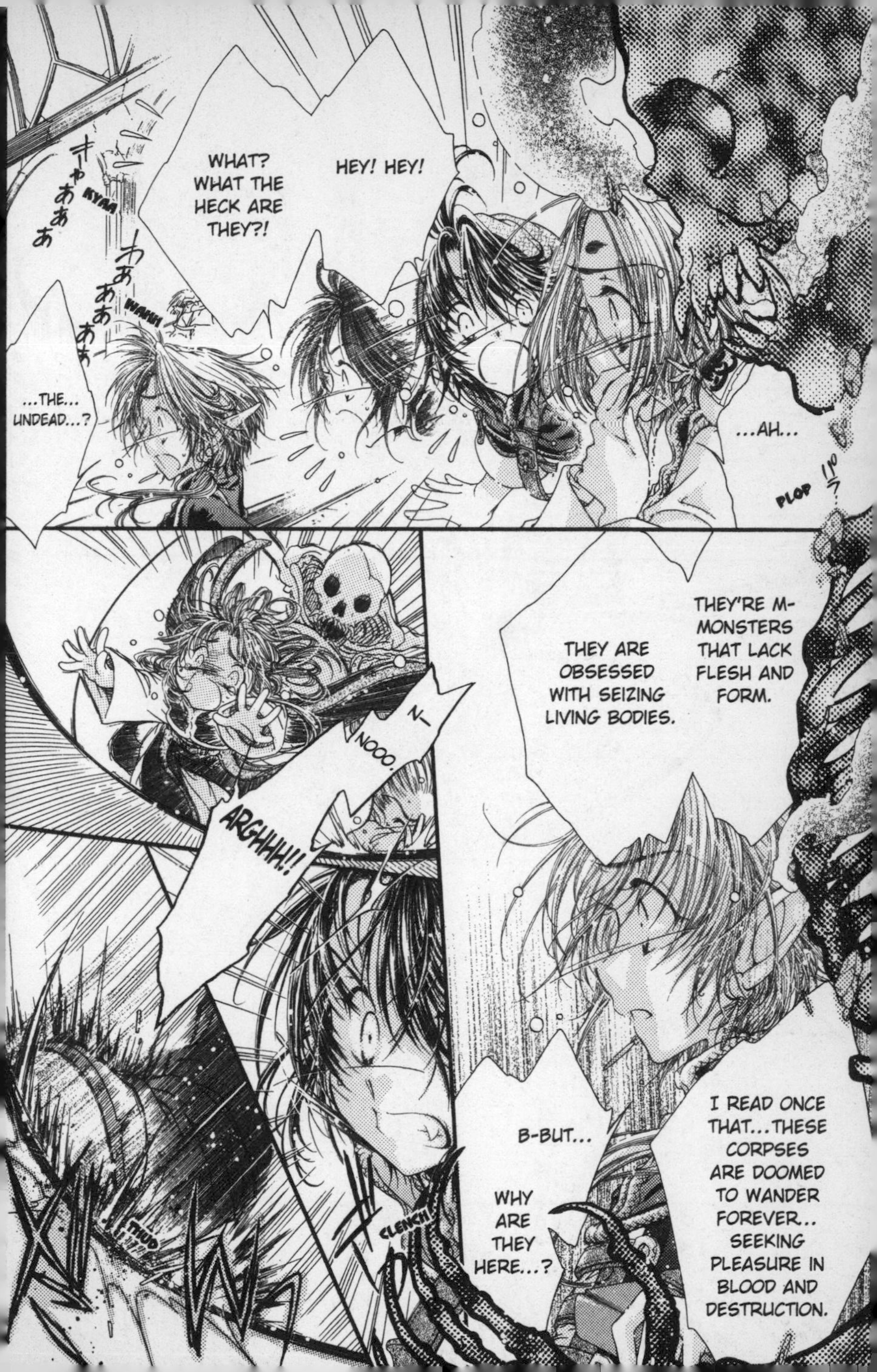
HEY! HEY!
WHAT? WHAT THE HECK ARE THEY?!
キャあああ
KYAA
...AH...
わあああああ
WAHH
...THE... UNDEAD...?
PLOP
THEY'RE M-MONSTERS THAT LACK FLESH AND FORM.
THEY ARE OBSESSED WITH SEIZING LIVING BODIES.
I READ ONCE THAT...THESE CORPSES ARE DOOMED TO WANDER FOREVER.. SEEKING PLEASURE IN BLOOD AND DESTRUCTION.
B-BUT...
WHY ARE THEY HERE...?
N-NOOO.
ARGHHH!!
CLENCH
THUD

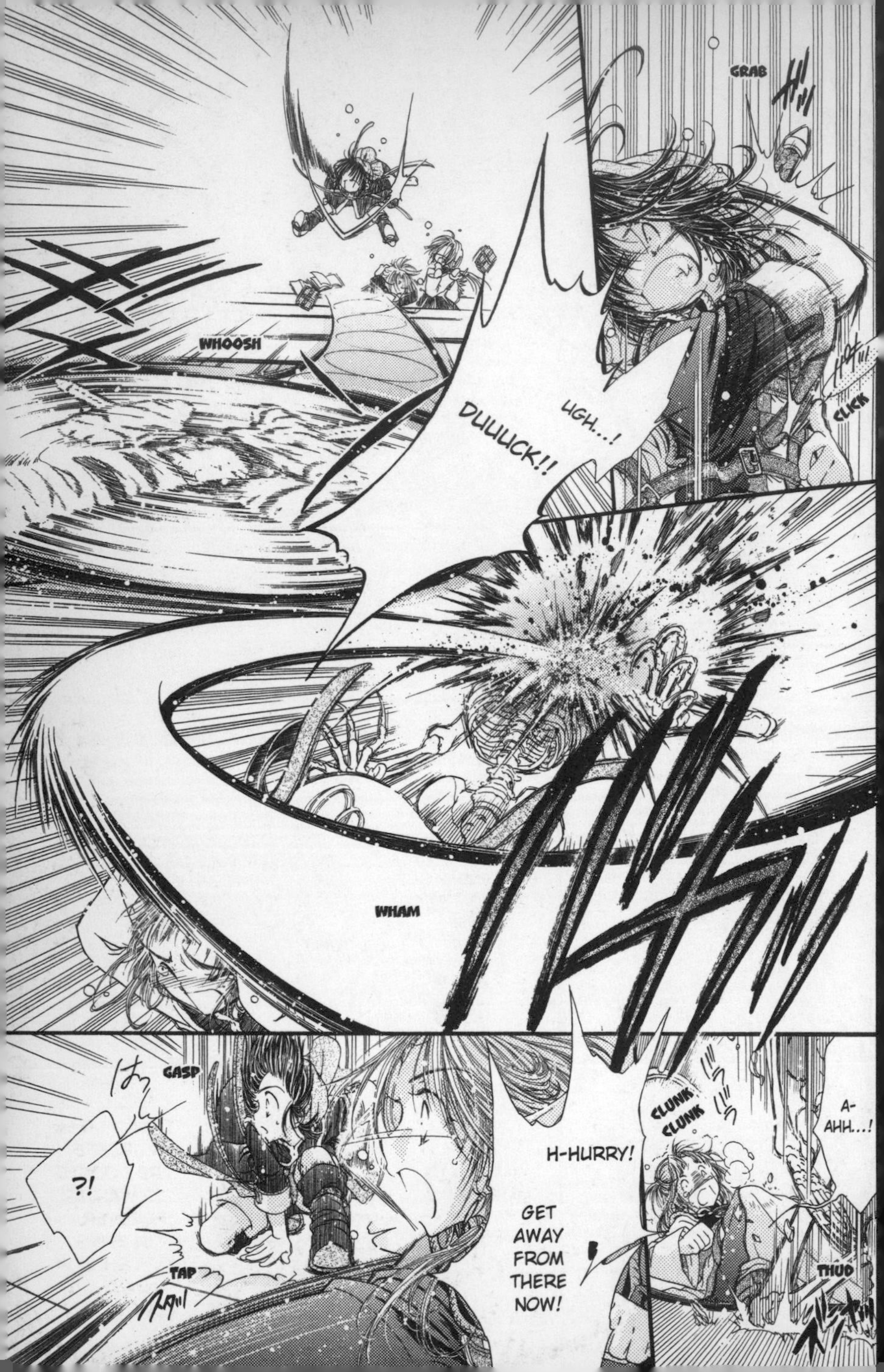
GRAB
UGH...!
CLICK
DUUUCK!!
WHOOSH
WHAM
A-AHH...!
CLUNK CLUNK
H-HURRY!
GET AWAY FROM THERE NOW!
THUD
GASP
?!
TAP

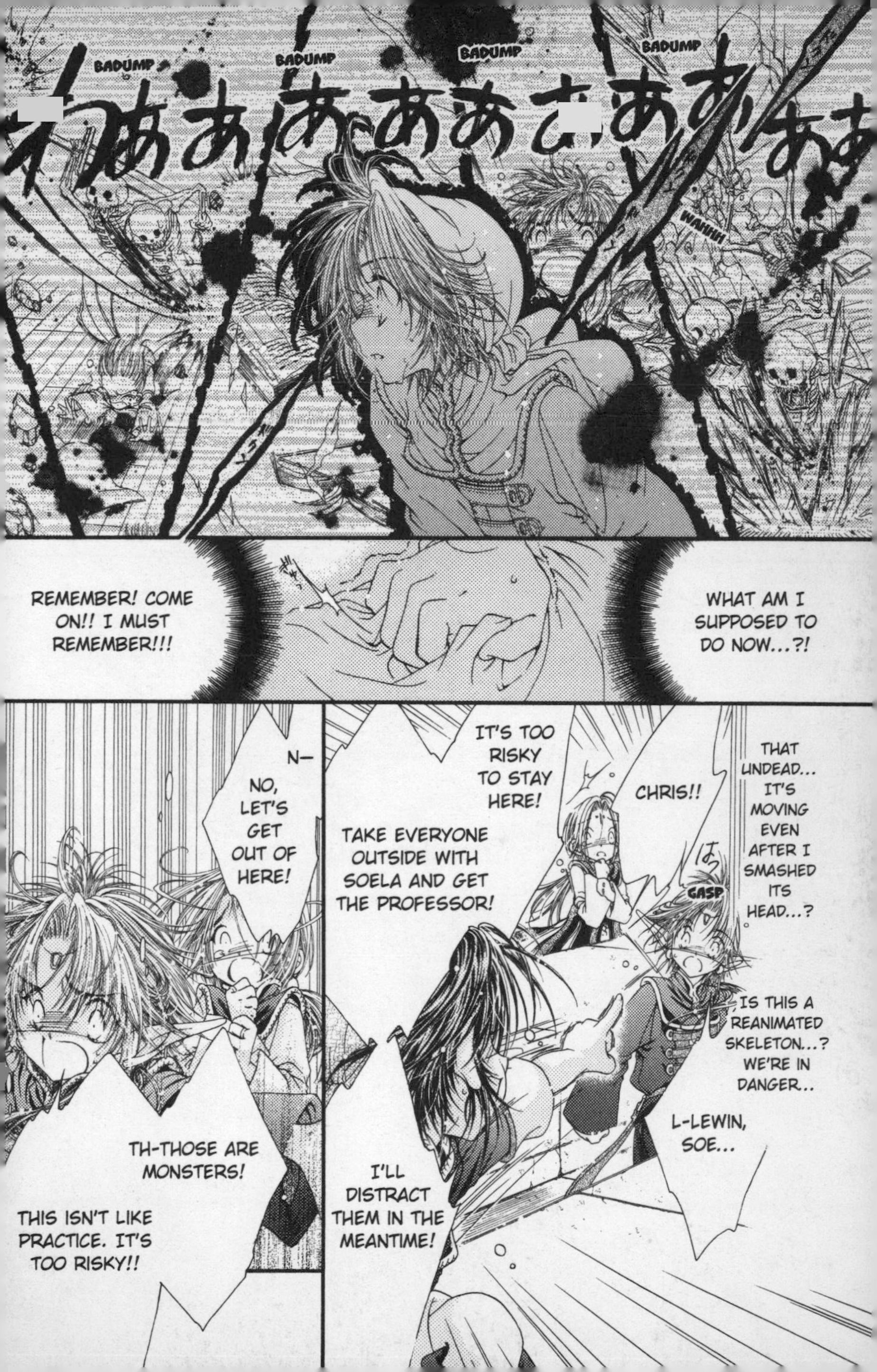
BADUMP
BADUMP
BADUMP
BADUMP
WAHHH
WHAT AM I SUPPOSED TO DO NOW...?!
REMEMBER! COME ON!! I MUST REMEMBER!!!
THAT UNDEAD... IT'S MOVING EVEN AFTER I SMASHED ITS HEAD...?
CHRIS!!
GASP
IT'S TOO RISKY TO STAY HERE!
TAKE EVERYONE OUTSIDE WITH SOELA AND GET THE PROFESSOR!
IS THIS A REANIMATED SKELETON...? WE'RE IN DANGER...
L-LEWIN, SOE...
I'LL DISTRACT THEM IN THE MEANTIME!
N— NO, LET'S GET OUT OF HERE!
TH-THOSE ARE MONSTERS!
THIS ISN'T LIKE PRACTICE. IT'S TOO RISKY!!

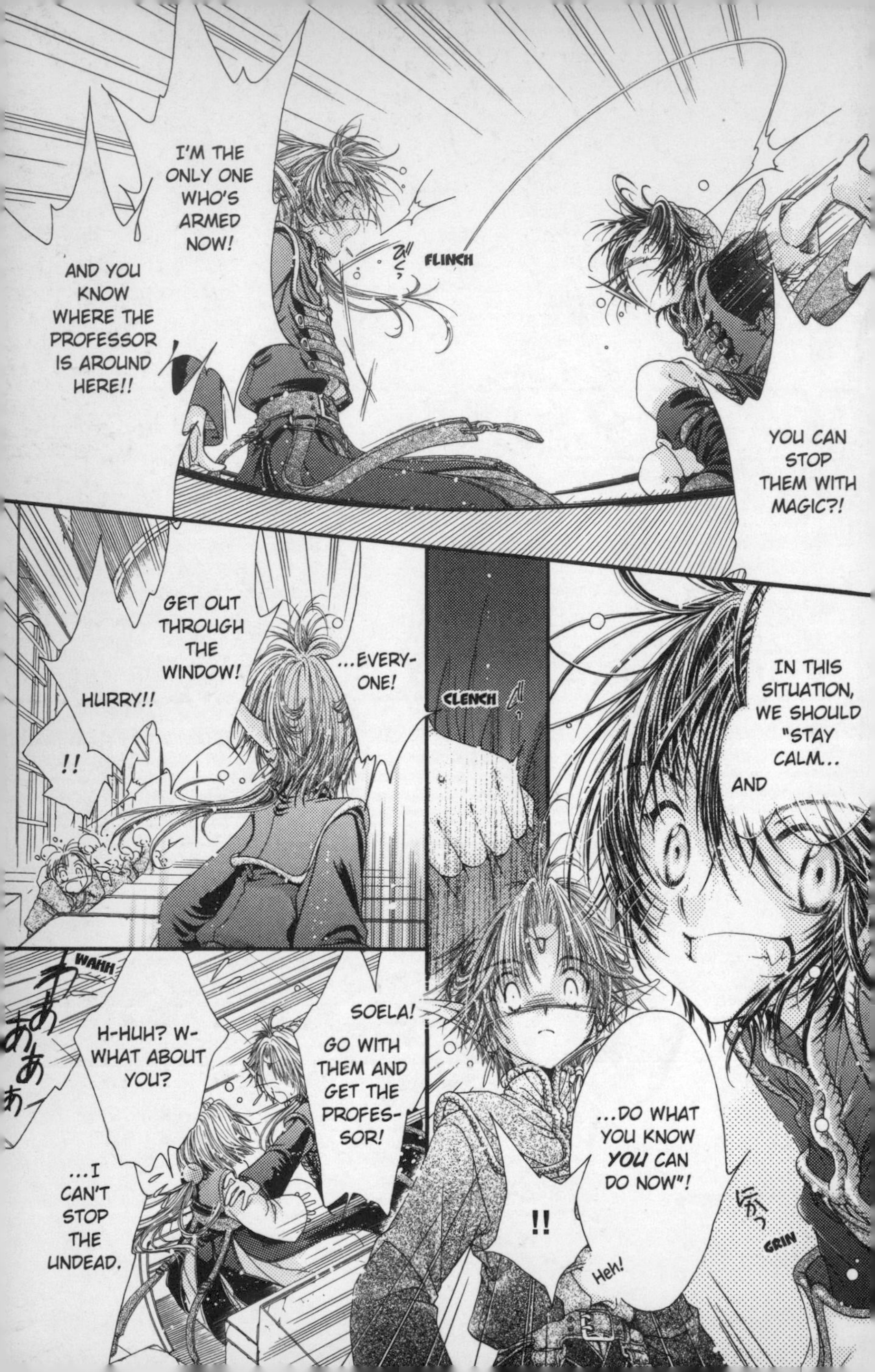
FLINCH
I'M THE ONLY ONE WHO'S ARMED NOW!
AND YOU KNOW WHERE THE PROFESSOR IS AROUND HERE!!
YOU CAN STOP THEM WITH MAGIC?!
IN THIS SITUATION, WE SHOULD "STAY CALM...
AND
...DO WHAT YOU KNOW *YOU* CAN DO NOW"!
GRIN
Heh!
!!
CLENCH
...EVERY-ONE!
GET OUT THROUGH THE WINDOW!
HURRY!!
!!
SOELA!
GO WITH THEM AND GET THE PROFES-SOR!
H-HUH? W-WHAT ABOUT YOU?
...I CAN'T STOP THE UNDEAD.
WAHH

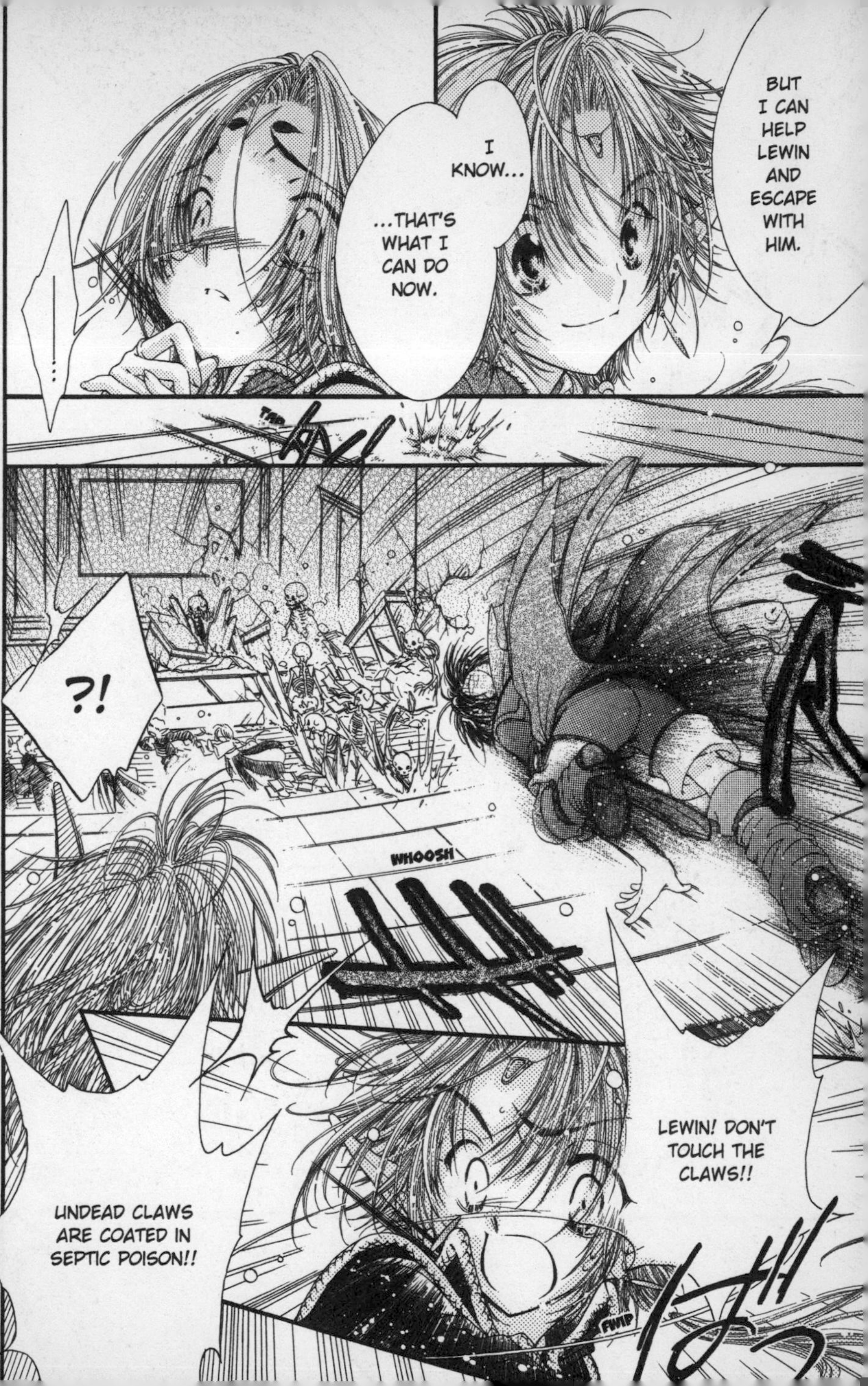
BUT I CAN HELP LEWIN AND ESCAPE WITH HIM.
I KNOW...
...THAT'S WHAT I CAN DO NOW.
...!
TAP
?!
WHOOSH
LEWIN! DON'T TOUCH THE CLAWS!!
UNDEAD CLAWS ARE COATED IN SEPTIC POISON!!
FWIP

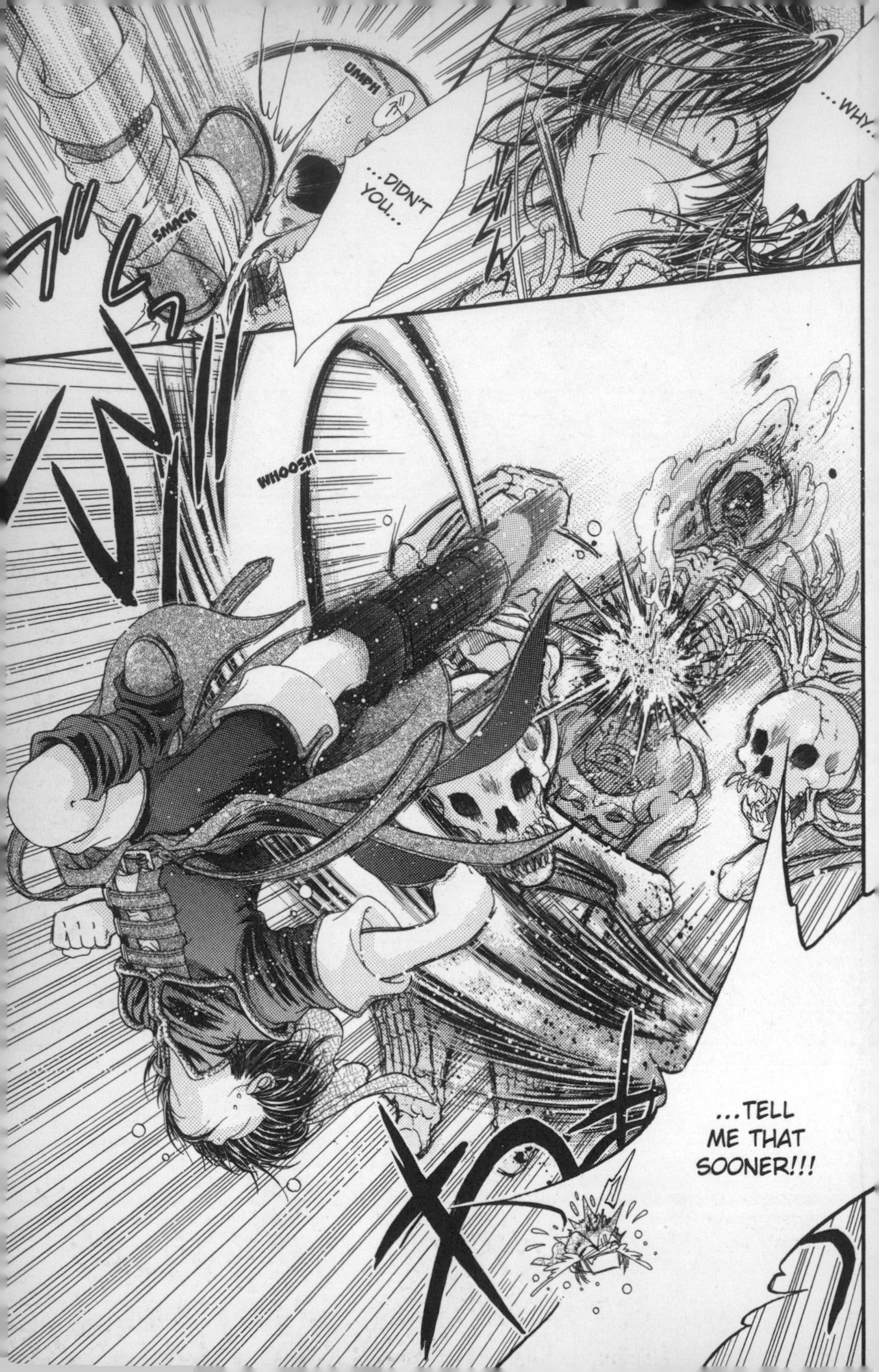
...WHY...
UMPH
...DIDN'T YOU...
SMACK
WHOOSH
...TELL ME THAT SOONER!!!

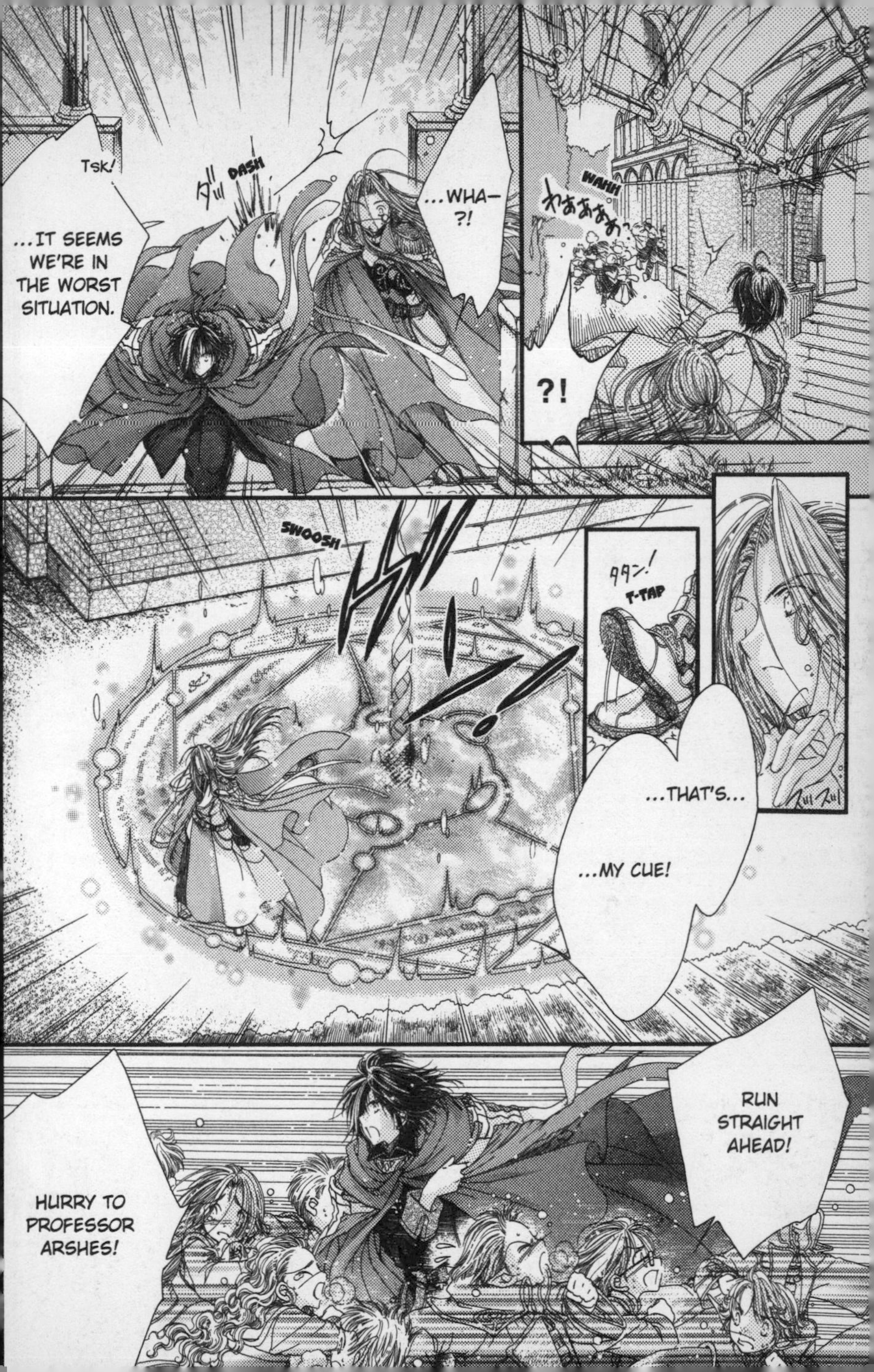
WAHH
?!
...WHA—?!
DASH
Tsk!
...IT SEEMS WE'RE IN THE WORST SITUATION.
T-TAP
SWOOSH
...THAT'S...
...MY CUE!
RUN STRAIGHT AHEAD!
HURRY TO PROFESSOR ARSHES!

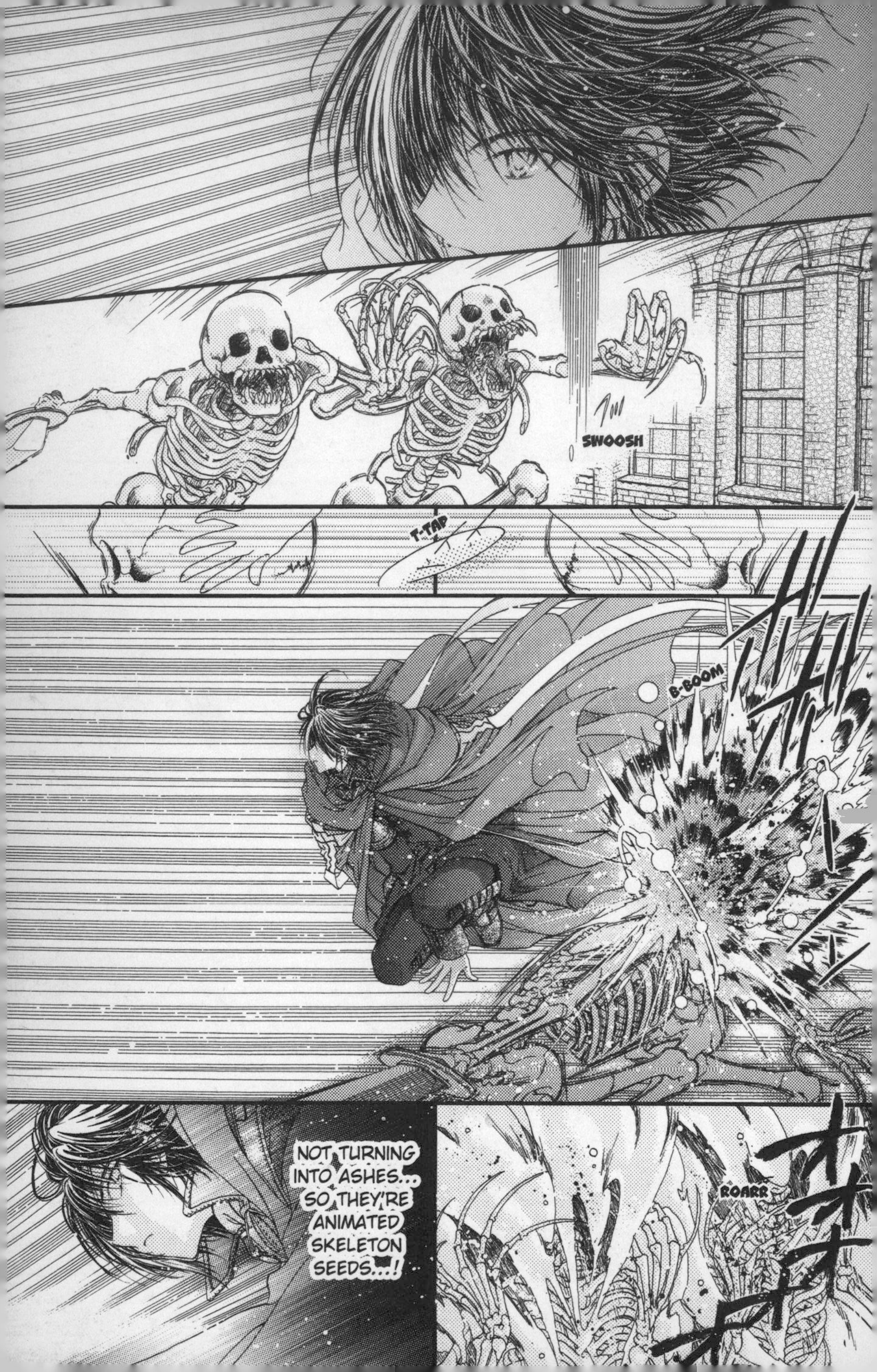
SWOOSH
T-TAP
B-BOOM
ROARR
NOT TURNING INTO ASHES... SO THEY'RE ANIMATED SKELETON SEEDS...!

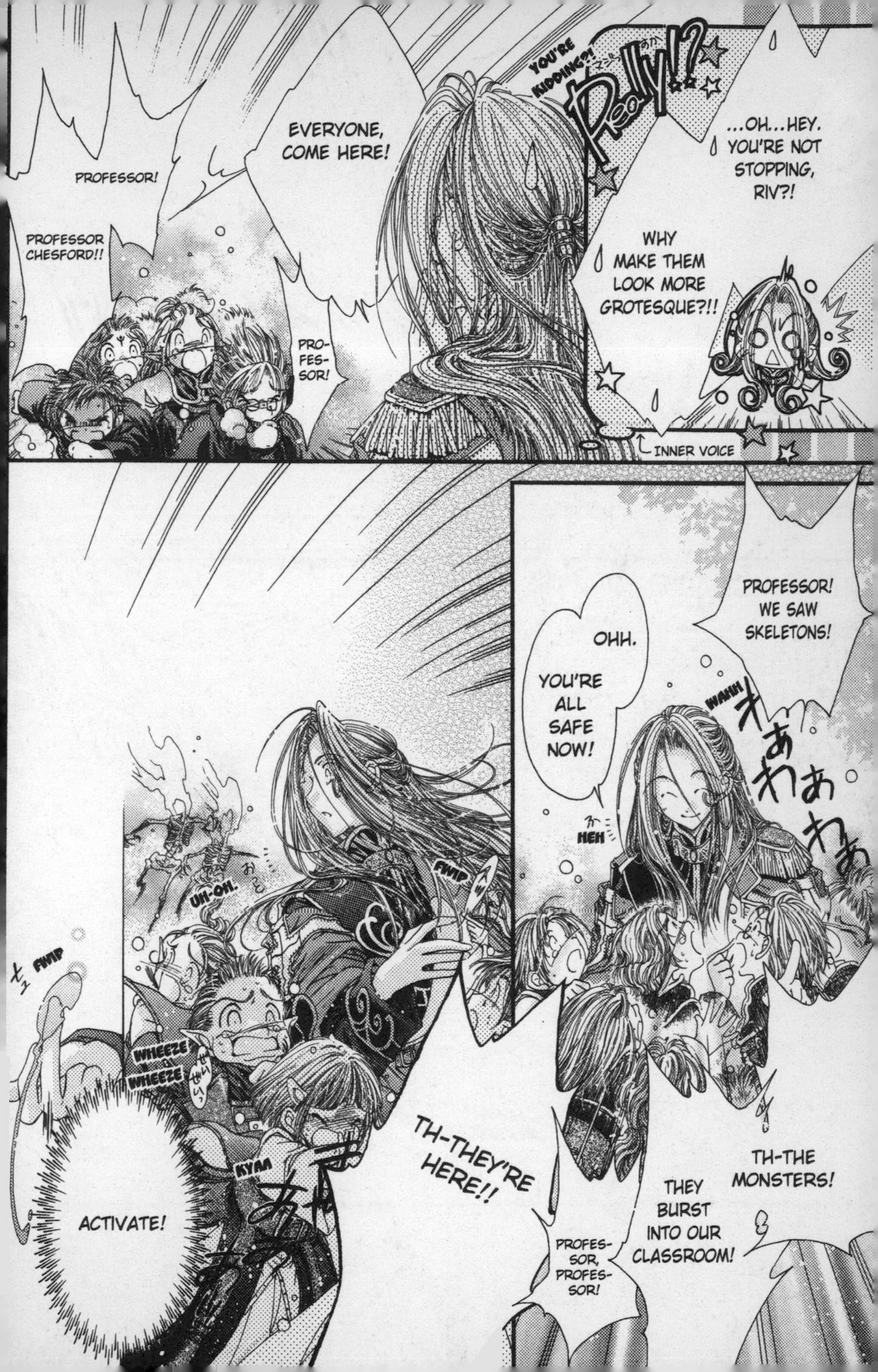
...OH...HEY. YOU'RE NOT STOPPING, RIV?!
WHY MAKE THEM LOOK MORE GROTESQUE?!!
INNER VOICE
YOU'RE KIDDING?!
Really!?
EVERYONE, COME HERE!
PRO-FES-SOR!
PROFESSOR!
PROFESSOR CHESFORD!!
PROFESSOR! WE SAW SKELETONS!
WAHH
OHH.
YOU'RE ALL SAFE NOW!
HEH
TH-THE MONSTERS!
THEY BURST INTO OUR CLASSROOM!
PROFES-SOR, PROFES-SOR!
TH-THEY'RE HERE!!
FWIP
UH-OH.
FWIP
WHEEZE
WHEEZE
KYAA
ACTIVATE!

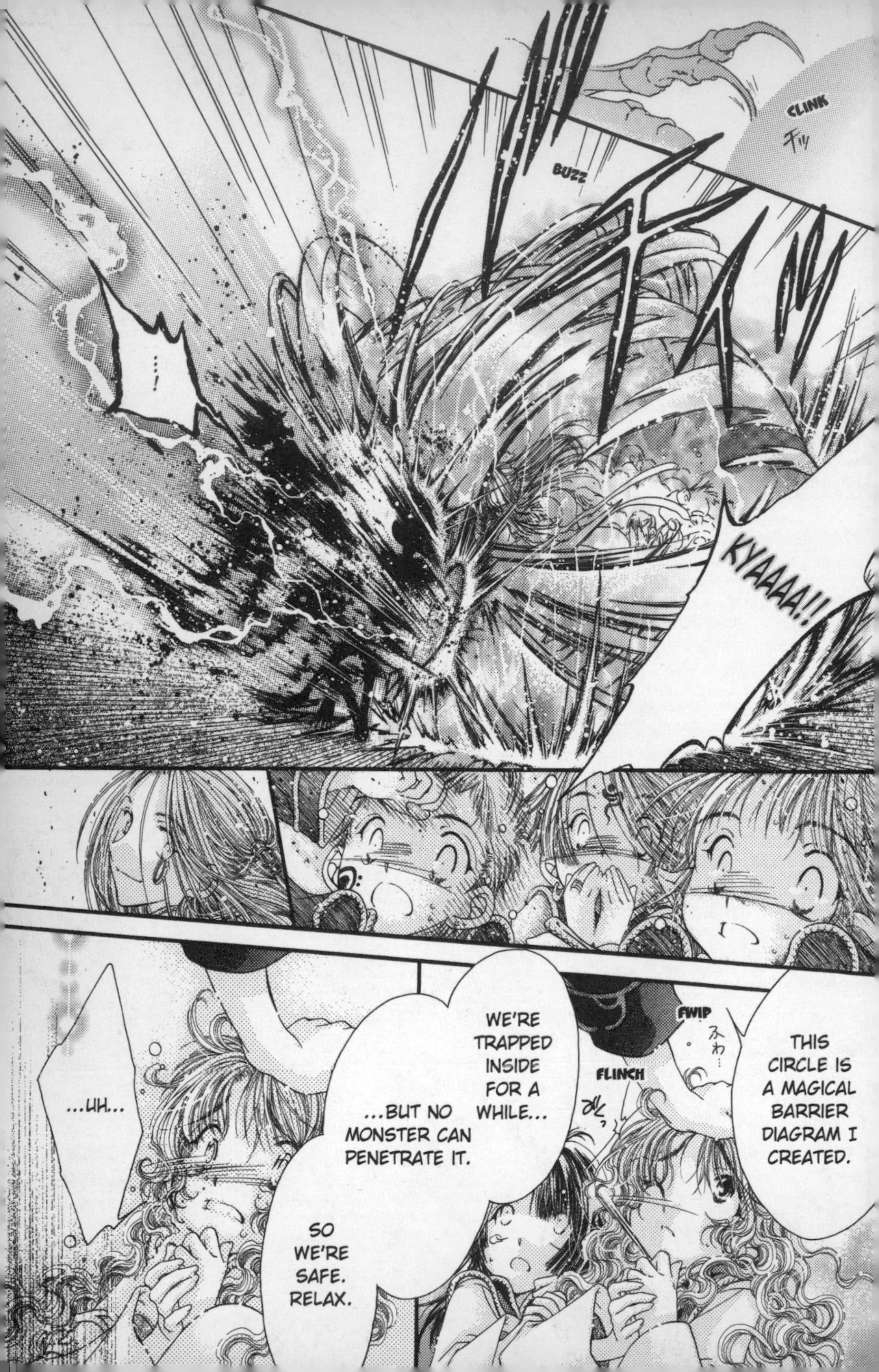
CLINK
ギッ
BUZZ
KYAAAA!!
...!
THIS CIRCLE IS A MAGICAL BARRIER DIAGRAM I CREATED.
FWIP
ふわ…
FLINCH
びくっ
WE'RE TRAPPED INSIDE FOR A WHILE...
...BUT NO MONSTER CAN PENETRATE IT.
SO WE'RE SAFE. RELAX.
...UH...

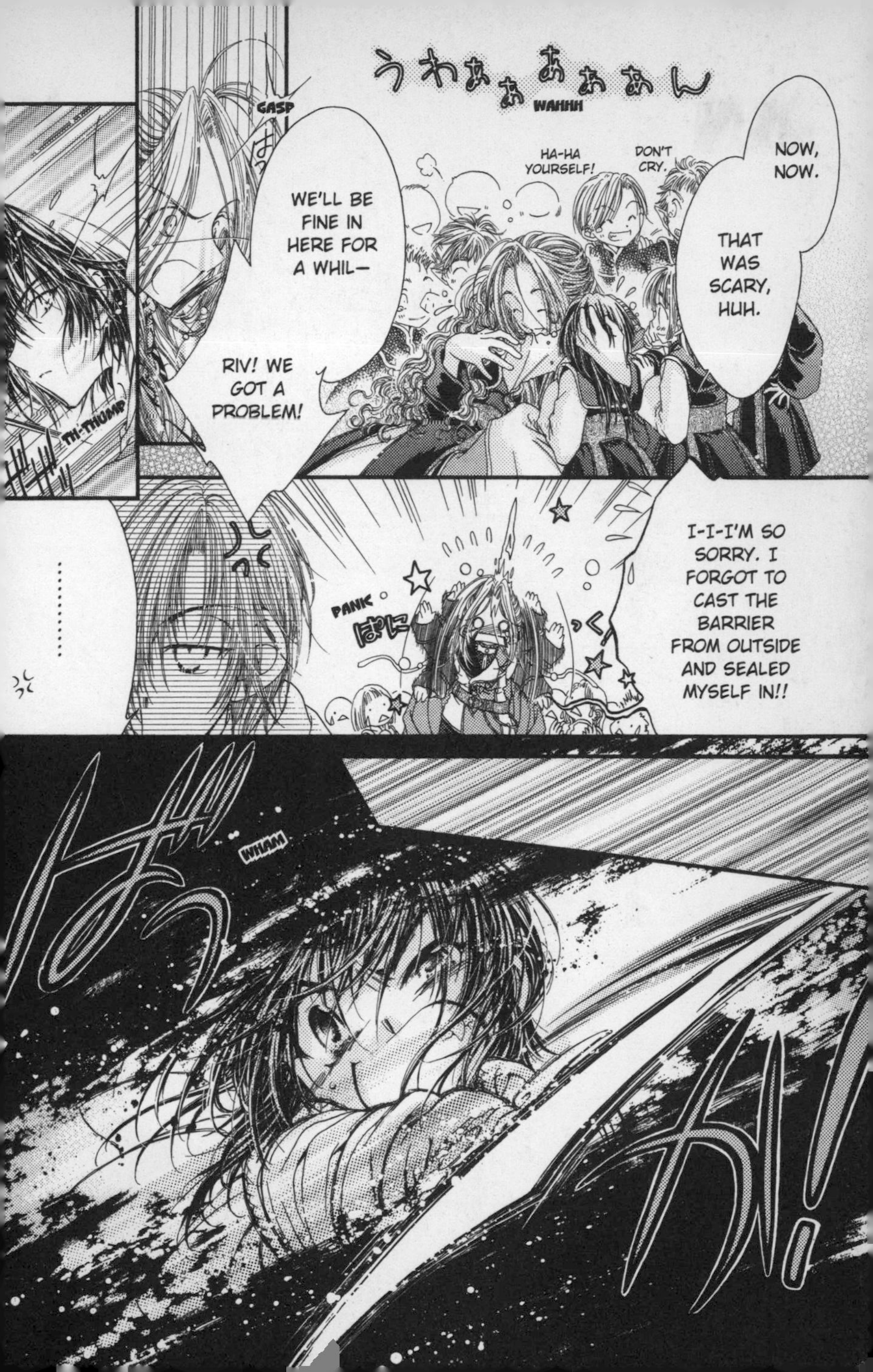
うわぁぁあぁあん
WAHHH
NOW, NOW.
THAT WAS SCARY, HUH.
DON'T CRY.
HA-HA YOURSELF!
GASP
WE'LL BE FINE IN HERE FOR A WHIL—
RIV! WE GOT A PROBLEM!
TH-THUMP
I-I-I'M SO SORRY. I FORGOT TO CAST THE BARRIER FROM OUTSIDE AND SEALED MYSELF IN!!
PANIC
ぱにっく
......
WHAM

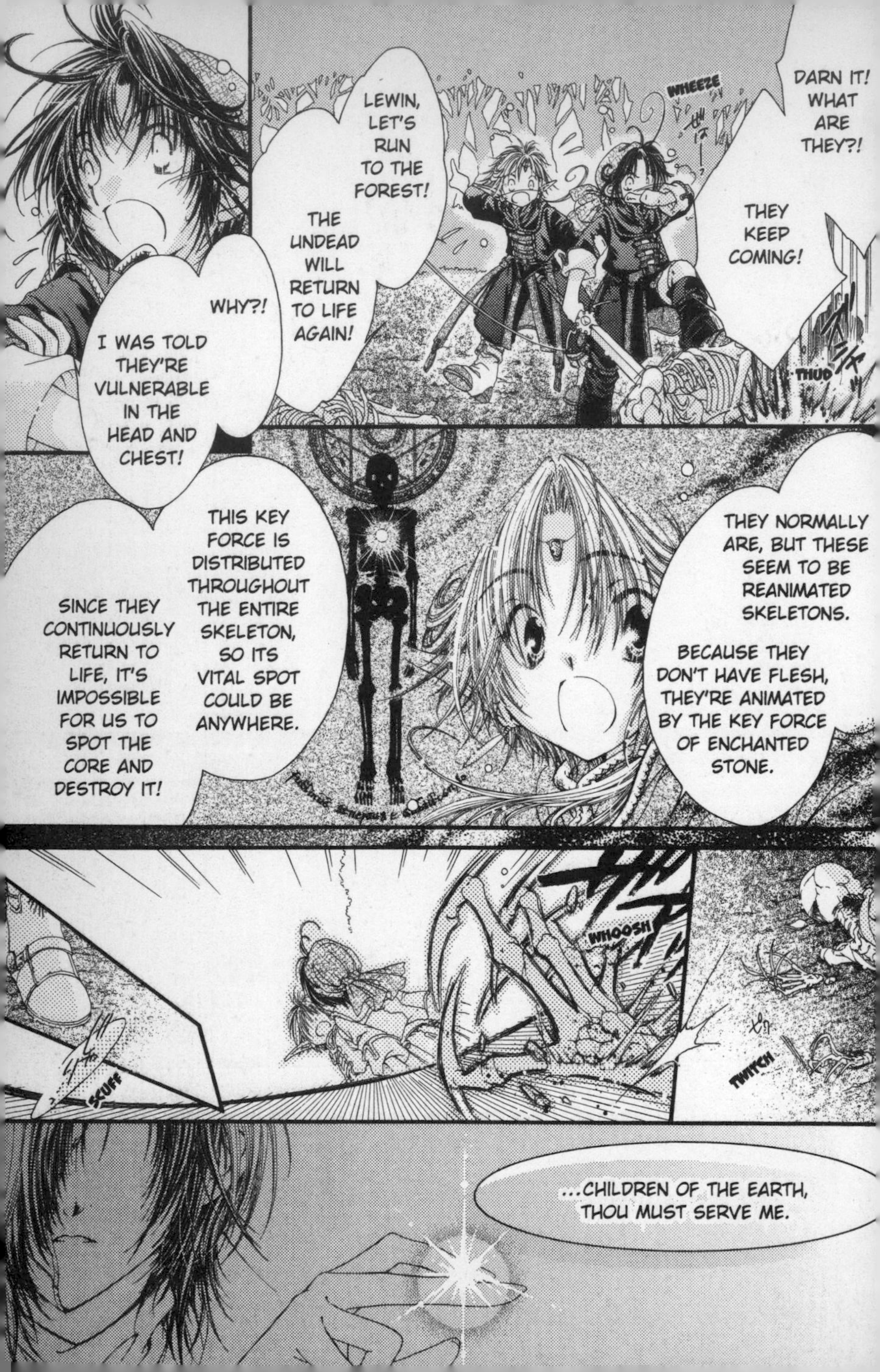
DARN IT! WHAT ARE THEY?!
THEY KEEP COMING!
THUD
WHEEZE
LEWIN, LET'S RUN TO THE FOREST!
THE UNDEAD WILL RETURN TO LIFE AGAIN!
WHY?!
I WAS TOLD THEY'RE VULNERABLE IN THE HEAD AND CHEST!
THEY NORMALLY ARE, BUT THESE SEEM TO BE REANIMATED SKELETONS.
BECAUSE THEY DON'T HAVE FLESH, THEY'RE ANIMATED BY THE KEY FORCE OF ENCHANTED STONE.
THIS KEY FORCE IS DISTRIBUTED THROUGHOUT THE ENTIRE SKELETON, SO ITS VITAL SPOT COULD BE ANYWHERE.
SINCE THEY CONTINUOUSLY RETURN TO LIFE, IT'S IMPOSSIBLE FOR US TO SPOT THE CORE AND DESTROY IT!
TWITCH
WHOOSH
SCUFF
...CHILDREN OF THE EARTH, THOU MUST SERVE ME.

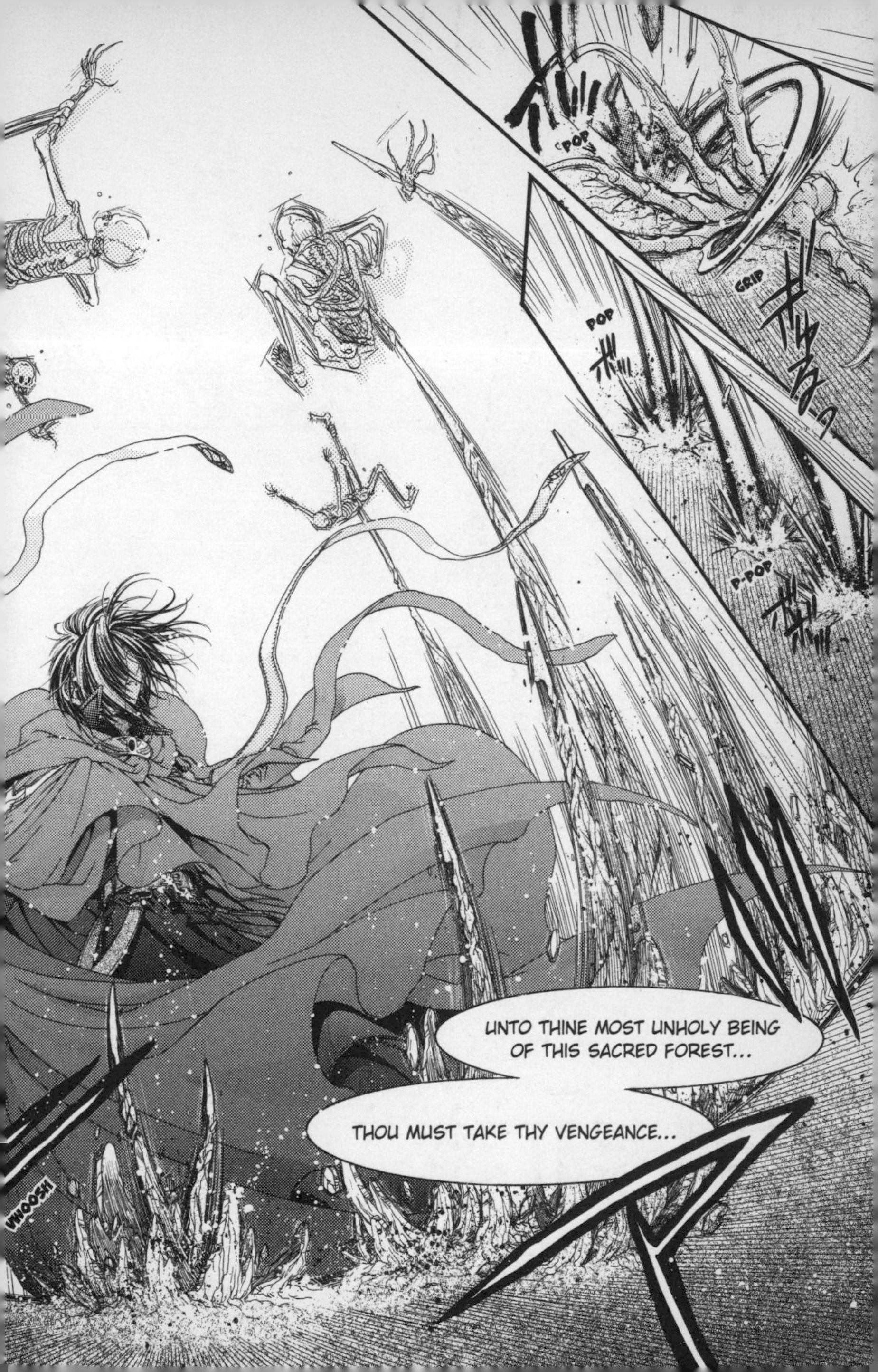
POP
GRIP
POP
P-POP
UNTO THINE MOST UNHOLY BEING OF THIS SACRED FOREST...
THOU MUST TAKE THY VENGEANCE...
WHOOSH

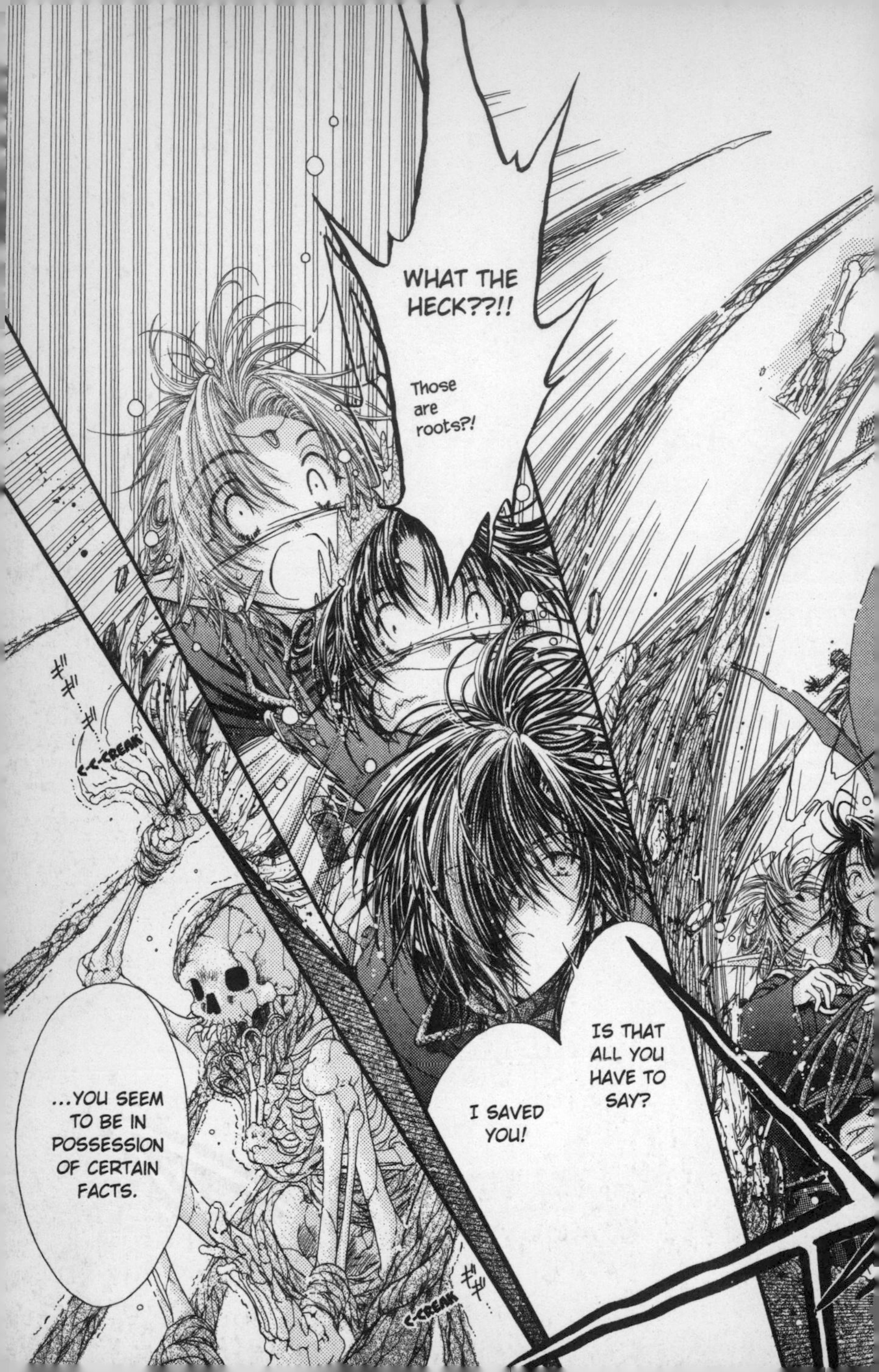
WHAT THE HECK??!!
Those are roots?!
IS THAT ALL YOU HAVE TO SAY?
I SAVED YOU!
ギギ…ギ
C-C-CREAK
...YOU SEEM TO BE IN POSSESSION OF CERTAIN FACTS.
ギギ…
C-CREAK

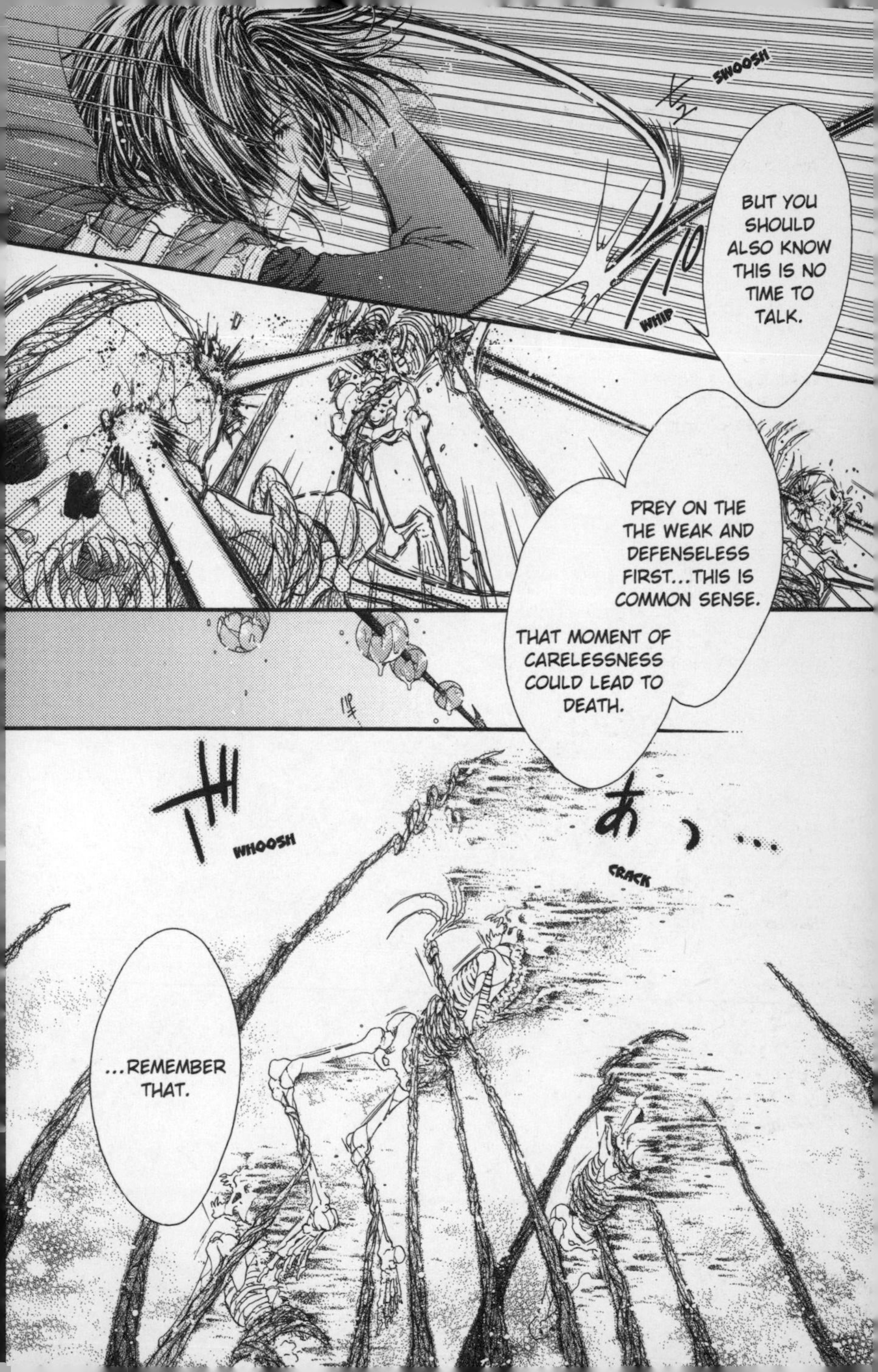
SWOOSH
BUT YOU SHOULD ALSO KNOW THIS IS NO TIME TO TALK.
WHIP
PREY ON THE THE WEAK AND DEFENSELESS FIRST...THIS IS COMMON SENSE.
THAT MOMENT OF CARELESSNESS COULD LEAD TO DEATH.
あっ...
CRACK
WHOOSH
...REMEMBER THAT.

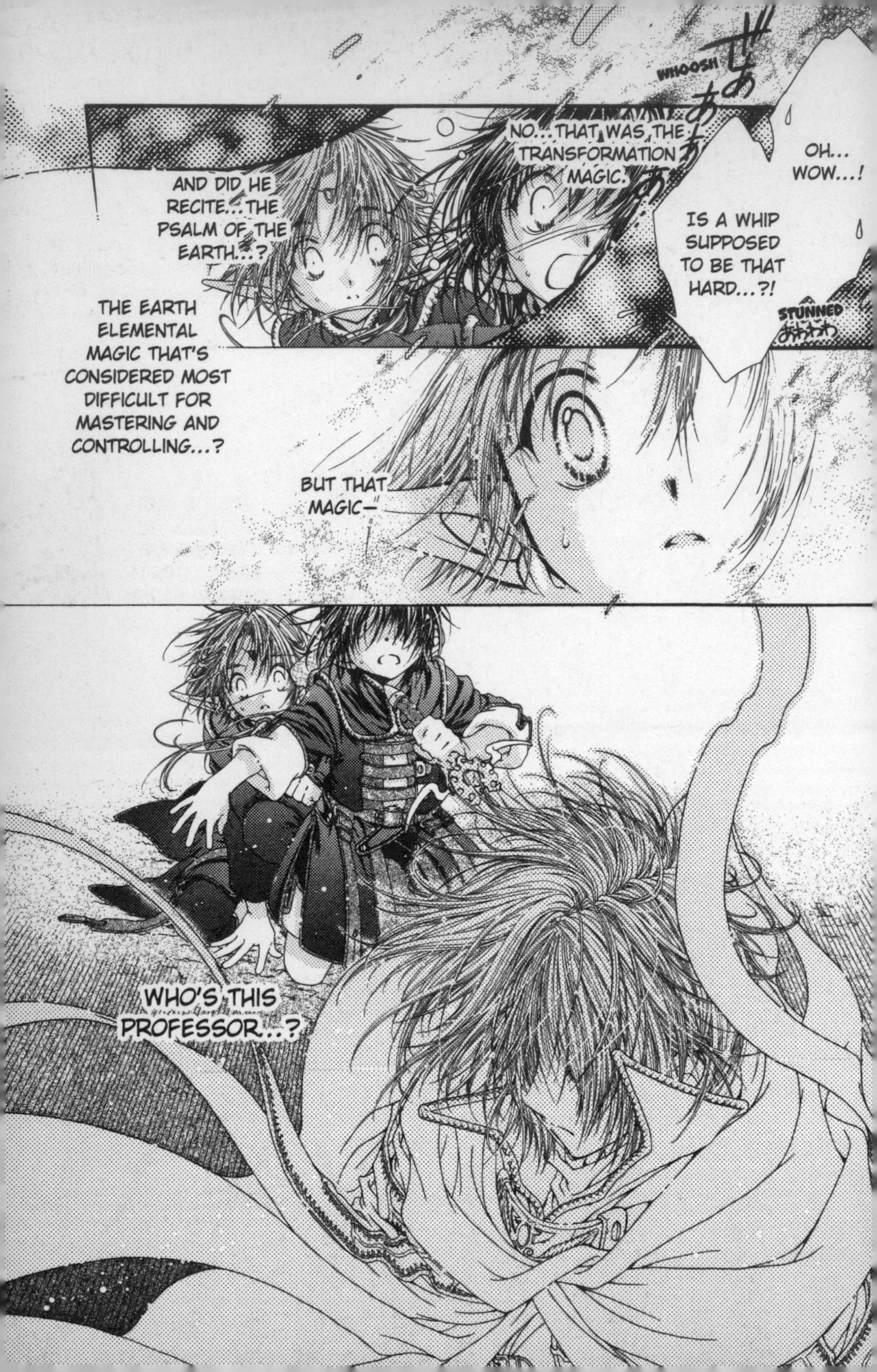
WHOOSH
OH... WOW...!
IS A WHIP SUPPOSED TO BE THAT HARD...?!
STUNNED
NO... THAT WAS THE TRANSFORMATION MAGIC.
AND DID HE RECITE... THE PSALM OF THE EARTH...?
BUT THAT MAGIC—
THE EARTH ELEMENTAL MAGIC THAT'S CONSIDERED MOST DIFFICULT FOR MASTERING AND CONTROLLING...?
WHO'S THIS PROFESSOR...?

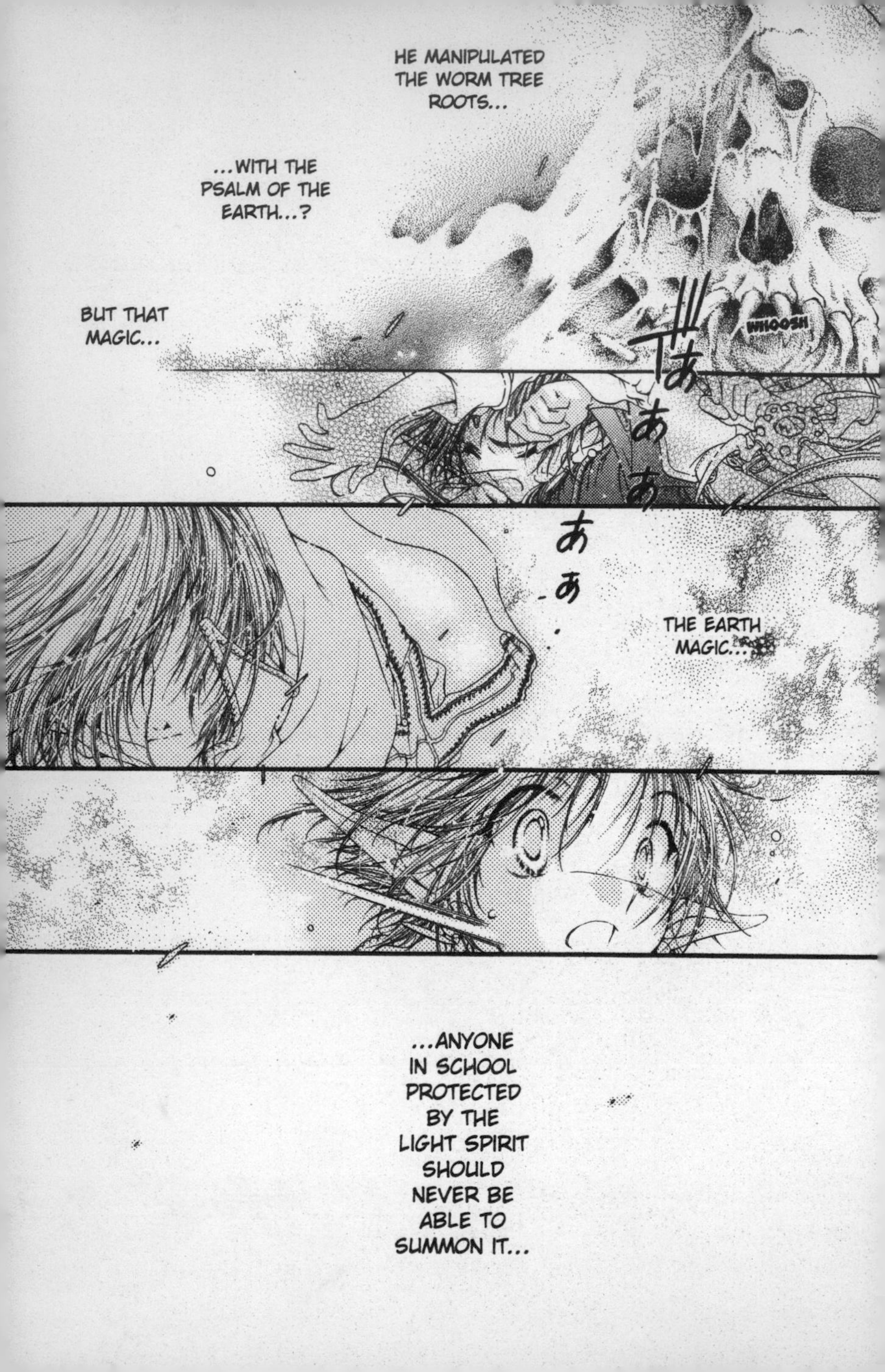
WHOOSH
ドあああああ
HE MANIPULATED THE WORM TREE ROOTS...
...WITH THE PSALM OF THE EARTH...?
BUT THAT MAGIC...
THE EARTH MAGIC...
...ANYONE IN SCHOOL PROTECTED BY THE LIGHT SPIRIT SHOULD NEVER BE ABLE TO SUMMON IT...

WHO'S THIS
PROFESSOR..?!

5th Bell: Aim of the Attack

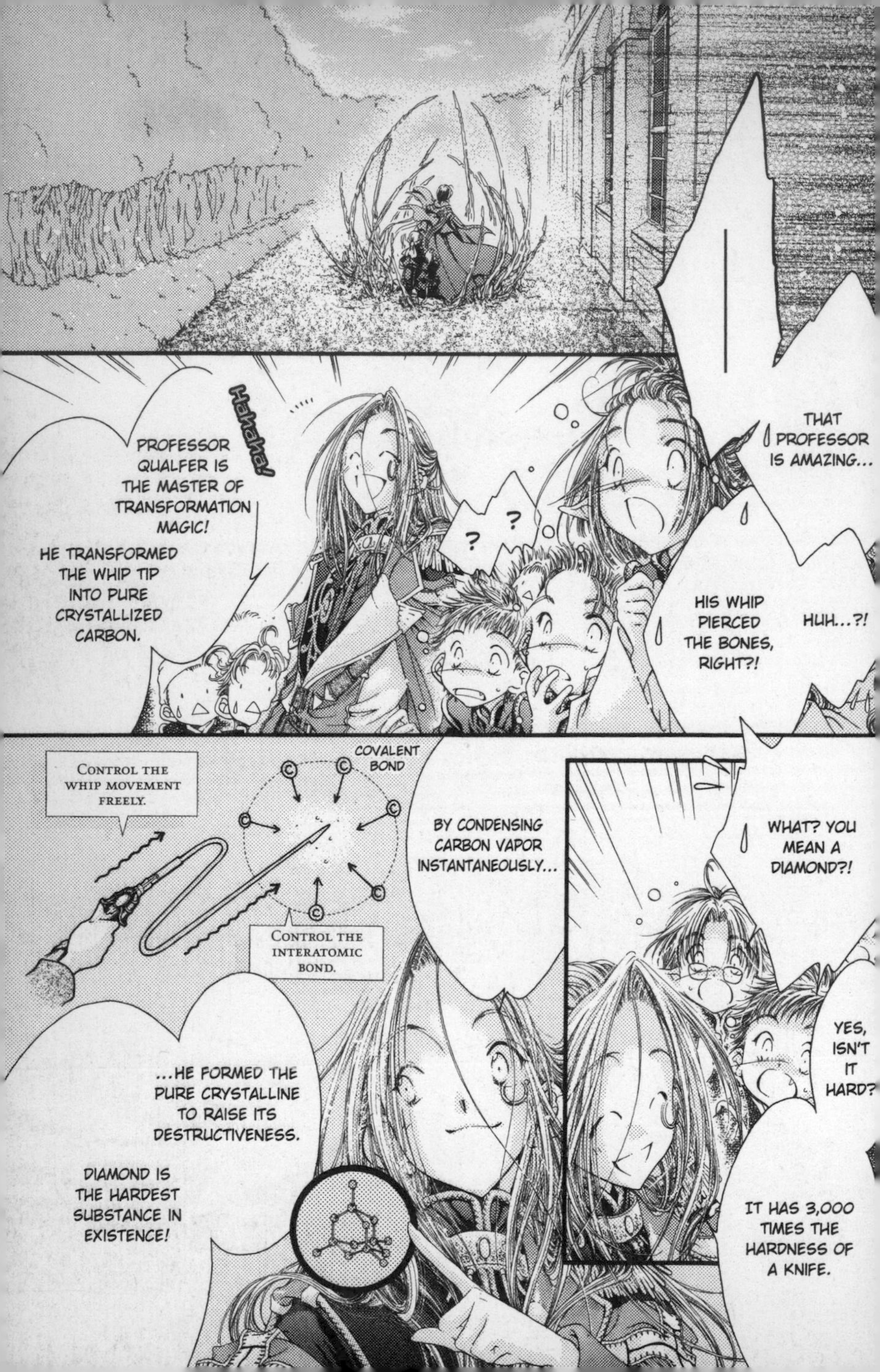
THAT PROFESSOR IS AMAZING...
HUH...?!
HIS WHIP PIERCED THE BONES, RIGHT?!
?
?
Hahaha!
PROFESSOR QUALFER IS THE MASTER OF TRANSFORMATION MAGIC!
HE TRANSFORMED THE WHIP TIP INTO PURE CRYSTALLIZED CARBON.
WHAT? YOU MEAN A DIAMOND?!
YES, ISN'T IT HARD?
IT HAS 3,000 TIMES THE HARDNESS OF A KNIFE.
BY CONDENSING CARBON VAPOR INSTANTANEOUSLY...
COVALENT BOND
Control the whip movement freely.
Control the interatomic bond.
...HE FORMED THE PURE CRYSTALLINE TO RAISE ITS DESTRUCTIVENESS.
DIAMOND IS THE HARDEST SUBSTANCE IN EXISTENCE!

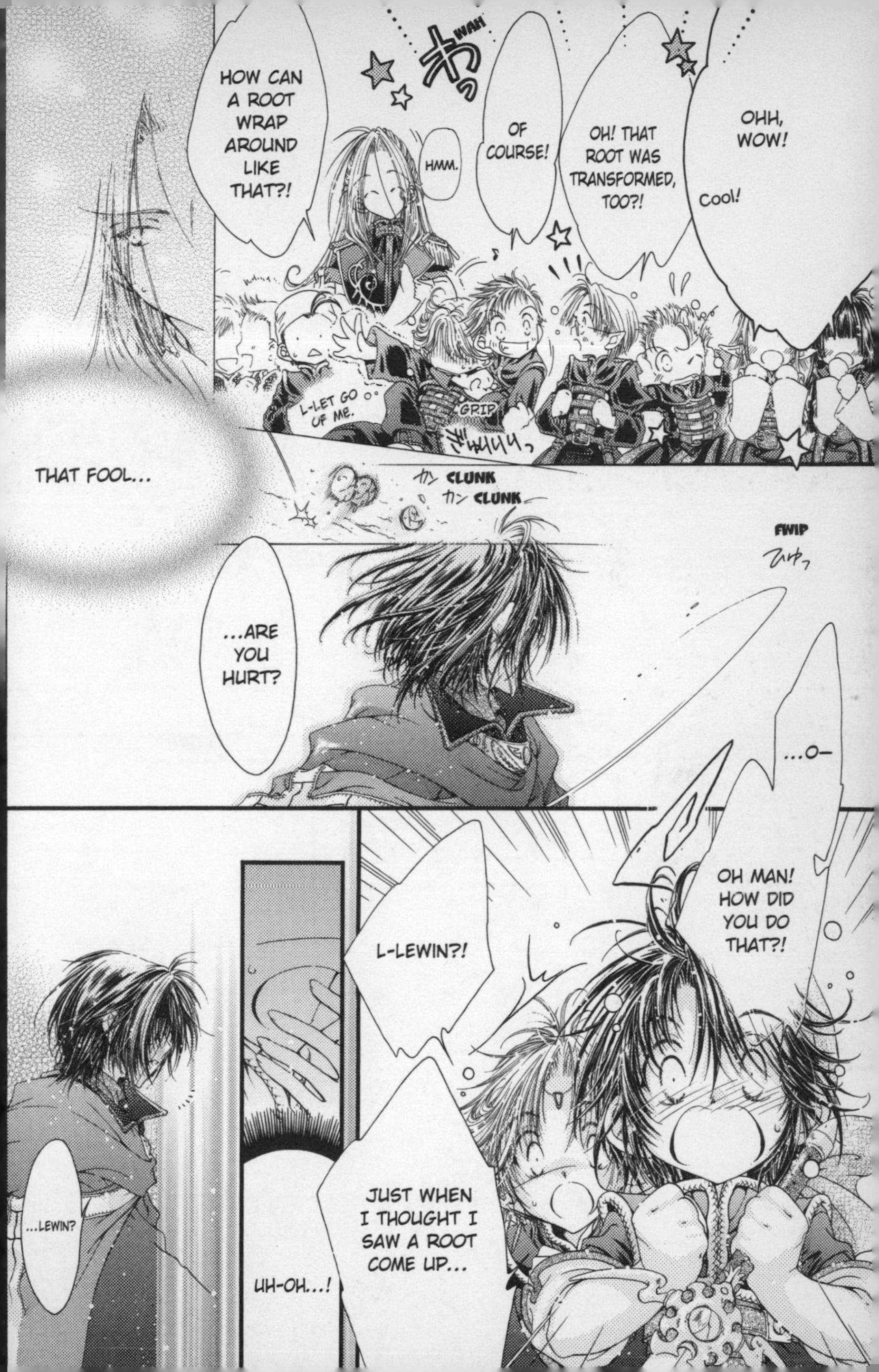
OHH, WOW!
Cool!
OH! THAT ROOT WAS TRANSFORMED, TOO?!
WAH
OF COURSE!
HMM.
HOW CAN A ROOT WRAP AROUND LIKE THAT?!
GRIP
L-LET GO OF ME.
CLUNK
CLUNK
FWIP
...O-
...ARE YOU HURT?
THAT FOOL...
OH MAN! HOW DID YOU DO THAT?!
L-LEWIN?!
JUST WHEN I THOUGHT I SAW A ROOT COME UP...
UH-OH...!
...LEWIN?

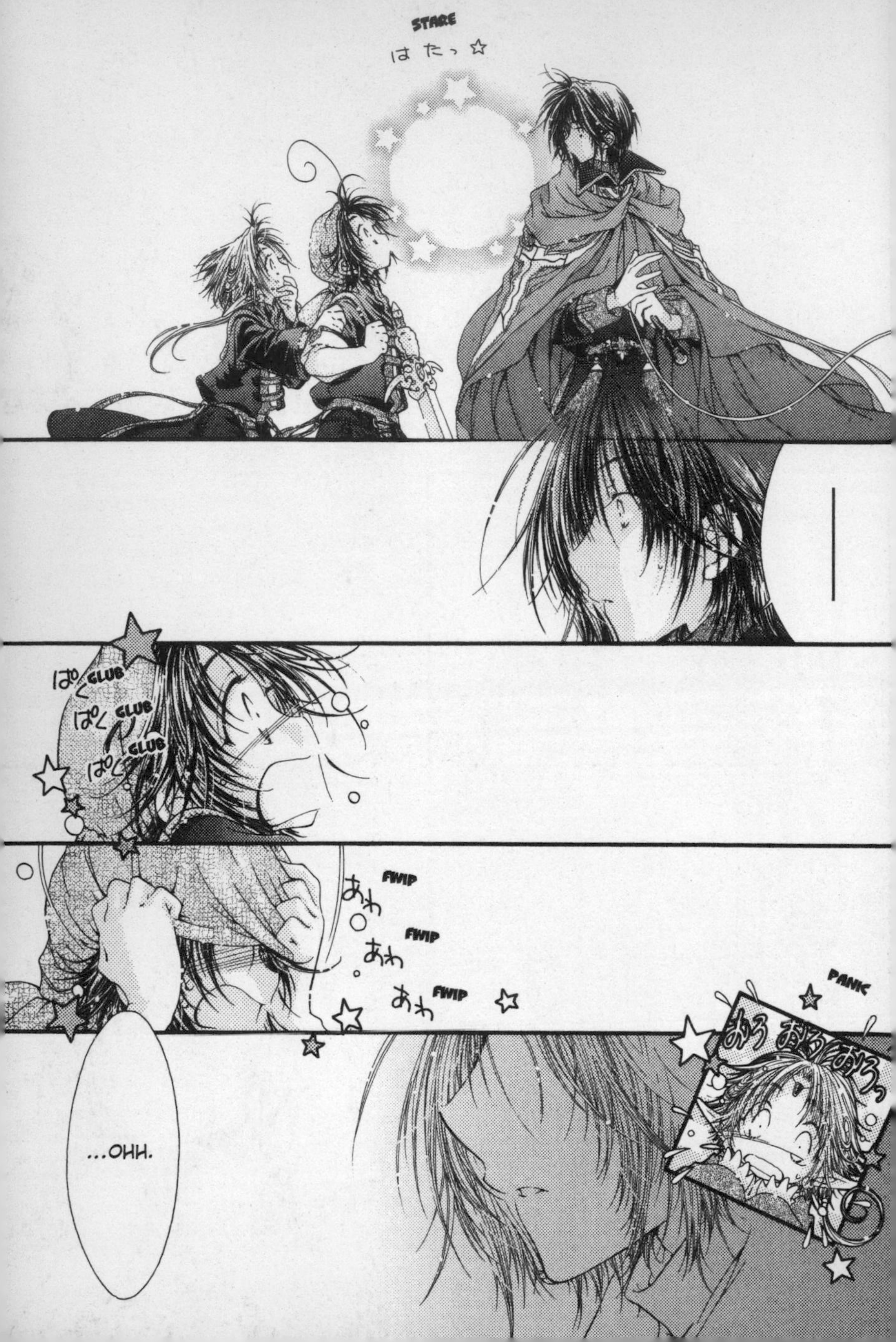
STARE
はたっ☆
ぱく GLUB
ぱく GLUB
ぱく GLUB
あわ FWIP
あわ FWIP
あわ FWIP
PANIC
おろ おろ おろっ
...OHH.

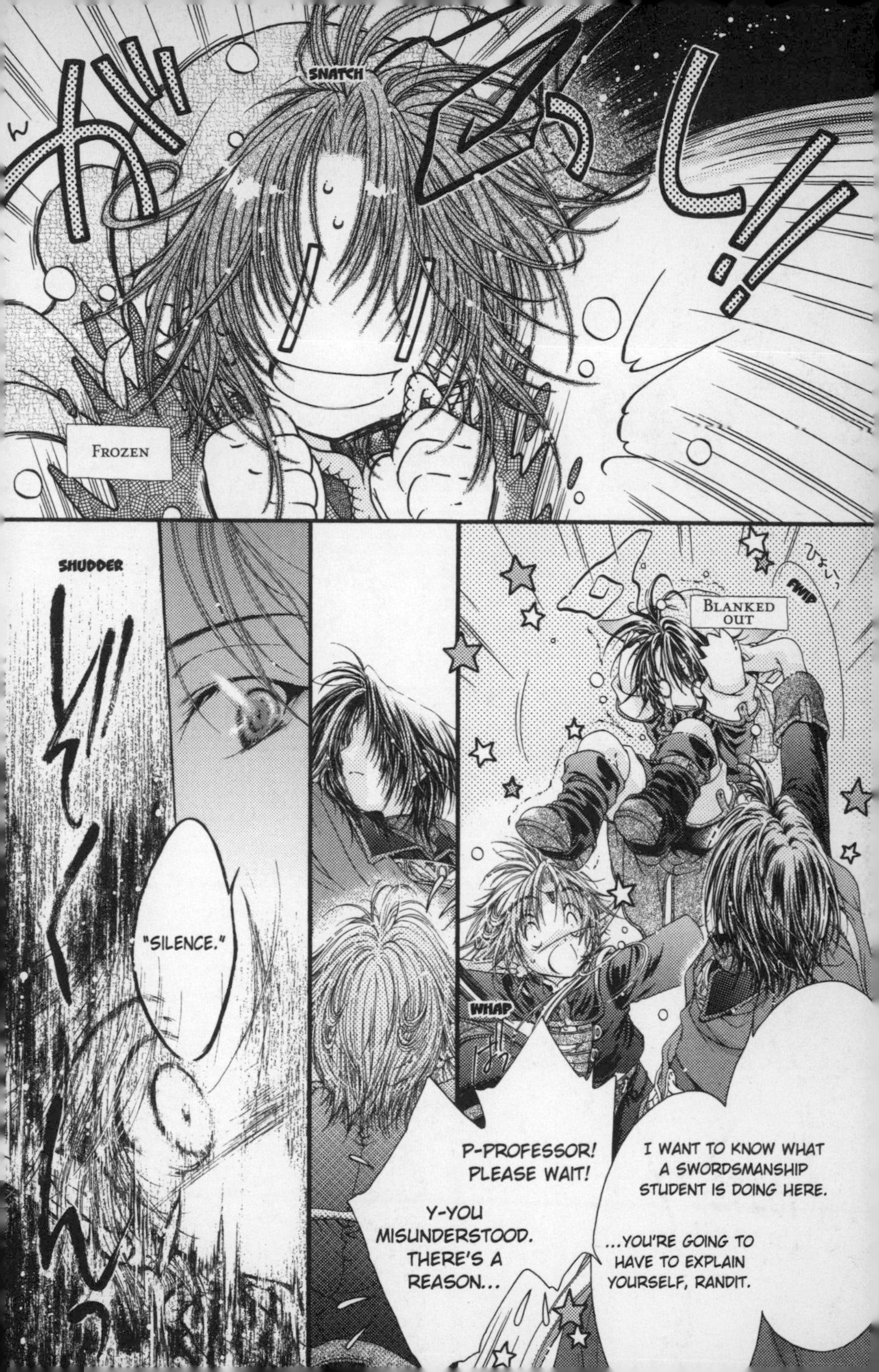
SNATCH
Frozen
FWIP
Blanked out
WHAP
I want to know what a swordsmanship student is doing here.
...you're going to have to explain yourself, Randit.
P-Professor! Please wait!
Y-you misunderstood. There's a reason...
Shudder
"Silence."

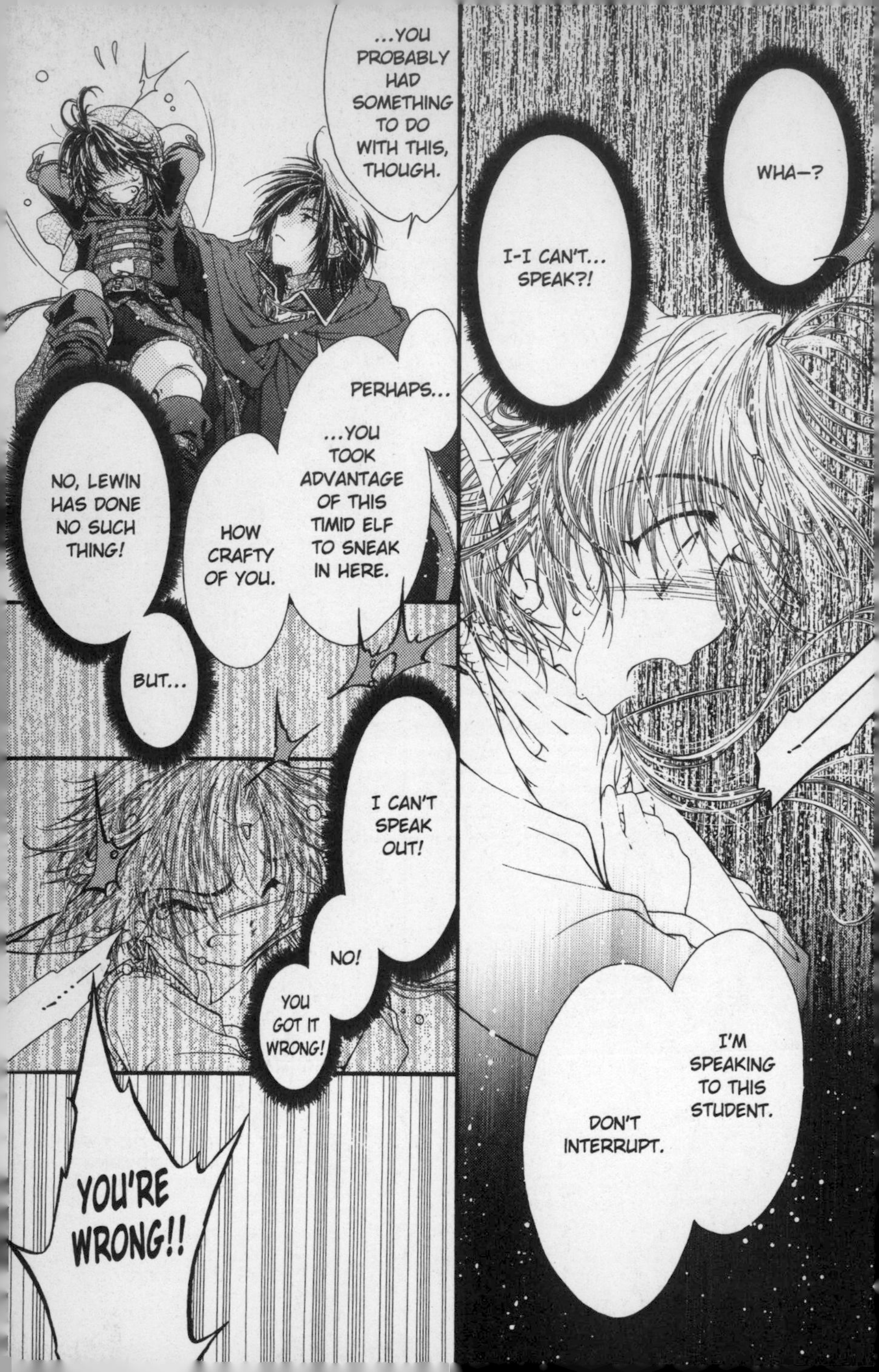

WHA—?
I-I CAN'T... SPEAK?!
I'M SPEAKING TO THIS STUDENT.
DON'T INTERRUPT.
...YOU PROBABLY HAD SOMETHING TO DO WITH THIS, THOUGH.
PERHAPS...
...YOU TOOK ADVANTAGE OF THIS TIMID ELF TO SNEAK IN HERE.
HOW CRAFTY OF YOU.
NO, LEWIN HAS DONE NO SUCH THING!
BUT...
I CAN'T SPEAK OUT!
NO!
YOU GOT IT WRONG!
YOU'RE WRONG!!

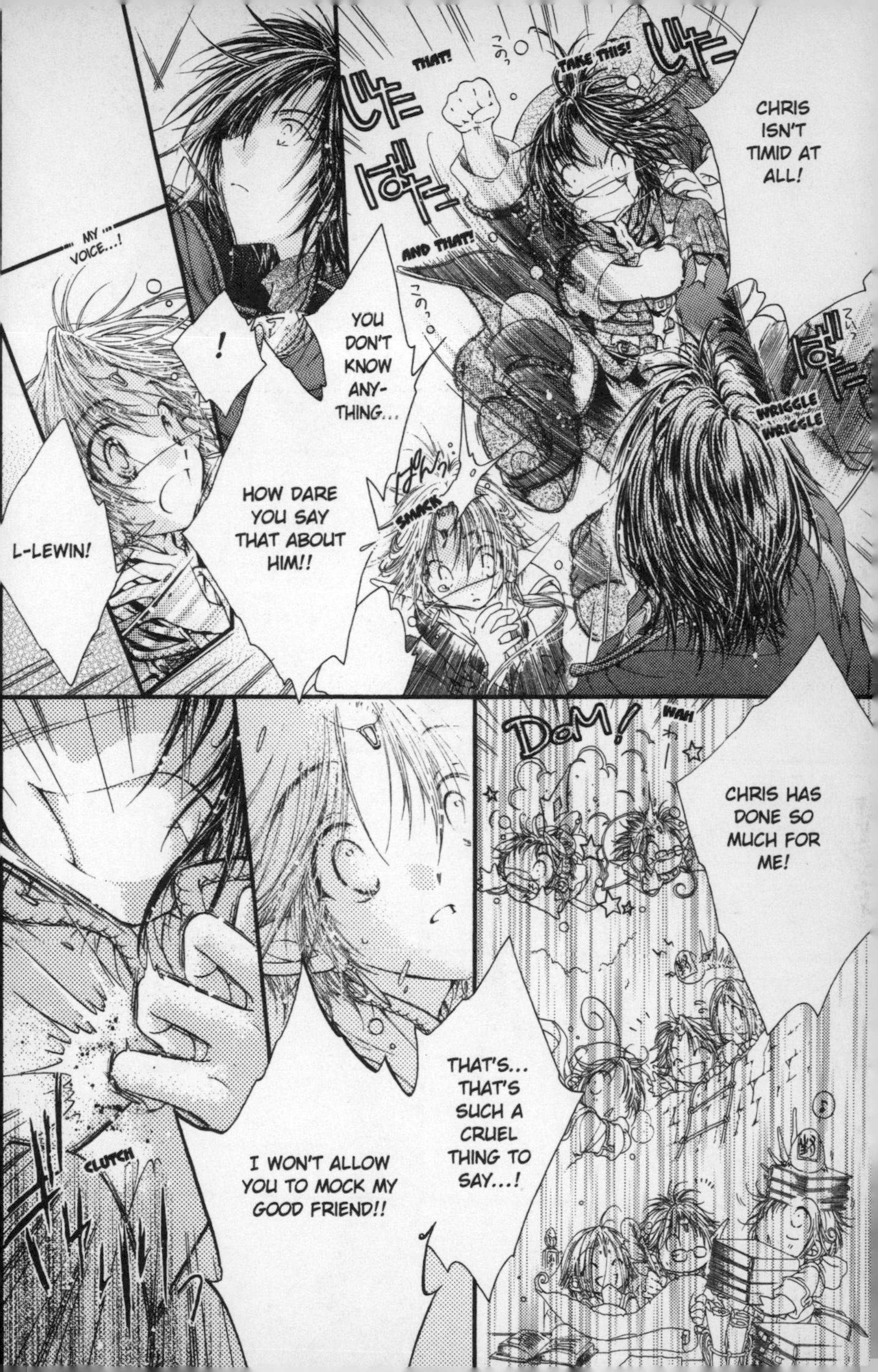
TAKE THIS!
CHRIS ISN'T TIMID AT ALL!
THAT!
AND THAT!
WRIGGLE WRIGGLE
YOU DON'T KNOW ANYTHING...
SMACK
HOW DARE YOU SAY THAT ABOUT HIM!!
MY... VOICE...!
!
L-LEWIN!
DoM!
WAH
CHRIS HAS DONE SO MUCH FOR ME!
THAT'S... THAT'S SUCH A CRUEL THING TO SAY...!
I WON'T ALLOW YOU TO MOCK MY GOOD FRIEND!!
CLUTCH

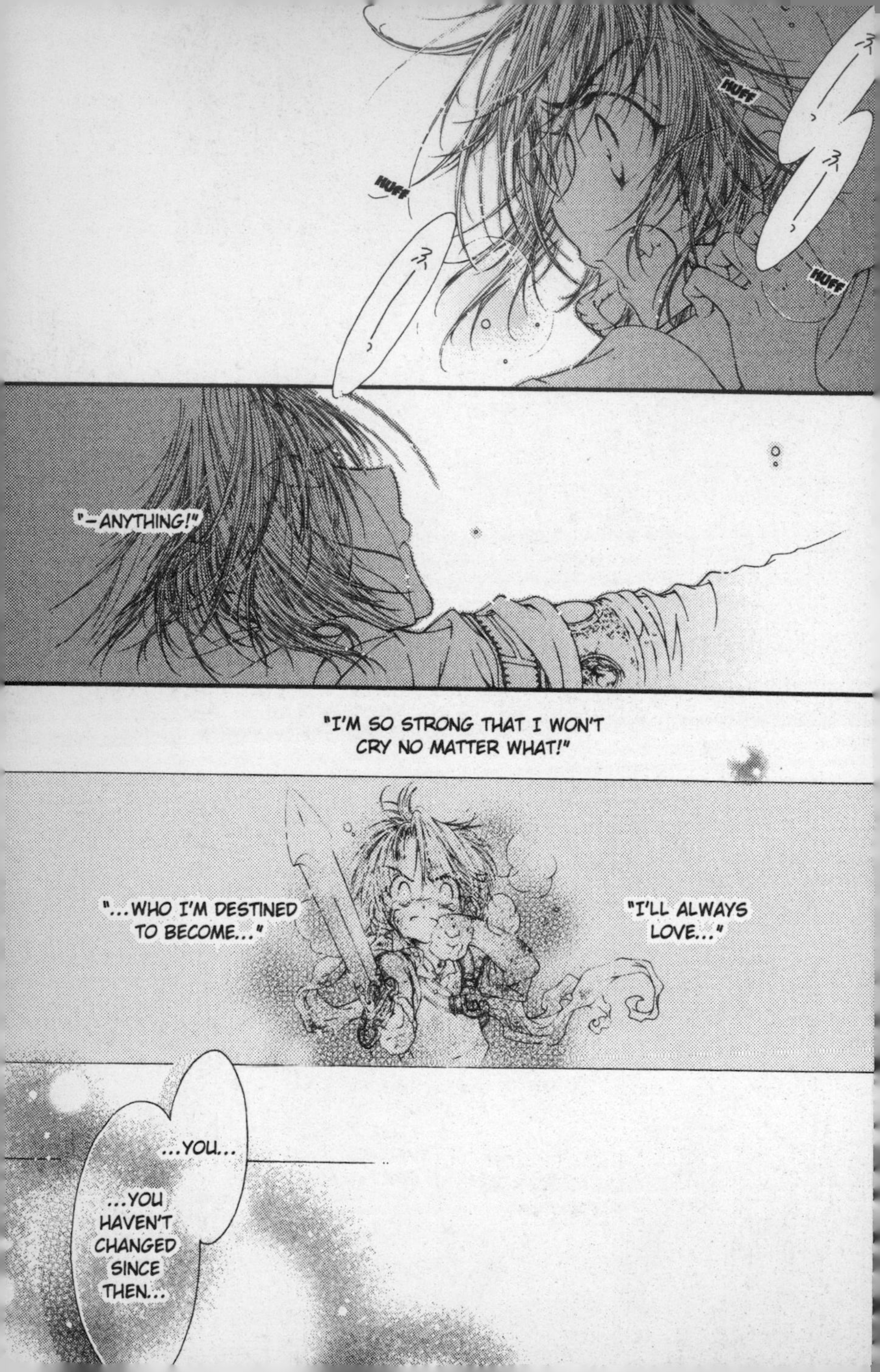

スーっ
スーっ
HUFF
HUFF
HUFF
スーっ
"—ANYTHING!"
"I'M SO STRONG THAT I WON'T CRY NO MATTER WHAT!"
"I'LL ALWAYS LOVE..."
"...WHO I'M DESTINED TO BECOME..."
...YOU...
...YOU HAVEN'T CHANGED SINCE THEN...

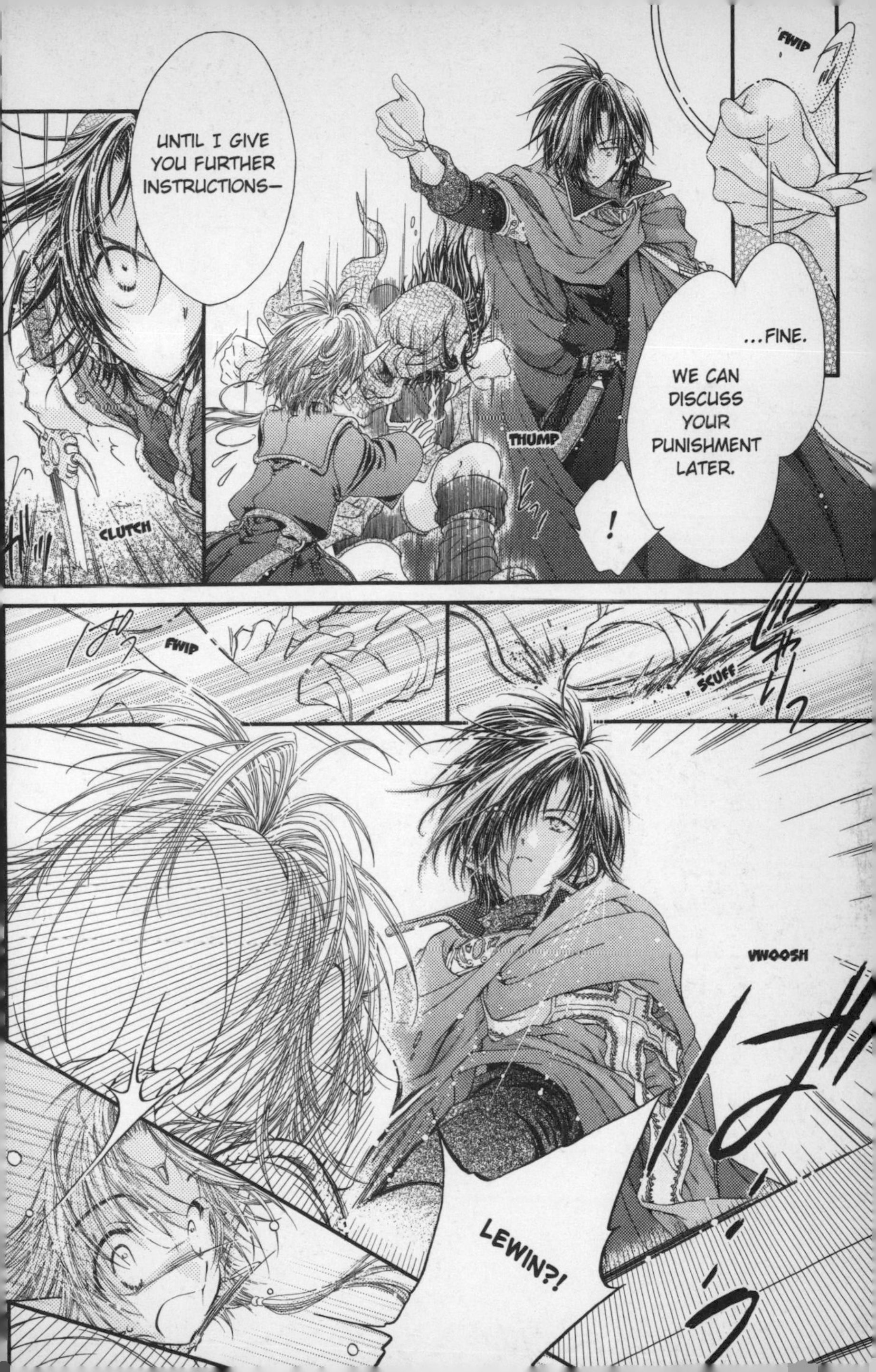
FWIP
...FINE.
WE CAN DISCUSS YOUR PUNISHMENT LATER.
!
THUMP
UNTIL I GIVE YOU FURTHER INSTRUCTIONS—
CLUTCH
SCUFF
FWIP
VWOOSH
LEWIN?!

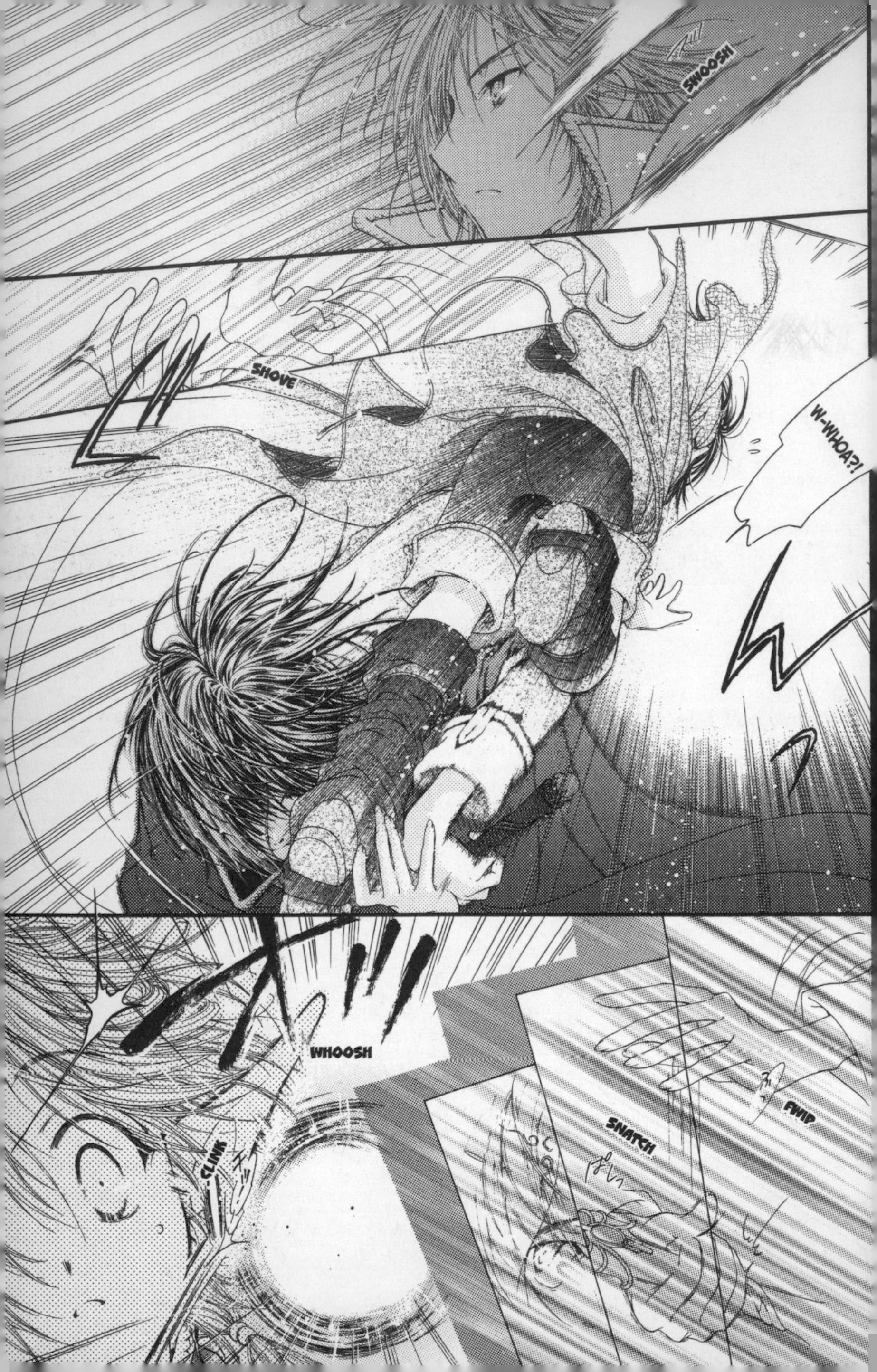
SHOOSH
W-WHOA?!
SHOVE
FWIP
SNATCH
WHOOSH
CLINK

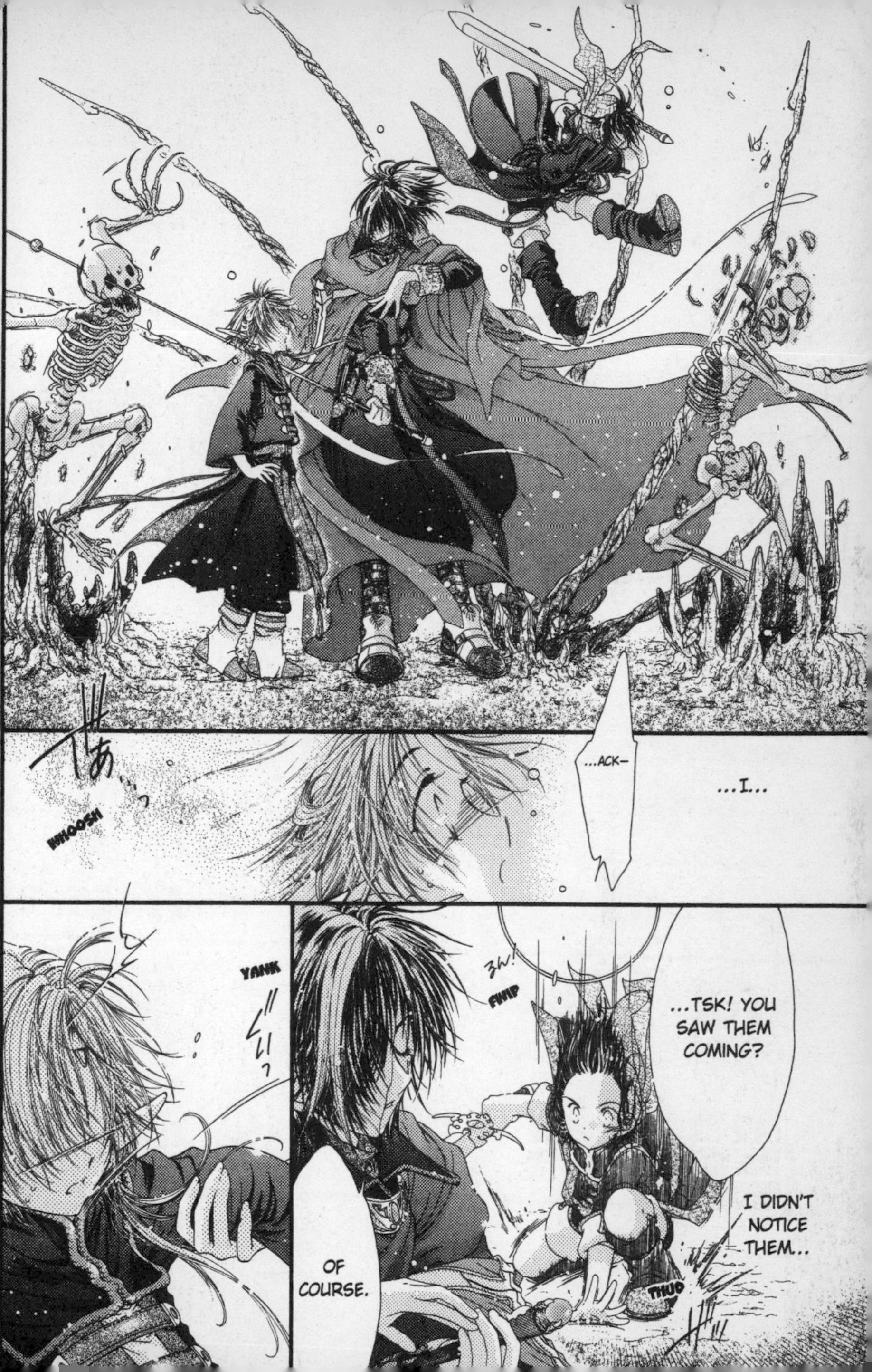
...I...
...ACK–
WHOOSH
...TSK! YOU SAW THEM COMING?
FWIP
I DIDN'T NOTICE THEM...
THUD
OF COURSE.
YANK

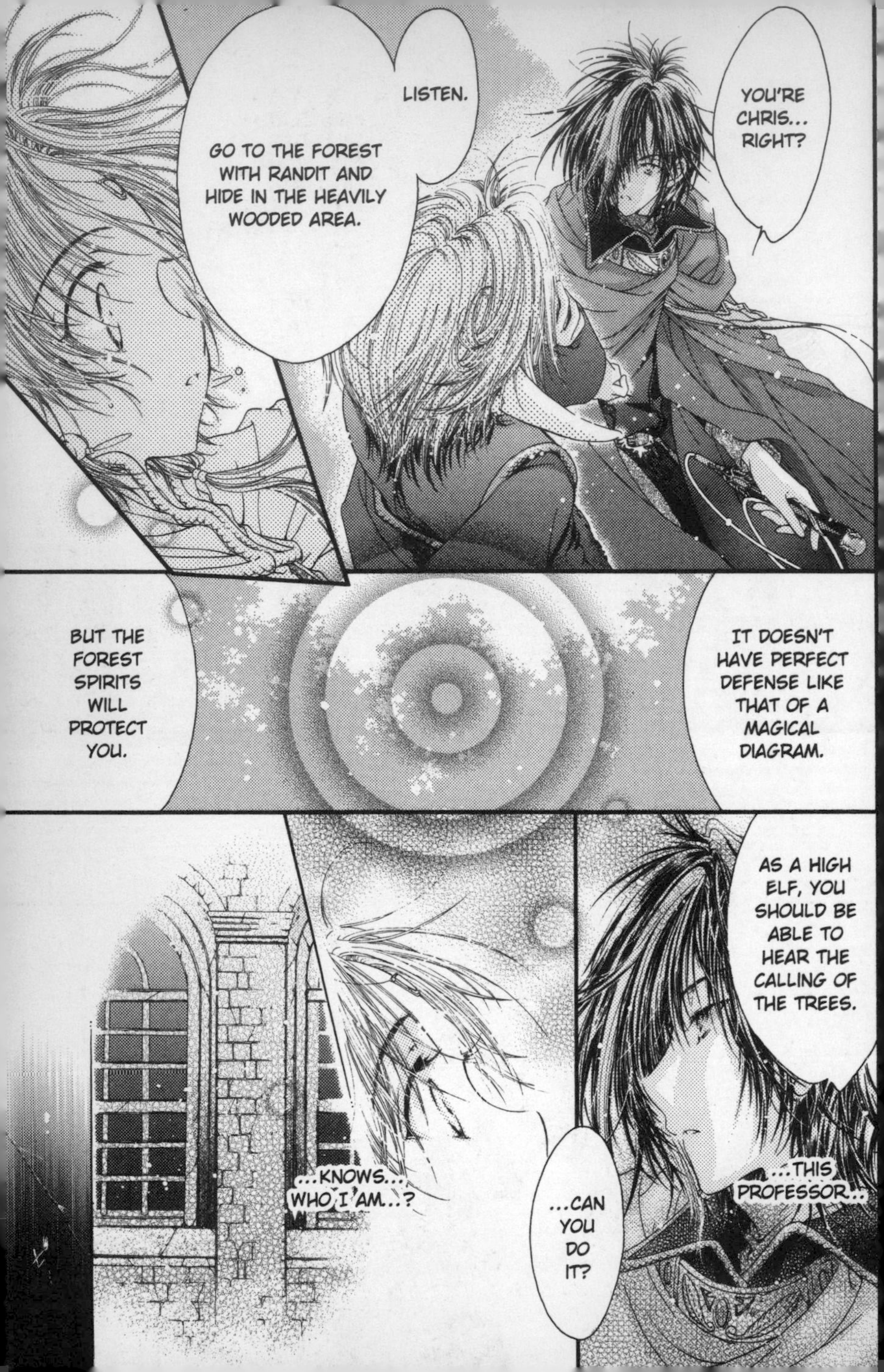
YOU'RE CHRIS... RIGHT?
LISTEN.
GO TO THE FOREST WITH RANDIT AND HIDE IN THE HEAVILY WOODED AREA.
IT DOESN'T HAVE PERFECT DEFENSE LIKE THAT OF A MAGICAL DIAGRAM.
BUT THE FOREST SPIRITS WILL PROTECT YOU.
AS A HIGH ELF, YOU SHOULD BE ABLE TO HEAR THE CALLING OF THE TREES.
...CAN YOU DO IT?
...THIS PROFESSOR...
...KNOWS... WHO I AM...?

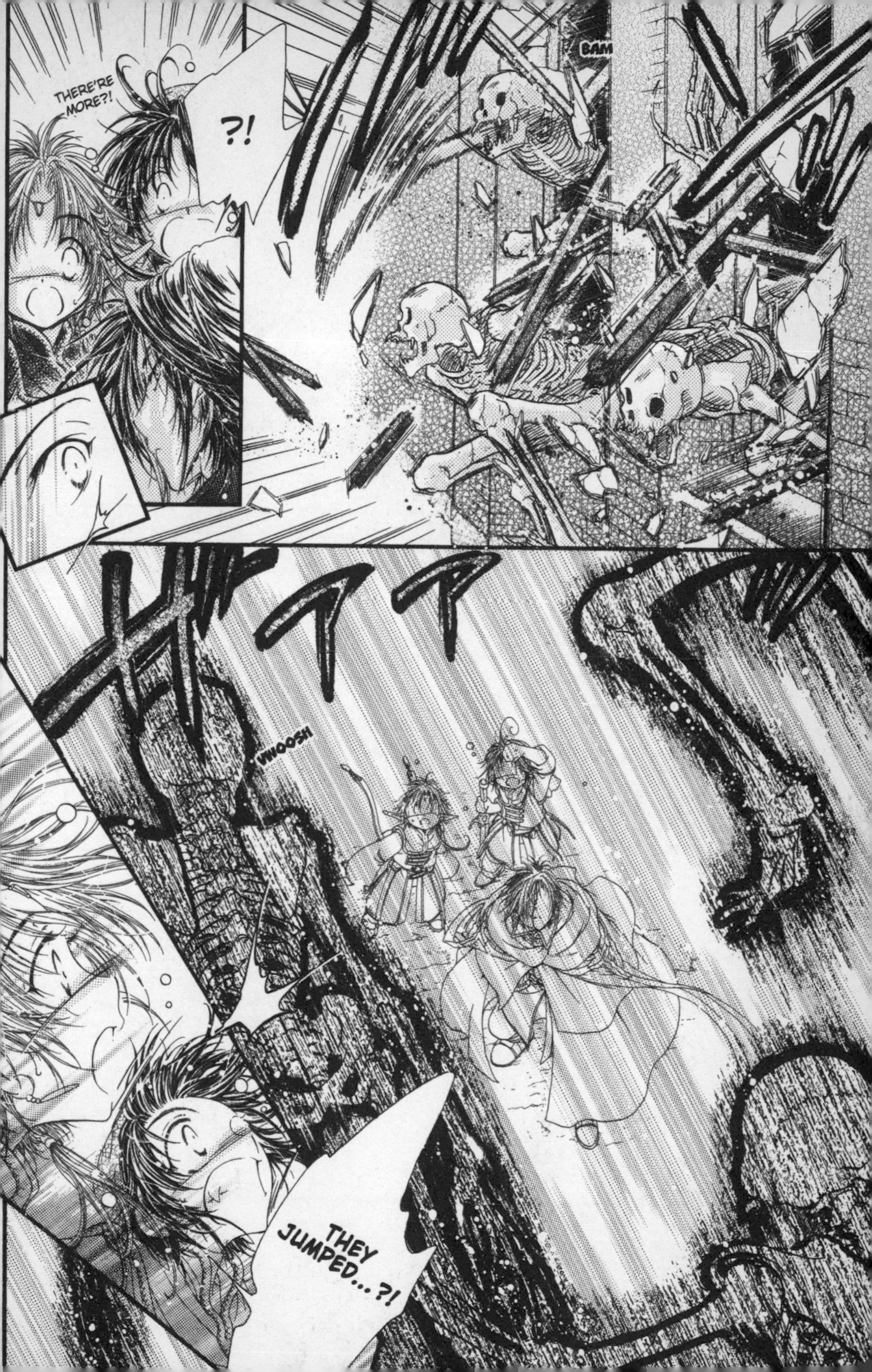
BAM
?!
THERE'RE MORE?!
WHOOSH
THEY JUMPED...?!

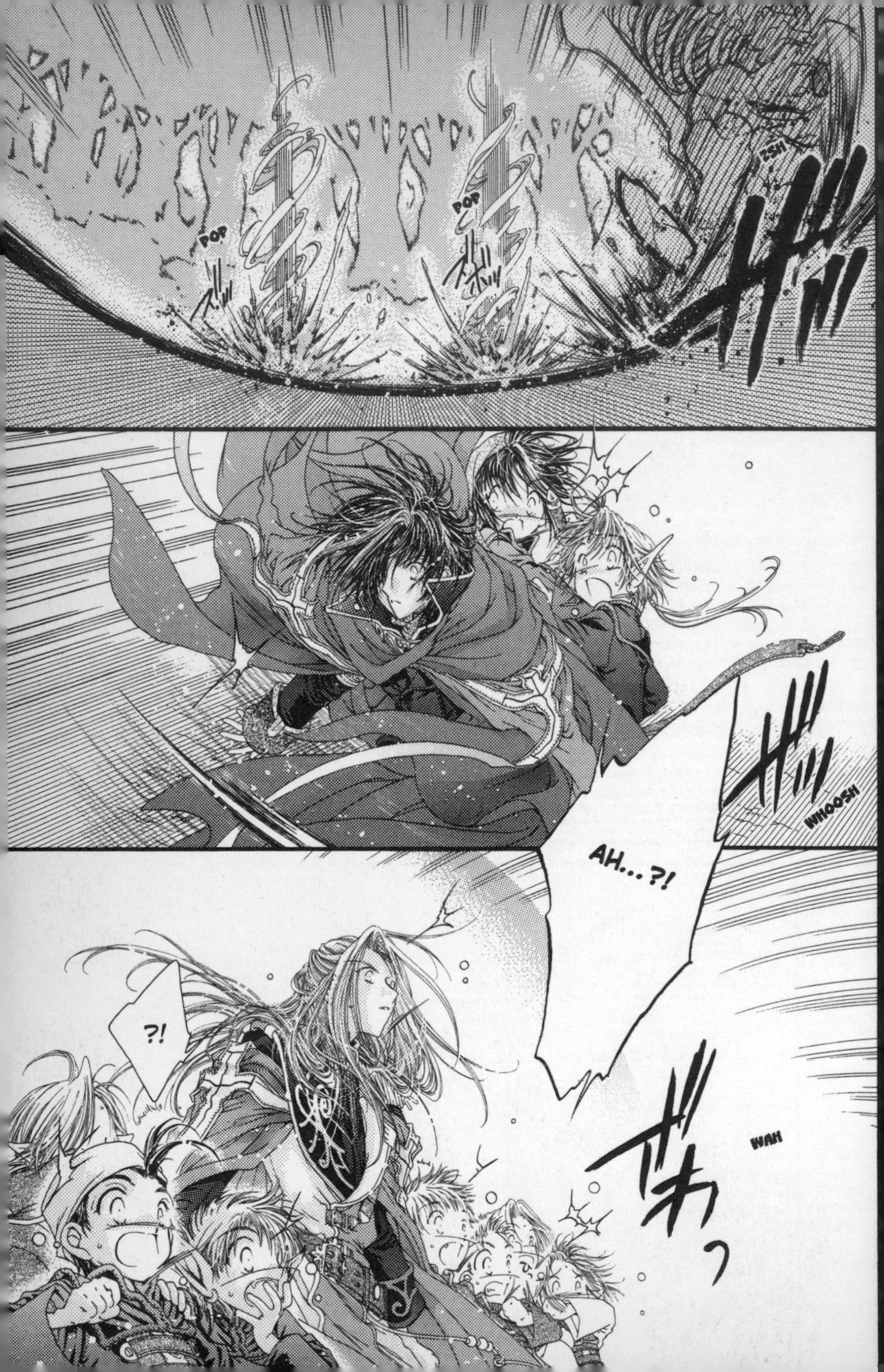
ZSH
POP
POP
WHOOSH
AH...?!
WAH
?!

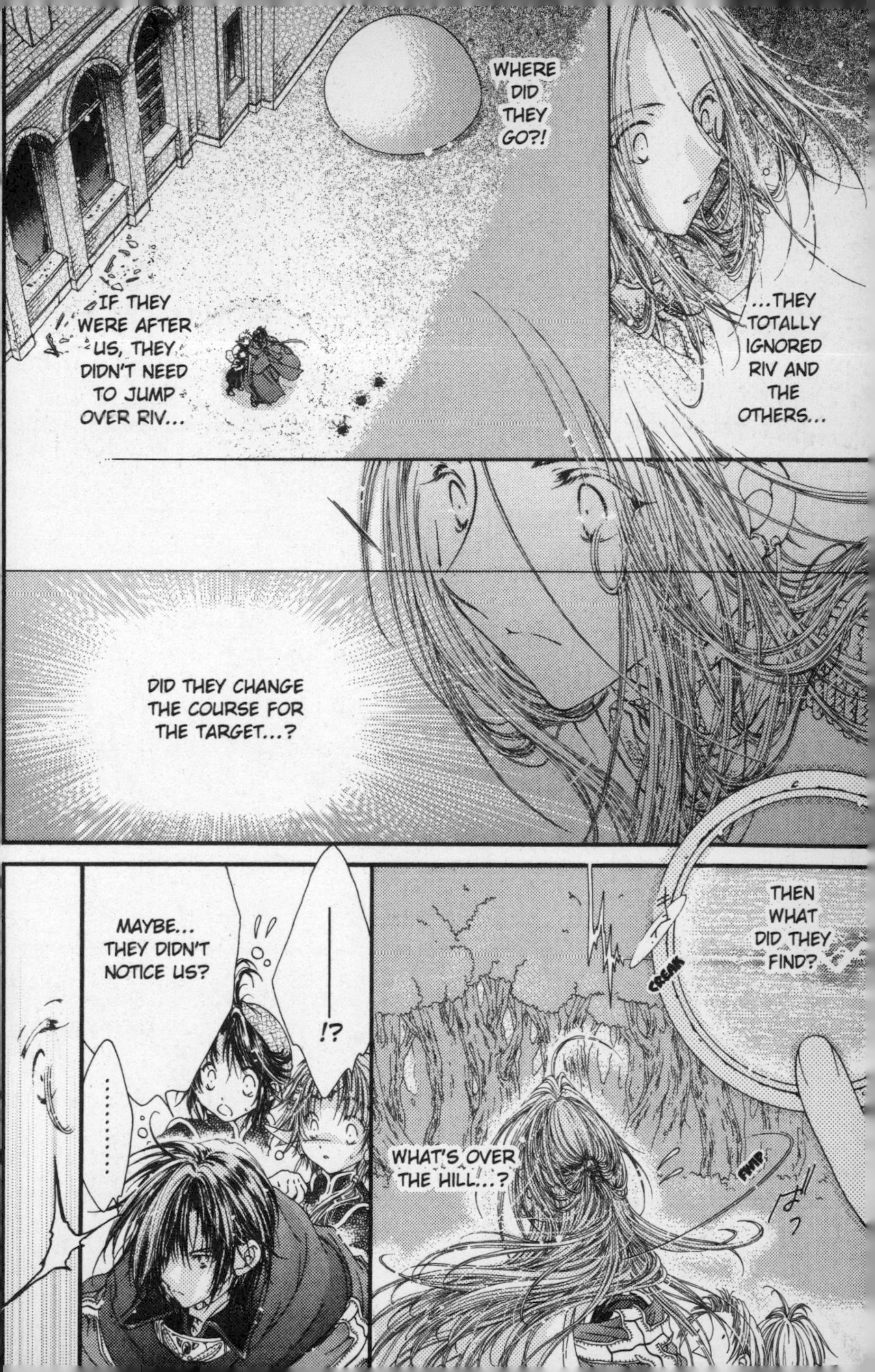
...THEY TOTALLY IGNORED RIV AND THE OTHERS...
WHERE DID THEY GO?!
IF THEY WERE AFTER US, THEY DIDN'T NEED TO JUMP OVER RIV...
DID THEY CHANGE THE COURSE FOR THE TARGET...?
THEN WHAT DID THEY FIND?
CREAK
WHAT'S OVER THE HILL...?
FWIP
!?
MAYBE... THEY DIDN'T NOTICE US?
......

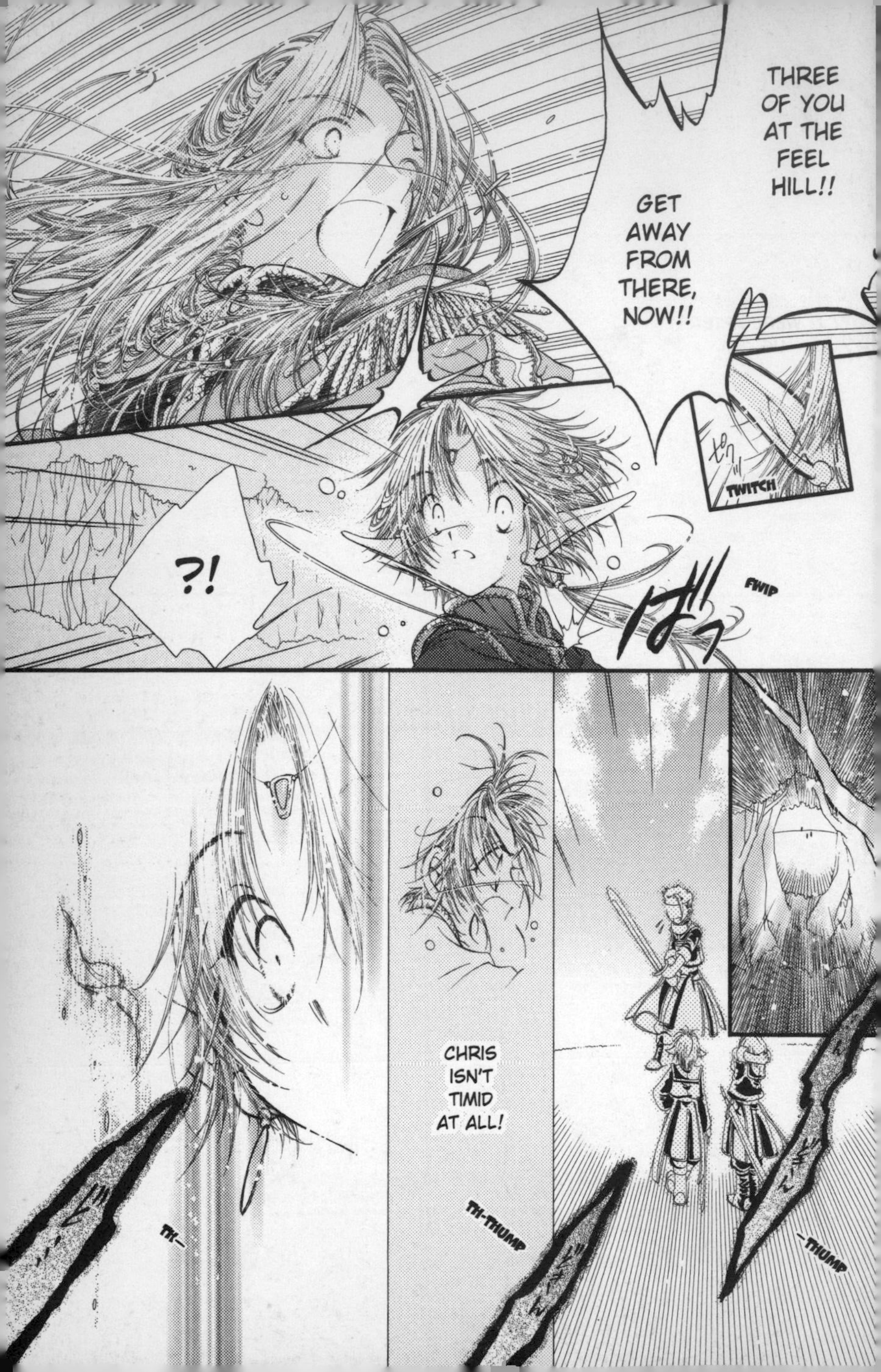
THREE OF YOU AT THE FEEL HILL!!
GET AWAY FROM THERE, NOW!!
TWITCH
FWIP
?!
-THUMP
CHRIS ISN'T TIMID AT ALL!
TH-THUMP
TH-

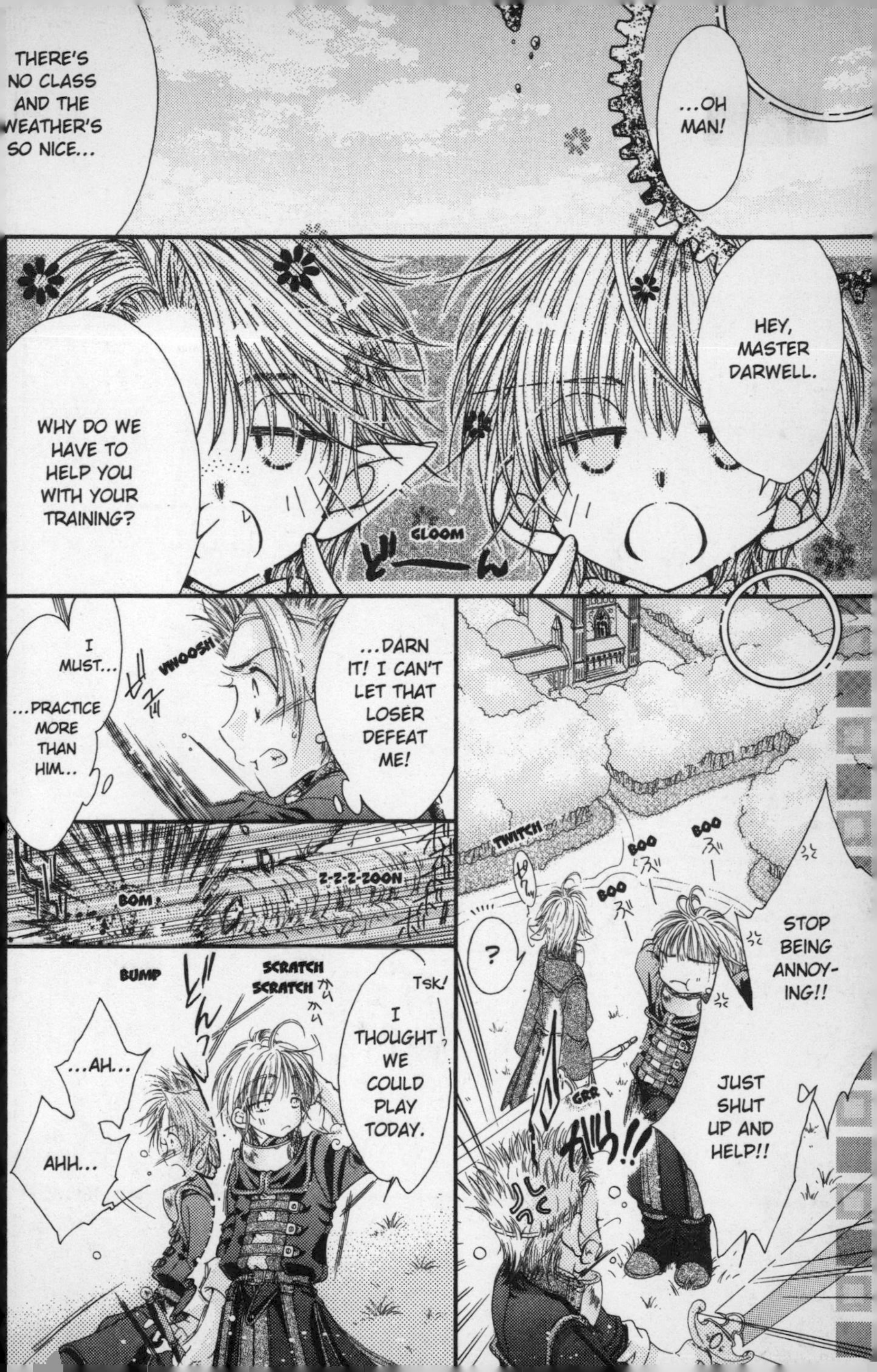
...OH MAN!
THERE'S NO CLASS AND THE WEATHER'S SO NICE...
HEY, MASTER DARWELL.
WHY DO WE HAVE TO HELP YOU WITH YOUR TRAINING?
GLOOM
TWITCH
BOO
BOO
BOO
?
STOP BEING ANNOY-ING!!
JUST SHUT UP AND HELP!!
GRR
...DARN IT! I CAN'T LET THAT LOSER DEFEAT ME!
WHOOSH
I MUST...
...PRACTICE MORE THAN HIM...
Z-Z-Z-ZOON
BOM
Tsk!
I THOUGHT WE COULD PLAY TODAY.
SCRATCH SCRATCH
BUMP
...AH...
AHH...

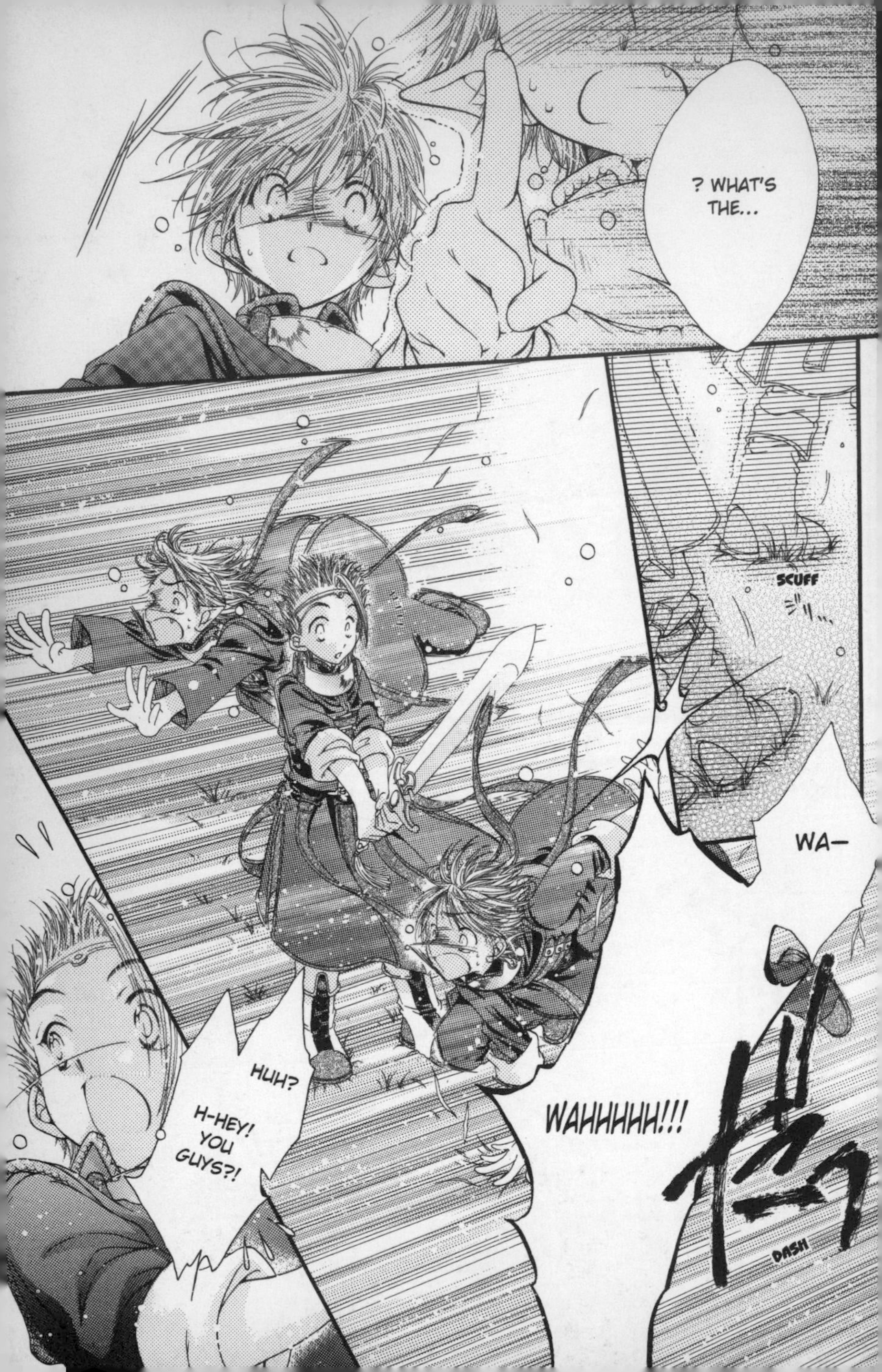
? WHAT'S THE...
SCUFF
WA—
WAHHHHH!!!
DASH
HUH?
H-HEY! YOU GUYS?!

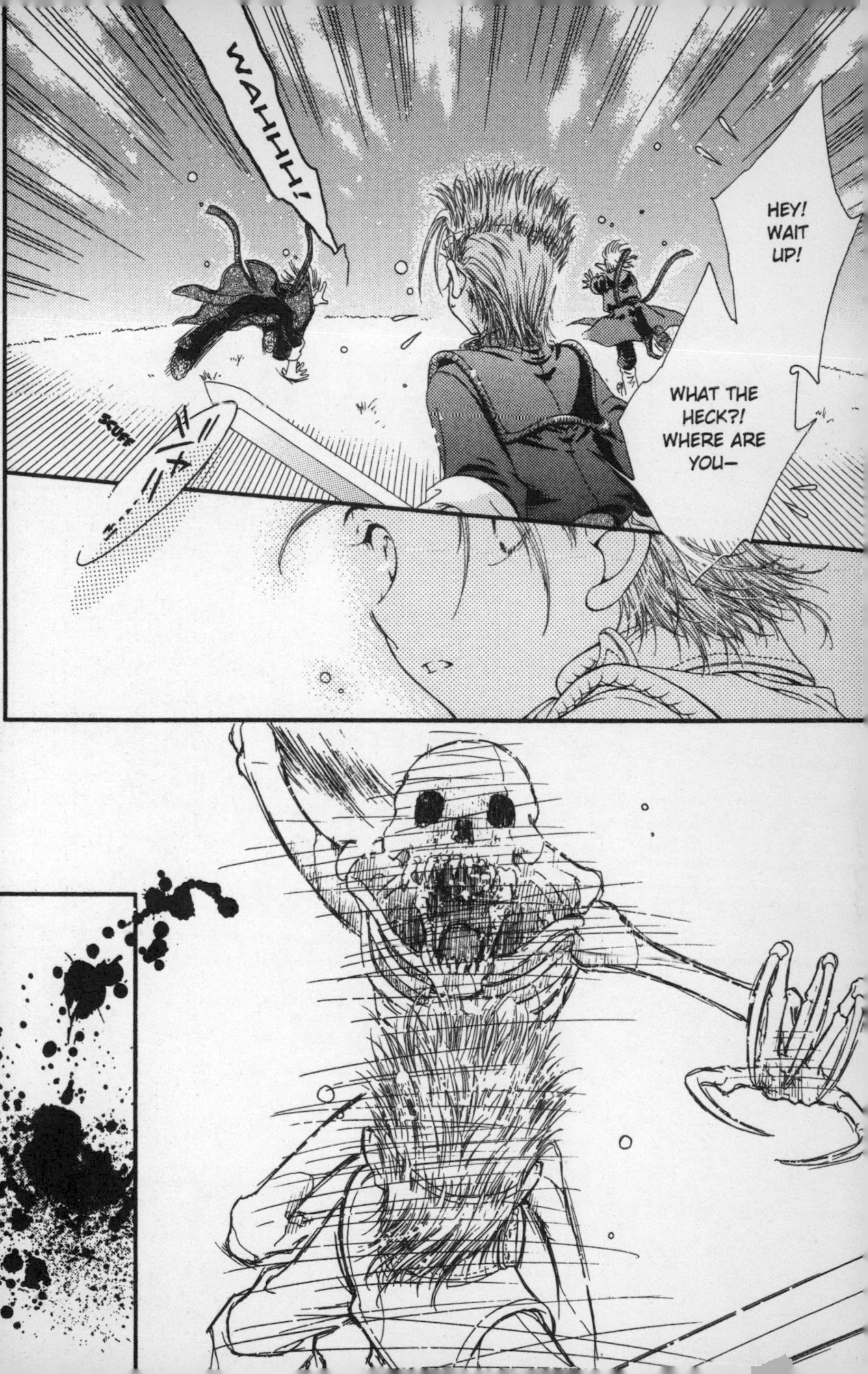
HEY! WAIT UP!
WAHHHH!
WHAT THE HECK?! WHERE ARE YOU—
SCUFF

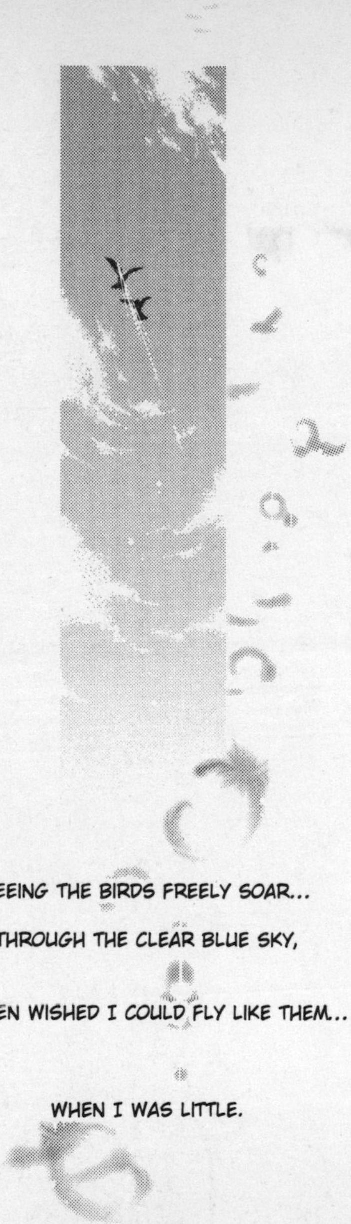
SEEING THE BIRDS FREELY SOAR...
THROUGH THE CLEAR BLUE SKY,
I OFTEN WISHED I COULD FLY LIKE THEM...
WHEN I WAS LITTLE.

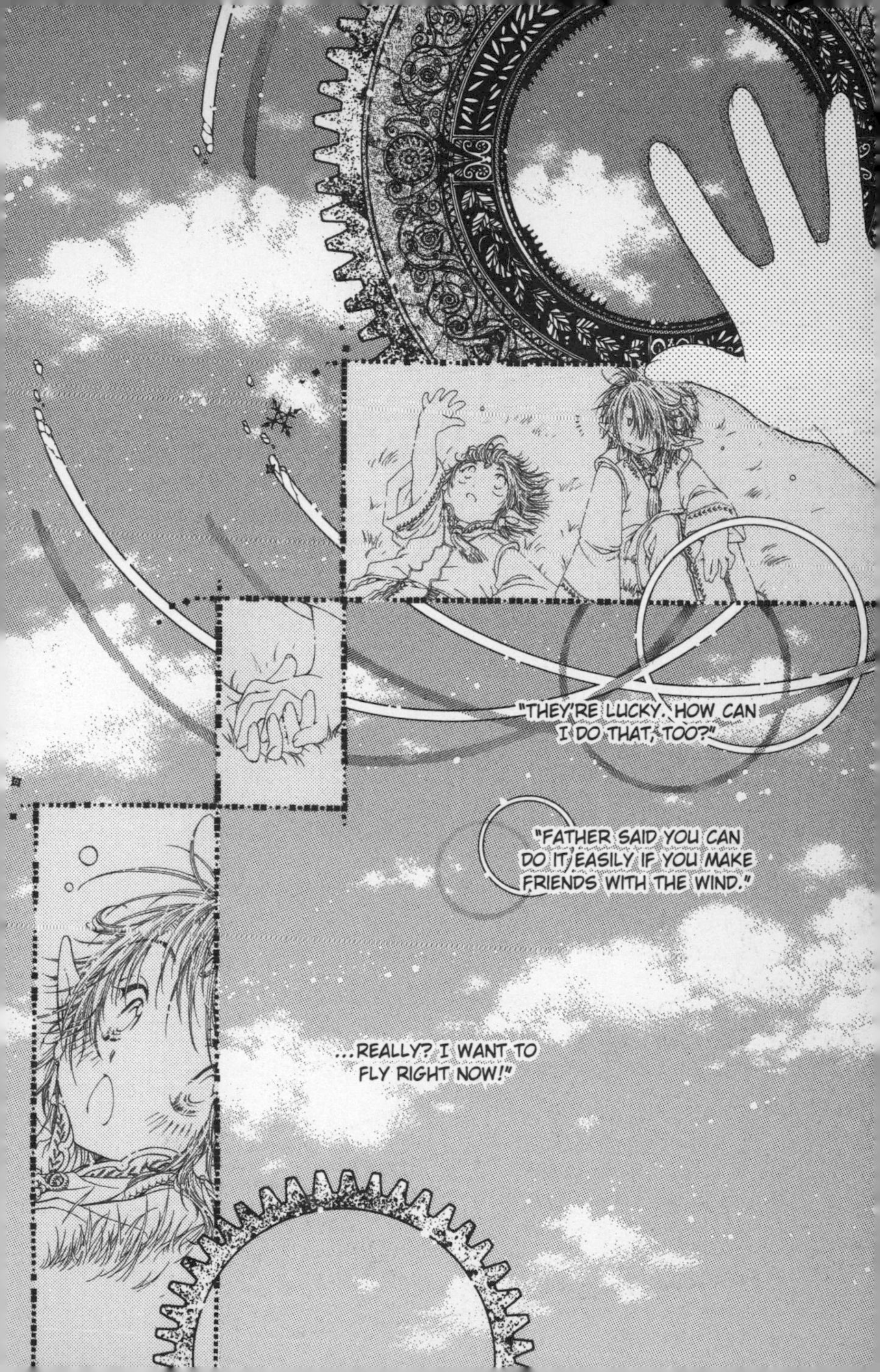
"THEY'RE LUCKY. HOW CAN I DO THAT, TOO?"
"FATHER SAID YOU CAN DO IT EASILY IF YOU MAKE FRIENDS WITH THE WIND."
...REALLY? I WANT TO FLY RIGHT NOW!"

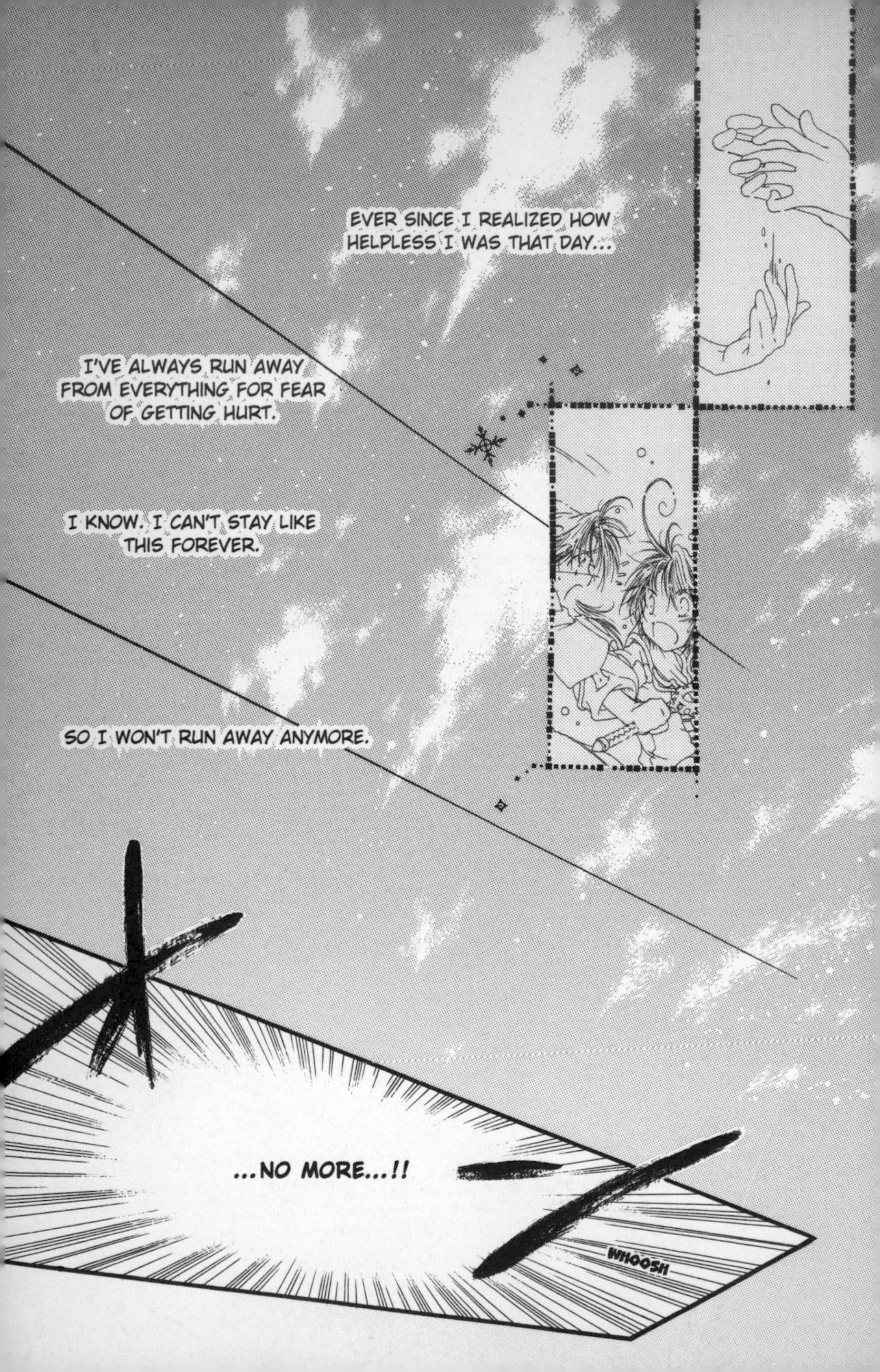
EVER SINCE I REALIZED HOW HELPLESS I WAS THAT DAY...
I'VE ALWAYS RUN AWAY FROM EVERYTHING FOR FEAR OF GETTING HURT.
I KNOW. I CAN'T STAY LIKE THIS FOREVER.
SO I WON'T RUN AWAY ANYMORE.
...NO MORE...!!
WHOOSH

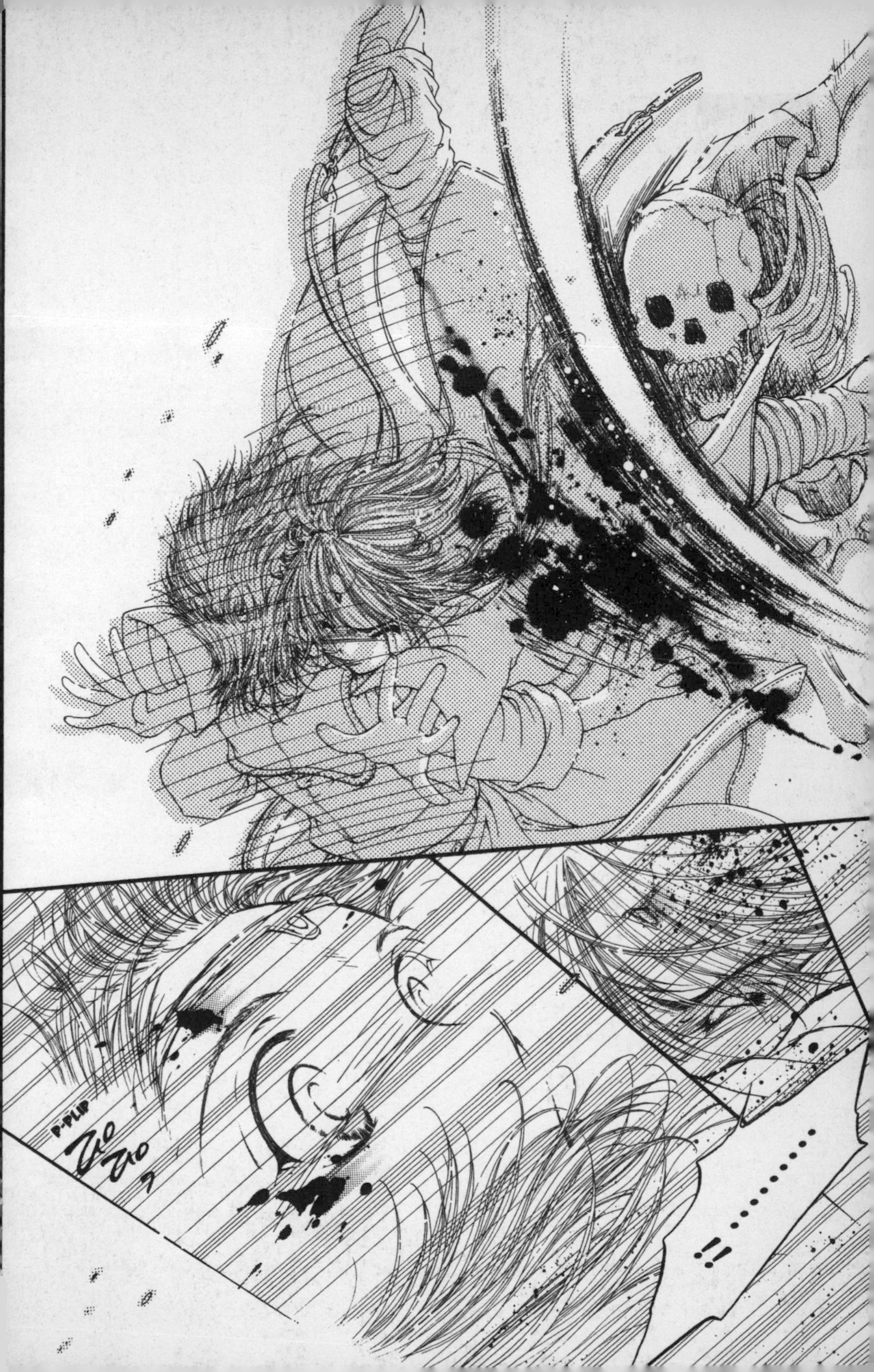
....
!!
P-PLIP

6th Bell: Undefeated

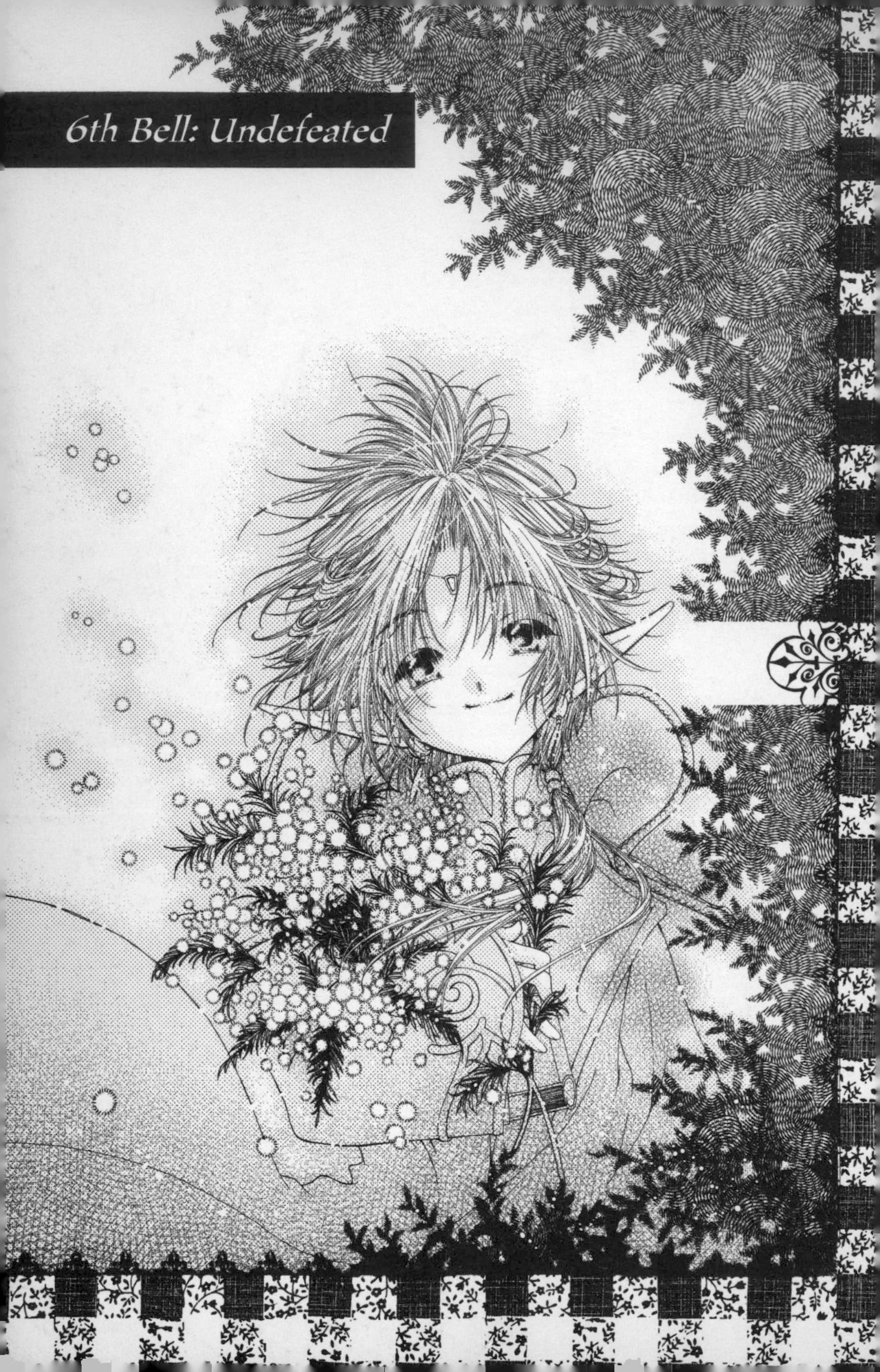

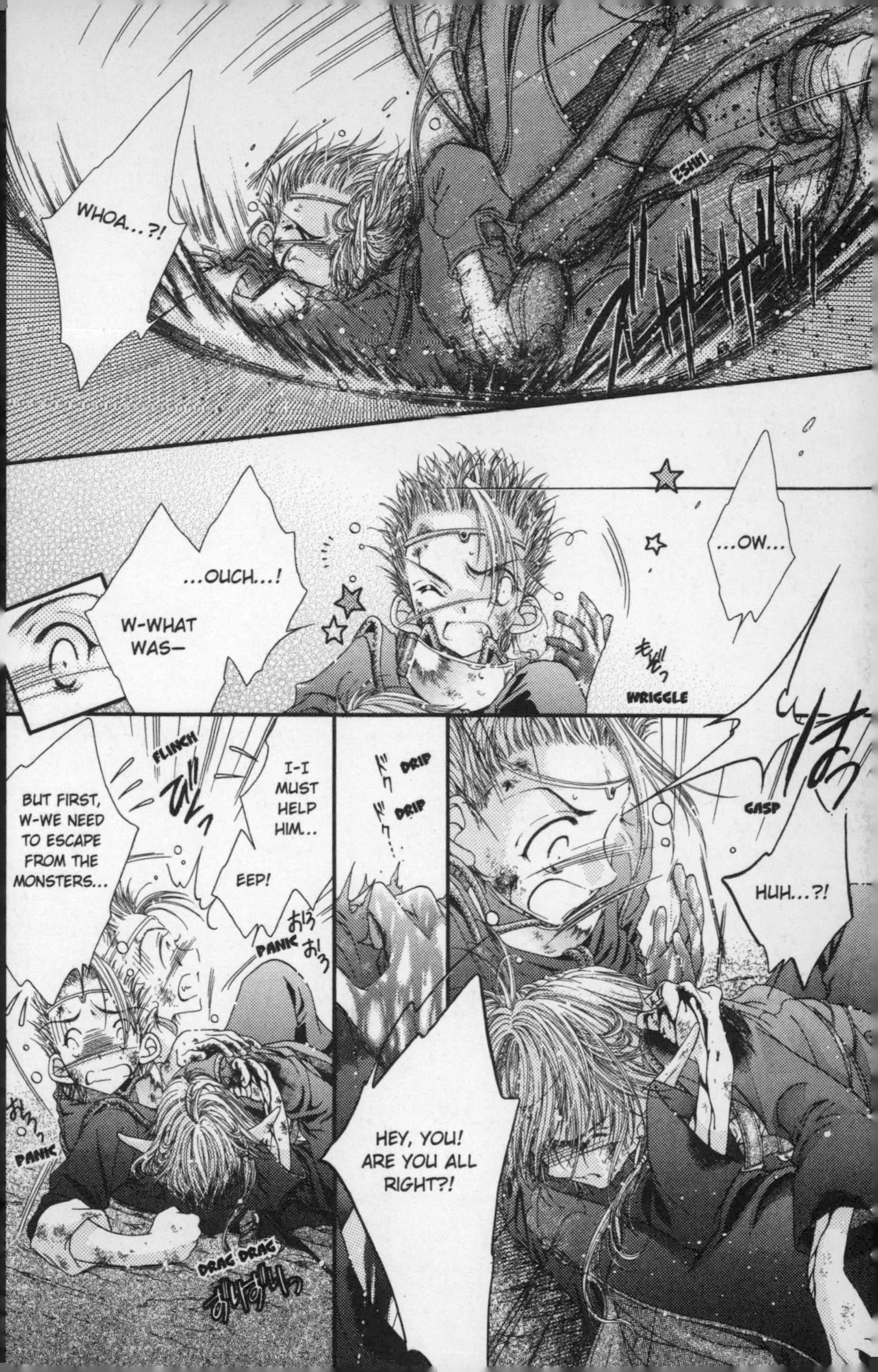
ZSHH
WHOA...?!
...OW...
WRIGGLE
...OUCH...!
W-WHAT WAS—
GASP
HUH...?!
HEY, YOU! ARE YOU ALL RIGHT?!
DRIP
DRIP
I-I MUST HELP HIM...
FLINCH
EEP!
BUT FIRST, W-WE NEED TO ESCAPE FROM THE MONSTERS...
PANIC
PANIC
DRAG DRAG

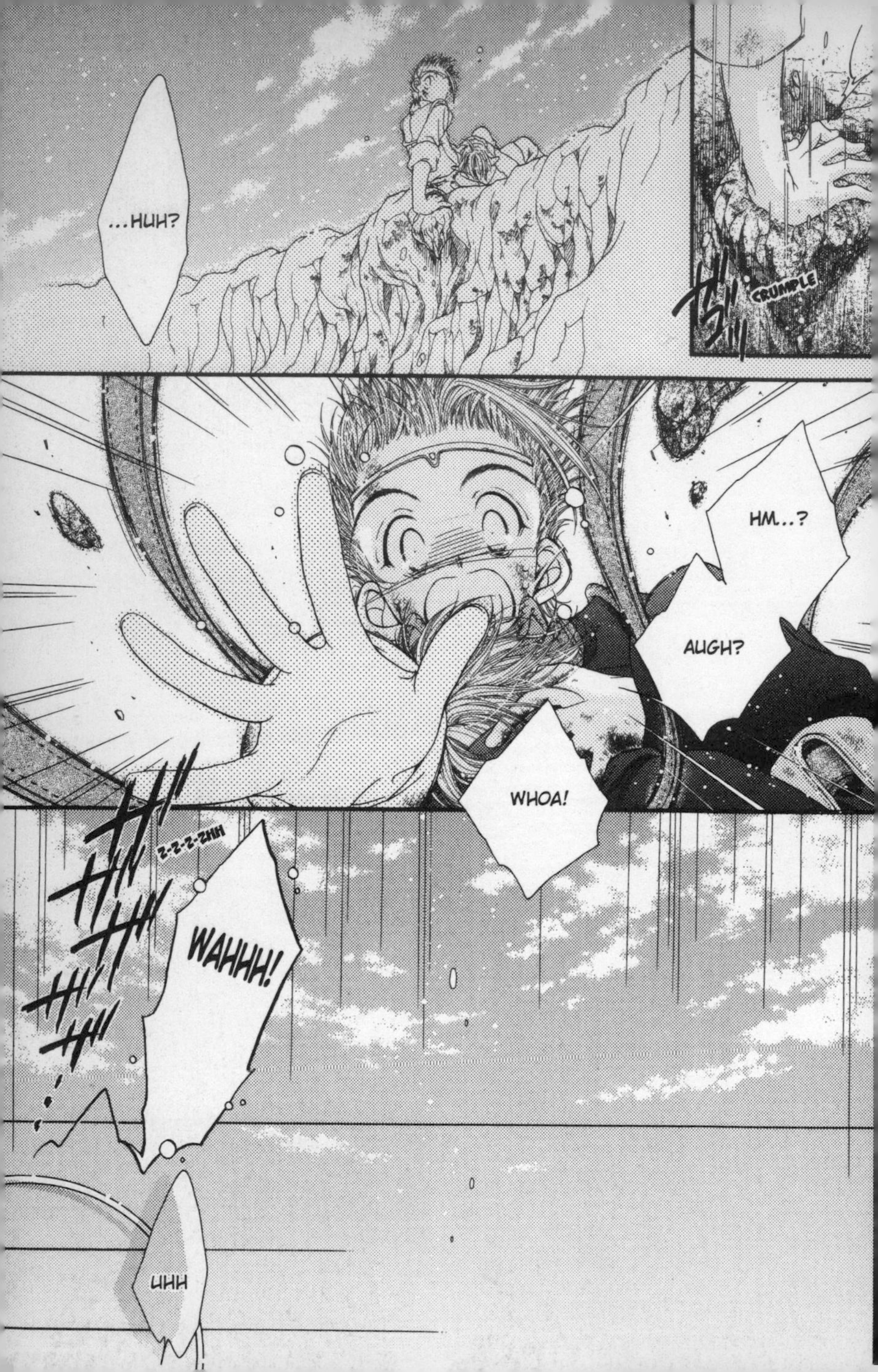
CRUMPLE
...HUH?
HM..?
AUGH?
WHOA!
Z-Z-Z-ZHH
WAHHH!
UHH

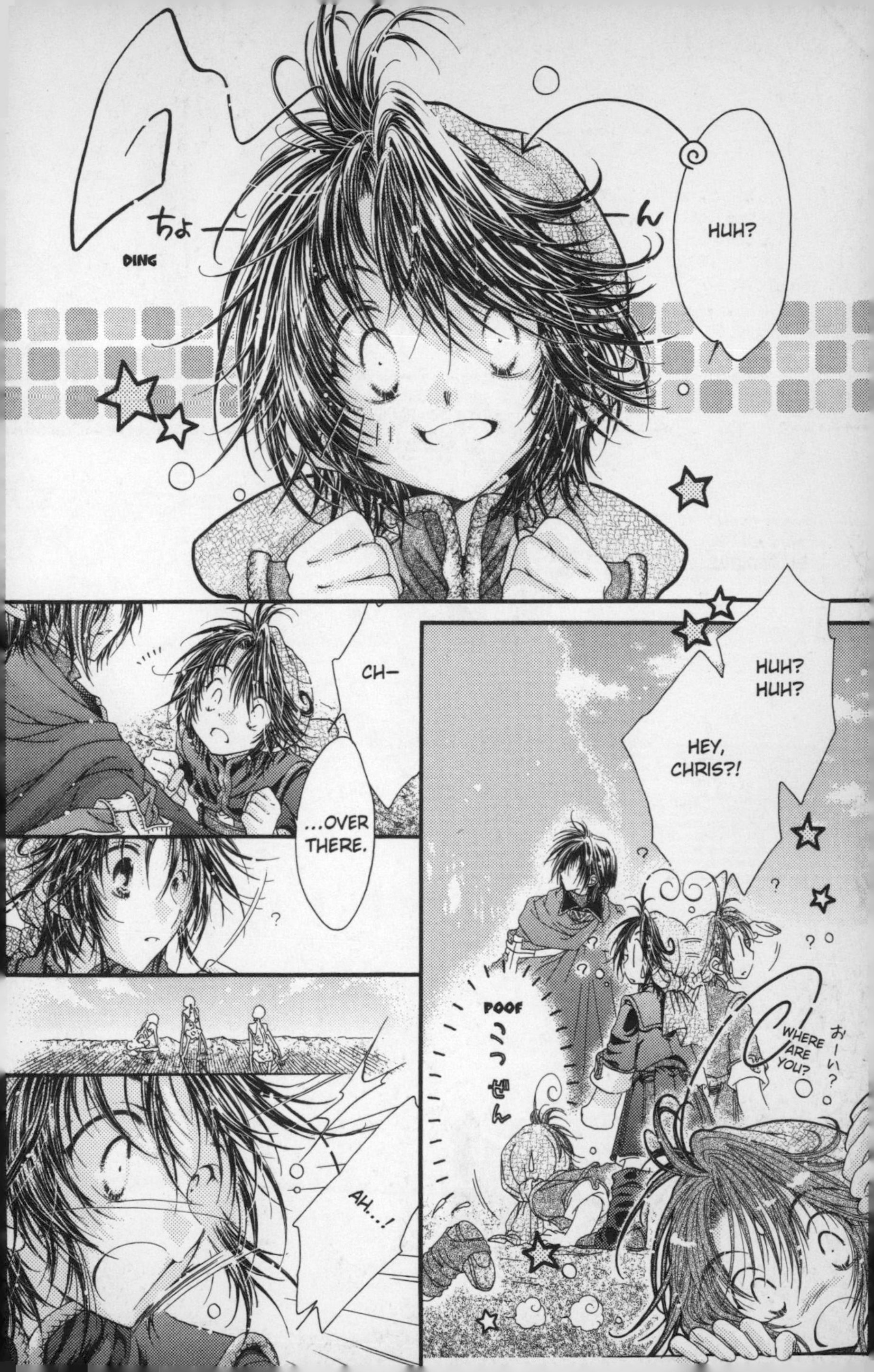
ちょーーん
DING
HUH?
HUH? HUH?
HEY, CHRIS?!
WHERE ARE YOU?
おーい?
POOF
こつぜん
CH—
...OVER THERE.
AH...!

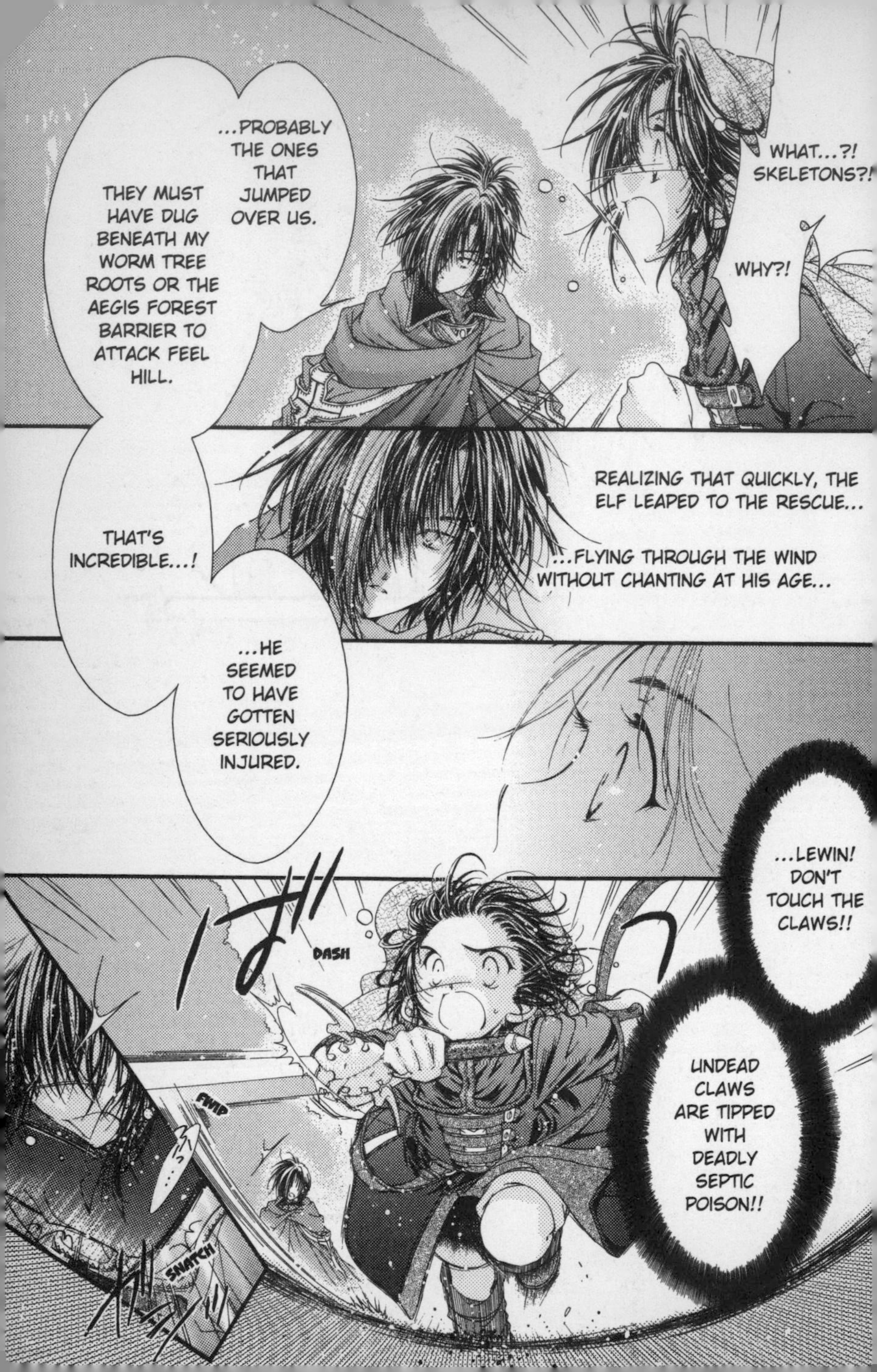
WHAT...?! SKELETONS?!
WHY?!
...PROBABLY THE ONES THAT JUMPED OVER US.
THEY MUST HAVE DUG BENEATH MY WORM TREE ROOTS OR THE AEGIS FOREST BARRIER TO ATTACK FEEL HILL.
REALIZING THAT QUICKLY, THE ELF LEAPED TO THE RESCUE...
...FLYING THROUGH THE WIND WITHOUT CHANTING AT HIS AGE...
THAT'S INCREDIBLE...!
...HE SEEMED TO HAVE GOTTEN SERIOUSLY INJURED.
...LEWIN! DON'T TOUCH THE CLAWS!!
UNDEAD CLAWS ARE TIPPED WITH DEADLY SEPTIC POISON!!
DASH
FWIP
SNATCH

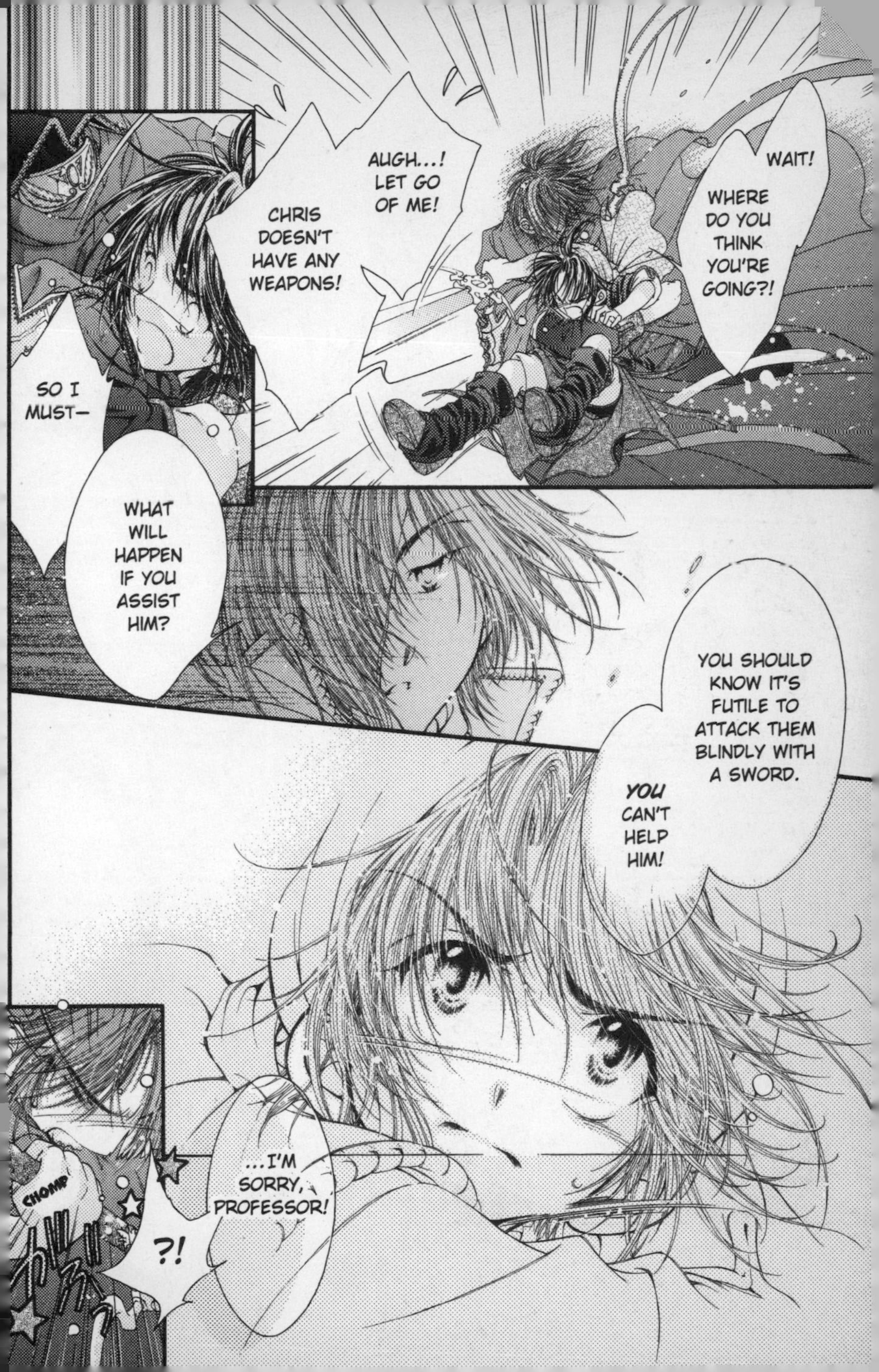
WAIT!
WHERE DO YOU THINK YOU'RE GOING?!
AUGH...! LET GO OF ME!
CHRIS DOESN'T HAVE ANY WEAPONS!
SO I MUST—
WHAT WILL HAPPEN IF YOU ASSIST HIM?
YOU SHOULD KNOW IT'S FUTILE TO ATTACK THEM BLINDLY WITH A SWORD.
YOU CAN'T HELP HIM!
...I'M SORRY, PROFESSOR!
?!
CHOMP

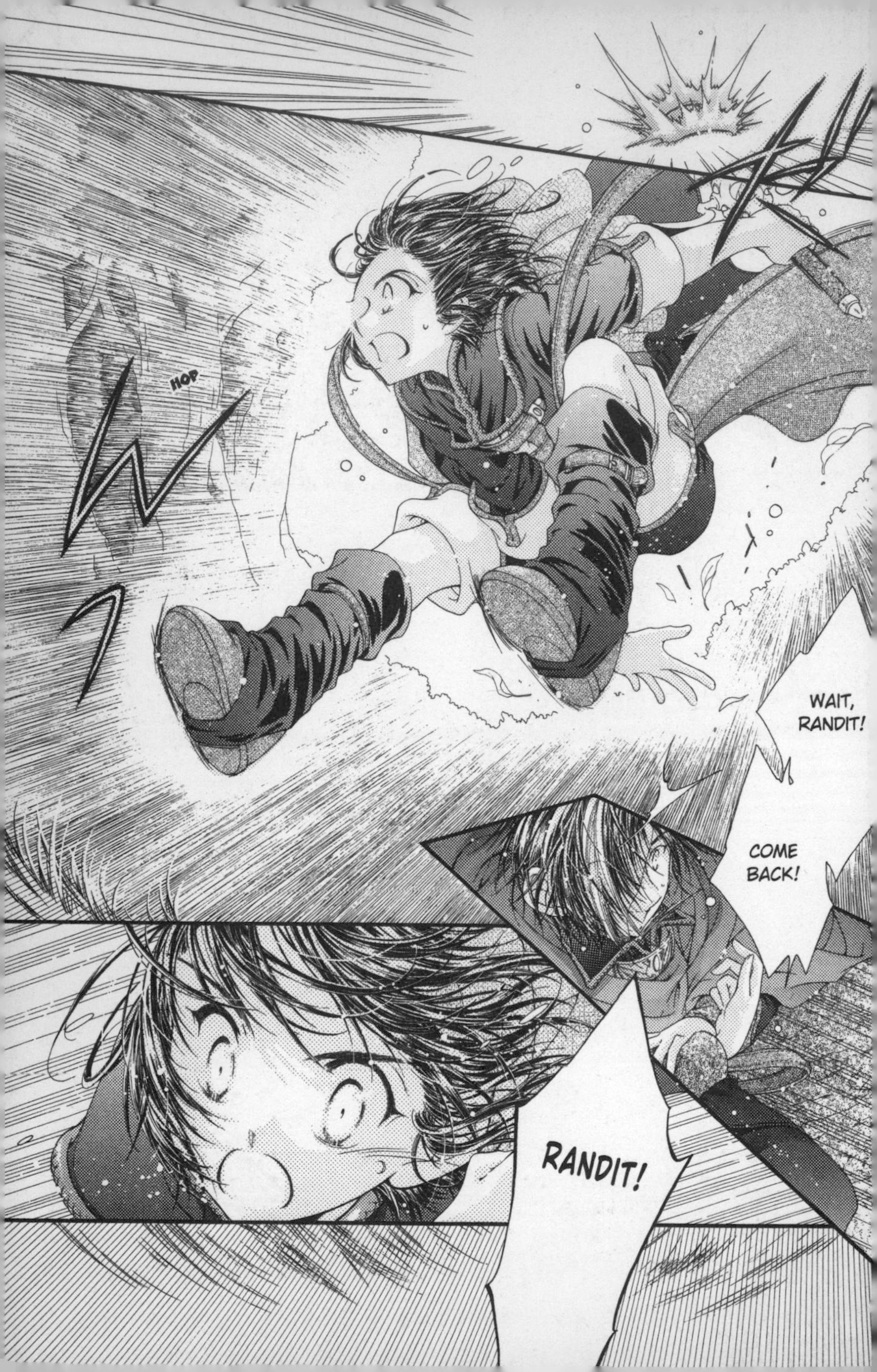
HOP
WAIT, RANDIT!
COME BACK!
RANDIT!

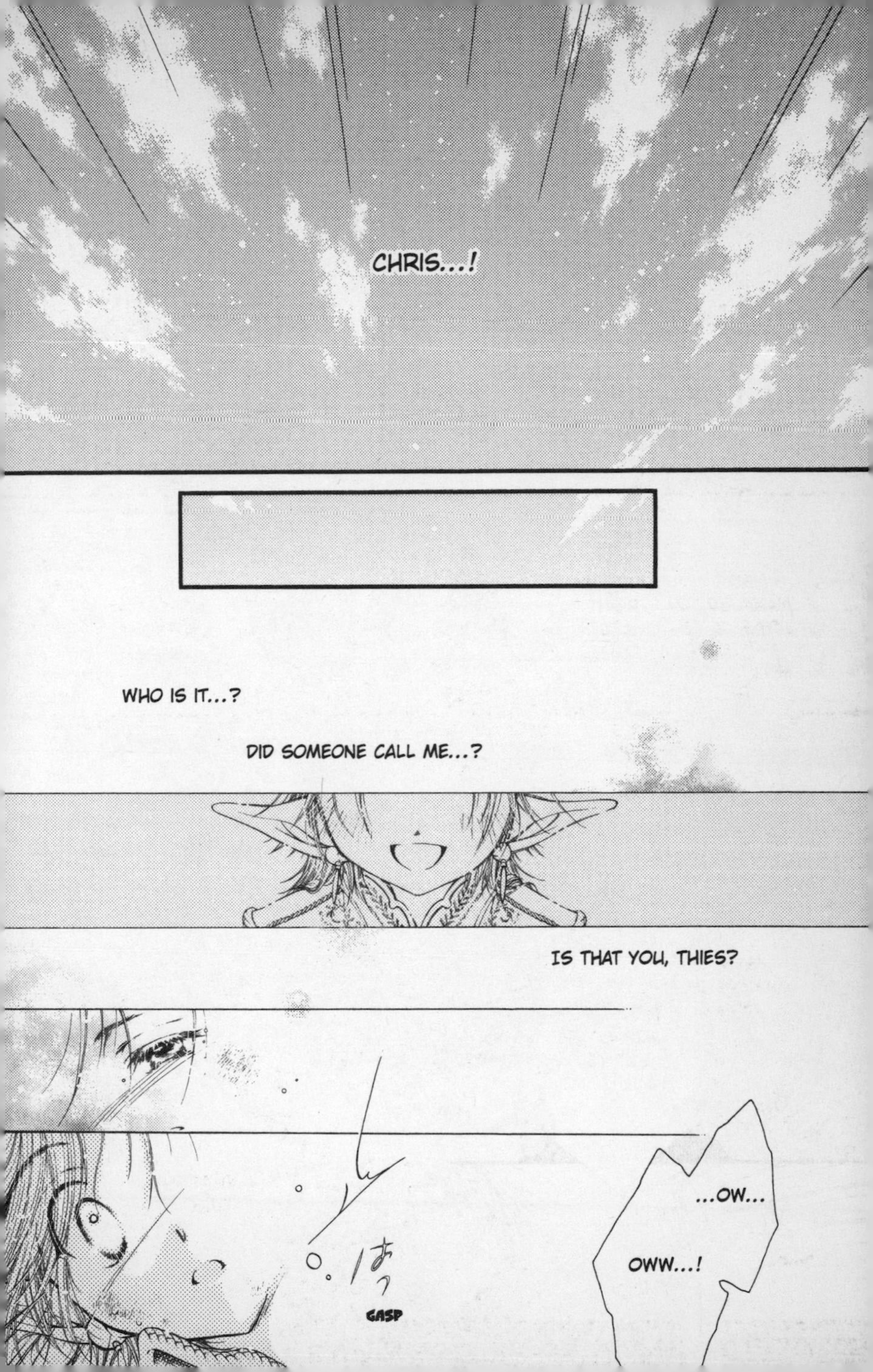
CHRIS...!
WHO IS IT...?
DID SOMEONE CALL ME...?
IS THAT YOU, THIES?
...OW...
OWW...!
はっ
GASP

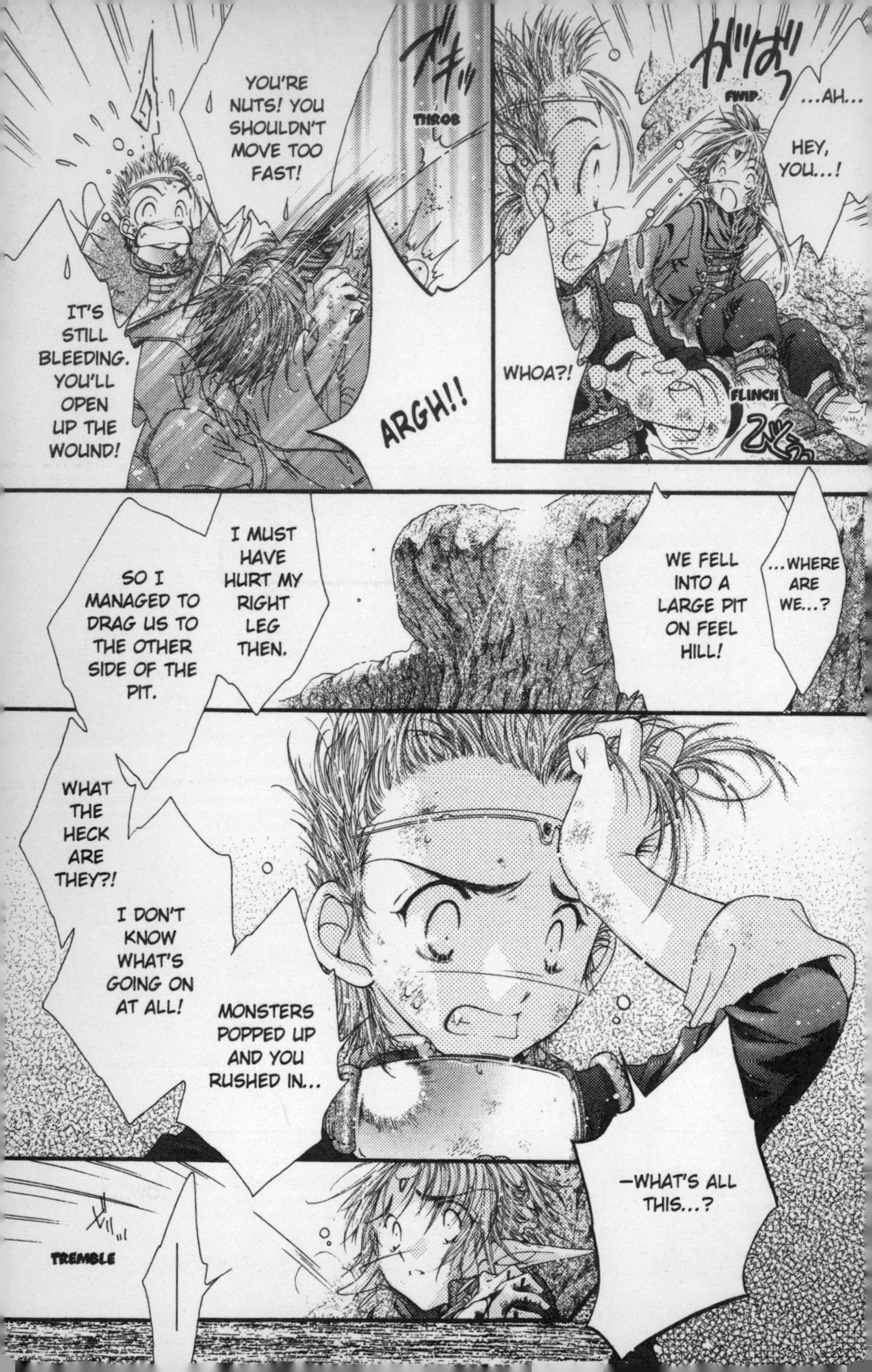
FWIP
...AH...
HEY, YOU...!
WHOA?!
FLINCH
YOU'RE NUTS! YOU SHOULDN'T MOVE TOO FAST!
THROB
IT'S STILL BLEEDING. YOU'LL OPEN UP THE WOUND!
ARGH!!
...WHERE ARE WE...?
WE FELL INTO A LARGE PIT ON FEEL HILL!
I MUST HAVE HURT MY RIGHT LEG THEN.
SO I MANAGED TO DRAG US TO THE OTHER SIDE OF THE PIT.
WHAT THE HECK ARE THEY?!
I DON'T KNOW WHAT'S GOING ON AT ALL!
MONSTERS POPPED UP AND YOU RUSHED IN...
—WHAT'S ALL THIS...?
TREMBLE

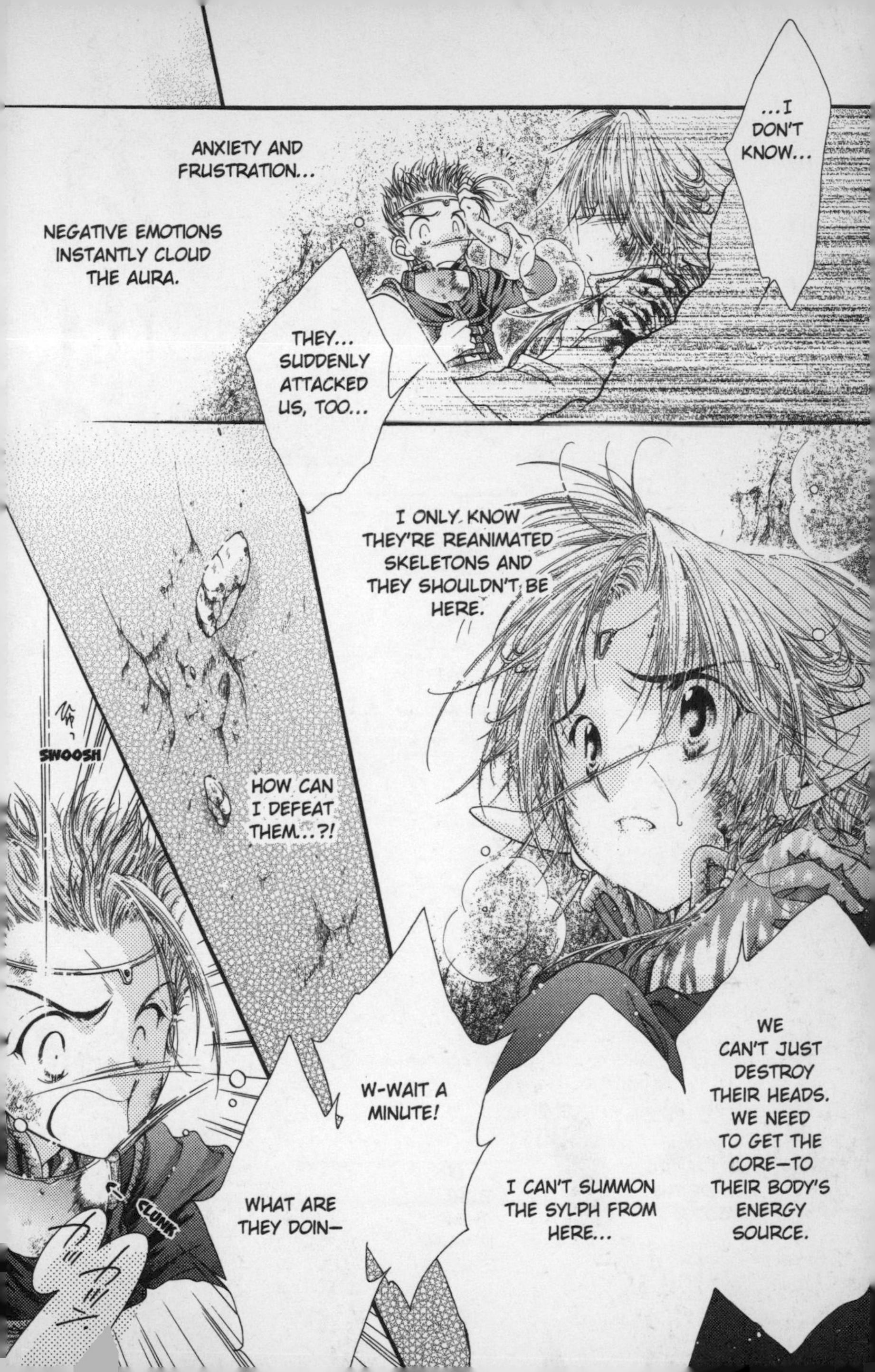
...I DON'T KNOW...
THEY... SUDDENLY ATTACKED US, TOO...
ANXIETY AND FRUSTRATION...
NEGATIVE EMOTIONS INSTANTLY CLOUD THE AURA.
I ONLY KNOW THEY'RE REANIMATED SKELETONS AND THEY SHOULDN'T BE HERE.
HOW CAN I DEFEAT THEM..?!
WE CAN'T JUST DESTROY THEIR HEADS. WE NEED TO GET THE CORE—TO THEIR BODY'S ENERGY SOURCE.
I CAN'T SUMMON THE SYLPH FROM HERE...
SWOOSH
W-WAIT A MINUTE!
WHAT ARE THEY DOIN—
CLUNK

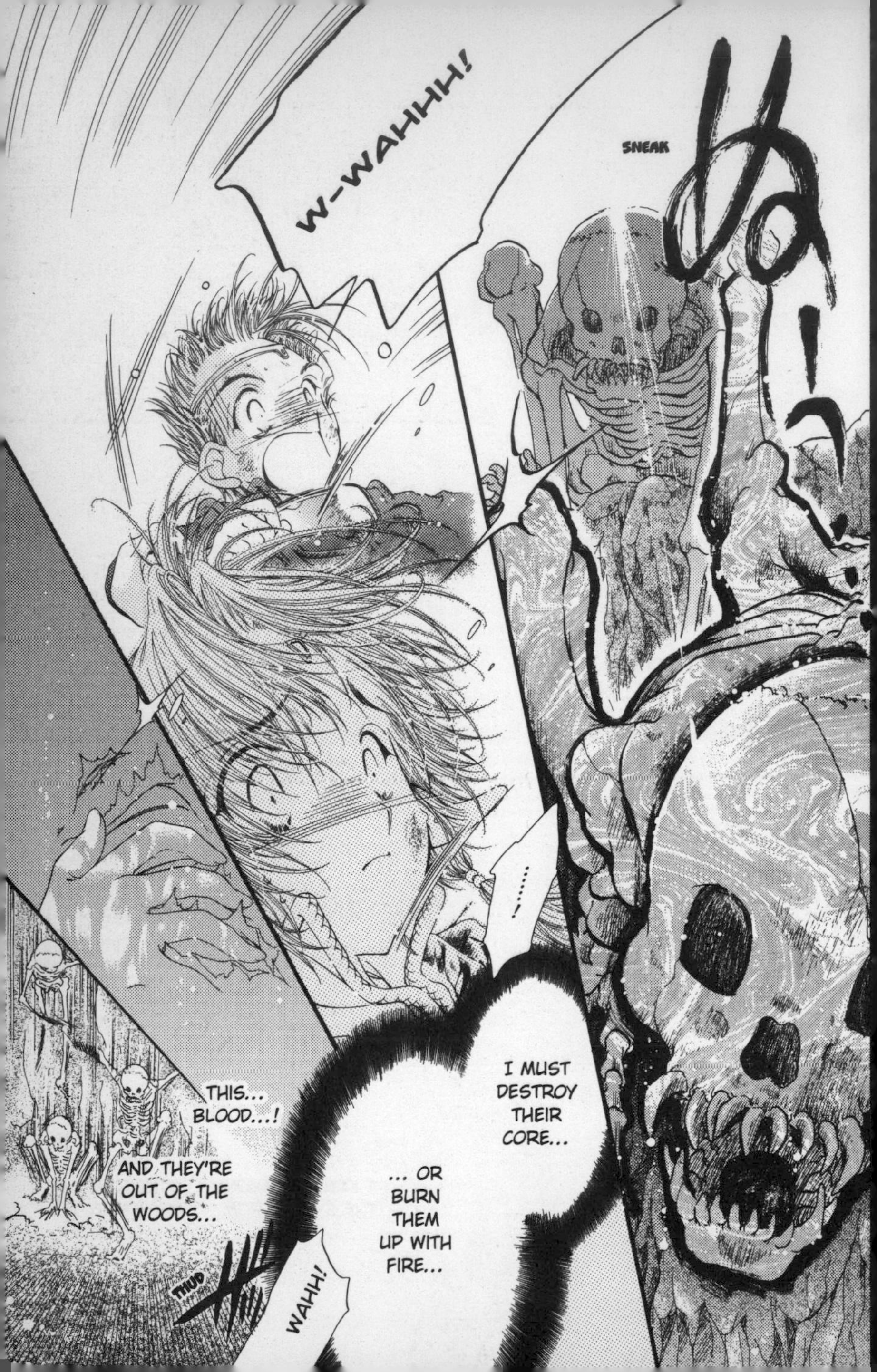
SNEAK
W-WAHHH!
......!
I MUST DESTROY THEIR CORE...
... OR BURN THEM UP WITH FIRE...
WAHH!
THUD
THIS... BLOOD...!
AND THEY'RE OUT OF THE WOODS...

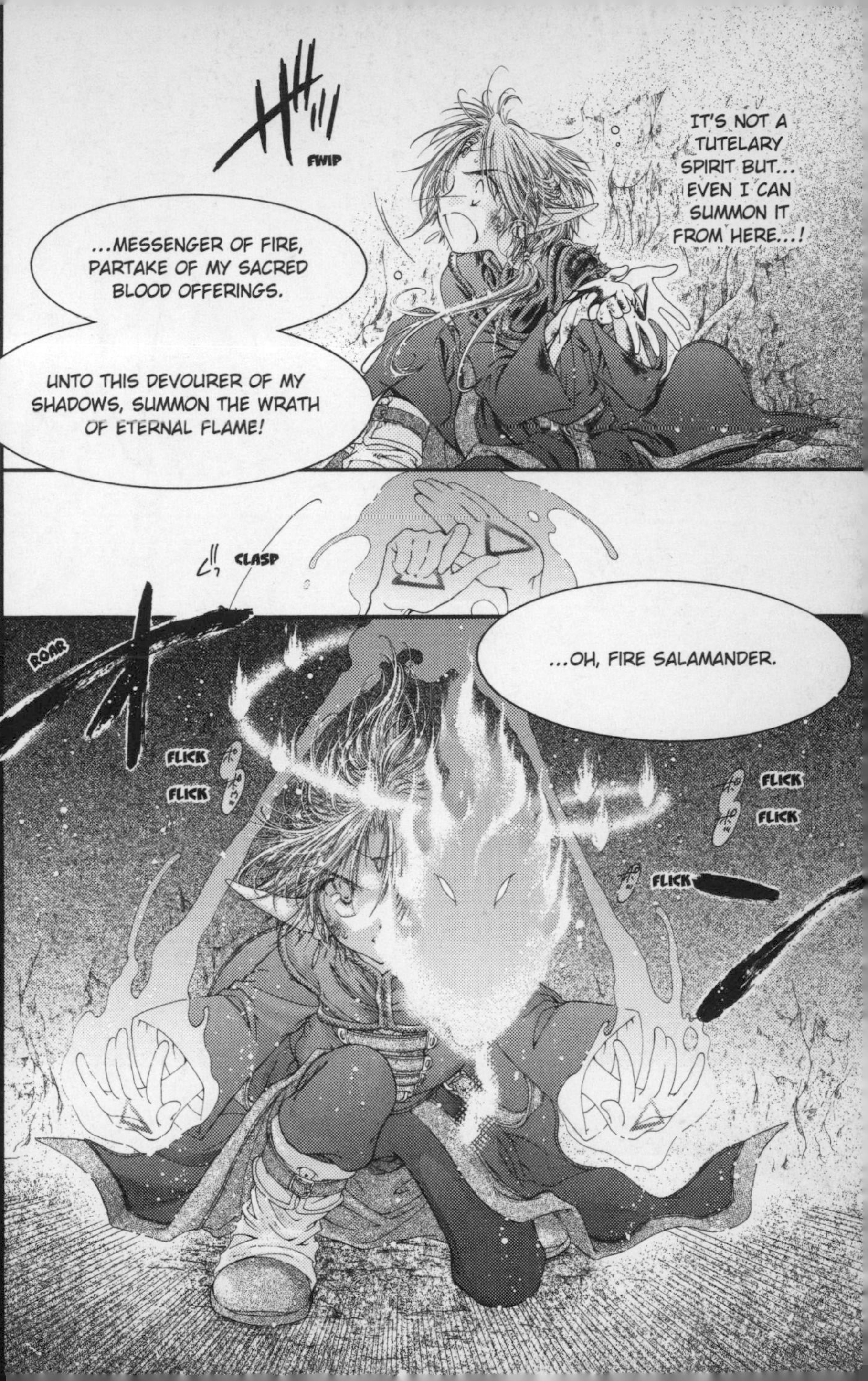
IT'S NOT A TUTELARY SPIRIT BUT... EVEN I CAN SUMMON IT FROM HERE...!
FWIP
...MESSENGER OF FIRE, PARTAKE OF MY SACRED BLOOD OFFERINGS.
UNTO THIS DEVOURER OF MY SHADOWS, SUMMON THE WRATH OF ETERNAL FLAME!
CLASP
...OH, FIRE SALAMANDER.
ROAR
FLICK
FLICK
FLICK
FLICK
FLICK

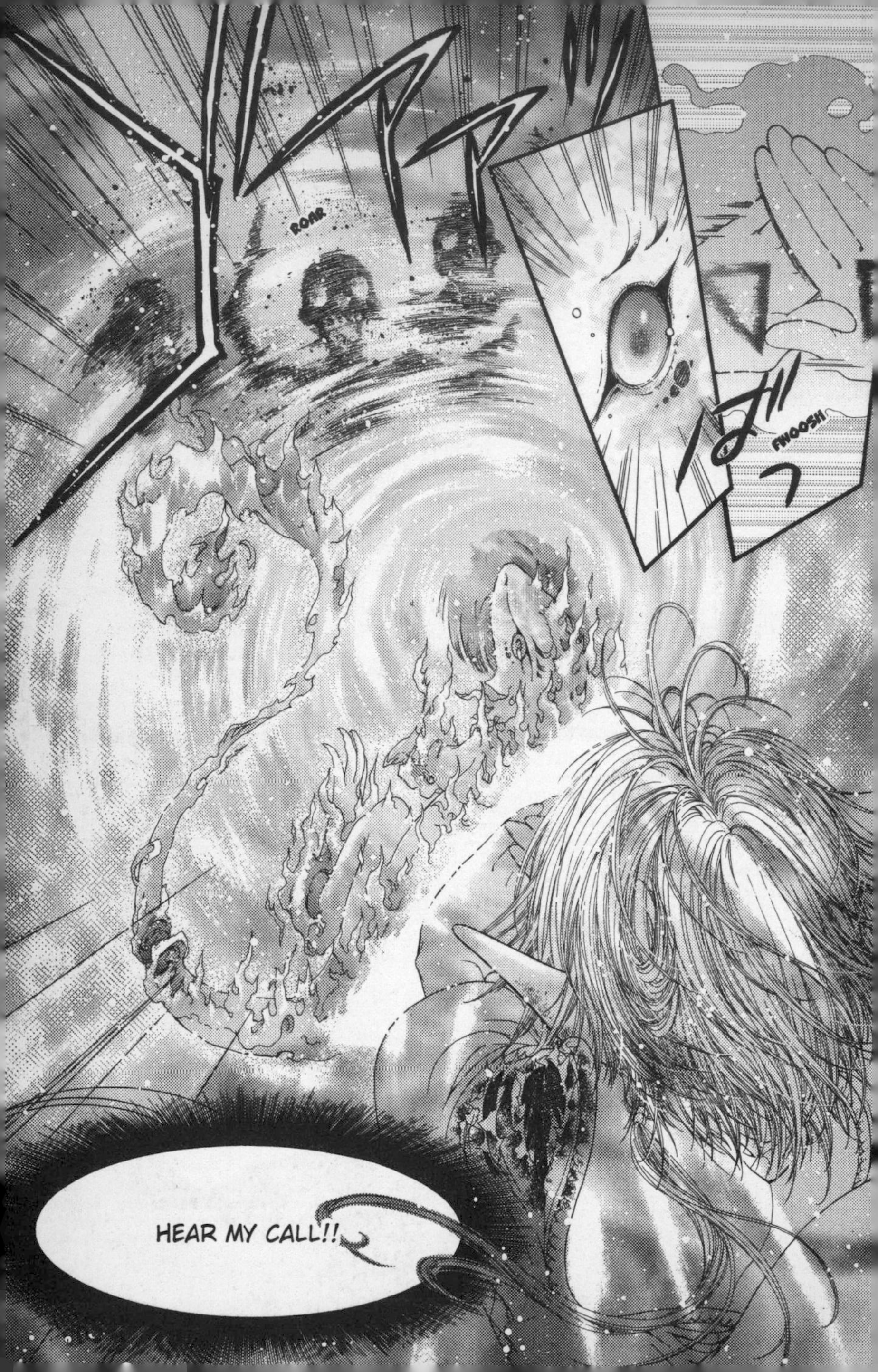
FWOOSH
ROAR
HEAR MY CALL!!

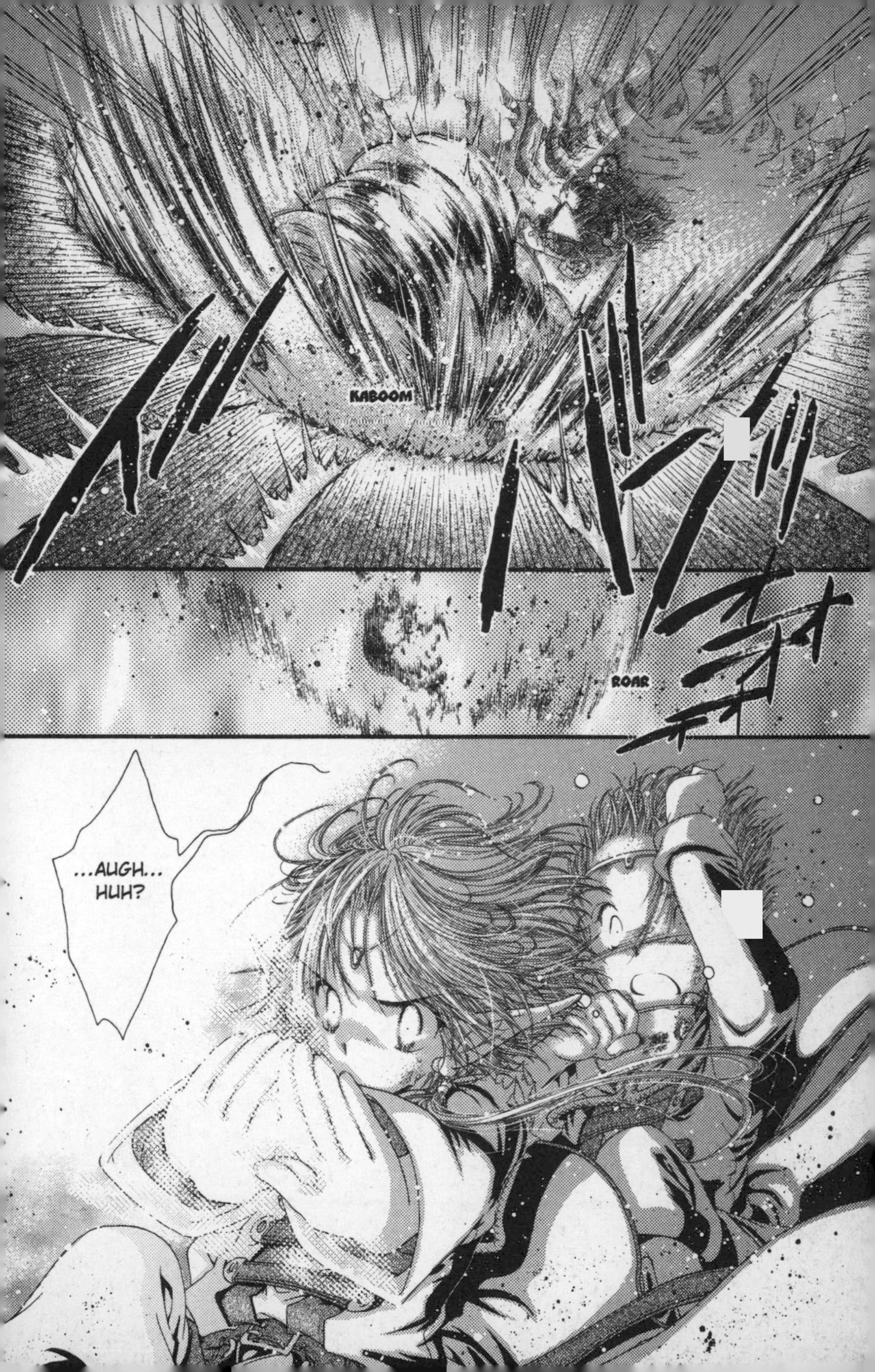
KABOOM
ROAR
...AUGH... HUH?

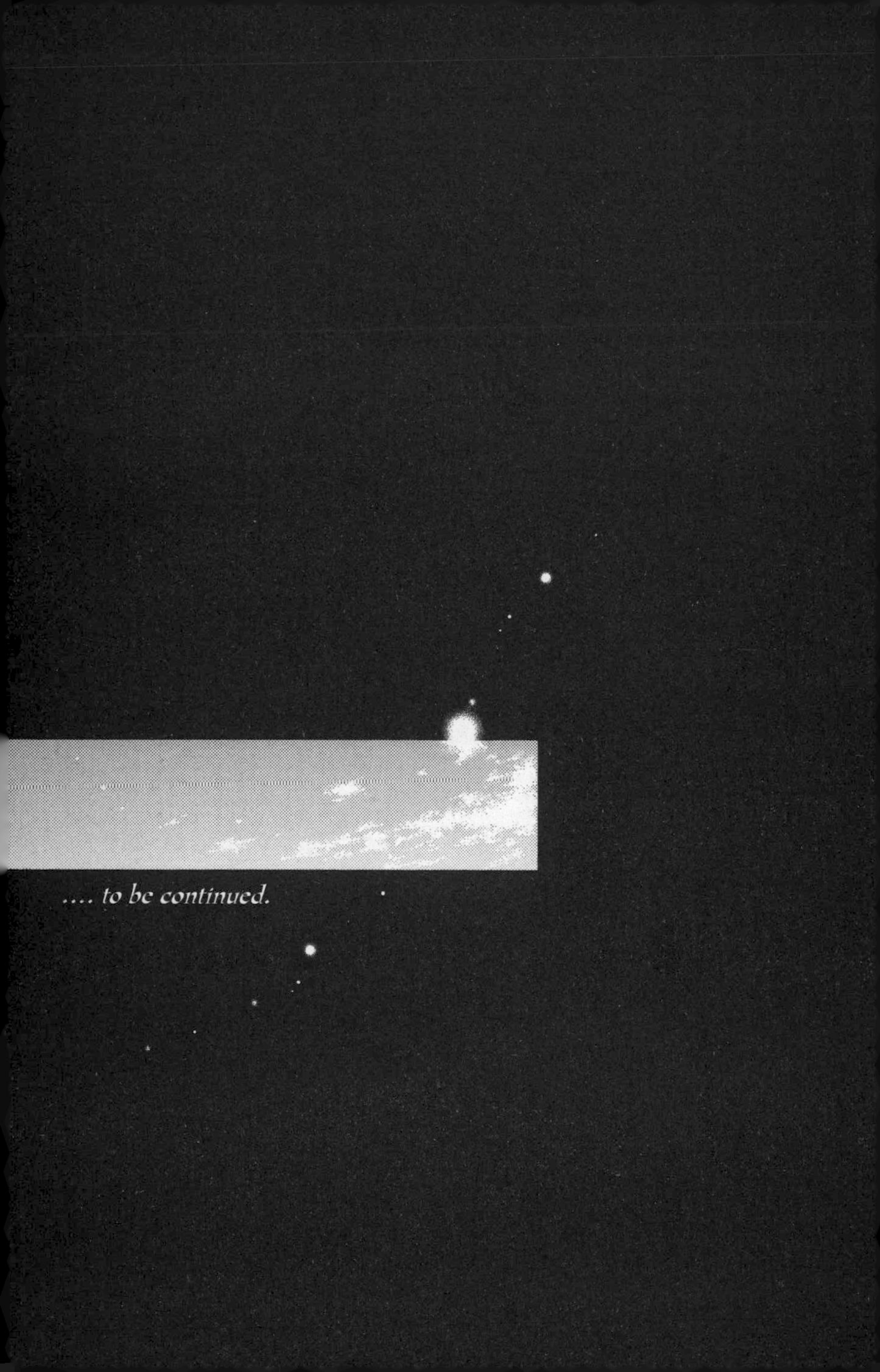
.... to be continued.

Aventura
Character Profiles

Lewin Randit

Birthday: **July 28**
Eye Color: **Garnet**
Protective Element: **Fire**

"If my main character is going to be a boy, I want someone energetic"—that's when Lewin popped into my head. (Laughs) I only drew his silly curly hair out of fun in the beginning— what can you do to make it look like that?

Chris Cottenburg

Birthday: **April 5**
Eye Color: **Peridot**
Protective Element: **Wind**

As a result of meeting Lewin, Chris really showed off his positive attitude in the *3rd Bell*. (Laughs) Though he claimed he doesn't know magic, he is the heir of an archbishop back home in Nemophily Land. He secretly has a tragic past. I was hoping I could show his growth as he overcomes it.

Soela Evenport

Birthday: **March 20**
Eye Color: **Aquamarine**
Protective Element: **Water**

I've never drawn this kind of character—the wimpy, shy youngest child. I'm putting a conscious effort into giving her a softer expression we don't see in a boy...It's very difficult.

To answer a question I'm asked all the time, Wotis is male. What's inside is a secret. (Laughs)

Special Thanks!

Ryuya (3. 4. 5. 6 bells)
You Yukinagi (4. 5. 6 bells)
Shimomo (5 bells)
Rika Sugiyama (Editor)

and You !!

Qualfer Riventzel
(Black Kylin Keeper)

Birthday: **September 23**

Eye Color: **Amethyst**

Subjects in Charge: **General Swordsmanship, Magical Astronomy**

Professor Qualfer's unexpected popularity makes me real nervous when drawing him. (Laughs) By halting his aging with the Mask Curse, Professor Qualfer appears young, but he's Professor Arshes's age. His name and birthday were actually decided afterward. Along with the Mask Curse, he is filled with many mysteries...

Chesford Arshes
(Scarlet Sorceror)

Birthday: **October 20**

Eye Color: **Sunstone**

Subjects in Charge: **Barrier Magic, Seal Magic**

As I aimed for a different character from Professor Qualfer, Professor Arshes came to me naturally. (Laughs) His sweet tooth led to his being a good baker, and he'd always bring baked goods to his students. He's a hard worker who was given the title "the Scarlet Sorceror" at his late older brother's request.

Milieu Rouge Tresor
(Indigo Witch)

Birthday: **November 3**

Eye Color: **Amber**

Subject: **Healing Magic**

Milieu Rouge is a professor who is in the same team with the two listed above. Coming from a family of ice witches, she studied witchcraft accordingly. But then she switched courses to become a healing witch—out of desperation to save her older sister, who remains under the seal.

Milieu Rouge is one of the few professors who knows Rejuvenation Magic. Her older sister's seal is significantly related to the Mask Curse.

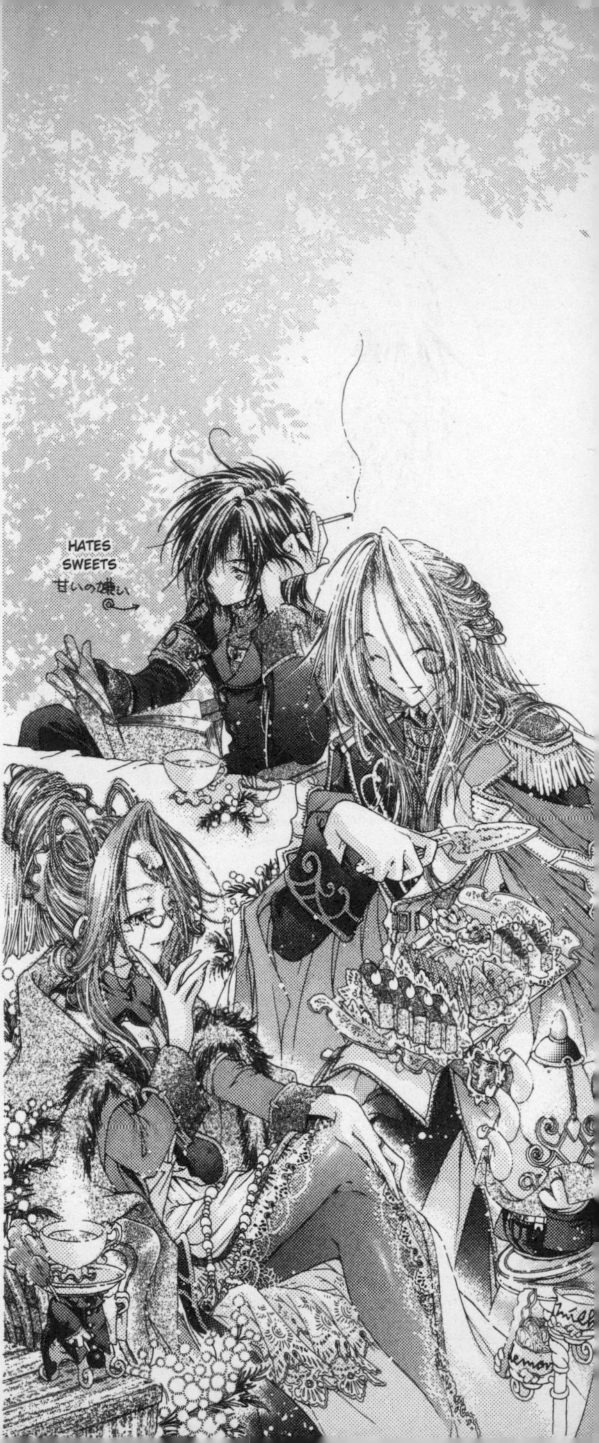
HATES SWEETS
lemon

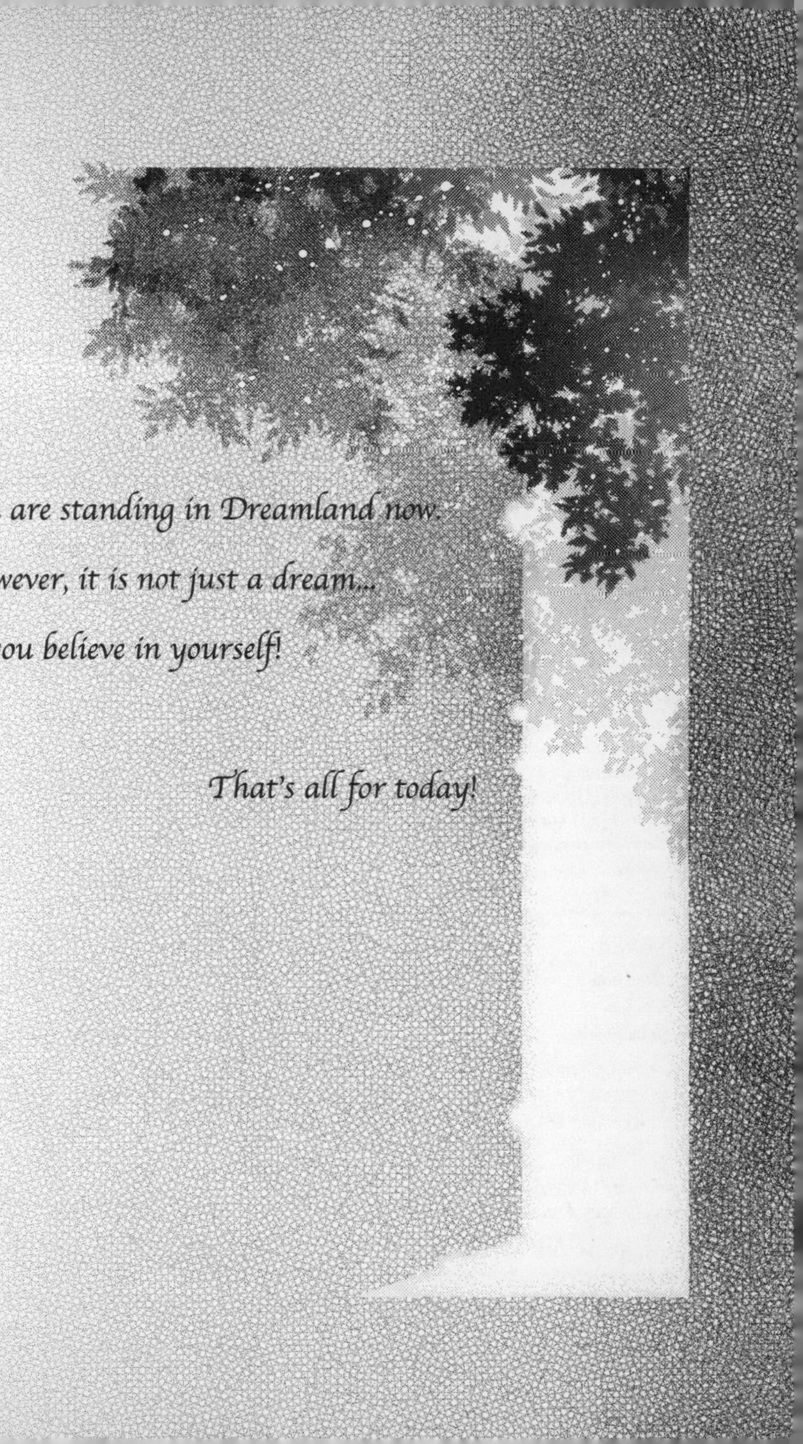

You are standing in Dreamland now.

However, it is not just a dream...

If you believe in yourself!

That's all for today!

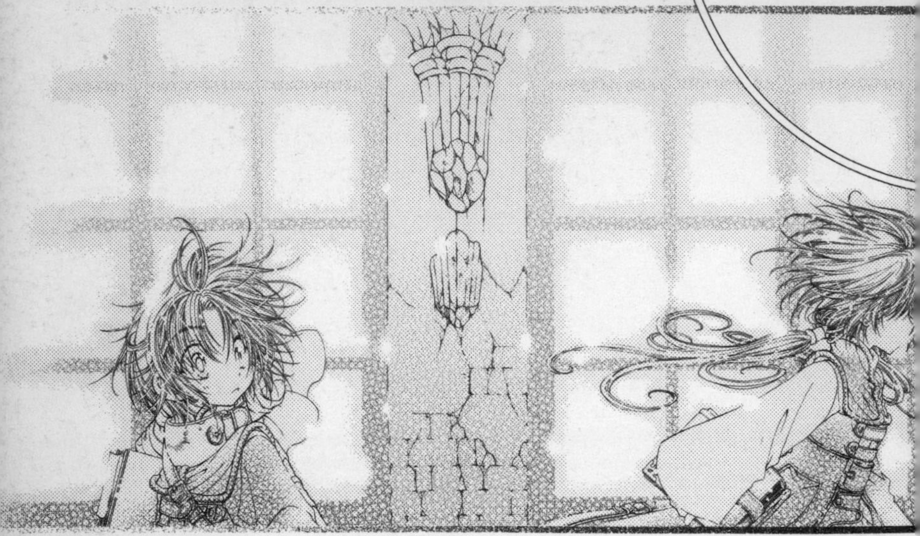

I dedicate this book to my mother in Heaven, who loved my work more than anyone.

And I dedicate it to my father in Heaven as well.

To my older brother, all of my relatives, friends, and readers, I was able to create this book *Aventura* only with your kindness and support.

I am overwhelmed with gratitude that cannot be described in any words. Though I fail to offer anything, I hope I can show how I feel through my work. I have only been causing inconvenience to everyone, but I will do my best.

I thank, from the bottom of my heart, the editorial department for this opportunity, my editor for cooperating with an illustrator like me, and everyone who reads this book.

2006. April. 翠川しん Shin Midorikawa

Translation Notes

Japanese is a tricky language for most Westerners, and translation is often more an art than a science. For your edification and reading pleasure, here are notes on some of the places where we could have gone in a different direction, or where a Japanese cultural reference is used.

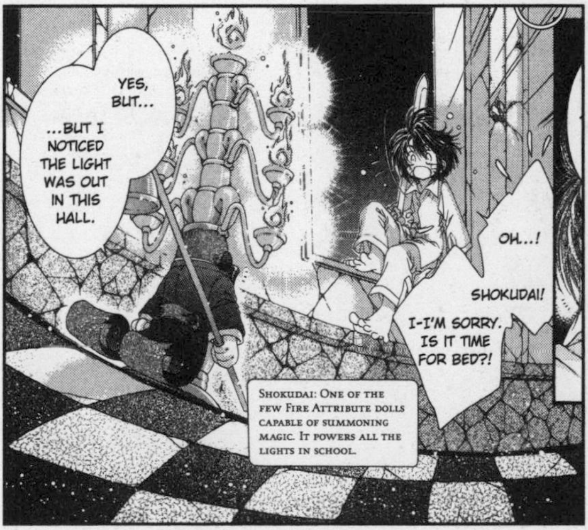
OH...!
SHOKUDAI!
I-I'M SORRY. IS IT TIME FOR BED?!
YES, BUT...
...BUT I NOTICED THE LIGHT WAS OUT IN THIS HALL.
SHOKUDAI: ONE OF THE FEW FIRE ATTRIBUTE DOLLS CAPABLE OF SUMMONING MAGIC. IT POWERS ALL THE LIGHTS IN SCHOOL.

Shokudai, page 25

Shokudai means "candleholder" in Japanese.

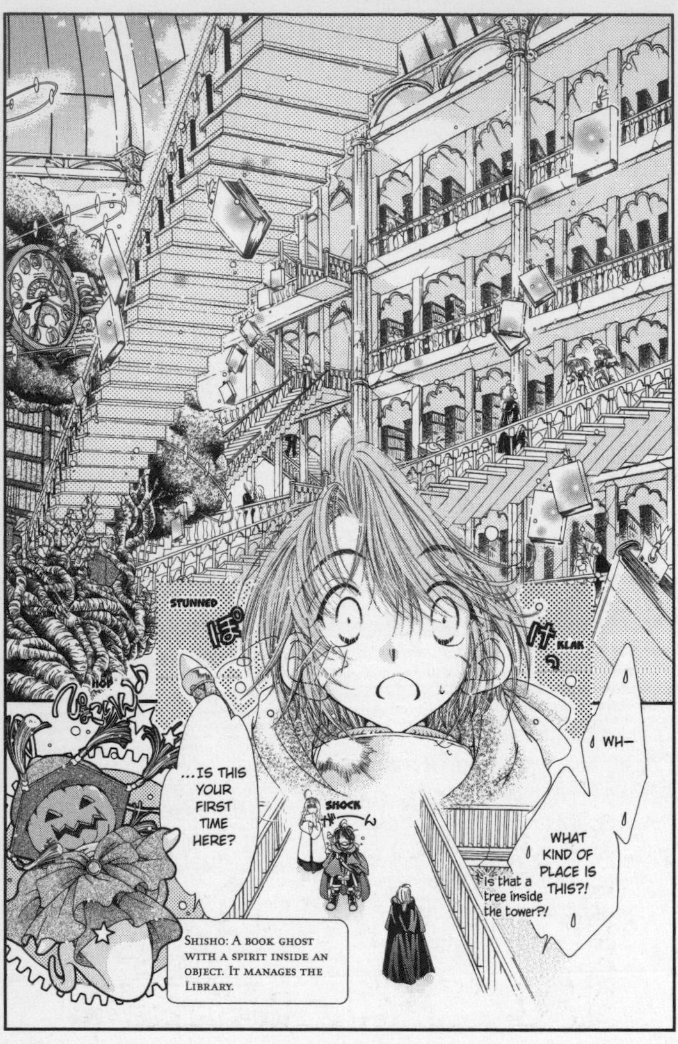
KLAK
STUNNED
WH—
WHAT KIND OF PLACE IS THIS?!
Is that a tree inside the tower?!
SHOCK
...IS THIS YOUR FIRST TIME HERE?
HOP
Shisho: A book ghost with a spirit inside an object. It manages the Library.

Shisho, page 28

Shisho means "librarian" in Japanese.

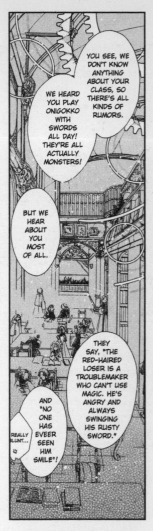

YOU SEE, WE DON'T KNOW ANYTHING ABOUT YOUR CLASS, SO THERE'S ALL KINDS OF RUMORS.
WE HEARD YOU PLAY ONIGOKKO WITH SWORDS ALL DAY! THEY'RE ALL ACTUALLY MONSTERS!
BUT WE HEAR ABOUT YOU MOST OF ALL.
THEY SAY, "THE RED-HAIRED LOSER IS A TROUBLEMAKER WHO CAN'T USE MAGIC. HE'S ANGRY AND ALWAYS SWINGING HIS RUSTY SWORD."
AND "NO ONE HAS EVEER SEEN HIM SMILE"!
REALLY BLUNT...

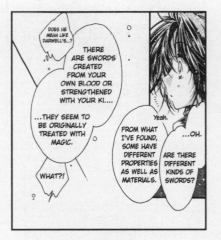

Onigokko, page 34

This is the Japanese version of the playground game tag. The person who is "it" is called the *oni* or ogre.

...OH.
ARE THERE DIFFERENT KINDS OF SWORDS?
FROM WHAT I'VE FOUND, SOME HAVE DIFFERENT PROPERTIES AS WELL AS MATERIALS.
Yeah.
THERE ARE SWORDS CREATED FROM YOUR OWN BLOOD OR STRENGTHENED WITH YOUR KI....
...THEY SEEM TO BE ORIGINALLY TREATED WITH MAGIC.
DOES HE MEAN LIKE DARWELL'S...?
WHAT?!

Ki, page 58

The Japanese word *ki*, literally translated, means "spirit." However, it is best described as "psychic energy," here used to enhance the strength of the magical sword, as Chris explains to Lewin.

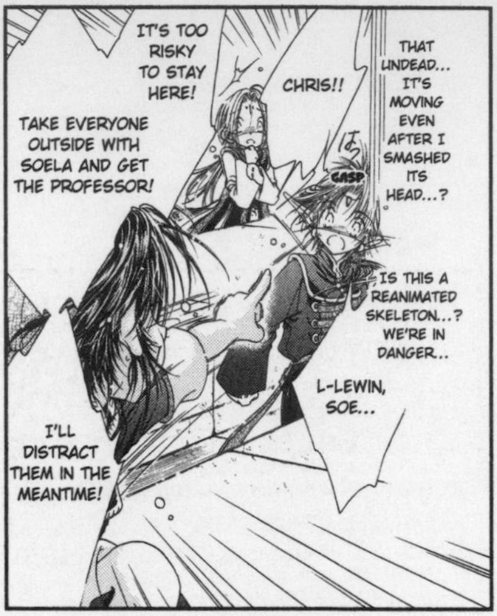
THAT UNDEAD... IT'S MOVING EVEN AFTER I SMASHED ITS HEAD...?
CHRIS!!
IT'S TOO RISKY TO STAY HERE!
TAKE EVERYONE OUTSIDE WITH SOELA AND GET THE PROFESSOR!
GASP
IS THIS A REANIMATED SKELETON...? WE'RE IN DANGER...
L-LEWIN, SOE...
I'LL DISTRACT THEM IN THE MEANTIME!

Reanimated skeleton, page 116

The word actually used in the original was "marionette." However, we felt "reanimated skeletons" better conveys the sense of "controlled undead."

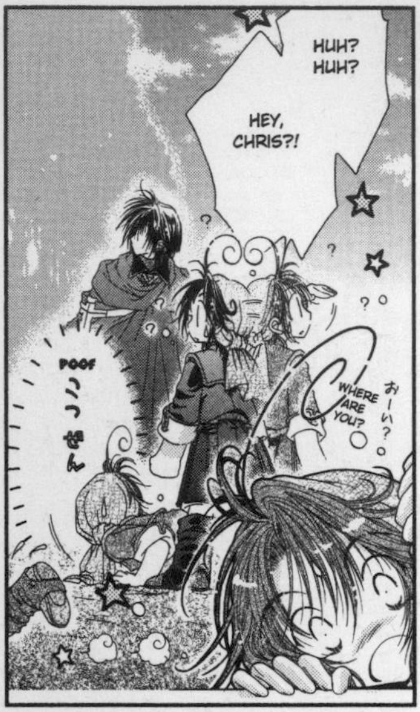
HUH? HUH?
HEY, CHRIS?!
WHERE ARE YOU?
おーい？
POOF
こつぜん

Poof, page 158

The word actually used is *kotsuzen*, which means "suddenly" or "all at once." Since the bubble indicates the empty space where Chris was, we thought that *poof* best communicated the sense of a sudden disappearance.

Kylin, page 171

A *kylin* is a Chinese mythical creature that combines the features of a dragon, lion, deer, and ox.

We're pleased to present you with a preview of volume 2. Please check our website (www.delreymanga.com) to see when this volume will be available in English. For now you'll have to make do with Japanese!

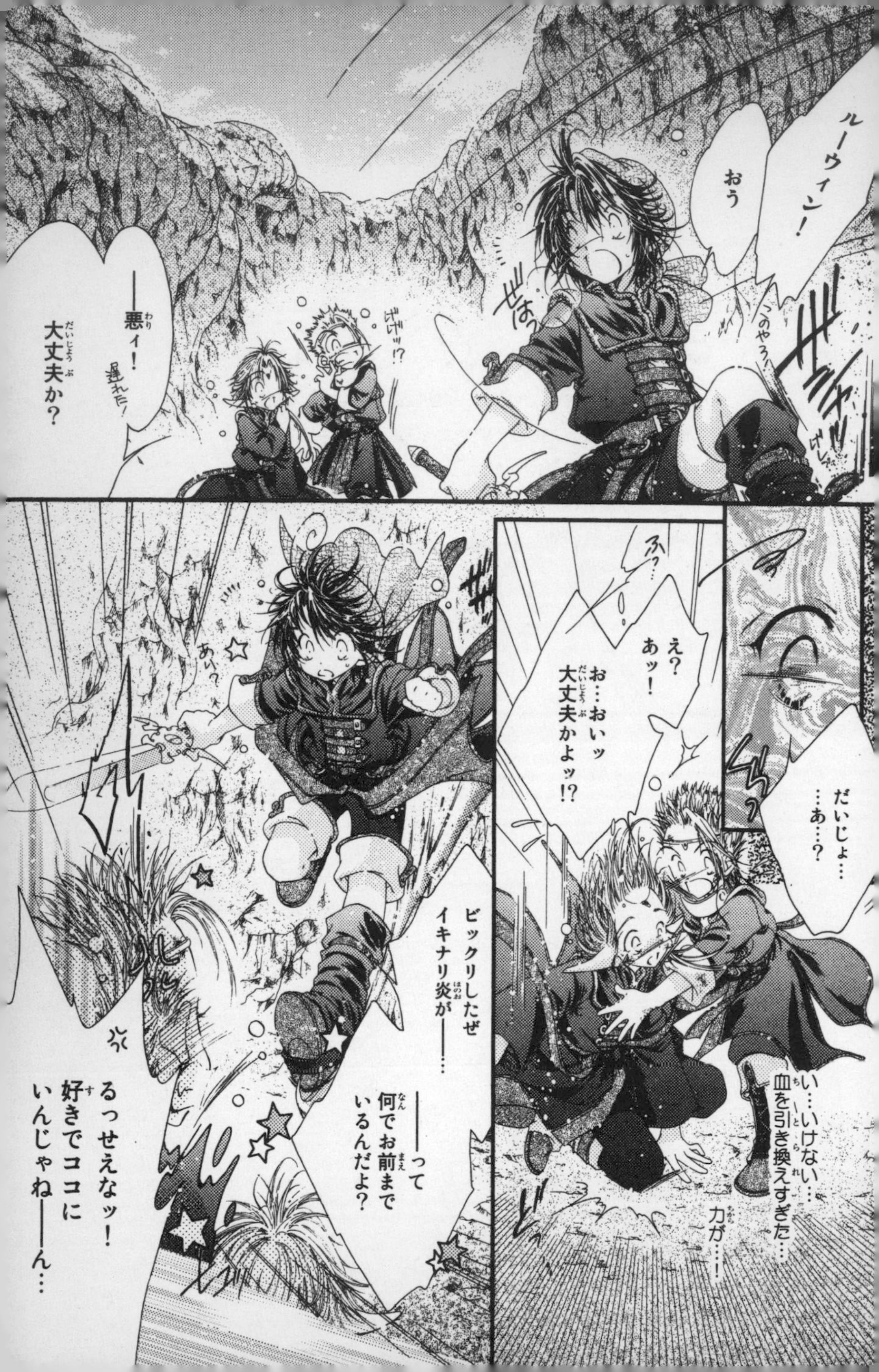
ルーウィン！
おう
ぜはっ
げげッ!?
――悪ィ！
遅れた！
大丈夫か？
だいじょ…
…あ…？
ふっ…
え？
あッ！
お…おいッ
大丈夫かよッ!?
い…いけない…
血を引き換えすぎた…
力が…！
ビックリしたぜ
イキナリ炎が――…
――って
何でお前まで
いるんだよ？
るっせえなッ！
好きでココに
いんじゃね――ん…

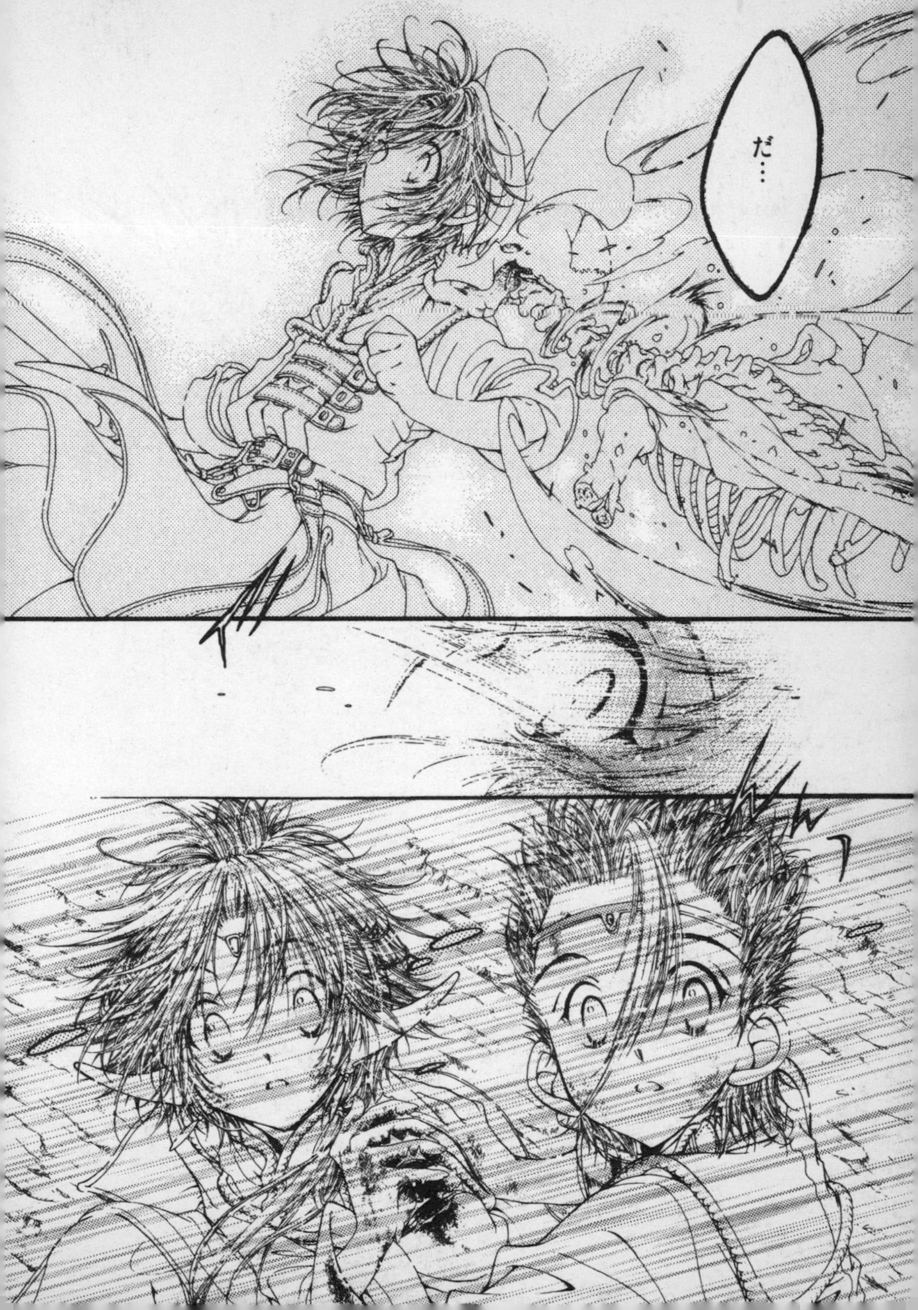
だ…

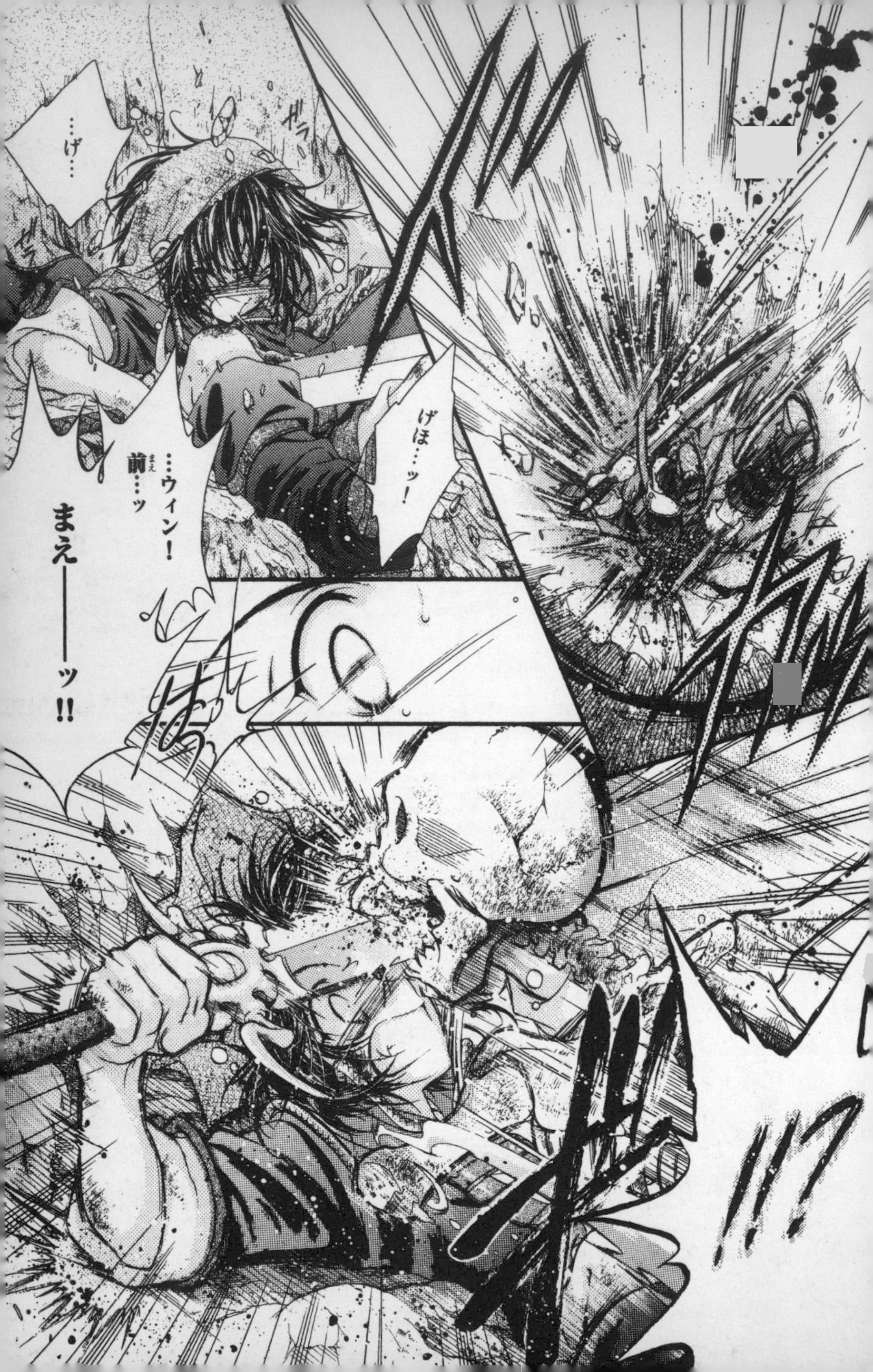

げほ……ッ!
……げ……
……ウィン! 前……ッ
まえ————ッ!!
!!?

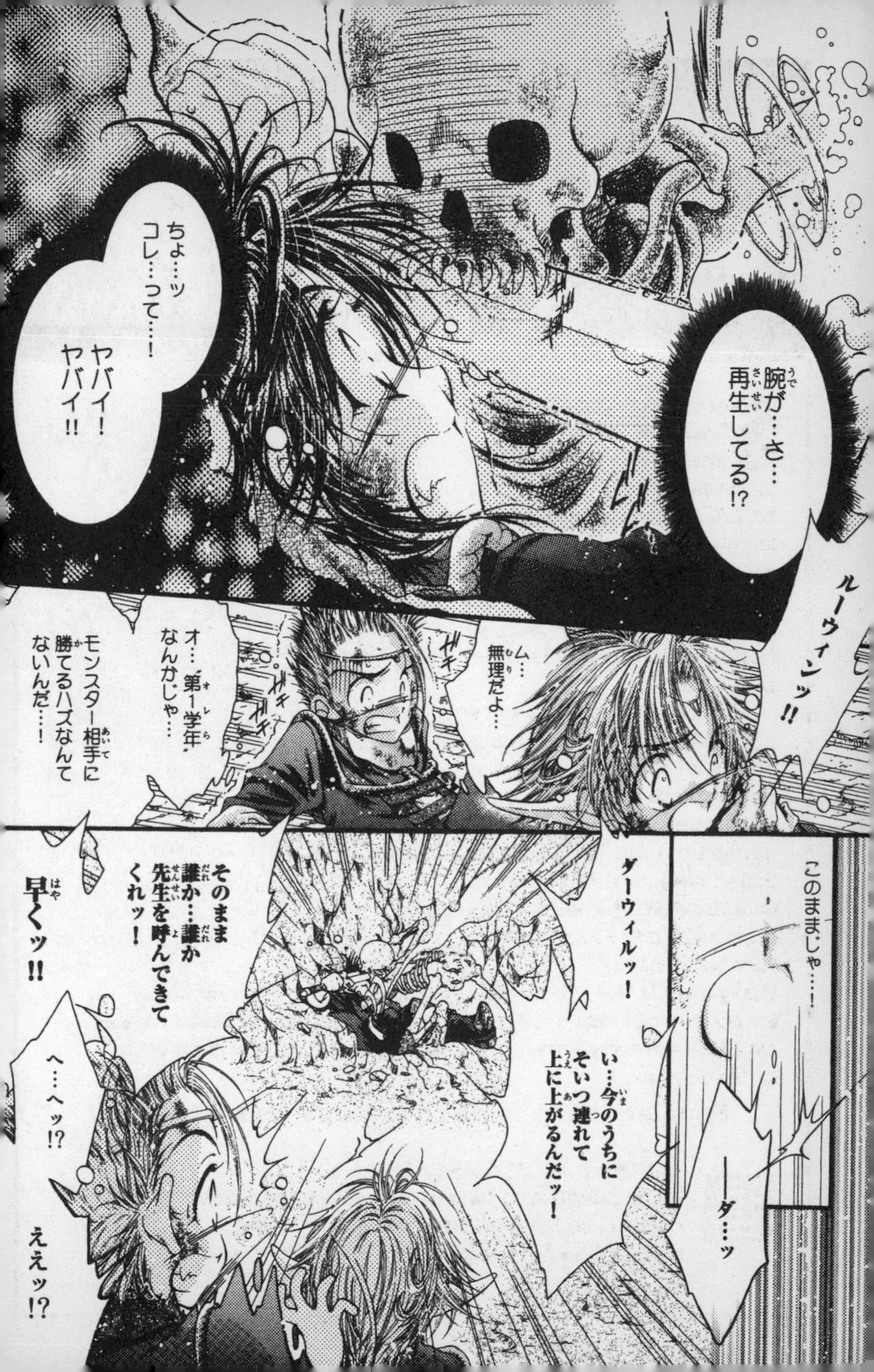
腕が…さ…再生してる!?
ちょ…ッコレ…って…!ヤバイ!ヤバイ!!
ルーウィンッ!!
ム…無理だよ…
オ…第1学年なんかじゃ…モンスター相手に勝てるハズなんてないんだ…!
このままじゃ…!
ダーウィルッ!
そのまま誰か…誰か先生を呼んできてくれッ!
早くッ!!
い…今のうちにそいつ連れて上に上がるんだッ!
ーダ…ッ
へ…ヘッ!?
ええッ!?

KAGETORA

BY AKIRA SEGAMI

MISSION IMPOSSIBLE

The young ninja Kagetora has been given a great honor—to serve a renowned family of skilled martial artists. But on arrival, he's handed a challenging assignment: teach the heir to the dynasty, the charming but clumsy Yuki, the deft moves of self-defense and combat.

Yuki's inability to master the martial arts is not what makes this job so difficult for Kagetora. No, it is Yuki herself. Someday she will lead her family dojo, and for a ninja like Kagetora to fall in love with his master is a betrayal of his duty, the ultimate dishonor, and strictly forbidden. Can Kagetora help Yuki overcome her ungainly nature . . . or will he be overcome by his growing feelings?

Ages: 13 +

Special extras in each volume! Read them all!

SHIKI TSUKAI

MANGA BY TORU ZEKU
ART BY YUNA TAKANAGI

DEFENDING THE NATURAL ORDER OF THE UNIVERSE!

The *shiki tsukai* are "Keepers of the Seasons"—magical warriors pledged to defend the planet's natural order against those who would threaten it.

When 14-year-old Akira Kizuki joins the *shiki tsukai,* he knows that it'll be a difficult life. But with his new friends and mentors, he's up to the challenge!

Special extras in each volume! Read them all!

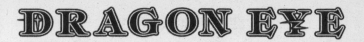

DRAGON EYE

BY KAIRI FUJIYAMA

HUMANITY'S SECRET WEAPON

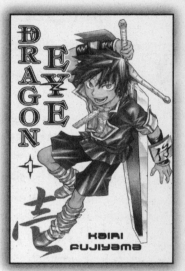

Dracules—bloodthirsty, infectious monsters—have hunted human beings to the brink of extinction. Only the elite warriors of the VIUS Squad stand as humanity's last best hope.

Young Leila Mikami is one of the squad's most promising recruits, but she's not only training to battle the Dracules, she's determined to find the magical Dragon Eye, a weapon that will make her the most powerful warrior in the world.

DRAGON
EYE
1
壱
侍
KAIRI
FUJIYAMA

Special extras in each volume! Read them all!

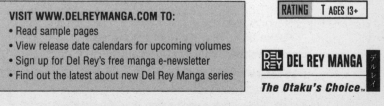

VISIT WWW.DELREYMANGA.COM TO:

- Read sample pages
- View release date calendars for upcoming volumes
- Sign up for Del Rey's free manga e-newsletter
- Find out the latest about new Del Rey Manga series

RATING T AGES 13+

DEL REY MANGA デルレイ

The Otaku's Choice™

TOMA

止まれ

[STOP!]

You're going the wrong way!

Manga is a completely different type of reading experience.

To start at the *beginning*, go to the *end!*

That's right! Authentic manga is read the traditional Japanese way—from right to left, exactly the *opposite* of how American books are read. It's easy to follow: Just go to the other end of the book, and read each page—and each panel—from right side to left side, starting at the top right. Now you're experiencing manga as it was meant to be!